The 1883 Philadelphia Athletics:
AMERICAN ASSOCIATION CHAMPIONS

Edited by PAUL HOFMANN and BILL NOWLIN

Associate editors BOB LEMOINE and LEN LEVIN

Society for American Baseball Research, Inc.
Phoenix, AZ

The 1883 Philadelphia Athletics: American Association Champions
Edited by Paul Hofmann and Bill Nowlin
Associate editors Bob LeMoine and Len Levin

ISBN 978-1-970159-69-1 ebook
ISBN 978-1-970159-70-7 paper
Library of Congress Control Number: 2022904179

The front cover photograph depicts the 1883 Philadelphia Athletics: (top, left to right) Harry Stovey, George Bradley, Mike Moynahan, Lon Knight; (center, left to right) Bob Blakiston, Cub Stricker, Jud Birchall, Bill Crowley, Jersey Bakley; (bottom, left to right) Bobby Mathews, John O'Brien, Fred Corey, Ed Rowen. Not pictured: Daniel "Jumping Jack" Jones and Al Hubbard. Courtesy of Ed Achorn.
Back cover illustrations by Schell and Hogan, "The Grand Torch-Light Parade in Philadelphia," *Harper's Weekly*, October 13, 1883. Courtesy of John Thorn.

Book design: Rachael E. Sullivan
Cronkite School at ASU
555 N. Central Ave. #416
Phoenix, AZ 85004
Phone: (602) 496-1460
Web: www.sabr.org
Facebook: Society for American Baseball Research
Twitter: @SABR

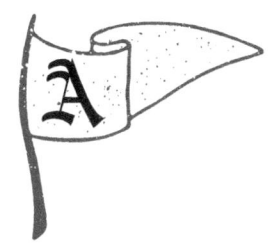

CONTENTS

OTHER ARTICLES / PIECES

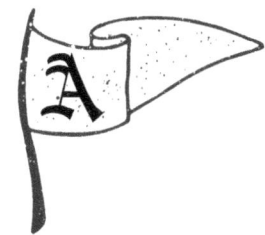

INTRODUCTION

By Paul Hofmann

It has been nearly 140 years since the Athletic Club of Philadelphia captured the attention of the city and the 1883 American Association championship in what was at the time the closest major-league pennant in baseball history. The team contained a core of players who hailed from the City of Brotherly Love and came together to win the city's first major professional championship.

The team not only brought the city its first major sports championship, a year earlier it ushered in a new era of major-league baseball in Philadelphia. The city had gone five years without a major-league franchise, since a previous Athletic Club of Philadelphia was expelled from the National League after the 1876 season for failing to complete its league schedule.

Determined to take on the Association head-to-head, the National League returned to Philadelphia in 1883 with the Philadelphia Quakers.[1] The Quakers finished in last place with a dismal record of 17-81, 23 games behind the seventh-place Detroit Wolverines. Meanwhile, the Athletic Club, with its 25-cent admission and free-flowing alcohol, were setting all sorts of attendance records as they pursued the Beer and Whiskey League pennant.

There are two seminal works that examine the American Association and the 1883 pennant race. David Nemec's *The Beer and Whiskey League* presents a chronological history of the Association from 1882 to 1891, of which the Athletic of Philadelphia was a mainstay franchise. Similarly, Edward Achorn's *The Summer of Beer and Whiskey* provides an in-depth look at one of the most exciting pennant races in baseball history. Both are wonderful reads. This book serves as a companion read to those books. Related to the SABR BioProject, this publication reveals who these players were.

To be sure, 1883 was a different time in Philadelphia, America, and the world. The Gilded Age was in full swing and the country was experiencing rapid economic growth in the Northern and Western United States. Base ball was among the many industries that benefited from this growth. While the business of baseball was evolving quickly, the game was in the process of being woven into the fabric of American culture.

Philadelphia, like many of the mid-Atlantic and Northeastern cities, was growing quickly. Fueled by immigrants from Europe, which resulted in cramped neighborhoods, and the Industrial Revolution, the city experienced a seemingly never-ending number of industrial fires in 1883. No fewer than 12 headline-grabbing fires swept through sawmills, textile factories, and other businesses, resulting in hundreds of thousands of dollars in damage and loss of property and life. Philadelphia also entered the electrical age when underground electrical wiring was installed to light a four-block business area on Market Street.[2]

Daily Graphic, courtesy of John Thorn.

Heavy Streak of Batting

Nationally, there was a lot happening in 1883.

Life expectancy in the United States was about 40 years of age, largely due to an infant mortality rate of more than 40 percent and little formal training of medical practitioners. It was not until 1885 that the age of modern medicine was introduced – a period that saw the growth of medical technology, the rise of academic medicine, new organizational standards, government support in the form of licensing regulations, and the acceptance of germ therapy – that medical care was transformed and life expectancy began to increase.[3]

Chester A. Arthur was the president of the United States. Arthur was one of a few US presidents who was never elected to the office. He became president on September 20, 1881, after President James A. Garfield was assassinated at Union Station in Buffalo, New York.

The Metropolitan Opera opened in New York City.

On January 16, Congress passed the Pendleton Civil Service Reform Act, establishing the United States civil service in an attempt to end the long-honored patronage system that awarded government jobs to political supporters.

The first electric lighting system utilizing overhead wires began service in Roselle, New Jersey, on January 19. The system was built by Thomas Edison as part of an experiment to prove that an entire community could be lit by electricity.

The first vaudeville theater opened, in Boston on February 28, ushering in a new era in American entertainment that would become an opportunity for the game's biggest stars to cash in on their fame during the offseason.

The Brooklyn Bridge opened to traffic on May 24 after 13 years of construction.

On June 2 the first night baseball game involving a professional team took place in Fort Wayne, Indiana, when the Quincys, a professional team from Illinois in the Northwestern League squared off against a team from Methodist College (Fort Wayne). Seventeen huge lights were placed around League Park, casting shadows on the field that made it difficult to see the ball, as the Quincys defeated the college team 19-11 in a seven-inning affair.[4]

On Friday, June 29, the Olympic Team of Philadelphia celebrated its 50th anniversary with a game on the team's grounds, at Eighteenth and Cumberland streets. The team, founded in 1833, was the oldest organization of players in the country.[5]

The world's first rodeo, a distinctly American form of entertainment, was held, in Pecos, Texas, on the Fourth of July.

Disaster struck Rochester, Minnesota, when a destructive tornado ripped through the city on August 21. Out of the destruction emerged the famed Mayo Clinic.

The University of Texas at Austin opened its doors on September 15.

On October 15, the Supreme Court of the United States declared part of the Civil Rights Act of 1875 to be unconstitutional, allowing individuals and corporations to continue discriminating on the basis of race.

The United States created four time zones on November 18.

Preacher, abolitionist, and women's rights advocate Sojourner Truth died on November 26 in Battle Creek, Michigan.

The first telephone exchange was created between two major US cities, New York and Boston.

William "Buffalo Bill" Cody created Buffalo Bill's Wild West Show.

Bernard Kroger established the first Kroger grocery store in Cincinnati.

There were significant international events that occurred in 1883, many of which probably went unnoticed by many Americans.

Carlo Collodi published *The Adventures of Pinocchio* in Italy. Years later, Walt Disney adapted the character for the 1940 animated Disney classic.

In late August, the volcanic island of Krakatoa in the Dutch East Indies (modern Indonesia) erupted, destroying 163 surrounding villages and killing more than 36,000 residents.

German scientist Robert Koch discovered the bacteria that cause cholera.

On October 4 the Orient Express train began to run between Paris and Giurgiu, Romania.

Germany became the first country to launch a national health-insurance system when it created the Sickness Insurance Law.

The genesis of this book dates back to 2005 when my grandmother passed away. Among her belongings was an envelope with my name on it that contained the December 23, 1887, obituary of Jud Birchall from the *Philadelphia Inquirer*. A few questions immediately came to mind. Who was Jud Birchall? How did my grandmother come to possess Birchall's obituary? And why did she keep it all those years? The first question is answered in this book.

In 2007 I completed my first bio for the SABR BioProject. The subject was Jud Birchall. While conducting research for the bio, I discovered the 1883 Athletic Club of Philadelphia and learned about its epic pennant race with the Browns. While no member of this team has been enshrined in the National Baseball Hall of Fame in Cooperstown, there was no shortage of nineteenth-century star power in the lineup. Harry Stovey established the major-league single-season home run record with 14 in 1883 and at one time was the major-league leader in career home runs. Right-hander Bobby Mathews, winner of 297 games (the most among any hurler not in the Hall of Fame), revived his career with the first of three consecutive 30-win seasons. Rookie sensation Jumping Jack Jones, player-manager Lon Knight, and others each have unique life stories told in this book.

This book contains 18 biographical sketches, including those of the three co-owners and 15 Athletic players.[6] This publication also highlights 10 games, from the Athletics Opening Day shutout victory over the Allegheny of Pittsburgh – the only time the team shut out an opponent all season– to the pennant-clinching victory against the Louisville Eclipse in late September. Three additional essays, a season timeline, and forensic analysis of the season by the numbers provide additional context.

One item we struggled with was balancing historical authenticity with conformity to modern usage. You will find teams referred to by the contemporary name of the day as well as how they are referred to in many modern publications. For example, the Athletic of Philadelphia and Philadelphia Athletics are synonymous in this publication. The official names of 1883 American Association member teams were as follows:

Athletic of Philadelphia
St. Louis Browns
Cincinnati Red Stockings
Metropolitans of New York
Eclipse of Louisville
Columbus Buckeyes
Allegheny of Pittsburgh
Baltimore Orioles

A work like this would not be possible without the contributions of volunteer authors, fact checkers, and editors. Each gave of their precious time to bring a unique perspective to their subjects. I would feel remiss if I did not thank each of them by name. In no particular order, I would like to thank Pamela Bakker, Jerrold Casway, Richard Hershberger, Bill Johnson, Bill Nowlin, Mike McAvoy, Brian Engelhardt, Richard Riis, Dalton Mack, Rich Bogovich, Bill Ryczek, Chris Jones, Brian McKenna, John Zinn, Joel Rippel, Bob LeMoine, Len Levin, Tim Hagerty, Michael Huber, Paul Doutrich, Michael Wagner, Gregory Wolf, Clifford Blau, Matt Albertson, Donna Halper, Eric Miklich, and Dan Fields.

A special acknowledgment is due Bill Nowlin, co-editor of this book, and associate editors Bob LeMoine and Len Levin. Bill worked tirelessly, as he always does, to ensure that the work stayed on track through completion. Bob's meticulous fact-checking of each article ensured that the book is as factually accurate as possible, while Len's editing and polishing of each article greatly enhanced the quality of the final product. Without their collective efforts, this SABR publication would not have been completed.

As for the other two questions – how my grandmother came into possession of this obituary and why she kept it all these years – they remain unsolved mysteries. My grandparents were both natives of Philadelphia, both from the Germantown area of the city. My grandfather was born in 1912 and my grandmother was born in 1917, 25 and 30 years after Birchall's death, respectively. Their grandparents (my great-great-grandparents) would have been contemporaries of Birchall and his siblings. The number of generations that have passed and my family's rather complex family tree suggests these may always remain a mystery.

It is our hope you will enjoy this publication and through it come to learn a bit more about the men who brought the first major-sports championship to the City of Philadelphia. Long live the 1883 Athletic Club of Philadelphia!

NOTES

1   The Quakers was the original name of the National League's Philadelphia Phillies.

2   "Philadelphia History," Retrieved from ushistory.org.

3   Michael Bliss, *The Making of Modern Medicine: Turning Points in the Treatment of Disease* (Chicago: The University of Chicago Press, 2011), 1.

4   "Under the Midnight Sun," *Fort Wayne* (Indiana) *Daily Gazette*, June 3, 1883: 8.

5   "Olympic Ball Club," *Philadelphia Inquirer*, June 30, 1883: 2.

6   Co-owner Charlie Mason appeared in one game for the team.

THE BALLPARK

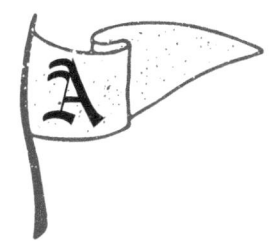

THE JEFFERSON STREET BALL PARKS (1864-1891)

By Jerrold Casway

The Philadelphia ballparks situated at Jefferson and Master Streets, between 27th and 25th Streets, have a significant historic importance for our national pastime. Originally, this plot of land was known as the Jefferson Parade Grounds. It was used as a bivouac and training site in the years leading up to the Civil War.[1]

In the antebellum era, the major Philadelphia teams – the Athletics, Olympics, Mercantiles, and Keystones – found it difficult to secure suitable playing grounds in the city. Because of the community's opposition to recreational sports, Philadelphia ball clubs were forced to play in Camden, New Jersey or across the Schuylkill River above the Fairmount Avenue Bridge near Harding's Inn and Tavern. With baseball's growing popularity, playing grounds soon encroached the outskirts of the city at 32nd and Hamilton and 11th and Wharton. It was not until the early war years that playing fields appeared at more accessible sites such as 10th and Camac Lane and 18th and Master Street. Eventually residential pressures compelled the Olympic and Mercantile ball clubs in 1864 to lease from the city "a handsome piece of ground at the north side of the Spring Garden Market" at 25th and Jefferson.[2]

Each club had two days a week for their practice. For a cost of about $1,500, the Olympics immediately built a clubhouse along Master Street and made substantial improvements by leveling and re-sodding the playing surface. The first game was played on Wednesday, May 24, 1864, between picked nines from Pennsylvania and New Jersey for the benefit of the United States Sanitary Commission. Without an enclosing fence, 2,000 spectators, paying 25 cents for admission, established the field's boundaries. The only field-sitting was for ladies who sat behind the players' bench.[3] This ballpark was marked by certain features. Along the third-base/Master Street side was the grass embankment of the old Spring Garden Reservoir. Trees also disrupted the playing site, and until the grounds were enclosed, neighborhood animals wandered onto the field of play. Parking for horse carriages was in the left field foul territory, and no elevated reporters' seating box existed until 1871.[4] Visible behind the 27th and Master home plate intersection on the Girard College campus was the towering Greek-styled Founders Hall with its Corinthian columns.[5]

The Jefferson Grounds experienced a significant overhaul when the city's best team, the Athletics, relocated there for the inaugural 1871 National Association of Professional Base Ball Players season. The Athletics had previously prospered at a popular site at 17th Street between Columbia and Montgomery Avenues before a housing development forced them to move to the Jefferson Grounds. Almost immediately, the Athletics tore down the old wooden grandstand and the encircling fence that had been erected in 1866. The new tenants re-sodded and leveled the playing surface, erected a 10-foot vertical slatted fence, and built a pair of tiered pavilions that abutted near the original home plate area on the corner of 25th and Master. Bleacher benches extended along the outfield lines. This rebuilt ball field held over 5,000 fans. This figure doubled during major ball games, when spectators lined up in front of the outfield fences and stood on wooden boxes that supported unstable raised wood planks. Those attendees who could not gain admission purchased

25-cent roof-top seats on neighboring houses, or sat on the branches of overhanging trees. These fans were termed "tree frogs," and were likened to "living fruit."[6]

Initially, the ball park was popular with women, but they eventually were turned off by the cursing, drinking, and the tobacco juice splashes on their dresses. Management tried to curb this rowdy behavior and attempted to attract fans with a music bandstand.[7] There was even talk in the off-season about having football games at Jefferson Grounds.[8] For the 1872 season, the champion Athletics resurfaced the infield, particularly the irregularly graded shortstop area. If these modifications were not completed in time for the new season the Athletics intended to schedule early-season games across the Delaware River in Gloucester, New Jersey.[9]

During the Athletics' third season at the Jefferson Grounds, alarms were raised over the possibility that the site would be sold to housing developers. The Athletics' directors were upset because they claimed to have invested over $7,000 on the ball field. After much debate and lobbying the politicians relented and the sale did not go through.[10] A subsequent concern was the building of additional cheap seats in the outfield. In 1874 this need intensified when the grounds welcomed a new tenant, the Philadelphia Centennials (also known as the Quakers or Fillies). The new club had the field every Monday and Thursday. The Athletics took the site on Wednesdays and Saturdays.[11] Prints of the playing grounds from a home plate perspective portrayed a wooden porched-styled construction.[12]

In spite of the clubs' successes the ball park was losing money. The tenant teams compensated by raising ticket prices and erecting a new interior fence that could be plastered with paying advertisements. But the prevalence of gambling and drinking at the ball field kept people away.[13] Eventually, the expenses of park maintenance and renovation exceeded revenues. They could not even afford a tarpaulin to cover

Courtesy of John Thorn.

The new reconfigured A.A. grounds focused at 27th and Jefferson. Note Founders Hall from Girard College over the center field fence.

the infield.[14] It was hoped that the Athletics' affiliation with the new National League in 1876 might save the old ball field. But the well-worn Jefferson Park did not appeal to fans and with low income and poor attendance the Athletics could not afford to remain in the new League. The unaffiliated and homeless Centennials now shifted their games to 24th Street and Ridge Avenue, Recreation Park, and the expelled Athletics' rump team in 1877 played unsanctioned games wherever they could find a ball field. It was obvious that more revenue could be made by turning part of the Jefferson Grounds over to residential developers. It took the creation of the American Association in 1882 to revive the Athletics and the old Jefferson Park ball field.

The Athletics initially played their inaugural Association season at Oakdale Park at 11th and Cumberland. This leisure recreation site had a large lake and an adjoining playing field, used early on for cricket. Some distance from the Jefferson/Columbia ball-playing corridor, the Oakdale grounds had been in use since 1866.[15] After nearly a decade the ball field became downtrodden until the displaced Olympics revived the grounds [1877-1881]. It was thus an ideal place for the revitalized Athletics to re-establish themselves.

Once the contracts had been signed, the Athletics razed the "old and unsightly" existing structure and replaced it with an upgraded wooden grandstand that held 2,000 spectators. The grounds were re-sodded and enlarged and open outfield benches were re-built for another 2,000 fans. A new fence was also erected for the start of the 1882 season.[16] Despite these renovations the ball field could not accommodate the large crowds that embraced the new Athletics. As a result, the Athletics decided to relocate back to the Jefferson Street ball field. Unfortunately, the original two-block 25th Street square site no longer existed. The city had committed the eastern portion to a new high school and 26th Street was cut through the original ball grounds. But the Athletics, recognizing the transportation convenience of the site, negotiated an initial lease for $1,000 for the remaining 27th Street remnant. As a result, the former center-field space became the new home plate area for the Association's Jefferson Street ball field.[17]

On the corner of 27th and Jefferson, the Athletics constructed "the handsomest ball grounds in the country."[18] The corner was backed up by a semi-circular two-tiered grandstand. Painted white and adorned in

Scorecard from home game, 1883 Philadelphia (vs. St. Louis) American Association.

"ornamental … fancy cornice work," the pavilions' occupants enjoyed arm-chair seating behind a wire-mesh screen. The structure eventually was topped by 32 private season boxes, each holding five people, and a 22-person press box. The grandstand sat 2,200 people and open benches bordering the outfield held more than 3000 fans.[19]

After a successful 1883 championship season, the ballpark's capacity was increased to 15,000. Special features abounded. The Oakdale flagstaff was planted at the 27th and Master Street corner[20], a private external staircase for box ticket holders was erected, a ladies room, with a female attendant, was set up and a bandstand, linking the third-base pavilion and outfield seats, was erected. The outfield benches were fronted by a horizontal slatted barrier and the left-field fence held a scoreboard and advertisements. Towering over the left-field benches was the Jefferson Street Mission Church. In the distance, beyond center field, was the still-visible Founders Hall on the Girard College campus.[21]

The new Athletics and their renovated ball field were overseen by a popular local triumvirate, Charles "Pop" Mason, Lew Simmons, and Billy Sharsig. They raised funds to finance the franchise and redesigned the grounds to suit their needs and limited budget. Each served a term as team manager, but Sharsig managed the ball club for five out of the eight years at Jefferson Street. The Athletics' record for these years was 519-464 for a .528 percentage. For most of their tenure at Jefferson Street the team was competitive and held their own attendance-wise against the National League Phillies. Their popularity was due to ballplayers like Bobby Mathews, Henry Larkin, Harry Stovey, and Louis Bierbauer. But Mason and Simmons recognized that the financial well-being of the franchise would be enhanced by Sunday ball playing. Unfortunately, Pennsylvania "Blue laws" forbade games on the Christian Sabbath. To counter this restriction Mason and his partners revived an old practice of scheduling games in Gloucester, New Jersey. Fans would assemble early on a Sunday morning at the South Street ferry and take a 45-minute crossing to Gloucester. Games were contested at a site next to the centrally-located race track that was served by horse trolleys. Radiating from this sporting juncture were saloons, betting parlors, fishcake stands, and other hostelries. One editorial called Gloucester "a nineteenth-century Sodom."[22]

The Athletics began the 1886 season with an advertisement claiming to be the "oldest playing organization in the United States." They asserted how they gave the Jefferson Street patrons "honest ball playing" when they posted the opening season schedule of games. These contests began at 4:00 P.M. and admission remained at 25 cents. Even the train schedule from Broad Street was publicized.[23] Despite this confidence, the ball field was again threatened by city officials. These ambitious politicians were deterred when they were reminded that no one except the Athletics was willing to pay the $2,000 lease for the grounds.[24] Once this issue was settled the Athletics re-dedicated their resources to repairing the grounds. They raised the infield, put in new cinder paths and purchased "an immense canvas to cover the entire infield."[25] Two years later, Mason and Simmons, looking for revenue, changed the ticket prices. General admission became 50 cents, and for an extra quarter women and their escorts could sit on cushioned seats in parts of the grandstand.[26] This new revenue was intended to cover the expenses of erecting a new fence, replacing old floorboards and re-painting the pavilions.[27] In spite of these changes, the growing threat of a players' strike put the Athletics and their ball park in jeopardy.

In 1890, the players' Brotherhood union brought a player strike team to Philadelphia. This anticipated rivalry moved the Pennsylvania Railroad to offer the Athletics a new ball field at a more competitive location with easy access from the Broad Street Station. It was rumored that the club was offered a five-year free lease if they moved to a site in West Philadelphia on the other side of the river below the Fortieth Street Bridge.[28] Rather than lose or alienate their existing fan base, the Athletics turned down this speculative offer. Instead the Athletics, in grounds which had been updated in a number of seasons, prepared for the 1890 strike season, competing against two Philadelphia ball clubs in different leagues. The season, as expected, was a hardship for the American Association Athletics. Attendance waned and expenses mounted. By the end of the year the Athletics had new management and the Jefferson Street grounds were on the verge of being eclipsed.

By the middle of the strike season the Athletics were plagued by pre-existing financial woes. In 1888, this condition moved Mason, Simmons, and Sharsig to seek new investors, like H.C. Pennypacker and his partner William Whitaker. But during the strike season of 1890 the club's problems mounted. In one instance, a suit for almost $300 was brought against the franchise in the Court of Common Pleas by carpenters who were not fully paid for their work on the pavilions.[29] The ball club also owed $1200 in back rent and $1435 for lumber purchases. To pay these outstanding debts the grandstand, inside fence, seats, flagstaff, ticket boxes and office furniture , appraised at $765 were sold at the end of the season for $600.[30] Sometime during these dealings, the Wagner brothers, J. Earle and George, wholesale meat distributers, took over the defunct franchise. Previously, the Wagners were stockholders in the city's Player League team. After the Jefferson Street field's sheriff sale, the Wagners shifted players from the three city ball clubs and set up their reconvene team at the Players League ball field, Forepaugh Park and Broad and Dauphin Streets.

The Athletics played one more season in Philadelphia before merging with the new National League Washington ballclub that previously played in the American Association. It was a better end than what was in store for the Jefferson ball field. Vacant and partially denuded during the 1891 season, the ballpark was set ablaze by neighborhood youngsters in November. A good deal of lumber, stored for carpenters repairing the surviving outside fence, fed the flames.[31] A month latter the Wagners' offices on Vine Street burned down. Fortunately, the office safe, with the club's records, tickets, and contracts, survived the fire.[32] By the following summer the old Jefferson Street grounds, behind a new "substantial fence" were converted into an enclosed "pleasure park" and playground.[33]

By the mid-1890s there was speculation that a new baseball association would take over the Jefferson Street site.[34] The future owners of the American League Athletics, Ben Shibe and Connie Mack, pondered the advantages of revisiting the old 27th Street ball field.[35] They investigated the options of a new annual lease, but investors did not want to commit $30,000, necessary for preparing the ball park, to a short-term lease. Nor were neighboring residents and the new 25th Street School happy with the prospect of a new ball park and its anticipated crowds.[36] As a result, the inaugural American League Athletics located to 29th and Columbia while the Jefferson Street site hosted leisure activities and an occasional Buffalo Bill Wild West Show.[37]

Today a memorial plaque to Billy Sharsig is mounted at the 26th Street recreation center and kids play on a softball field set on the grass and dirt of one of Philadelphia's oldest and most important ball playing sites.

NOTES

1   *Sunday Dispatch*, March 27, 1859.

2   *Sunday Mercury*, May 16, 1866 and March 3, 1872.

3   *Sunday Mercury*, May 22, 1864; *Philadelphia Inquirer*, May 25, 1864. Olympics club house, c. 1866. Baseball Hall of Fame Library, Olympics Folder: B 13.55.

4   *Evening City Item*, May 15, 1871.

5   Painting by A. Kollner, 1865 in Logan Library, Philadelphia. See also T. Eakins painting, 1875, "Baseball Players," at Rhode Island School of Design, Providence, Rhode Island.

6   *Sunday Dispatch*, September 15, 1872 and June 11, 1871; *Philadelphia Inquirer*, April 11, 1871.

7   *Sunday Dispatch*, April 7, 1873.

8   *Sunday Dispatch*, November 21, 1871.

9   *Sunday Dispatch*, April 7, 1872 and April 28, 1872.

10 *All Day City Item*, May 23, 1873.

11 *Sunday Dispatch*, January 25, 1874.

12 *The Daily Graphic*, April 30, 1873 and April 18, 1874.

13 *All Day City Item*, February 10, 1875; February 28, 1875; May 3, 1875.

14 *All Day City Item*, July 30, 1875.

15 *Sunday Mercury*, November 4, 1866.

16 *Sunday Item*, March 26, 1882.

17 By the end of the first year the Committee on City Property gave the Athletics a three-year renewable lease at $2000 a year. This agreement stood unless the new high school was built. In that case the city had to give the ball club a three-month notice of the forfeiture. *Sunday Dispatch*, December 9, 1883; *Philadelphia Press*, January 17, 1883; *Sunday Dispatch*, February 4, 1883,

18 *Sunday Item*, April 8, 1883 and April 1, 1883.

19 *Sunday Item*, April 8, 1883; *Sunday Dispatch*, January 14, 1883; *Philadelphia Record*, April 1, 1883.

20 *Philadelphia Record*, March 29, 1883.

21 *Frank Leslie Illustrated Newspaper*, October 6, 1883 and Gilbert & Bacon picture, 1884, Baseball Hall of Fame, B. 164.65. See also *Philadelphia Record*, March 29, 1883 and March 31, 1883. The late Larry Zuckerman calculated that the ball park's dimensions were 288-440-352. Zuckerman to J. Casway, August 7, 1999.

22 *North American*, August 28, 1899; May 5, 1893; *Philadelphia Inquirer*, October 10, 1898.

23 *Sporting Life*, March 31, 1886.

24 *Sporting Life*, May 5, 1886.

25 *Sporting Life*, November 17, 1886.

26 *Sporting Life*, April 25, 1888.

27 *Sporting Life*, February 20, 1889.

28 *Sporting Life*, October 16, 1889; *The Sporting News*, October 19, 1889,

29 *North American*, June 26, 1890; *Sporting Life*, June 28, 1890.

30 *North American*, October 18, 1890; *The Sporting News*, October 18, 1890; *Cleveland Plain Dealer*, October 15, 1890.

31 *Sporting Life*, November 28, 1891.

32 *Sporting Life*, December 12, 1891.

33 *Sporting Life*, June 18, 1892; *Sunday Item*, June 19, 1892; *The Sporting News*, October 27, 1894.

34 *Sporting Life*, October 27, 1894.

35 *The Sporting News*, September 23, 1900 and November 24, 1900.

36 *Philadelphia Press*, December 20, 1900.

37 *Philadelphia Press*, May 13, 1901; *Sunday Item*, May 11, 1902.

OWNERSHIP/MANAGEMENT

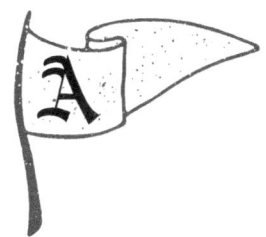

CHARLIE MASON

By Tim Hagerty

Charlie Mason was a co-owner and, for one game, a player for the 1883 American Association pennant-winning Philadelphia Athletics. He held other jobs throughout his baseball career and was an innovator, credited with conceiving the ladies day promotion and the rule that gave batters first base after they were hit by a pitch.

Charles Edward Mason was born on June 25, 1853, in New Orleans. It's difficult to confirm his parents' names or at what point in his childhood he moved from Louisiana to the Northeast. "Little is known of Mason's early life," is how one author phrased it.[1]

Mason attended Williams College in Williamstown, Massachusetts, in the early 1870s and played for baseball teams in nearby Adams and Pittsfield, Massachusetts, while there.[2] He was primarily a first baseman and outfielder and he hit and threw right-handed. His professional debut came in 1875 with the short-lived Philadelphia Centennials of the National Association, who folded on May 24 after a home loss in front of only 100 fans. Mason batted .234 with three RBIs as the Centennials went 2-12 in their only major-league season.

The Centennials' demise left Mason seeking a new team to play for. He and teammate Sam Field joined the National Association's Washington Nationals, another bumbling club that folded at midseason with a 5-23 record. Mason batted .091 (3-for-33) with the Nationals, but he remained persistent and played for a third team in 1875, finishing the season with the Ludlows in Kentucky.[3]

Mason's offensive and defensive skills earned him additional playing opportunities. One appraisal said he could "do good execution with the bat, being especially effective at critical junctures, and also a very clever baserunner. He, however, more particularly excels at first base, where he has few if any superiors, pluckily facing and holding the swiftest and wildest throwing, some of his catches and stops being extraordinary."[4]

He signed a one-year, $700 contract with the National Association's Philadelphia White Stockings on December 3, 1875, but was left without a job when the league disbanded on February 2, 1876.[5] Mason ended up splitting the 1876 season with

Charlie Mason, 1887

CHARLES E. MASON.

Image from New York Clipper, June 26, 1880.

Charles E. Mason

the independent Philadelphia Pearls and a club in Harrisburg, Pennsylvania.

It was also in 1876 that Mason umpired his only major-league game.[6] He was behind the plate for the Louisville-Philadelphia contest at the Jefferson Street Grounds on May 26, and the box score referred to him as "Mr. Mason."[7]

Mason played for two International Association teams in 1877, the Lynn Live Oaks and Rochester. While with Lynn, Mason was a teammate of curveball pioneer and future Hall of Famer Candy Cummings.

In 1878 Mason played for the Philadelphia Athletics when they weren't a major-league team.[8] He traveled west in 1879 to play for the Northwestern League's Davenport (Iowa) Brown Stockings, a team that included another future Hall of Famer, gloveless defensive virtuoso Bid McPhee. In 1880 and 1881, Mason was back in Philadelphia playing outfield for the Athletics.

By 1882, Mason was "the owner of a saloon and bookie joint"[9] and was ready to expand his portfolio. He partnered with sporting-goods salesman Billy Sharsig and minstrel show performer Lew Simmons to secure a ballpark lease and put up the money required to enter the major-league American Association. The three owners became known as "The Triumvirate" and

brought major-league baseball back to Philadelphia for the first time since 1876.

Mason's primary job at first was acquiring players. He "scoured the states himself and brought some of the best players obtainable to the A's."[10] Nineteenth-century scouting required negotiating with minor-league clubs to purchase desired players, a process illustrated in this newspaper description: "Mr. Mason came from the East. He visited Haverhill and tried to purchase the services of (Chippy) McGarr, the noted short stop. The Haverhill management refused to deal, however, but Mr. Mason has every promise that McGarr will sign with the Athletics for next season."[11]

On the Fourth of July in 1883, Mason was the central figure in a scene that would be inconceivable in modern major-league baseball. The Athletics were in Louisville for a doubleheader and Philadelphia catcher Jack O'Brien passed out from sunstroke in the sixth inning of the first game. Cub Stricker moved from second base to fill in at catcher and other Athletics repositioned, leaving Philadelphia without a right fielder or any bench players.

Mason was in the stands watching the situation unfold and he decided to volunteer his services. He rolled up his pants, walked through the gate and went to right field "doffing his plug hat and striped coat."[12] He caught a fly ball barehanded and got two late-game at-bats, going 1-for-2 with an RBI single.

With a roster partially constructed by Mason, the Athletics went 66-32 in 1883 and led the American Association in hits and runs. They competed in a tight pennant race down the stretch and edged the second-place St. Louis Browns by one game, clinching the title at Louisville on September 28 in their next to last game of the season. It was an especially memorable day for Mason, who married Kate Bayne Cook in Philadelphia on the same day the Athletics secured the pennant in Louisville.[13]

The team returned to Philadelphia and received a torchlight parade with celebratory flags flying.[14] Players attended a banquet and received personalized gold badges to commemorate their championship. Mason gave star player Harry Stovey a gold watch and chain because Stovey's "extraordinary grace and drive had sustained the club during its crucial final six weeks."[15]

The league championship was good for business. Mason and his partners made a $50,000 profit in 1883. "Fans flocked to Athletics' park, and, playing in a league still in its early stages, the triumvirate balanced very large revenues against small player payrolls and benefited from the (Association's) lack of a percentage system for determining visiting teams' gate shares, which would have enabled other clubs to share in the Philadelphia gravy," one historian observed.[16]

"Back in 1883 we did our own accounting," Mason explained. "With my partners, Simmons and Sharzig [sic], I sat in our dingy little ticket office down at the old Athletics Park, 26th and Jefferson streets, and there we counted the quarters, dimes, nickels and pennies – yes there were 'coppers' in our receipts – and the money was placed in three equal piles. When the three partners were satisfied the count was correct, each pocketed his third of the day's receipts."[17]

Mason continued working as an Athletics executive before moving to the dugout in 1887 for the only major-league managing assignment of his career. The Athletics were 26-29 and in fifth place on June 29 when manager Frank Bancroft was fired and replaced by Mason. Philadelphia went 38-40 for the remainder of the season under Mason, who was not brought back to manage in 1888. Sharsig replaced him and became the Athletics' fourth manager in four years.

The Triumvirate wasn't thriving financially as it had in 1883 and "by the fall of 1887 they had to reorganize to take in new investors from among the Philadelphia business community."[18] Mason's role with the Athletics faded in 1888 and he moved on to a new, ambitious plan – indoor baseball.

Mason booked the main building on the state fairgrounds in Philadelphia and arranged a full-size infield there. The indoor outfield was much smaller than ballpark outfields, but Mason counterbalanced the small dimensions by using deadened baseballs with cork centers. There were ground rules specific to the indoor facility, like batters receiving automatic doubles on balls hit into the stands.

The first Mason-organized indoor game was held on Christmas Day in 1888 and players from the two major-league teams in Philadelphia participated. The game was a disappointment; only 2,000 people came to the arena with a capacity of 5,000. "The number of posts and braces in the building also acted as a drawback, and the bad light rendered the catching of a swiftly thrown ball difficult and hazardous business," the *Boston Globe* noted.[19]

Mason returned to outdoor baseball in the spring of 1889, managing the minor-league Philadelphia Giants of the Middle States League while simultaneously serving as the league's president.[20] In 1890

he managed the Eastern Interstate League team in Allentown, Pennsylvania, where future Hall of Famer Hughie Jennings was one of his players.

Mason also showed honesty in Allentown on days he had to leave the dugout to be a fill-in umpire. A hometown sports reporter wrote, "Charley [sic] Mason is one of the few managers in the country who can go in and umpire a thoroughly impartial, first-class game, in which his team is one of the contestants. Some managers would seize upon this golden opportunity to help his team out, but Charley Mason is not built that way."[21]

His disposition was also praised in an article of unknown provenance found in his National Baseball Hall of Fame Library player file: "His coolness in critical emergencies, and his judgement in availing himself of every point of play offered may also be mentioned as marked characteristics. In all of his professional career he has maintained the reputation of a hard-working and reliable player."[22]

Late in his life, Mason worked as a clerk,[23] a superintendent of a ballclub,[24] and a ballpark cashier.[25] He died at his home in Germantown, Pennsylvania on October 21, 1936, at age 83. He was survived by his second wife, Sarah A. MacGregor, daughters Anna and Margaret, and sons Charles and William. William was "the star pitcher of the Wildwood, N.J. independent team" as a teenager.[26]

Obituaries credited Mason with multiple noteworthy innovations. "'Ladies' Day' was conceived by Mason when he noticed that women didn't attend ballgames," one of his obituaries noted. "They were

public domain

Mason and family

invited by the Athletics management, so they came in large numbers and evinced interest."[27]

Mason certainly could have come up with the Athletics' ladies day promotion on his own, but at least one SABR historian pointed out that other clubs offered women free admission in the mid-1860s, long before Mason worked in Philadelphia.[28]

The *Philadelphia Inquirer* credited Mason with another significant development: "The ruling, still in force today, that a batter hit by a pitched ball should take first base, was suggested by Mr. Mason."[29] Other summaries were more skeptical. One author described Mason as "claiming to have suggested the hit by pitch rule."[30]

It's hard to determine if the hit-by-pitch rule was exclusively Mason's brainchild. The concept was discussed at the American Association's annual convention at Cincinnati's Grand Hotel on December 12-13, 1883, but Mason wasn't there; the Athletics were represented by Simmons and Sharsig. Those same two delegates represented the club, without Mason, at the American Association's next meetings, March 4-5, 1884, in Baltimore, where the concept was revisited.[31] The hit-by-pitch rule was approved and officially added to the American Association's constitution on July 23, 1884, in Columbus, Ohio.[32]

So Mason wasn't present for the key league meetings that decided the hit-by-pitch rule, but he was considered the baseball expert among the Triumvirate, so it's possible he pushed the idea to Sharsig, Simmons, or other colleagues leading up to the decisive meetings.

Rulebook innovator or not, Charlie Mason made his mark on nineteenth-century baseball, especially the 1883 American Association champions.

SOURCES

In addition to the sources cited in the Notes, the author used Baseball-Reference.com, Newspapers.com, and Retrosheet.org.

NOTES

1 David Nemec, *Major League Baseball Profiles, 1871-1900, Volume 2: The Hall of Famers and Memorable Personalities Who Shaped the Game* (Lincoln, Nebraska: Bison Books, 2011), 171.

2 John M. Flynn, "Connie's Classy Combination Completely Curbs the Cardinals," *Berkshire County Eagle* (Pittsfield, Massachusetts), October 2, 1930.

3 Nemec, 171.

4 "Charles E. Mason," unidentified clipping in Mason's Baseball Hall of Fame Library player file.

5 "1875 Charles Mason Philadelphia White Stockings National Association Player's Contract," robertedward-auctions.com, December 3, 1875, 2012 auction.

6 "Charlie Mason," Retrosheet.org player page.

7 "That Drawn Game," *The Times* (Philadelphia), May 27, 1876.

8 "Ball and Bat," *The Times* (Philadelphia), August 10, 1878.

9 Nemec, *The Great Encyclopedia of Nineteenth-Century Major League Baseball* (Tuscaloosa, Alabama: University of Alabama Press, 2006), 219.

10 "'Pop' Mason Dies; Gave A's First Title," *Atlanta Constitution*, October 23, 1936.

11 "No New Players for the Athletic," *The Times* (Philadelphia), July 2, 1886.

12 "A Sudden Change," *Louisville Courier-Journal*, July 5, 1883.

13 Marriage certificate, Pennsylvania Marriages, 1709-1940, FamilySearch.org.

14 John Thorn, "A Pictorial Chronology of Baseball in the 19th Century, Part 10: 1883," *Our Game*, June 17, 2019.

15 Edward Achorn, *The Summer of Beer and Whiskey* (New York: Public Affairs Press, 2006), 240.

16 Nemec, *Major League Baseball Profiles, 1871-1900*, 180-181.

17 Stoney McLinn, "Charley Mason Responsible for Hit Batsman Receiving Free Ticket to Initial Sack," unidentified publication, article found in Mason's Baseball Hall of Fame Library player file.

18 Nemec, *Major League Baseball Profiles, 1871-1900*, 181.

19 "Base Ball Indoors," *Boston Globe*, December 26, 1888.

20 Paul Browne, *The Coal Barons Played Cuban Giants: A History of Early Professional Baseball in Pennsylvania, 1886-1896* (Jefferson, North Carolina: McFarland, 2013), 78.

21 "Grand Stand Chat," *Harrisburg Telegraph*, June 28, 1890.

22 "Charles E. Mason," unidentified clipping in Mason's Baseball Hall of Fame Library player file.

23 US Census Bureau, 1900 US Census.

24 US Census Bureau, 1910 US Census.

25 US Census Bureau, 1930 US Census.

26 Unidentified clipping in Mason's Baseball Hall of Fame Library player file, August 21, 1915.

27 "Mason, Old A's Manager, Dies," *Philadelphia Evening Bulletin*, October 22, 1936.

28 Peter Morris, *A Game of Inches: The Stories Behind the Innovations That Shaped Baseball* (Chicago: Ivan R. Dee, 2010), 426.

29 "Charles E. Mason," *Philadelphia Inquirer*, October 24, 1936.

30 Browne, 79.

31 "The American Base-Ball Association at Baltimore," *St. Louis Post-Dispatch*, March 5, 1884.

32 "That Star Chamber Session," *Cincinnati Enquirer*, July 24, 1884.

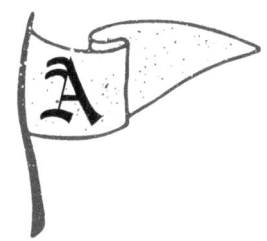

LEW SIMMONS

By Michael McAvoy

INTRODUCTION

Lew Simmons was a popular performer as a minstrel entertainer both before and after his time in baseball management. One of many persons who linked the theater with nineteenth-century baseball, Simmons was a noted banjoist, a professional comedian of great repute, and an end man with the tambourine in the minstrel show.[1] There is considerable evidence that Simmons was a baseball fan his entire life.

Simmons gave up minstrelsy when owning a baseball club offered better returns. Between 1882 and 1887, he embraced active partnership with Charles Mason and William Sharsig to own the Philadelphia franchise in the American Association. Simmons managed his club, represented its interests in the American Association, and represented the Association's interests in its conferences with the National League to create what we know today as major-league baseball, or Organized Baseball, including the recognition of territory, respect for player contracts, an early form of player reserve, and a means to settle disputes. David Nemec observes, "[I]n AA councils Simmons was the most prominent in the ownership group. The presence of a successful professional comedian must have given a unique dimension to meetings of AA bigwigs. Simmons, not surprisingly, was a genial fellow always ready with a story, but was taken seriously in AA councils. ..."[2] Simmons was best recalled from that era as part of the triumvirate ownership group with Mason and Sharsig. He was the business manager of the pennant-winning 1883 club that captured the AA pennant in the most exciting pennant race to that point in baseball history. For Philadelphia baseball fans, Simmons sought another championship, but they had a long wait until the 1910 World Series champions under another owner and manager, Connie Mack, whose club Simmons passionately followed.

When the returns in baseball decreased, Simmons sold his economic interests in the Athletics. Failing in business, Simmons successfully returned to minstrel performances.

Simmons was born on August 27, 1838 at New Castle, Pennsylvania.[3] In an early recollection, Simmons fell into the flooded Shenango River. At grave danger, P. Ross Berry, a teenaged African American, saved Simmons. Berry later settled in Youngstown, Ohio, and whenever Simmons visited Youngtown, he would visit with Berry in his rooms

LEW SIMMONS

Courtesy of John Thorn.

Lew Simmons

23

or at the theater. Simmons commemorated his fortune by wearing on his watch chain a personalized Masonic charm, the reverse of which was engraved with an African American man rescuing a White male child.[4]

By 1842, the family moved to Warren in northeastern Ohio, where his father, William, worked as a cooper, or barrel maker.[5] There, Simmons experienced an event that shaped and guided him for the remainder of his life:

"When I was about 6 years of age my father took me to a circus and we stayed for the minstrel performance that closed the show. One of the players did a blackface stunt and played the banjo. That caught my youthful fancy. I had a fairly good singing voice and immediately took up the study of the banjo."[6]

Simmons reflected, "[T]he instant I saw that man with the banjo, I told my father that some day I was going to play one, too." Simmons's father purchased a banjo for him.[7] Simmons enjoyed a childhood of performance on stage and with music. He and a dozen other boys would rehearse a play, and then perform at a benefit. Around 1851, Ed Slocum arrived in Warren with a dream to manage a show, and quickly put together a minstrel trio that included young Simmons and his banjo.[8] Slocum later became Simmons's business partner during the 1870s.[9]

When Simmons was 13, the family moved to Massillon, Ohio, where he worked as a hotel bellboy, then sold papers on the Pittsburgh, Fort Wayne and Chicago Railroad. The family thereafter moved to Lockport, New York, near Buffalo and alongside the Erie Canal. There, Lew learned his father's profession, that of a cooper.[10]

Ambitions beyond manual labor and town life led Simmons to seek fame and fortune as an entertainer. At 18 he left home to join Yankee Robinson's Circus, then touring from Bloomington, Illinois.[11] He was paid $20 a month for physical tasks, but Robinson allowed him to play the banjo in a small minstrel show if he put up the tent.[12]

At the end of the 1858 season, the circus broke up its tour outside Indianapolis, where Simmons spent the winter. The Empire Minstrels, one of those traveling troupes common in that time period, also broke up at Indianapolis around the same time, and Simmons learned from them how to improve his banjo play. When a funny banjo solo was met with audience disapproval, Simmons declared afterward, "That was a pretty bad reception, boys, but it don't scare me. I'll be at the top of the heap yet."[13] Simmons was determined to reach the top of his craft. In the spring of 1859, he

moved to Detroit to play the banjo professionally at Beller's Music Hall, where he earned $1 and four beer tickets a night.[14] There was some interchange between theater and baseball in that era and Simmons was an example of the mixture.[15] He claimed to have first played baseball at Detroit around 1859.[16]

Simmons returned home in 1859, but he was determined to make it on his own and in show business. By the summer, he left for New York City with his banjo and – just in case – his cooper's tools.[17] He began his full-time minstrel career on December 19, 1859, playing the banjo at Frank Rives' Melodeon Theatre on 539 Broadway for $8 a week. Simmons was good enough that Rives quickly increased his pay to $15 a week, then put him on a year's contract at $25 per week, three nights in New York, and three at Rives' Philadelphia theatre.[18] No more nightly earnings or beer tickets for Simmons! This move introduced Simmons to Philadelphia's theater scene.

During the Civil War, Simmons sang popular patriotic songs and performed in burlesques in places like Boston, Chicago, New York, and Philadelphia.[19] He never mentioned military service in his interviews, and none was provided in his obituary.

Simmons continued to play baseball as an amateur during the 1860s, playing first in New York, then in Philadelphia, where he played games with the Athletic Club.[20] Simmons joined the Athletic Club in 1865, and during 1866-1867, he claimed to have played in one of its nines against well-known amateur clubs like the Haymakers and the Mutuals.[21] When Oakdale Park opened on July 30, 1866, Simmons later proudly noted that the record books showed he scored 10 runs and recorded an out in one game.[22] This early association with amateur baseball was one he would often refer to when he became a baseball magnate, as if his old-time involvement in the game provided him with the credibility to be taken seriously by his partners, colleagues, players, press, and fans.

How did Lewis Simmons become involved in owning the Philadelphia Athletics? Some backstory. Billy Sharsig, Charles Mason, Horace Phillips, and Chick Fulmer – the shortstop – were at times partners in the 1881 version of the Athletics. These owners contributed to the transition of professional baseball in Philadelphia from unorganized and independent teams into a market controlled by organized baseball. This Athletics club was a member of the short-lived 1881 Eastern Championship Association. Much like associations other than the National League, its existence lacked stability. After the season, the Athletics went on a Western tour and the team's owners noted the large crowds that appeared for many of its exhibitions.[23] Philly crowds were often large but the Eastern Championship Association was unstable, which likely led Sharsig and Mason to seek entry into the National League. In mid-August, Phillips met with William Hulbert and applied for admission of the Athletics; however, within two weeks, the Athletics withdrew the application and released manager Phillips.[24] Soon after the departure of Phillips, Simmons joined the partnership with Mason, Sharsig, and Fulmer. As an amateur player of some repute, he likely jumped at the opportunity for a chance to own and manage a baseball team, especially given the risks he'd taken in show business. The Athletics soon became the Philadelphia entry in the new American Association.

How Simmons became an owner is not entirely clear. The most consistent story is that he partnered with Fulmer, Mason, and Sharsig after a $200 payment for Phillips' quarter-interest.[25] Simmons recalled, "I paid the three $200 in gold, and you should have seen them scramble to divide it."[26] Soon, due to political difficulties, Fulmer fled Philadelphia and surrendered his partnership interest. Rather than take a risk as an owner in a new association, Fulmer had signed a contract to play shortstop for the Cincinnati American Association club.[27] The partnership of Sharsig, Mason, and Simmons became the famous triumvirate of the 1883 Athletics with Simmons often its most public representative.

Simmons became the business manager of the Athletics.[28] Bill James describes the typical manager of the 1880s as "[a] young entrepreneur … Some of these, like Cap Anson, stayed in baseball until circumstances forced them out. But more of them, best represented by John Montgomery Ward, were on their way to some other destination."[29] Simmons had come by a different route. Except for the 1884 season, until 1887, sportswriters referred to him as manager of the Athletics, and this reference was clearly related to the business position.[30] By early December of 1881, Simmons was established in the Athletics headquarters at 135 North Eighth Street, and plans were announced to erect a new fence and seating for 1,000 at the old-time Athletics home of Oakdale Park. Season tickets with a reserved seat were offered for $10, and they were reportedly going fast.[31]

Though Simmons claimed to have left minstrelsy after he became manager of the Athletics, neither engaged contractually with an organized company nor performing for a regular theater program, he continued

to entertain for money. Akin to the modern speakers bureau, Simmons used his musical and comedic talents with his newfound fame as an Athletics club owner to offer his services as an event performer. After taking on the management of the Athletics, Simmons continued to perform with Thatcher's Minstrels, on tour as late as May 1882.[32]

The triumvirate enjoyed early financial success. The partners split $15,000 at the end of the 1882 season. Simmons observed that his share of the profits exceeded the cumulative shares from the time he managed the theater.[33] After the 1882 season, he appeared in benefits and toured with the Arch Street Opera House Minstrels.[34]

Simmons continued to play baseball, too. He was the captain of the troupe of Courtright and Hawkins' Minstrels. The minstrels – in costume – defeated the Athletics 21-18 in an exhibition game on October 2, 1882, in front of 1,000 fans at Oakdale park.[35]

Seeking a pennant and greater profits, the triumvirate upgraded the 1883 Athletics with players who had National League experience. Simmons engaged Fred Corey (Worcester), Alonzo Knight (Detroit), Bobby Mathews (Boston), Mike Moynahan (League Alliance Philadelphia), Ed Rowen (Boston), and Harry Stovey (Worcester).[36] Before the start of the 1883 season, the triumvirate incurred $15,000 debt to pay advance money, lease new grounds, and construct the enclosed

Sheet music cover for traditional song as sung by Simmons.

stands.[37] Using his show-business contacts, Simmons obtained a loan of $16,000 from Adam Forepaugh of Forepaugh's Circus.[38]

The 1883 race was one of the first to have an uncertain outcome heading into the final week of the season. In 1902 Simmons reflected on how he tried to buy a pennant for his 1883 Athletics. Using the promise of gifts, he encouraged an opposing club to beat the St. Louis Browns, owned by Chris Von der Ahe, who had to add his own encouragement to the Athletics' opponents:

"I was more or less superstitious. ... I rounded up [the Pittsburgh players] and made a speech, saying that if they would win but one game in Saint Louis, I would buy each and every player a $25 overcoat. ... They never got the coats – they did not win a game....

"Von der Ahe telegraphed from Saint Louis that he would give a $50 suit of clothes to every man on the Louisville team if they beat us four straight. Henry Pank, owner of the Louisvilles, sent smiling Guy Hecker in against us that day and the man who is now selling groceries in Oil City certainly did pitch the ball the first game. ... The next day was one to make angels weep." [39]

To capture the pennant, the Athletics needed either a single win at Louisville in their final series of the season, or St. Louis to lose a game in their series against the Allegheny club:

"When I saw we were gone I rushed up to Pank and shouted loud enough to be heard all over the stand: 'I will give you $1,000 cash to put a man we can hit in there tomorrow.'

"This, coupled with the fact that in the eighth inning with men on second and third and two runs needed to win the game, I had rushed out to Rowen at bat and promised him $500 for a hit which would score both men, set the people thinking I was crazy. I was almost crazy. ..."[40]

Such behavior today would earn Simmons some grief from the league offices, including a permanent ban from Organized Baseball, but times were different then. Simmons fondly recalled the hit by Moynahan that scored the winning runs: "I was so near a nervous wreck that I didn't even have enough voice to yell. ... I gave a kid a dollar to chase that ball down for me, and I kept it for years."[41] Simmons had an appreciation for game relics before there were memorabilia collectors.

Their season was highly profitable, with the triumvirate splitting $51,000.[42] From just two seasons of ownership, Simmons had cleared $22,000. More than

the money, Simmons especially enjoyed the limelight brought to him as a baseball magnate and the adulation he received from Philadelphia's baseball-crazed public. Politicians attended their games. Thousands of fans clamored to watch. Simmons truly loved being its fulcrum:

"I was in the game up to my neck and was having the time of my life, making money and friends and enjoying good things. Then I got too blooming ambitious – didn't want only a million, but several million, all at once."[43]

After the championship season, Simmons turned down a reported offer of $50,000 for his one-third partnership interest. He expected the Athletics to earn more than $75,000 in 1884.[44] With his newfound wealth, Simmons purchased a $10,000 house and fruit farm in Vineland, New Jersey.[45] And he closely supervised improvements to the ballpark's grandstand and private boxes.[46] However, 1883 was the high point in both the field and bank for his baseball work.

The triumvirate soon learned that the talent in other Association clubs was catching up with that on the Athletics. Increasing the competitive pressure, their National League competitor, owned by Al Reach, quickly improved under Harry Wright's management. Wright's club began its practice at the beginning of April 1884. Athletics players were seen around town but not always at their ballpark. An observer who appeared at Athletics Park to watch practice and discovered only two players present inquired why. Simmons answered that the players would practice "when we can control our team," after April 15, when their contracts began.[47]

The 1884 baseball preseason was exciting, with lots of Hot Stove League intrigue, the entrance of a new major league, the Union Association, and franchise expansion in the American Association from eight clubs to 12. Simmons opposed this expansion.[48] His opposition was likely due to increased competition for players, which would increase salaries and lower the level of available talent, reduce the number of home games, and require greater travel expenses. Simmons sought unsuccessfully to strengthen the Athletics by negotiating with players under contract to Union Association clubs, those players not subject to Organized Baseball's reserve rules. He actively wooed Fred Dunlap, the former Cleveland superstar.[49] In a major coup, Simmons separated Billy Taylor from Henry Lucas's St. Louis Union Club.[50] Although the Athletics management acquiesced to an Eastern League entry in Philadelphia, Simmons was on record as opposing it, and he appeared to understand fully well the likely degradation in his franchise's value when the city already had League and Union Association competitors: "There is enough base ball in this city without it."[51]

The Athletics' 1884 season was disappointing both in the field (61-46, 14 games out of first place) and in its finances. These failures resulted in conflict between the owners and the players. Simmons blamed manager Lon Knight, whom he viewed as ineffective, and he announced that he would manage the Athletics in 1885.[52] In what would become an unfortunately common management practice on his part, Simmons bad-mouthed the players. A postseason interview in *Sporting Life* was reprinted in other newspapers and caused a blowup in the baseball world.[53] Simmons went full bore and publicly blamed Knight for poor management, complained that the players did not follow team rules, and said the club's profits were down $20,000. Simmons blamed the team's budding star Harry Stovey for at least one lost game:

"Lon Knight was too easy for a manager. The men were allowed too many privileges, and more than one game was lost that would have been won had the men been in proper condition. That story about Stovey being injured by a falling scaffold at Ninth and Chestnut streets was very lame. The simple fact is that Stovey was intoxicated and Knight refused to allow him to play."[54]

With his reputation at stake, Stovey immediately replied in *Sporting Life* with a denial and an announcement that he would not play under Simmons.[55] Now facing the loss of their star player, the partners Sharsig and Mason worked to contain the damage:

"There will be no more experiments, and Mr. Alonzo Knight will manage and Mr. Harry Stovey captain the team. Under the circumstances the prospects we consider very flattering. Mr. Simmons' claim that his management won the championship in 1883, was simply one of his midnight dreams."[56]

Simmons did not back off and replied, "Facts are facts and speak for themselves."[57] Self-reflecting on his own hubris, he connected his thoughts of his importance within minstrelsy to those of player threats to not play for him:

"The trouble is with the players, they think they're indispensable, but that's where they make a grand mistake. Suppose Stovey or Knight should die, would the Athletic Club stop playing ball? Well, I guess not. I had that idea myself when I left the minstrel business,

but the sun rises and sets just the same, and the show keeps moving along without me."[58]

From the end of the 1884 season, there was little evidence that Simmons performed on the stage. Instead, he focused on managing the Athletics. Simmons managed the 1885 Athletics and Stovey played for him. That season Simmons again spoke ill of his players. Some, he said, failed to earn their salaries and others he threatened to release.[59] His remarks failed to have the desired effect, and the triumvirate were dissatisfied with the playing outcome of the 1885 season. *Sporting Life* wrote that Simmons suffered "an uncontrollable temper." There was a push to replace him with a professional baseball manager, and *Sporting Life* opined that the Athletics could do worse than Frank Bancroft. This was ironic. According to *Sporting Life*, Bancroft was an excellent business manager, but the triumvirate already enjoyed good home revenues and received their guarantee for road dates, therefore Bancroft's natural talents would be of no use. And even worse, his social skills were unsuited to player management.[60]

At the 1885-1886 winter meetings, a reporter for *Sporting Life* wrote of Simmons:

"Lew is original, usually has a good story to tell, and is for war with the League for breaking the Reserve Rule, etc., but he wants no trouble, consequently when he is shown that there will be sure enough trouble if the war comes, he is not for it yet."[61]

Simmons appeared to be a person who said what was on his mind or what he believed in, but in the end, he was a team player. He expressed conflict, but he preferred to get along.

In preparing for 1886, the triumvirate shifted their strategy in composing a roster. As the National League Phillies improved with young talent developed under Wright's tutelage, the triumvirate understood fully well how the reserve rule protected the Phillies' investment in that development. The triumvirate resolved to sign fewer older and experienced players and instead sought younger talent. Those players who proved themselves, the triumvirate would reserve. This is a practice many clubs follow today: Develop a promising young roster, fill in the pieces with veterans, then start over. While Simmons was not in favor of the youth movement, he went along with the experiment.[62]

Simmons managed the 1886 club, but it was unsuccessful. In a seemingly frenetic attempt to win, Simmons gave prospects regular tryouts and released underperforming contracted players, continually reordering the Athletics lineup.[63] With the team suffering through a stretch of losses during a midsummer road trip, a correspondent reported, "Lew Simmons remarked to me the other day that he wouldn't know how to feel if his boys would happen to win the game."[64] As the losing took its toll on him, Simmons reportedly lost 20 pounds.[65] The *Sporting Life* correspondent exclaimed, "It's worth the price of admission to sit within range when his club is getting the worst of it, and particularly when the boys make bad blunders."[66] Simmons again used the press to embarrass his players. He said that he would play in a game because he and Sharsig "can improve upon the work of the regular club batteries."[67]

After the 1886 season, the triumvirate declared the youth movement experiment a success. Younger players like second baseman Lou Bierbauer and catcher Wilbert Robinson were quickly developing into effective starters.[68] However the work of their free-agent veterans (Joe Start and George Bradley) was judged unsatisfactory. Simmons came around, too: "Old players, why, they're chestnuts."[69] Other clubs took notice and some sold their rights to veterans and signed younger talent.[70] Heading into the 1887 season, Simmons provided public support for this strategy:

"I don't take as much stock in 'old blood' as some people do, for I think young fellows if properly handled and if they have had some fair experience, can do just as well as anyone. We have got a good bit of new blood in our team for the coming season and we are going to do excellent work."[71]

The 1886 season proved to be Simmons's last in the Athletics' business management; Mason and Sharsig blamed him for the poor financial performance at home games.[72] It was very likely Simmons had too many other responsibilities, including his vaudeville and minstrel performances, for him to be successful in baseball management during the 1886 season.

Simmons was not independently wealthy, so he lived off what he earned as an owner. When the club neither paid its own expenses nor provided him income, he decided he had to sell his interest. However, once he sold his economic interest in the Athletics, Simmons was unable to get back into Organized Baseball. There is evidence that he tried to reenter baseball, his name linked to a new American Association league with a franchise in Philadelphia, but nothing eventuated.

Simmons continued to be a baseball fan in general. He wasn't just partial to the Athletics. When his Athletics were on the road, Simmons was often at the National League park, where he could be found in his favorite seat in the top row of the lower deck of the pavilion.[73] He was often noted as present at the team's Opening Day ceremonies.[74]

Unlike Sharsig, who had a long and professional career in Organized Baseball, Simmons's flame burned bright and fast. While he was in baseball, he was the most visible and active of the triumvirate.

The Reach guides show that Simmons held the offices of secretary in 1883, secretary and treasurer in 1884, secretary in 1885, secretary and manager in 1886, and president in 1887.

A review of the American Association guides shows that Simmons was a director of the Association in the seasons of 1882, 1883, 1885, 1886, and 1887, the Association's vice president in 1884, and a member of the schedule committee in 1885 and 1886.

Simmons was both a leader and an innovator. In 1906 he claimed that he introduced the practice of making more than one ball available for a game. He noted the custom of playing with a single ball and the time spent waiting by players and fans for the return of the ball when the batter hit it into the stands or out of the park. With a bit of humor, Simmons stated:

"In a moment of brilliant inspiration it occurred to me that we might as well have two balls in the game, so that if one was put out of play the other could be used. I reasoned that it was a waste of time for some 15,000 spectators to play thumbs while the ground keeper was digging a lost baseball out of the tall grass, so I surprised the fans by introducing two balls. It made a great hit, and I was voted a good fellow and a very smart man for having thought of it. I always will believe that for this one thing alone the fans of the country owe me an inexhaustible debt of gratitude."[75]

In addition to the extra ball, Simmons claimed two additional innovations. One related to fan experience: He had a net placed behind the home-plate area to protect spectators from passed and batted balls. The other was a change in the rules which penalized the pitcher for striking the batter with a pitched ball.[76]

A change in the rules that Simmons did not later claim, but one in which he clearly had a role, was the elimination of the foul bound, which called it an out when a foul ball was caught on the first bounce. Once on record favoring the foul bound, Simmons changed his view and seconded the motion to end the foul-bound rule.[77]

After selling his interest in the club and losing money on a failed baseball tour of Cuba, Simmons cast about for something permanent. He worked briefly for a machine-oil firm[78] and for a book publisher.[79]

He also operated cigar stores and opened a saloon, all the while keeping an interest in show business.

FAMILY LIFE

On September 9, 1863, Simmons married Mary Blaber, about 18 years old, in New York City.[80] Their 10-week-old daughter, Mary, died on November 30, 1868, of capillary bronchitis.[81] A son, Lewis Jr., also died.[82] Mary died on April 26, 1897, of pneumonia, at the age of 51. An adopted daughter, Anna Francis, survived.[83] When 20 years old, Anna married Charles B. Connolly on September 2, 1903.[84] Anna and Charles produced a large family.

On May 13, 1905, Simmons, then 66 years old, married Sarah "Sallie" Rhoda, 40, of Allentown, in Philadelphia, where he lived at 17 North 60th Street.[85] His comedic minstrel sketch first performed during the winter of 1897-1898, was "Sally Is the Girl for Me," which could be a coincidence. Once married, Simmons and Sallie lived in Allentown at 501 N. 8th Street.[86] Sallie died on February 10, 1920.[87]

Simmons was related to two professional baseball players. Joe Quest, a member of the 1886 Athletics, was also from New Castle, Pennsylvania. Simmons was related by marriage to Arlie Latham of the St. Louis Browns;[88] he was the uncle of Latham's wife.

Simmons was a member in Philadelphia's LuLu Temple Ancient Arabic Mystic Shrine, which had 2,000 members,[89] and also an active member of the fraternal organization the Benevolent and Protective Order of Elks.[90] As a founding member of Philadelphia's "Jolly Corks," its members, including Simmons, founded Lodge No. 2 at Philadelphia on March 12, 1871.[91] Simmons was said to visit with the Elks lodge wherever one was located at the place he performed on tour.[92]

Simmons's life ended violently. While on the vaudeville circuit tour performing his comedic sketch *Get on The Band Wagon*, Simmons was in Reading, Pennsylvania, as part of a program at the Orpheum Theatre. On September 2, 1911, during the busy noon hour, he walked to his hotel to meet his wife, Sallie, who usually traveled with him when he was on tour. As he crossed the street, Simmons was struck by an ice team being driven the wrong way in the street. According to one eyewitness report, one of the horses struck Simmons in the face and the wagon crushed his ribs.[93] All accounts report that a moment after he was knocked down, he was struck by a brewery truck. Loaded with beer kegs, the truck dragged Simmons

up to 50 feet. Simmons's injuries included a broken right leg, a fractured left arm, a crushed breast, and the splintering of every rib on his left side.[94] Simmons died five minutes after admission to the Homeopathic Hospital.[95] For the cause of death, the death certificate says, "Accidentally killed by being run over by an automobile. Shock, fractures, and internal hemorrhages."[96] Simmons was buried in Fairview Cemetery in Allentown.[97]

THANK YOU

For sharing information, thoughts, and ideas, I thank James E. Brunson III, Richard Hershberger, Tom Shieber, L.M. Sutter, John Thorn, and Robert Warrington.

SOURCES

Sources included the following:

Achorn, Edward. "The Minstrel Star," in *The Summer of Beer and Whiskey* (New York: Public Affairs, 2013).

Le Roy, Edward. "Lew Simmons" (obituary), *New York Clipper*, September 16, 1911.

Reach's Official American Association Base Ball Guide for 1883 to 1888.

Sutter, L.M. "'I'm an Actor, You Bet' (1888)," in *Arlie Latham: A Baseball Biography of the Freshest Man on Earth* (Jefferson, North Carolina: McFarland, 2012), 86.

NOTES

1   "Toboyne Township," *Newport* (Pennsylvania) *News*, August 28, 1886: 8; "Old-Time Minstrels," *Philadelphia Times*, November 27, 1887: 6.

2   David Nemec, *Major League Baseball Profiles, 1871-1900: The Hall of Famers and Memorable Personalities Who Shaped the Game* (Lincoln: University of Nebraska Press, 2011), 180-181.

3   "Lew Simmons," *New York Clipper*, September 16, 1911.

4   "Lew Simmons' Close Call," *New Castle* (Pennsylvania) *News*, April 3, 1901: 12.

5   Brothers Dallas Simmons (8 years) and Thomas Simmons (4 years) were recorded born in Ohio in the 1850 Census. United States Census, 1850, *Family Search*, https://www.familysearch.org/ark:/61903/1:1:MX3Z-QBM, accessed July 2020.

6   "Sport Comment," *St. Louis Star and Times*, February 2, 1910: 8.

7   "Lew Simmons at the Orpheum," *Allentown Leader*, September 28, 1909: 1.

8   "Years of Burnt Cork," *Philadelphia Times*, September 10, 1893: 16.

9   "Seen and Heard in Many Places," *Philadelphia Times*, October 19, 1895: 8.

10   "Lew Simmons at the Orpheum."

11   "Old Yankee Robinson," *Bloomington* (Illinois) *Pantagraph*, September 13, 1881: 4; "Sport Comment," *St. Louis Star and Times*, February 2, 1910.

12   "Lew Simmons at the Orpheum."

13   "Years of Burnt Cork."

14   "Years of Burnt Cork."

15   L.M. Sutter, *Arlie Latham: A Baseball Biography of the Freshest Man on Earth* (Jefferson, North Carolina: McFarland, 2012), 86.

16   "Won Quakers' Only Pennant," *Detroit Free Press*, April 10, 1902: 9.

17 "Lew Simmons at the Orpheum"; "Sport Comment."

18 "Years of Burnt Cork"; "Lew Simmons at the Orpheum"; "Sport Comment."

19 "Years of Burnt Cork"; *Philadelphia Times,* April 5, 1895: 34.

20 "Veteran Baseball Player Tells How Athletics Won the Pennant," *Salt Lake Tribune,* August 16, 1910: 10.

21 "Won Quakers' Only Pennant"; "Sport Comment." Simmons played baseball on ice skates for the Athletics during the winter of 1866-1867. *New York Clipper,* January 6, 1883.

22 *Philadelphia Times,* August 7, 1887: 14.

23 Robert D. Warrington, "Philadelphia in the 1881 Eastern Championship Association," *Baseball Research Journal* (SABR), Spring 2019, volume 48, number 1: 78-85.

24 Brock Helander, "Prelude to the Formation of the American Association," https://sabr.org/research/prelude-formation-american-association. Al Reach soon hired Phillips in late October to manage the 1882 Phillies, who would become a member of the League Alliance after Reach was outmaneuvered for a franchise in the American Association. Robert D. Warrington, "Philadelphia in the 1882 League Alliance," *Baseball Research Journal* (SABR), Fall 2019, volume 48, number 1: 105-124.

25 "Base Ball," *Nashville Tennessean,* December 13, 1886: 8; "Won Quakers' Only Pennant"; "How He Won the Pennant," *Butte Miner,* April 15, 1902: 9, printed in the *Pittsburgh Dispatch;* "Sport Comment"; "First Owner of Athletes Here," *Spokane Spokesman Review,* May 28, 1910: 14. See Sutter for a summary of other stories recorded over the years.

26 "How He Won the Pennant."

27 Fulmer was reported to be in political difficulties that necessitated his leaving Philadelphia. See "Sporting Business," *Cincinnati Enquirer,* March 14, 1882: 2. A sportswriter claimed that Fulmer, who aspired to have a career in Philadelphia politics, had to leave town due to his conflict with two influential political leaders. "The Old Sport's Musings," *Philadelphia Inquirer,* May 23, 1909: 15; November 24, 1909: 10; "Clean Sport a Good Investment," *Butte Daily Post,* December 16, 1909: 7.

28 "Sporting Matters," *Buffalo Morning Express and Illustrated Buffalo Express,* November 29, 1881: 4.

29 Bill James, *The Bill James Guide to Baseball Managers from 1870 to Today* (New York: Scribner, 1987), 19.

30 "Lew Simmons will hold on to the management of the Athletic club, notwithstanding the frequent reports to the contrary." "Sporting Topics," *Fall River* (Massachusetts) *Daily Herald,* July 17, 1882: 1.

31 "The Athletic Nine," *Philadelphia Times,* December 4, 1881: 2.

32 "Amusement Notes," *Reading* (Pennsylvania) *Times,* May 4, 1882: 4.

33 "Speed and Skill," *Buffalo Evening Republic,* March 19, 1884: 1.

34 "Amusements," *Wilmington* (Delaware) *Morning News,* January 20, 1883: 1; "Sporting News," *Buffalo Evening News,* March 31, 1883: 5.

35 Frank Moran, one of Simmons' former minstrel partners, umpired. Sam Weaver and Jack O'Brien of the Athletics served as the minstrels' battery. For the Athletics, an off-duty police officer pitched and Moran ordered him to provide slow tosses across the plate. "Minstrels Playing Baseball," *Philadelphia Inquirer,* October 3, 1882: 2.

36 "Won Quakers' Only Pennant"; "How He Won the Pennant."

37 "How He Won the Pennant."

38 James E. Brunson III, "A Mirthful Spectacle: Race, Blackface Minstrelsy, and Base Ball, 1874-1888," *NINE,* vol. 17, no. 2 (2009): 13-29.

39 "How He Won the Pennant."

40 "How He Won the Pennant."

41 "First Owner of Athletes Here."

42 "Sport Comment." Sharsig's obituary gives the amount as $63,000. "Mr. Sharsig Dead," *Allentown Leader,* February 3, 1902: 2.

43 "Simmons," *Fort Worth Star Telegram,* March 14, 1906: 7.

44 "Won Quakers' Only Pennant."

45 "Sports and Pastimes," *Brooklyn Daily Eagle,* March 23, 1884: 4.

46 "Base Ball," *Philadelphia Times,* March 2, 1884: 8.

47 "A Contrast," *Sporting Life,* April 16, 1884: 5.

48 "Diamond Chips," *St. Louis Post-Dispatch,* June 6, 1884: 5.

49 "Diamond Chips," *St. Louis Post-Dispatch,* June 16, 1884: 8.

50 "Notes," *Louisville Courier-Journal,* July 11, 1884: 8.

51 "Forty-Eight Out of Sixty," *Wilmington News Journal,* August 9, 1884: 1.

52 "Base Ball," *Philadelphia Times,* November 1, 1884: 3; "Base Ball Gossip," *Philadelphia Times,* November 23, 1884: 8.

53 "Base Ball Notes," *Lancaster* (Pennsylvania) *Intelligencer,* December 3, 1884: 3; "Base Ball Notes," *Detroit Free Press,* December 7, 1884: 11.

54 "Lew Simmons Talks," *Sporting Life,* November 26, 1884: 3.

55 "Harry Stovey Expresses Himself," *Sporting Life,* December 3, 1884: 3.

56 "Trouble in the Camp," *Sporting Life,* December 3, 1884: 3.

57 "Notes and Comments," *Sporting Life,* December 10, 1884: 5.

58 "Lew Simmons Talks."

59 "Diamond Dust," *St. Louis Post-Dispatch,* May 12, 1885: 5. "Diamond Dots," *Lancaster Daily Intelligencer,* July 21, 1885: 1.

60 *Sporting Life,* September 2, 1885: 5.

61 "From the Falls City," *Sporting Life,* January 13, 1886: 2.

62 "The Young Bloods," *The Sporting News,* November 20, 1886: 7.

63 "Base Ball Briefs," *Lancaster Daily Intelligencer,* June 21, 1886: 1; July 1, 1886: 1; "East vs. West," *Brooklyn Daily Eagle,* July 30, 1886: 2; "Hart's Case," *Chattanooga Daily Times,* August 4, 1886: 5; "A Letter from Billy Explaining the Matter," *Chattanooga Daily Times,* August 10, 1886: 5.

64 "From St. Louis," *Sporting Life,* July 21, 1886: 4.

65 "Base Ball," *Camden* (New Jersey) *Morning Post,* July 19, 1886: 1.

66 "Local Jottings," *Sporting Life,* July 14, 1886: 8.

67 "The Diamond Sport," *Louisville Courier-Journal,* July 9, 1886: 6.

68 "The Young Bloods."

69 "The Young Bloods."

70 "The Young Bloods."

71 "Local Ball Gossip," *Philadelphia Times,* February 27, 1887: 11.

72 "The Athletic Club," *Philadelphia Times,* November 7, 1886, 11; "Opening of the Season," *Philadelphia Inquirer,* March 31, 1887: 2.

73 "All the Players in Good Condition," *St. Louis Globe-Democrat,* May 29, 1887: 9; "Won in the Ninth," *Philadelphia Times,* August 26, 1887: 4.

74 "Who Were There," *Philadelphia Inquirer,* April 15, 1899: 10.

75 "Simmons," *Fort Worth Star Telegram,* March 14, 1906: 7.

76 "Dean of Minstrels Was Pioneer of Baseball," *Seattle Star,* January 2, 1909: 2. "The American Association," *Sporting Life,* December 19, 1883: 2; "The American Association Convention," *New York Clipper,* December 22, 1883: 672. At a special meeting in 1884, the Association directed the umpires to enforce the rule giving the batter a base when struck with the ball thrown by the pitcher. "That Special Meeting," *Cincinnati Enquirer,* July 20, 1884: 10.

77 "Base-Ball," *Cincinnati Enquirer,* March 3, 1885: 8; *Chicago Tribune,* June 8, 1885: 3.

78 "Base Ball Notes," *Philadelphia Times,* February 17, 1889: 16.

79 "Lew Simmons as a Book Peddler," *Wilmington Morning News,* May 16, 1889: 4.

80   United States Census, 1860, *Family Search*, https://www.familysearch.
      org/ark:/61903/1:1:MCHP-P3H, accessed July 2020; "Lew Simmons."

81   Pennsylvania, Philadelphia City Death Certificates, 1803-
      1915, *Family Search*, https://www.familysearch.org/
      ark:/61903/1:1:JKSW-36N, accessed July 2020.

82   United States Census, 1870, *Family Search*, https://www.family-
      search.org/ark:/61903/1:1:MZRF-VGM, accessed July 2020. The
      1867 city directory also provides this address. Ancestry.com, *U.S.
      City Directories, 1822-1995* [database online], Provo, Utah, USA:
      Ancestry.com Operations, Inc., 2011, accessed July 2020.

83   "Mrs. Simmons Dead," *Allentown Leader*, May 7, 1897: 4;
      "Died," *Philadelphia Times*, April 29, 1897: 5; "Lew Simmons
      Killed at Reading," *Allentown Morning Call,* September 4, 1911:
      11; "Lew Simmons." David Nemec states that Mary gave birth to
      Annie in 1882. *Major League Baseball Profiles*, 180-181.

84   Pennsylvania Civil Marriages, 1677-1950, *Family Search*, https://www.
      familysearch.org/ark:/61903/1:1:QKJ4-3JWY, accessed July 2020.

85   New York, New York City Marriage Records, 1829-1940, *Family
      Search*, https://www.familysearch.org/ark:/61903/1:1:2489-
      2BN, accessed July 2020. See also, "Lew Simmons
      Married," *Allentown Morning Call,* May 20, 1905: 5.

86   "Lew Simmons to Be Buried Here," *Allentown
      Morning Call,* September 5, 1911: 5.

87   Sarah Elizabeth Rhoda, *Family Search*, https://www.familysearch.
      org/tree/person/details/LL3J-M9Q, accessed July, 2020.

88   "High Priced Horses," *Pittsburgh Press*, March 1, 1886:
      2; "Arlie Latham Dies at 93, Longest Living Player,"
      The Sporting News, December 19, 1952: 13.

89   "Mystic Shrine," *Wilkes-Barre Times Leader*, March 7, 1892: 3.

90   Ellis, Charles Edward, *An Authentic History of the Benevolent and
      Protective Order of Elks* (Chicago: self-published, 1910), 352.

91   "The Elks Are Now of Age," *Philadelphia Times,* March 13, 1892: 4.

92   "Veteran Baseball Player Tells How Athletics Won the Pennant."

93   "Old-Time Minstrel Man Is Killed on Street,"
      Reading Times, September 4, 1911: 5.

94   "'Lew' Simmons Killed," *New York Tribune*, September 3, 1911: 7; "Minstrel
      Lew Simmons Killed by Auto Truck," *Tampa Tribune*, September 5, 1911: 5.

95   "Old-Time Minstrel Man Is Killed on Street."

96   Pennsylvania Historic and Museum Commission; Harrisburg,
      Pennsylvania; *Pennsylvania (State). Death certificates, 1906–1967*;
      Certificate Number Range: *085971-089710, from* Ancestry.com,
      Pennsylvania, Death Certificates, 1906-1967 [database online], Provo,
      Utah, USA: Ancestry.com Operations, Inc., 2014, accessed July 2020.

97   "Lew Simmons Killed at Reading"; "Lew Simmons Laid to Rest,"
      Allentown Morning Call, September 7, 1911: 10; Historical Society
      of Pennsylvania; Philadelphia, Pennsylvania; *Historic Pennsylvania
      Church and Town Records, from* Ancestry.com, *Pennsylvania and New
      Jersey, Church and Town Records, 1669-2013* [database online], Lehi,
      UT, USA: Ancestry.com Operations, Inc., 2011, accessed July 2020.

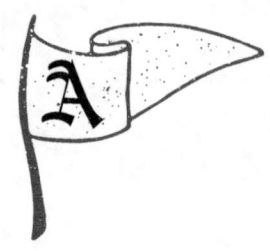

BILL SHARSIG

By Jerrold Casway

The name Billy Sharsig rings familiar to only a select number of baseball chroniclers. Nevertheless, he played a prominent role in late nineteenth-century baseball annals. He is known for founding the American Association Athletics, a team that revived Philadelphia's historic Athletics appellation. His actions also allowed the city to fill the professional baseball vacuum that existed after the National League dismissed the Athletics' predecessor for not going on a 1876 Western road trip.

For the next four years the remnant Athletics, in its various semipro forms, competed only when they could arrange games. It was at this juncture that a number of diehard baseball enthusiasts strove to bring back professional baseball to the country's second largest city. The eventual vehicle for this rebirth was a maverick league that offered Sunday baseball, beer sales, and cheap ticket prices. Taking advantage of this opportunity was a mixed-matched group of baseball boosters – Billy Sharsig, Charlie Mason, and Lew Simmons. These men, from different backgrounds, were linked by their passion for the game and the lure of investment profits.

The moving spirit of this troika was Billy Sharsig. Born in Philadelphia in 1855, he was the son of refugees from Prussia who settled in the Kensington section of Philadelphia, where his father set up a successful dye factory.[1] His father's hope was for Billy to follow in his footsteps. Young Billy, however, had other aspirations. He was attracted to show business and was titillated by the sport of baseball. Through his theatrical ventures, Sharsig gained entrepreneurial experience that left him with little money for anything else. Nevertheless, he was driven by the investment potential of returning professional baseball to Philadelphia.

Until the advent of the American Association in 1882, Sharsig maintained his baseball interest through local amateur and semipro ballclubs. In the late 1870s he played right field and caught for the Eckford, Shibe, and Defiance teams of Philadelphia. Eventually, he assumed administrative roles with each ballclub. By 1880, the 25-year-old Sharsig, with the help of Horace Phillips, a former major-league manager, revitalized what was left of the defunct Athletics baseball club.[2] To raise money for this project, Billy tried in vain to persuade his father to finance this venture. Legend has it that Billy's mother rescued him with personal savings she kept in socks. Sharsig also got some preliminary backing from two sporting associates named Slater and McCartney.[3]

With no place to affiliate, Sharsig in 1881 set up local exhibitions and arranged for a profitable Midwest tour. By the end of the ball season, the Athletics' fortunes began to change. First, there was renewed interest in setting up a new professional league among the cities earlier abandoned by the National League. This opportunity played into Sharsig's two trump cards. He had a new access to money, allowing him to be the major investor in the revived Athletics, and he held the lease to the old Oakdale Park Grounds with its 11th and Huntingdon ball field. Situated among newly built residential houses south of Lehigh Avenue, the park was noted for its lake and picnic groves. The Oakdale playing field traced its grounds to the postwar National Association years.[4]

In anticipation of admittance to the new Association, Sharsig had the Oakdale grounds resodded and leveled. The old grandstand was replaced with three linked porched pavilions holding 2,000 spectators, and the playing field was enclosed with a new wood-slatted fence. Part of the renovations was a new main entrance on Lehigh Avenue, 2,000 outfield benched seats, a handsome dressing room, a press box, and private offices at the rear of the main pavilion.[5]

During the franchise's development stage, Sharsig sought out more wizened partners. Slater and McCartney had cut their ties with the club and Sharsig came upon and welcomed Charlie Mason aboard. Mason, born in New Orleans, was two years older than Sharsig. As a youngster Mason played amateur ball in his hometown and at neighboring Williams College. By the mid-1870s, the athletically gifted Mason found himself in Philadelphia, playing for a number of semipro ball clubs. Eventually, he played right field and caught for old National Association teams in Philadelphia and Washington. When the Association folded, Mason played for independent professional teams in Pennsylvania, Iowa, and Massachusetts. This career path led to him signing up with the independent Athletics that was later subsumed to Sharsig's 1881 pre-American Association Athletics.

Outside of baseball, Mason ran a cigar store and a local saloon. Initially his main function with Sharsig and the Athletics involved scouting and signing prospects. When necessary, he filled in as manager for the city's new Association ballclub. The final piece to the franchise's puzzle was a theatrical acquaintance of Sharsig, Lew Simmons.

Simmons was the oldest member of the Athletics' governing triumvirate. He was born in New Castle in western Pennsylvania in 1838. But baseball was not Lew's cherished pastime. He was a talented musician and minstrel entertainer. Strumming his banjo in blackface, he made quite a name for himself. He opened his own theater in Philadelphia, published a popular minstrel songbook and traveled widely with his musical routines. Despite these successes, he maintained a real passion for baseball. He played with the original Athletics after the war and helped popularize winter ice baseball. It wasn't until Sharsig and Mason's reconstituted Athletics materialized that Simmons turned his attention back to baseball.

Simmons knew that Sharsig and Mason were looking for another investor with baseball aspirations. Simmons not only met their criteria, but he also played a role in getting the Athletics an Association franchise.[6] It was said that he got a $16,000 investment from Adam Forepaugh, who operated a popular local circus.[7] He also used his outgoing and convivial manner at Association meetings to smooth the way for the Athletics' acceptance. These successes got him invited as an Association delegate to a February 1883

conference with National League officials. This meeting resulted in an agreement about the reserve rule and the issue of the number of protected players. This success earned the Association a tacit recognition from the senior circuit.

Without deprecating Mason and Simmons, Billy Sharsig remained the central figure in the Athletics' organization. The 1882 American Association season had seen the Athletics emerge as the only professional ballclub in Philadelphia. Now it was up to Sharsig to rekindle the city's love of baseball. His greatest obstacle was getting the local papers to cover the Athletics because, as one newspaper said, "Billy ... We have no time to talk about a dead crow."[8] But the city and its newspapers changed their attitudes after the 1882 season. The *Philadelphia Item* was more optimistic when it remarked how the Athletics were entering a wedge to the return of the game.[9]

Sharsig and his associates had assembled a respectable and competitive ballclub. George "Jumbo" Latham was the field captain and first baseman; off-field business was managed by Sharsig and Simmons. Mason oversaw the grounds and continued scouting players. Throughout most of the season, the Athletics stayed in contention and finished the year 41-34, in second place, 11½ games behind Cincinnati. Oakdale Park hosted capacity crowds as baseball in the Quaker City recovered its former luster. The Athletics' success also convinced the National League that it should

Bill Sharsig.

rethink its relationship with the city. By the end of 1882, Philadelphia was granted Worcester, Massachusetts' "right to franchise." This new National League team became the Philadelphia Phillies. The season was also a profitable one for Sharsig's Athletics. The size of the profit was hard to determine because the team kept no books and the troika daily divided up each ballgame's take. It was alleged that the Athletics cleared about $22,000 for the year.[10]

The 1883 American Association responded to the league's popularity by adding two teams to the six-club organization. This expansion pleased Sharsig and his associates. But the new season was played at a different location. Sharsig was notified that his Oakdale lease was up and that the site would be sold to enterprising housing developers. This transaction left the ballclub with few alternatives. Sharsig, however, was fortunate to get a $1,000 lease from the city for what remained of the old National Association grounds at 27th and Jefferson. On this truncated site, the Athletics constructed "the handsomest ball grounds in the country."[11]

Once the new home site was resolved, the triumvirate focused their attention on signing players and organizing the ballclub for the 1883 season. After evaluating their salaried expenses, they agreed that they needed more talented players to compete for the Association's pennant. The Athletics were determined to sign the best available players. The *Philadelphia Evening Item* wrote, "The man who stops to question the cost of a thing that will benefit the club or please the public is an idiot and will soon find himself left [out]."[12] As a result, only four players from the 1882 team were retained. The two most significant signees were pitcher Bobby Mathews and first baseman Harry Stovey. A number of native Philadelphians made up the other roster spots. With Lon Knight serving as field captain, Sharsig selected the effusive Simmons as the off-field manager. These changes cemented the team's relationship with the city as the 1883 season began with great promise.

Many believed that the Athletics were "ushering in a new popular age."[13] The telling sign for Sharsig and his associates was a preseason exhibition series between the Athletics and the nascent National League Phillies. Both organizations were stunned by its success. In six games, 50,000 tickets had been sold.[14] Extra security was needed for each game. The enclosed playing fields were lined six persons deep. At one point the Athletics used ladders to get late-arriving ticket-holders into the ballpark.

The Athletics began the 1883 season winning 18 of 21 games. But as the season progressed pitchers tired and injuries mounted. By the beginning of September, the Athletics held a half-game lead over St. Louis with a four-game series ahead of them and with first place at stake. With pitchers still ailing, Lew Simmons signed a 20-year-old dental student Daniel Jones for $500 a month. Jones pitched and won two games in this series. He excited the crowds by his occasional "jumping jack" pitch, whereby he would leap in the air to throw his fastball. Thanks to his signing, the Athletics took three out of four games from St. Louis to open a 2½-game lead. More than 50,000 fans attended these games. With the city's second pennant in view, the Athletics finished the year with a 13-game road trip.

Responding to the importance of the road trip, Sharsig and Charlie Mason took leave of their businesses and accompanied the ballclub. It was said that Mason was like "an old hen … [watching] her brood of children," keeping them on the straight and narrow.[15] The Athletics played well on the road and staked their claim by taking two out of three games from the Brown Stockings in St. Louis. Philadelphia only had to win a game in Louisville to clinch the pennant. Mason left the ballclub to look after celebrations in Philadelphia. Simmons, the off-field manager, was too unnerved by his self-imposed pressure and Sharsig was compelled to step in. After the Athletics lost the first two games in Louisville, Sharsig kept Simmons out of sight so as not to unnerve the players. When the Athletics won the last game, 7-6, Sharsig was overjoyed and telegraphed the wonderful results to Philadelphia. His telegram set off spontaneous celebrations in the Quaker City.

The train from Louisville carrying the champion Athletics was greeted at every stop by enthusiastic and celebrating fans. The closer they got to Philly, the bigger the welcoming crowds became. They arrived at the Broad Street Station in the early evening. Their greeting was unprecedented. People were "climbing on each other's shoulders" to catch a glimpse of their heroes.[16] The players followed a path cleared by the police and a marching band. The parade, viewed by an estimated 750,000, went on for more than a mile along Broad Street. The evening hour did not curtail the city's enthusiasm. The players' progress was illuminated by firing rockets, lighting Roman candles, and waving lanterns. Some accounts spoke about the roar of tens of thousands of applauding shouts and chants. The *Philadelphia Press* said, "[T]he bands played, hundreds of flags fluttered in the breeze. …

[T]he enthusiasm could not have been more real."[17] It was said that the parade took an hour and 10 minutes to pass the reviewing stand. By 11 P.M. the players escaped to Mercantile Hall for a grand celebratory banquet. Gold badges and performance gifts were awarded to the weary players. Billy Sharsig and his partners could not have been more thrilled by the city's reception. They were also pleased by their profit margin for the championship season. It was said to be about $78,320.[18]

Over the next four years, the ballclub and the Association faced many challenges, such as the emergence in 1884 of a rival league, the Union Association. Nevertheless, Sharsig and the Athletics persisted with profitable seasons despite fourth- to sixth-place finishes. During these seasons the ballclub benefited from the batting of Harry Stovey, Ted Larkin, and Denny Lyons. But aging pitchers and poor fielding negated their offensive advantages. The Association also labored under many rule changes and game practices. For Sharsig, the greatest problems were organizational. In 1884 and 1886 he split his managerial responsibilities with Charlie Mason and Lew Simmons. Sharsig still remained as the senior partner and in 1886 served as the club's president. A year later, he became the Athletics' managing secretary and made a critical decision for the sake of the franchise's unity when he bought out Mason and Simmons. After this transaction, he sold the surviving shares to local businessmen H.C. Pennypacker and William Whittaker.[19] He hoped this sale would stabilize the franchise, but it only compounded his problems. Neither man proved to be a good choice; they were neither frugal nor baseball-savvy. Sharsig needed all the support he could mobilize from his investors because of the challenging labor disputes that were on the professional baseball horizon.

The next two years, 1888 and 1889, laid the groundwork for the players' strike season of 1890. These years, with Billy Sharsig at the helm, saw the Athletics finish in third place with positive profit margins. These pre-strife years would have been an ideal time for Sharsig to liquidate his vulnerable Athletics stock. Unable, or perhaps unwilling, to transact such a sale, Sharsig held on to his franchise shares in the face of the threatening labor storm that hung over the Association.

Many of the Association's teams were ill-prepared for the pending economic labor struggle between the three professional baseball leagues. Ballplayers would abandon their teams, lured by excessive Players'

League contracts. Sharsig's Athletics were shaken by these raids. Four major players signed elsewhere – Stovey, Larkin, Lave Cross, and Lou Bierbauer. Sharsig had little choice but to reconstruct his ballclub with young players and well-worn veterans. He compounded his player problems when he refused to sign any contract-jumping players. He said they could not be trusted or depended upon.[20]

Remarkably, by mid-July Sharsig had his ballclub in first place. This success was fleeting. The Athletics finished in seventh place, 33½ games behind the Louisville Colonels. Sharsig's Athletics concluded the season by losing 22 straight games. The club, thanks to the profligate spending of William Whittaker, was more than $17,000 in debt. This condition resulted in a threatened players' strike if they were not paid. There was little Sharsig could do. Whitaker reacted by releasing all the players.[21] Sharsig did what he could by recruiting replacements of questionable skill.

He took this team on its last Western road trip of 1890 with only $245 in hand for expenses. The Athletic players were to be paid per diem from the gate receipts. Having survived this trek, Sharsig and the team returned to Philadelphia to discover that their home field, the Jefferson Street Grounds, had been sold out from under them in a sheriff's sale. To pay back rent and other outstanding expenditures, the team sold the seats, stands, and all furnishings. They raised only

Public domain.

Sharsig as manager of the 1889 Philadelphia Athletics.

$600, well short of what they owed.[22] Sharsig was powerless to offset what Whittaker and Pennypacker had spent on inflated salaries and personal expenses. But Sharsig was so well regarded that many of his former players proposed to play a benefit game on his behalf at Forepaugh Park.[23]

In the wake of the strike season, Billy Sharsig found himself to be a casualty and pawn in the settlement negotiations. To resolve the season's turmoil, the leaders of the three professional leagues gathered to reconcile their differences and settle their 1891 rosters. The Players' League Quakers of Philadelphia, run by two local meat wholesalers, Earle and George Wagner, brokered their cooperation by exchanging their franchise for the expired American Association Athletics.[24] Sharsig opposed this transaction, but he had very little leverage in these dealings. His capital assets were lacking and he had little choice but to sell his remaining stock and sign a contract to be the Athletics manager in 1891.

Sharsig's ballclub, however, was lacking two of its principal players, Harry Stovey and Lou Bierbauer. They were lost to the Athletics because of the inattention to player reserve contracts by the defunct Association and the negligence of the Wagner brothers.[25]

Sharsig's 1891 Athletics, playing at Forepaugh Park, the former home field of the Players' League Quakers, began the season 6-11. This disappointing start provided J. Earle Wagner a justification for terminating Sharsig's contract. George Wood, an outfielder from the Quakers ballclub, became the new manager.[26] Sharsig, who had little trust or affection for the Wagner brothers, countered that he had not signed a conditional player contract with an arbitrary release clause.[27] As a result, he sued the brothers for breach of contract. But the Wagners, with Sharsig out of the picture, ran the franchise as they pleased. After a fifth-place finish, the Wagners abandoned the Athletics and the American Association. They held on to their investment and with it finagled the purchase of the Washington American Association franchise before it was transferred to the newly expanded 12-team National League.[28]

Under Sharsig's direction the American Association Athletics' record was 244-218 (.528). He sacrificed his money and reputation to salvage his franchise and received little in return. Neither the Association nor the Wagners ever acknowledged their indebtedness to him.[29] This disregard was neither deserved nor warranted. After being cashiered, Sharsig had only his sterling reputation to show for his Association years. Nevertheless, he was still well regarded by his peers, and this steeled his determination to carve out a niche for himself in the reorganized world of professional baseball. The next decade proved this esteem true.

In 1892 Sharsig was hired to manage the Indianapolis team in the Western League. The following year the York team in the Pennsylvania State League took him on as manager. In 1894 he was re-engaged to manage Indianapolis. The next season Sharsig returned to the Pennsylvania State League to manage Hazelton. He not only won the pennant, but he also opened negotiations to resettle the franchise in Philadelphia. He hoped to gain access to the Phillies' ballpark when the Phils were on the road. For the next two years, Sharsig's Athletics represented Philadelphia in the Atlantic League. They did not draw well and were compelled to drop out of the league. They were replaced by an Allentown franchise that kept Sharsig at the helm for the next two years, 1896 and 1897.[30]

It was hoped that Sharsig's Allentown club could help keep the floundering Atlantic League solvent. Meetings were held and Sharsig again was fated to endure more disappointing setbacks.[31] Nevertheless, he was still recognized as a knowledgeable baseball contributor. In spite of having no ties to the National League, Sharsig was included in the National League's meetings that determined the new 60-foot-6-inch pitching distance.

Sharsig, despite his ballclub's demise, was not forgotten by his sporting associates. Ben Shibe, the owner of the American League's Athletics, had been affiliated with him during the American Association days. Ban Johnson, the president of the new American League, and Connie Mack, the Athletics' new manager, knew Sharsig from Western League and Atlantic League seasons. The input of these men certainly helped get him a position with the new American League Athletics.

Drawing on Sharsig's financial and administrative baseball experiences, the club hired him as its business manager. He also worked with Connie Mack on the development of the Athletics' playing field and the actual structure of Columbia Park.[32] But Sharsig was not a well man. He suffered from lower bowel and digestive problems, possibly colon cancer, that gave him great pain and constant discomfort.[33] On February 1, 1902, a year after he was hired by the Athletics, he died.[34] He was buried in Mt. Vernon Cemetery at 34th and Lehigh, 13 blocks from the Athletics' future home, Shibe Park. His funeral was attended by many baseball dignitaries. The coffin was covered by large floral wreaths from admirers and associates.[35] Billy Sharsig was only 47 when he died. His obituary in the *Inquirer* summed up his career, "that no man will ever hold the place he held in the estimation of the base ball going people of this good old town [Philadelphia]."[36]

NOTES

1   A *Sporting News* obituary said Sharsig was born in Gloucester, New Jersey. All other references, including his death certificate, say Philadelphia.

2   John Shiffert, *Base Ball in Philadelphia* (Jefferson, North Carolina: McFarland, 2006), 97-9, 246-7; *New York Clipper*, May 19, 1883; *The Sporting News*, September 28, 1895, November 21, 1896, February 8, 1902; *Spalding Scrapbook*, Hall of Fame, VI, 103.

3   *The Sporting News*, February 8, 1902; *Sporting Life*, February 8, 1902; Shiffert, 247; Edward Achorn, *The Summer of Beer and Whiskey* (New York: Public Affairs, 2013), 43.

4   Achorn, *The Summer of Beer and Whiskey* 41, 45; David Nemec, *The Beer and Whiskey League* (New York: The Lyons Press, 1994), 46; *Sporting Life*, February 8, 1902; *New York Clipper*, May 19, 1883; *The Sporting News*, February 8, 1902; *Philadelphia Press*, March 31, 1867; *Sunday Mercury*, November 4, 1866.

5   *Sunday Item*, March 26, 1882; *Philadelphia Public Record*, March 11, 1882.

6   Achorn, *The Summer of Beer and Whiskey*, 37-51; *New York Clipper* in Spalding Scrapbook, 1882: 682; Nemec, *Beer and Whiskey*, 45-6.

7   Ted Vincent, *Mudville's Revenge, The Rise and Fall of American Sports* (Lincoln, Nebraska: Bison Books, 1994), 164.

8   Edward Achorn, "Philly Teams for All Seasons," *Philadelphia Inquirer*, April 28, 2013; Achorn, *The Summer of Beer and Whiskey*, 43; *The Sporting News*, December 10, 1887.

9   *Philadelphia Item*, June 21, 1881.

10 It was reported that the triumvirate actually acted as ticket collectors, trusting no one to handle their gate receipts. Achorn, *The Summer of Beer and Whiskey*, 43.

11 *Sunday Item*, April 5, 1882.

12 *Philadelphia Evening Item*, June 24, 1883.

13 *New York Clipper*, April 7, 1883.

14 Achorn, *The Summer of Beer and Whiskey*, 51.

15 *Police Gazette*, December 23, 1883.

16 *Philadelphia Press*, October 2, 1883.

17 *Philadelphia Press*, October 2, 1883.

18 *Philadelphia Press*, October 20, 1883.

19 Nemec, *The Beer and Whiskey League*, 192; Shiffert, 248; J. Casway, "The Jefferson Street Ball Parks (1864-91)," *The National Pastime*, 2013: 16.

20 Sharsig file, National Baseball Hall of Fame, January 15, 1890.

21 *Philadelphia Inquirer*, September 13, 1890; Shiffert, 139.

22 Casway, 16; *Sporting Life*, October 18, 1890, November 28, 1891, and December 12, 1891; *The Sporting News*, October 18, 1890; *Cleveland Plain Dealer*, October 15, 1890.

23 *Sporting Life*, October 11, 1890.

24 For a good summary of these transactions, see Shiffert, 153-4, and Nemec, *The Beer and Whiskey League*, 220-1. In Sharsig's obituary, it was said that "[n]o man was harder hit by the Brotherhood Movement." *Philadelphia Inquirer*, February 3, 1902.

25 An analysis of this neglect and complicity is summarized in Shiffert, 153-4.

26 Shiffert, 155.

27 *Philadelphia Bulletin*, May 11, 1891.

28 Harold and Dorothy Seymour, *Baseball, The Early Years* (New York: Oxford University Press, 1960), 260-1; Shiffert, 157, 248.

29 *Sporting Life*, October 11, 1890; Sharsig file, Hall of Fame, December 6, 1890.

30 *The Sporting News*, September 28, 1895; November 21, 1896; January 16, 1897; February 8, 1902. Spalding Scrapbook, Hall of Fame, VI:, 103.

31 *The Sporting News*, February 15, 1902.

32 Norman Macht, *Connie Mack and the Early Years of Base Ball* (Lincoln: University of Nebraska Press, 2007), 194-5, 204-5.

33 *The Sporting News*, February 8, 1902.

34 Death Certificate, #3179, City of Philadelphia.

35 *The Sporting News*, February 8, 1902, and February 15, 1902. Sharsig's widow continued to work at the Athletics' ballpark, and their son enlisted in the Navy. *Sporting Life*, August 16, 1902.

36 *Philadelphia Inquirer*, February 3, 1902.

THE PLAYERS

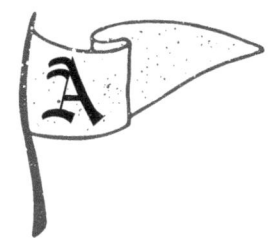

EDWARD ENOCH "JERSEY" BAKLEY

By William Johnson

He was accused of gambling on baseball early in his playing career. He was acknowledged to have a serious alcohol problem, one that may have contributed to his death at age 50. His professional pitching record, for six major-league seasons and four at the minor-league and independent levels, was 109-161. On first blush, and in any era of the professional game's long history, those numbers not only are unremarkable, but indicate that the pitcher was relatively ineffective. Yet modern metrics, applied to the greatest degree possible, given that the subject pitched in the late nineteenth century, value him with a Wins Above Replacement (WAR) rating of 1.1 for his major-league time.[1] That WAR estimate indicates that there is value in more closely examining the player and his career. A deeper dive into Jersey Bakley's record reveals details embedded within his professional baseball career that point to a better player than the raw numbers might suggest, and that in a sense underscore a life more complex than a simple obituary might convey.

Enoch Edward Bakley was born on April 17, 1864, in what was then called Blackwoodtown, New Jersey. Now called simply Blackwood, the community lies south-southeast of Philadelphia, across the Delaware river and about eight miles into New Jersey. (Hence his nickname, Jersey.) Enoch's father, Henry, fought in the Civil War as a private in Company D of the New Jersey Volunteer 25th Regiment.[2] Little is recorded about Enoch's early life, but according to the 1880 US Census, he and his father were both ironworkers in a local mill.[3] The work was hazardous but provided a living wage, and on July 16, 1882, Enoch married Barbara Carolyn Krantz, a daughter of German

Jersey Bakley, in 1886.

immigrants, in Gloucester City, New Jersey.[4] In 1883 their first child, Edward Jr., was born, and he was joined by sister Barbara in 1888 and brother John in 1890. The marriage did not last, and at some point between 1890 and 1896 (when Barbara remarried), the couple divorced.[5] Of note, Bakley's name was often spelled Bakely in newspaper accounts of his baseball activity.

In 1883, with a family, Enoch accepted a chance to pitch for the Pottsville Anthracites of the Interstate Association, about 85 miles northwest of Philadelphia. At 5-feet-8 and 170 pounds, Bakley pitched and played the outfield, although Pottsville used him primarily in the pitching box. The team was not very good, and finished 1883 with a 15-50 record under three different managers.[6] Bakley is credited with a 2-5 record during his short stint but posted an ERA of 2.95. The talent level was clear, and in May, the American Association's Philadelphia Athletics signed him to fill the void created by an injury to Bobby Mathews, who sprained his ankle trying to steal second base.[7] He made his major-league debut on May 11, 1883, in a 4-3 win over the Tim Keefe-led New York Metropolitans. Philadelphia scored four runs in the top of the first inning, giving the 19-year-old pitcher a cushion before he threw his first pitch. Bakley pitched well for four innings before giving up two runs in the bottom of the fifth and another in the sixth, but he held on for the win.[8]

Led by Harry Stovey, among others, the 1883 Athletics finished first in the league with a 66-32 record. The 19-year-old won five games before finishing with a 5-3 mark for the season, but spent much of the season on loan to both Pottsville and Harrisburg.[9]

Bakley jumped to the upstart, and short-lived, Union Association in 1884. Playing with the Philadelphia Keystones, Wilmington Quicksteps, and Kansas City Cowboys, he lost a league-leading 30 games while winning 16.[10] SABR historian Justin McKinney discovered that in 1884 Bakley originally signed a contract with the Littlestown, Pennsylvania, club of the Keystone Association in addition to his deal with the Philadelphia Keystones of the Union Association. Since the teenager had already taken money from Littlestown prior to signing with Philadelphia, he tried to feign illness in an attempt to void the Littlestown obligation.[11] The effort failed. Blacklisted under the National Agreement, Bakley tried to sign with Providence when the Keystones folded in August, but was denied reinstatement.[12] He played out the season in two brief stops in Wilmington and Kansas City.

After the Union Association dissolved, Bakley moved on to Portland (Maine) in the independent Eastern New England League, and the Albany Senators and Oswego Sweegs of the New York State League for 1885. In 1886, and again in 1887, the pitcher signed with the Rochester Maroons of the International League. (Some sources refer to it as the International Association.)[13]

In Rochester Bakley began to gain the attention of the news media for reasons beyond the baseball diamond. While gambling was neither sanctioned nor excluded from baseball at the time, the perception of players possibly throwing games was intolerable. At one point, there were rumors that Bakley was involved. In July 1886, in response to one reporter, Maroons manager Frank Bancroft said, "The statement that Bakley had been released or suspended on account of selling the game was wholly without foundation. He has only been temporarily suspended. He had been intemperate and was used up physically. … The club, as a whole, are total abstainers. No man can drink whiskey and play ball. …"[14]

With that single declaration, Bancroft both exonerated Bakley of any gambling charges, and identified what became the root of the pitcher's demise: alcohol. Throughout his career, certainly going forward from his time with Rochester, Bakley suffered from a drinking problem. In 1887 he and teammate Fred Lewis were arrested and fined $50 for public drunkenness, and the antics began to wear on his manager. For every game in which he homered and starred defensively, it seemed there were several games in which he appeared lost.[15] Rob Neyer, in the 1992 edition of *The Baseball Book*, encapsulated the pitcher's career in a precis of his tenure: "Bakely [sic] pitched six seasons in the major leagues for nine different teams. … The reasons for his transcience weren't much of a mystery. Bakely was a drunk, and not that great a pitcher besides. …"[16]

Yet Bakley did have a modicum of talent. In 1888 he began the first of three consecutive seasons in Cleveland —with different teams and each in a different league. The moribund Cleveland Blues, a team that had posted a 39-92 record in the American Association in 1887 and finished 54 games out of first, signed Bakley. The now 24-year-old won 25 games (against 33 losses) with a 2.97 ERA. In 1889 Bakley played for the Cleveland Spiders of the National League and lowered his ERA to 2.96, but won only 12 games. In 1890 he jumped to the Cleveland Infants of the new Players' League, but the demise of the latter, and his release by the Spiders, led him to Washington and then Baltimore in 1891.

Perhaps underscoring the athletic talent that Bakley squandered, *The Sporting News* reported that he was "once matched to fight Jack Dempsey, the Nonpareil [not the Jack Dempsey of twentieth-century renown].

Frank Bancroft called the fight off, and it is probably lucky for Bakley that he did, as he would not have escaped from a go with the redoubtable Jack without carrying some marks of the encounter."[17]

Several interesting events occurred during the 1890 season. On July 9 Bakley was an emergency substitute umpire for Harry Leach, who'd been knocked unconscious by a foul tip the day before.[18] Bakley had performed the task once before, in August 1888 in a game versus Kansas City,[19] and the 1890 game proved to be his final appearance as an umpire. Then, on September 3, in a makeup of a May rainout against Boston, Bakley gave up Harry Stovey's 100th career home run. That feat by Stovey made him the first member of baseball's figurative "100 Homer" club and earned Bakley a mention in the game's annals.[20]

In 1891, after losing 10 of his first 12 decisions, Bakley was released by Washington. Baltimore signed him almost immediately, and the pitcher enjoyed a renaissance of sorts with his new team, winning four of his first six starts. Unable to control his alcohol use, he was suspended without pay for disobeying club rules.[21] Within a week after his final appearance in an August 20 loss to Washington, Baltimore gave Bakley his last big-league release. According to the *Baltimore Sun,* "Bakely is said to have broken several promises made to the management of the club, and for this reason he was allowed to go."[22]

He remained in Baltimore and in 1895 joined the Allentown Goobers of the Pennsylvania State League. He pitched well initially, earning newspaper praise: "Bakely pitched the better game. He was steady, displayed considerable headwork and never allowed himself to get rattled by the loud coaching."[23] But the Goobers released him in late July, with a local correspondent for *The Sporting News* reporting, "Considerable regret is felt here over the release of Bakely. 'Jersey' was quite popular and he won more games for Allentown than any of the other pitchers. His jaunty step as he walked up to the pitcher's box was especially pleasing to the ladies, many of them attending games when they knew Bakely was going to pitch. He had such a bewitching smile also and it is to be regretted that his fondness for 'smiles' led to his release."[24]

In August, after a stint with Pottstown and now pitching for Reading, Pennsylvania, the tone changed, one paper reporting, "Jersey Bakely was the sweetest kind of tapioca, the locals batting him terrifically. In every inning Lancaster hit safely one or more times,

their total hits being twenty-four."[25] In short, after 13 years, Bakley's baseball career was over.

Out of baseball, uneducated, no longer married, likely an alcoholic, and still only 31, Bakley took jobs as a carpenter and rigger in the southern New Jersey/Philadelphia region over the next two decades.[26] On February 17, 1915, not quite 51 years old, Jersey Bakley died at his residence in Philadelphia. The death certificate cited chronic endocarditis as the primary cause, although there is no record of an autopsy being performed. He was buried at Greenmount Cemetery in Philadelphia on February 20.

On the diamond, Bakley had some terrific seasons, despite his career losing record. He finished second in National League ERA in 1889 (2.96), seventh in American Association wins in 1888 (25), twice in the top 10 in strikeouts in his respective leagues (sixth, with 226, in the 1884 Union Association, and fourth, with 212, in the 1888 American Association), and was still in the top 200 list for career complete games (with 191), as of 2020. His career, and his life, ended in ignominy, but Jersey Bakley certainly enjoyed a few afternoons in the sun, as well.

SOURCES

Much of the fundamental work on this biography was crafted by David Nemec and Steve Behnke, both members of the Society for American Baseball Research. The statistical information is taken from Baseball-reference.com, unless otherwise noted. Additionally, Justin McKinney provided information regarding Bakley's contractual issues in the Union Association in 1884.

NOTES

1   Jersey Bakley's page on Baseball-Reference.com: baseball-reference. com/register/player.fcgi?id=bakley001jer. Accessed October 16, 2020.

2   Henry H. Bakley, Find-a-Grave. findagrave.com/memorial/31137786/henry-h-bakley. Accessed October 16, 2020.

3   US Census: 1880. ancestry.com/imageviewer/collections/6742/images/4244461-00771?pId=179390. Accessed October 15, 2020.

4   New Jersey, Marriage Records, 1670-1965. search. ancestry.com/cgi-bin/sse.dll?indiv=1&dbid=61376&h=552813&queryId=9a49b2488offec1563e2033053232425&usePUB=true&_phsrc=vSy19&_phstart=successSource&requr=2550866976735 232&ur=0&lang=en-US. Accessed October 16, 2020.

5   This conclusion comes from the 1900 US Census, in which Barbara is married to a different man and having additional siblings for the three Bakley children. ancestry.com/imageviewer/collections/7602/images/4120424_00267?pId=31400663. Accessed October 16, 2020.

6   *Encyclopedia of Minor League Baseball, Third edition* (Durham, North Carolina: Baseball America, 2007), 141.

7   Edward Achorn, *The Summer of Beer and Whiskey* (New York: Public Affairs, 2013), 169-170.

8   The game description is from an unpublished biography of Jersey Bakley, and draws the news citation from "Another Close Contest," *Philadelphia Inquirer,* May 12, 1883: 2.

9   David Nemec, "Jersey Bakley," in *Major League Baseball Profiles: 1871-1900, vol. 1* (Lincoln, Nebraska: Bison Books, 2011), 244.

10   Union Association Pitching Leaders, Baseball-Reference.com: baseball-reference.com/register/leader.cgi?type=pitch&id=4b1eb341. Accessed October 16, 2020.

11   "Base Ball Notes," *Franklin Repository* (Chambersburg, Pennsylvania, April 30, 1884.

12   Justin McKinney, in a pending history of the Union Association; provided to the author on October 21, 2020.

13   "The Official Record," *The Sporting News*, December 4, 1886: 5.

14   "Five Runs and All Earned," *Rochester Democrat and Chronicle*, July 3, 1886: 6.

15   Bakley's home runs were infrequent, and they merited special notice when they occurred, such as on August 26, 1887. See "Hamilton Easily Beaten," *Rochester Democrat and Chronicle*, August 26, 1887: 7. The less glorious results, such as those reported in "Two Games to Toronto," *Rochester Democrat and Chronicle*, September 6, 1887: 6, with fielding gaffes and hitless afternoons, became more common as the years passed.

16   Rob Neyer, "Jersey Bakely," in *Bill James' The Baseball Book* (New York: Villard Books, 1992), 360-361.

17   *The Sporting News*, November 17, 1888: 5.

18   "Cleveland, 9; Boston, 7," *New York World*, July 9, 1890: 7.

19   Jersey Bakley, Retrosheet.org: retrosheet.org/boxesetc/B/Pbakej102.htm. Accessed October 17, 2020.

20   Baseball-Reference.com's listing of players hitting at least 100 home runs: baseball-reference.com/bullpen/100_Home_Run_Club. Accessed October 17, 2020.

21   "Bakely Turns Up Again," *Baltimore Sun*, July 15, 1891: 6.

22   "Wise and Bakely Released," *Baltimore Sun*, August 27, 1891: 6.

23   "The Season Opened," *Allentown* (Pennsylvania) *Morning Call*, May 2, 1895: 1.

24   "Fired All His Pitchers," *The Sporting News*, July 27, 1895: 7.

25   "Crawling Up Nicely," *Intelligencer Journal* (Lancaster, Pennsylvania), August 28, 1895: 1.

26   US City Directories, 1822-1995: Newark, New Jersey, City Directory, 1909, 321.

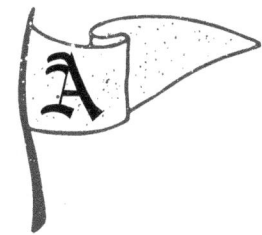

JUD BIRCHALL

By Paul Hofmann

Hidden in obscurity after his death more than 130 years ago, A.J. "Jud" Birchall was the starting left fielder and leadoff hitter of the 1883 American Association champion Athletic Club of Philadelphia. A local schoolboy who grew up in Philadelphia's Germantown neighborhood, Birchall had a three-year major-league career with the Athletics that culminated with one of the greatest pennant races in American Association history. Birchall and his teammates entertained large crowds at Jefferson Street Grounds during the 1883 season that ushered in a new era of baseball in Philadelphia and took the game to previously unseen heights of popularity.

Adoniram Judson Birchall was born on September 12, 1855, in Germantown to Elias Birchall, an immigrant from England, and Sarah (Lutz) Birchall, the daughter of a shoemaker of German extraction. Jud, as he would be known, was the 10th of 15 children born to the Birchalls between 1843 and 1863.[1] Of the 15 children, only eight survived to adulthood, including his older brother Edward, who was also a baseball player of local renown in Philadelphia. The elder of the baseball-playing Birchall brothers played left field for the Girard club of Philadelphia before embarking on a career as a civil engineer.

The well-documented business successes and philanthropic activities of Jud's father, as well as the wealth of information available about the family's history, gives us a glimpse into circumstances into which Jud was born.

Elias Birchall came to the United States with his parents when he was 6 years old. In early adulthood he became involved in manufacturing hosiery in Germantown. On December 8, 1842, he married Sarah Lutz, the daughter of Abraham and Elizabeth (Conver) Lutz, who were said to be "staid and fervent

Christians."[2] The senior Birchall enjoyed great success in the textile industry and, over time, acquired a sizable fortune. His prominent position in Germantown's commercial and social circles are an indication that Jud probably grew up in what would have been considered an upper-class family in late nineteenth-century Germantown. It is certain that young Jud's material needs were met and education, including religious instruction, was stressed in the home.

Jud, or A.J., was named after Adoniram Judson, an early American Baptist missionary, lexicographer, and Bible translator, best known for his missionary work

Jud Birchall with the Athletics ca. 1883 or 1884.

in Burma.[3] The Birchalls were active members of the Milestone Baptist Church. Elias served the church as a deacon, trustee, and choir leader, giving liberally of his time and financial resources – to his own detriment in his later years – for the advancement and support of the church.[4] Jud was raised with traditional nineteenth-century evangelical Protestant tenets that emphasized individual conversion, personal piety, Bible study, and public morality. Whether these were values he carried with him into adulthood is unclear.

Jud attended Rittenhouse Grammar School, a public school that served rich and poor families alike in the Germantown, Mt. Airy, Chestnut Hill, and Rittenhouse Town sections of Philadelphia.[5] His first amateur baseball experience came in 1869 as a member of the Americus Club.[6] This team was made up of members of the first senior class of Rittenhouse. Jud was one of only two players who were not members of the graduating class. Unlike his brothers, he never attended college and it is unknown how many years of formal education he completed. However, given his family's commercial interests, he was identified as having the offseason vocation of weaver.[7]

It is unknown if Birchall threw right- or left-handed or from which side of the plate he batted. However, we do know that by the spring of 1870 the 14-year-old boy had set out to pursue a career in baseball, which always seemed to bring him back to his hometown of Philadelphia. Birchall played for three different organizations that used the name Athletic Club of Philadelphia.

The early years of Birchall's baseball life were spent as an infielder, primarily at third base. He spent parts of 1870 with both the Athletics Jr. and United, one of the best amateur clubs in Philadelphia at the time. When the United disbanded, he joined the Germantown Alert and stayed with them until the end of the 1874 season.[8] In 1875 he went to Wilmington and played third base for the Delaware Quicksteps. That year, the Quicksteps barnstormed across the Midwest and played against the Chicago White Stockings and Cincinnati Red Stockings. Although the Quicksteps were considered an amateur club, they were a commercial venture and had a roster that included paid players playing alongside true amateurs. The Quicksteps were on the edge of professionalism and by every account were one of the finest amateur nines in the region. The experience of playing for the Quicksteps proved invaluable to the young infielder, providing him with his first taste of professional competition.

Jud remained with the Quicksteps during the 1876 season before returning to Philadelphia in 1877 to join the Fergy Malone-led Athletics of the League Alliance. This version of the Athletics was reborn as a semipro team after the club was expelled from the National League for failing to complete its entire schedule during the 1876 season. Birchall also began the 1878 season with the Athletics, which again played independently. However, a late May tailspin, which included defeats at the hands of local amateurs, necessitated a shake-up that resulted in Birchall being drafted by the International Association's New Bedford franchise, co-managed by Frank Bancroft.[9]

Bancroft, who honed his entrepreneurial skills in the theater industry, saw the moneymaking potential in baseball, and acquired Birchall in June. The 22-year-old third baseman joined future major-league stars George Gore, Roger Connor, and Harry Stovey on the New Bedford roster. While Birchall was with the club for just under a month, there was no shortage of baseball played. Bancroft treated his club like a theatrical group and reportedly scheduled 130 games that year. On the Fourth of July holiday, Bancroft scheduled a tripleheader for New Bedford and Hartford: an 8 A.M. game in New Bedford, an 11 A.M. game in Taunton, and a 4 P.M. game in Providence.[10] Four days later, Birchall left the New Bedford team. Where he played during the remainder of the 1878 season is unknown. Birchall once again played for the hometown Athletics in 1879.

In 1880 Birchall joined future Hall of Famer Dan Brouthers on the Baltimore club of the loosely organized National Association. Birchall, beginning his transition from third base to left field, divided the third-base and left-field duties with utilityman Joe Ellick. The Baltimore team disbanded on June 29 and Birchall once again returned to Philadelphia, finishing the season with the Globe club.

In February 1881 Birchall signed with the Athletics and began his third and final stint with the team. The Athletics were now part of the Eastern Championship Association (ECAS) and boasted a roster that included Jack O'Brien, Cub Stricker, and Charlie Mason – all of whom played a prominent role on the 1883 American Association championship team. Unlike his previous associations with the club, Birchall stuck with the Athletics for the next three seasons, becoming an integral part of a lineup that later included established major-league stars like first baseman Harry Stovey and ace right-handed pitcher Bobby Mathews.[11]

The Athletics joined the American Association in the fall of 1881 and on May 2, 1882, the 26-year-old Birchall made his major-league debut, patrolling left field and batting cleanup for the Athletics in Oakdale Park, located on Eleventh and Cumberland Streets.[12] Birchall went 2-for-4 with a walk and a run scored as the Athletics beat the Baltimore Orioles 10-7 in the first-ever American Association game. Birchall batted in the cleanup spot during the early part of season before moving to the leadoff spot he customarily occupied for the next year and a half.

During his rookie season, Birchall earned a reputation as a steady left fielder with a flair for making incredible catches. One such instance was during a game against the Cincinnati Red Stockings on June 1, when he made a spectacular game-saving catch that the *Philadelphia Inquirer* described as "the most wonderful ever witnessed on the ball field." With Philadelphia leading 3-0 in the top of the ninth, Cincinnati was threatening with runners on second and third and two down. Red Stockings first baseman Henry Luff sent a rocket to left field. The *Inquirer* recounted the play as follows:

"Luff hit a ball that traveled like a shot out of a cannon directly over Birchal's [*sic*] head. The later jumped fully three feet from the ground, and the ball struck his right wrist, bounded in the air, fell into his hand and then dropped, but before it reached the ground Birchal [*sic*] cleverly caught it with one hand, and the Cincinnatis were 'Chicagoed.'"[13]

Birchall enjoyed a fine rookie campaign. He appeared in all 75 of the Athletics' games that season, 74 in left field and one at second base. He finished the season with career highs in batting average, .263, and RBIs, 27, both fourth-best among the team's regulars. He also led the team in plate appearances, at-bats, and runs scored, while finishing second on the club in both hits and doubles. More importantly, he established himself as the Athletics' everyday left fielder and a reliable leadoff hitter.

Following his steady performance during his rookie year, much was expected of Birchall and the Athletics in 1883. In its annual Baseball Preview, *Sporting Life* tabbed the Athletics as the American Association favorites and highlighted Birchall's steady left-field play and excellent baserunning: "He is credited with some remarkable catches in his position, his running catches bring noteworthy. His great forte, however, is in base running, in which he leads the players of the country, and which has made him famous."[14]

Philadelphia Inquirer.

Birchall, *from* Philadelphia Inquirer, *December 23, 1887.*

Stolen bases did not become an official statistic until 1886, so Birchall's baserunning skills are difficult to assess in comparison with his contemporaries.

The 1883 season marked the Athletics' return to the newly renovated Jefferson Street Grounds, which the *New York Times* hailed as the prettiest ballpark in America. It was reported that landscape gardeners made the playing field as "level as a billiard table."[15] The Athletics' return to Jefferson Street Grounds presented a unique challenge to Birchall and the other Athletic outfielders. The ballpark, formerly known as Athletics Park, featured tight narrow corners in left and right fields and deep power alleys that met a cavernous 500 feet away in dead center field. The oddly-shaped ballpark tested outfielders' awareness of where they were at on the field and their range to cover the vast power alleys.

In addition to having the finest ballpark in America, Philadelphia also had a brand-new entry in the National League. For the first time Philadelphia was a two-team major-league city, marking the beginning of a period of unprecedented growth in the popularity of baseball in the city.

Birchall and his Athletics teammates were so well received by the city of Philadelphia, that by early June their NL counterparts received permission from the League to reduce admission from 50 cents to 25 cents to allow them to compete with their popular crosstown rivals. Amazingly, the Athletics drew more than 300,000 fans[16] to the Jefferson Street Grounds that season, including more than 45,000 for an early September four-game series with the second-place St. Louis Browns.

For Birchall the 1883 season marked the zenith of his major-league career. Although his batting average dipped 22 points from the previous year to .241, Birchall led the Association in both plate appearances and at-bats, establishing major-league records of 468 and 448, respectively.[17] He also ranked fifth in the Association in runs scored with 95. Batting in the leadoff position, Birchall often set the table for Lon Knight, O'Brien, and Stovey, who batted .304 and smacked 14 home runs that year.

Despite charging out of the gate to an 18-3 mark in May, the Athletics were later locked in a tight three-way pennant race with the St. Louis Browns and Cincinnati Red Stockings. On August 10, in the midst of a three-game series in New York with the Metropolitans, the Athletics clung to a slim two-game lead over the Browns and were facing future Hall of Famer and Metropolitans ace Tim Keefe. Trailing 3-1 in the eighth inning, Birchall, in his customary role as a table-setter, ignited a two-run rally with a base hit off Keefe and heads-up baserunning. With the game tied 3-3 in the 10th, Birchall smacked a long triple to right field and scored on Stovey's game-winning single, helping the Athletics maintain their slim lead over the Browns,

Not known for his power, Birchall hit only one home run in his major-league career. Fittingly, it came during the Athletics championship season and in the midst of the pennant race. On September 13, 1883, at Recreation Park in Columbus, Ohio, Birchall led off the game with an inside-the-park home run off right-hander Frank Mountain. The Athletics went on to win the game, 11-5, and opened up a seemingly safe 3½-game lead over the Browns, who dropped a 3-0 decision to the Baltimore Orioles the same day.

As the 1884 season opened, the Athletics and their fans anticipated another American Association pennant run. Birchall began the season in left field and batted in his customary leadoff spot, the catalyst of the returning offensive juggernaut. However, the Athletics quickly faltered and Birchall's playing time witnessed a dramatic fall-off. Birchall appeared in only 54 of the team's 107 contests, and by mid-May was dropped to the sixth and seventh slots in the Athletics batting order for the remainder of the season. Although he batted .258, his power numbers

had declined significantly – he recorded only four extra-base hits – and his fielding was nowhere near what it had been two seasons before. By the end of the season, Birchall rarely appeared in the Athletics lineup, replaced by Henry Larkin, and the Athletics had fallen to seventh place in the Association. At the end of the season, Birchall's major-league career came to a quiet end.

On January 1, 1885, Birchall married Emma Jane Pinkerton. Emma Jane was the daughter of John and Margaret Pinkerton, also of Germantown. The Pinkerton men were typically employed as blacksmiths while the women worked in the hosiery business. It is unclear when the romance between the two began, but it is hard to imagine the two hadn't known each other nearly their entire lives.

Despite not being offered a contract by the Athletics in 1885, Jud felt he still had some baseball left in him. So in the spring of that year, he left his then-pregnant wife in Philadelphia and headed to New Jersey, where he joined the minor-league Newark Domestics. Reunited with former Athletics teammate "California" Bob Blakiston, Birchall primarily played left field for the Domestics, who finished 42-49, good enough for fourth place in the financially struggling Eastern League. After the season Birchall returned to Philadelphia and prepared for the birth of his first child. On November 25, 1885, Jud and Emma Jean Birchall became the parents of a son, Judson Elias.

Jud Birchall appeared in 225 major-league games, compiling 254 hits in 1,007 at-bats for a .252 batting average. Although his major-league totals are modest and his career described as undistinguished by some baseball historians, the official statistics probably don't provide us with an accurate picture of the important role Birchall played in the Athletics' pennant-winning season of 1883. According to David Nemec, author of *The Beer and Whiskey League*, there was a distinct difference in philosophy between NL and AA official scorers, and the fact that Birchall played in the American Association "probably deducted 5-10 points from his batting average."[18] AA official scorers were typically stingy in awarding hits, while NL scorers tended to be more liberal in their scoring decisions.

In addition to the discrepancies and inaccuracies associated with statistics from this era (and the American Association in particular), stolen bases were not an official statistic until 1886. Consequently it is difficult, in any reliable manner, to quantify or compare Birchall's baserunning abilities. Yet, at the time of his death, his baserunning and "wonderful slides into second were still talked about in baseball circles."[19]

When compared to his contemporaries, Birchall's career fielding statistics would indicate that he was a slightly below average left fielder. His statistical plunge in fielding percentage following his outstanding rookie season of 1882, when he was one of the better left fielders in the Association, raises many questions.

Was this drop-off the result of the early signs of consumption that would eventually take his life? At least two independent sources suggest that Birchall's playing career was cut short due to failing health. However, the fact that he died more than three years after the end of his major-league career would indicate that the pulmonary trouble that led to his demise may not have been contracted or progressed far enough to begin impacting his playing ability. Therefore, baseball historians are left to search for other clues that may have contributed to his fall-off during a time when he should have been entering his prime.

It's possible that Birchall's off-field activities contributed to his fall-off. As with many teams during the 1880s, there were numerous reports of heavy drinking among the Athletics. In fact, the Athletics management expressed concerns about almost all of their players during the 1883 season, which resulted in management establishing a set of club rules that among other things addressed the primary vices of hard living associated with the Athletics and ballplayers of this era. However, no one player or group of players was mentioned by name, so it is difficult to know if this may have contributed to Birchall's decline.

His playing career complete and health beginning to fail, Birchall spent the next two summers umpiring in amateur leagues in and around Philadelphia.

On December 22, 1887, Jud Birchall succumbed to consumption (tuberculosis). He died quietly at his home on Main Street in Philadelphia and was buried in the Milestone Baptist Church Cemetery. The cemetery was later destroyed for construction and Birchall was reinterred in a common mass grave in Cheltenham, Pennsylvania.

After Birchall's death, Emma worked as a dressmaker. She and Judson moved in with her sister, Sarah Pinkerton. Judson grew up to be a haberdasher and

died in 1911 at the age of 25. In 1916 Emma married William Parsons, who worked for an electric storage company. The couple were married for at least 34 years, as the 1940 census shows them residing in Philadelphia.

SOURCES

In addition to the sources cited in the Notes, the author relied on Baseball-reference.com and Retrosheet.org.

NOTES

1 Willoughby H. Reed. *History and Genealogy of the Reed Family* (Norristown, Pennsylvania: Norristown Press, 1929), 206.

2 Reed, 205.

3 Fred Barlow, "Adoniram Judson, Worldwide Missions." Retrieved from wholesomewords.org/missions/bjudson1.html.

4 Reed, 207.

5 The school was named after David Rittenhouse (1732-1796), a noted American clockmaker, mathematician, astronomer, educator, and state politician. As an astronomer he is credited with calculating the transit of Venus as well as making a successful observation of the planet. In later years he was a vice provost and professor of astronomy at the University of Pennsylvania. He was also the first director of the United States Mint.

6 "A.J. Birchal [*sic*]," *Philadelphia Inquirer*, December 23, 1887: 1.

7 "The Base Ball Parade," *Times* (Philadelphia), October 2, 1883: 1.

8 "A.J. Birchal [*sic*]."

9 "General Notes and News," *Chicago Tribune*, June 16, 1878: 7.

10 "Base Ball," *Buffalo Courier*, July 4, 1878: 2.

11 Harry Stovey was the greatest power hitter in American Association. Bobby Mathews won 30 games in three consecutive seasons for the Athletics (1883-1885).

12 Jerrold Casway, "Jefferson Street Grounds," *National Pastime*, 2013: 14.

13 "Chicagoed" was the nineteenth-century term to describe a team that had been shut out. *Philadelphia Inquirer*, June 2, 1882.

14 The Athletics Club; the Men Who Will Strive for the American Association Championship," *Sporting Life*, April 15, 1883: 2.

15 M. Benson, *Ballparks of North America: A Comprehensive Historical Reference to Baseball Grounds, Yards and Stadiums, 1845 to Present* (Jefferson, North Carolina: McFarland & Company Publishers, Inc., 1989), 296.

16 Edward Achorn, *The Summer of Beer and Whiskey* (New York: Public Affairs, 2006), 243.

17 Birchall's major-league record for plate appearances and at-bats was broken in 1884.

18 David Nemec, personal correspondence, July 30, 2004.

19 "'Jud' Birchal [*sic*] Dead: The Famous Left Fielder of the Athletic Base Ball Club," *Times* (Philadelphia), December 24, 1887: 1.

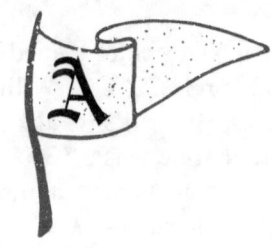

BOB BLAKISTON

By Bill Nowlin

There are a few mysteries surrounding Bob Blakiston. Was he right-handed or left-handed? Was he Robert J. or John Robert? Did he die on Christmas Day, or the 26th?

At least one thing is clear, however, he was one of the first San Francisco area ballplayers – if not the first – to play for a major-league team. We are indebted to the *San Francisco Chronicle* for a lengthy account of Blakiston's trailblazing career. The paper wrote in 1914, four years before the player's death, "Blakiston has the unique distinction of being the first local player to leave for other parts under salary, and his capable playing made such an impression with the Eastern managers that other Californians were called East."[1] The paper added, "Following Blakiston was the famous Jerry Denny, Pitcher Charlie Sweeney and his batterymate, Vincent Nava, known as 'Sandy Irwin.'"

Robert J. Blakiston was born on October 2, 1855, in San Francisco.[2] His father was John S. Blakiston, a sailmaker who lived much of his life on Clay Street in San Francisco. John was apparently Canadian by birth, a native of Quebec, and his wife, Catherine, was from South Carolina.[3] During his playing days, Blakiston claimed that his real name was Blackstone and that he was a descendant of the English legal luminary Sir William Blackstone.[4]

We are unable to supply details on his childhood or education, but can report that John S. Blakiston advertised his sailmaking shop in area newspapers, and for some period of time listed the business (see the 1880 City Directory, for instance) as J.S. Blakiston and Son. As a young man, Bob presumably worked alongside his father as a sailmaker.

Bob married Helena (Lena) Walcott on January 30, 1878, in San Francisco.[5] Blakiston and Lena, who was born in Massachusetts, shared a common cultural connection. Lena was the daughter of a Canadian father. There is no record of the couple having children.

In 1879 Bob appears occasionally in newspaper stories playing for the Californias in the four-team Oakland League.[6] The later 1914 *Chronicle* article provides some detail. The league embraced the Californias, the Athletics, the Stars, and the Mutuals, and "The Californias under the management of Harry Plate succeeded in annexing the championship by winning eighteen games and losing three."[7] Blakiston was the team's third baseman.

Two members of the team – pitcher William Sweeney and catcher Jack O'Brien – "were from Philadelphia and it was due to their clever battery work that the Californias proved to be the victors." League games were played in Oakland "on the old Fourteenth and Castro streets grounds in Oakland and were a drawing card from both sides of the bay."[8]

In 1880 Blakiston played some for the Unions of San Francisco, a team that did some degree of traveling. For instance, on March 12 they played a game against the Capital Citys of Sacramento at Agricultural Park, the downtown Sacramento horse racing track with an infield that doubled as a baseball field, winning 10-7 before a crowd of about 1,000.[9] During the regular season, however, he seemed to play for the Californias once more as he is found at least once, in August, playing first base for them. A July article in the *New York Tribune* refers to "the California nine" and has Blakiston as shortstop.[10] There is no context provided for the mention. Was the team touring in the East? We do not know.

The only mention we find of Blakiston in 1881 is in the *Eureka* (Nevada) *Daily Sentinel,* which says he would be playing third base for the Albion Club, which was apparently situated in Eureka.[11] They played three games on successive days against the Austins, at the Miners Union picnic at a location about 35 miles from Eureka, winning the first game, 20-15, but dropping the second, 13-8, before winning the third, 25-10. Blakiston had three hits in each game.[12] The games were considered to have been for the state championship and the *San Francisco Examiner* later agreed, writing that Blakiston had "assisted in winning the State Championship."[13] In the following weeks, he appeared on a couple of "picked nines" playing for other teams.

It was for the 1882 season that Blakiston first forayed East. How his signing came to pass we do not know, but the Eureka paper reported that catcher, and future Athletics teammate Ed Rowen had signed to play for "the Bostons" in 1882 and that Blakiston and his wife departed on the same train leaving Eureka and heading east on January 26.[14]

In early May 1882, Blakiston was playing third base for the Athletics of Philadelphia. He played for them for all of 1882 and 1883 and most of 1884. New York Giants famed manager John McGraw said that as a boy he had seen Blakiston play ball in the American Association.[15]

The *Chicago Daily News* reported in mid-1882 that "O'Brien, Cub Stricker, and Blakiston, of the Athletics, have received offers from a league club for next season."[16] It appears that Blakiston, instead, may have intended to return to California after the 1882 season. The *Philadelphia Record* was quoted as writing, "Two weeks ago the *Record* announced that of the Athletic nine who were likely to remain with the club next season were Messrs. Latham, Stricker, Birchall, O'Brien, and Blakiston. It is now certain that the first payers named have been re-engaged, while Blakiston would have been if he had not promised to go back to California."[17]

Blakiston enjoyed a good season playing for the Athletics in 1882, with home games played at Philadelphia's Oakdale Park. Playing for manager Jumbo Latham, the team finished second in the American Association with a 41-34 record, but a full 11½ games behind the dominant Cincinnati Red Stockings (55-25). Blakiston played in 72 of the team's 74 games and hit .228 with 20 RBIs and 40 runs scored. He was not among the team leaders in any category, but wasn't the low man, either, except in on-base percentage. He demonstrated little power, with only five extra-base hits.

Bob Blakiston with the 1883 Athletics.

He appeared in 38 games in the outfield (four in center and 34 in right), 34 at third base, and one at second base. In total Blakiston committed 45 errors in 223 chances, for a .798 fielding percentage. He was second on the team in errors only to Cub Stricker's 52, though Stricker handled twice as many chances.

By late October, Blakiston had rethought his decision to return to California and arranged to return to the Athletics for 1883. The Athletics added a great deal of talent during the offseason, including slugger Harry Stovey, pitcher Bobby Mathews, and Rowen, who for all intents and purposes had become Mathews' personal catcher. Great things were expected of Blakiston and the Athletics when the team arrived in New Orleans in December for preparatory training for the 1883 season.[18]

The *Philadelphia Times* characterized Blakiston before the 1883 season: "a good batter and excellent fielder, but at times he throws very wildly."[19] *Sporting Life* echoed the *Times's* assessment of Blakiston's fielding prowess and erratic arm in its season preview: "He excels in stops and pickup of hot balls, some of his work in this line last year being remarkable. He was however a little off in his throwing."[20] The article went on to describe him as a "fair batter and good base runner."[21]

Playing under new manager Lon Knight, with the Jefferson Street Grounds as their home, the 1883 Athletics won a league-leading 67.3 percent of their games (66-32) in a pennant race that couldn't have been much tighter. They finished first, only one game ahead of the second-place St. Louis Browns. Blakiston again played multiple positions – outfield (37 games), first base (6), and third base (5). His fielding improved considerably, though he appeared in only 48 games (35 of them as a center fielder), accepting just 109 chances with 15 errors (.862). At the plate, he had 176 plate appearances and improved his batting average from .228 to .246. Nine of his teammates had more plate appearances. His 26 RBIs ranked eighth on the club.

As the season progressed, Blakiston continued to contribute. After taking two out of three from St. Louis in St. Louis on the weekend of September 21-23, the Athletics had a 3½-game lead with only four games left to play. Some 16,800 paying customers attended the final game, won 9-2 by the Athletics. They had four remaining in Louisville against the Eclipse, but St. Louis had only three games left on its schedule. The pennant was virtually theirs. The Browns won all three of their games, but the Athletics won the third of their games in Louisville, and that sealed it.

The 1883 season ended on September 30 with the Athletics winning the American Association pennant. The team returned to Philadelphia and on October 3,

BOB BLAKISTON

Bob Blakiston.

Public domain.

some 8,000 fans came out to an exhibition game (a 13-2 Athletics win over "the Philadelphias"). Before the game, gold watches and badges were presented to four Athletics players: Stovey, Stricker, George Bradley, and Blakiston.[22]

Under a recently adopted rule of the day, which later became known as the reserve clause, the day the 1883 season ended Blakiston's contract was automatically reserved for 1884. This meant that none of the other clubs in the American Association could bid for his services.[23]

The 1884 season was not a good one for the Athletics. The American Association had expanded from an eight-team league in 1883 to a 13-team league in 1884. The Athletics fell to seventh place and finished with a 61-46 record, 14 games behind the first-place Metropolitans of New York. The Athletics were said to have suffered from "sickness among the players and a lack of form by the twirlers."[24]

Blakiston primarily played in the outfield and played at least one game at each infield position. However, his playing time was cut significantly and he appeared in only 32 games, less than 30 percent of the Athletics' 107 games. His batting average improved to .258, and his fielding, particularly in the outfield, continued to improve. His reduced playing time was more of a case of the team simply having what Lon Knight deemed to be better options. In the first part of September, both Blakiston and little-used Frank Siffell were released.[25]

In his final month with the Athletics, there were two occasions in which Blakiston officiated as umpire – as the home-plate umpire on August 12 and as the first-base umpire on September 10. In the first instance, the two teams mutually agreed on Blakiston. The fact that he was chosen to umpire in an era when gambling was rampant is testament to his character. Both teams noted that he performed "in a satisfactory manner."[26]

Blakiston caught on with the Indianapolis Hoosiers (who finished in 12th place) and appeared in six games. Blakiston was 4-for-18 in the six games. After the season the Hoosiers traveled to Philadelphia to play an exhibition game against the Athletics. Blakiston played first base and led the Hoosiers' hitting attack by going 2-for-4 with a double and triple.[27] The *Intelligencer Journal* (Lancaster, Pennsylvania) wrote, "He played yesterday against his old club and carried off the honors of the day. Blakiston is a good ballplayer and should never have been released by the Athletics."[28] In early December, it was reported that he had offers from both Louisville and Kansas City.[29]

Blakiston signed with the National League's Buffalo Bisons for the 1885 season, but was released in mid- to late April, a little over a week before the regular season began. He was with the team long enough, however, for us to learn that he was right-handed. The *Buffalo Times* reported: "He is 28 years old, five feet seven inches in height and weighs 160 pounds. ... He is a right handed batter."[30] Blakiston is found in box scores umpiring the occasional game in Philadelphia – though neither AA nor NL games. And he was seen playing center field for Newark during the 1885 season. After the season, he returned home to California, where the baseball seasons were longer.

In 1886 Blakiston was said to have played for Rochester, but is also noted as playing the outfield for Binghamton.[31] He returned to California, and the November 20, 1886, *Sporting News* reported that Blakiston "is playing with the Greenhood and Morans of San Francisco."[32] He apparently settled in with them and played the 1887 season with the G&M's, too. The *Cleveland Leader* had a note in late May: "Bob Blakiston has become the champion first baseman of California. He plays the position perfectly by all accounts. That's the position he always wanted to play here, but he never got a fair chance."[33] Blakiston was reportedly named captain of the team.[34] Assigning him the captaincy was said to have resulted in "an improvement in the discipline of the club."[35] Box scores later in the 1887 season, however, show him playing right field and third base. And there was one game at the end of October in which he was the starting pitcher, later moving to third base and then right field.[36]

After being released by the G&M's in 1888, Blakiston played for Stockton, which won the pennant in the four-team California League. However, Blakiston was unable to finish the season on account of injuries he suffered in midseason.[37]

He became an umpire with the California League toward the end of 1888.[38] What prompted him to have incurred the displeasure of locals attending the games, we do not know, but the *Oakland Tribune* wrote that "the cranks are now dissatisfied with Blakiston's umpiring."[39] He quit umpiring on November 1.[40]

After 1888 Blakiston called it a career and went back to making sails at the Mare Island Navy Yard in Vallejo, California. The *San Francisco Chronicle* wrote, "Between this and participation in politics, he lost interest in playing."[41] Later he became a deputy assessor in San Francisco.[42]

Blakiston still remained somewhat active in baseball. He was seen with the Knickerbockers team of the California League in January 1889, and in February 1890, he was listed as an outfielder with the Knickerbockers.[43]

In his later years, Blakiston worked at a number of jobs. The 1910 census found him living with Lena in Solano County, California, and identified him as a watchman. San Francisco city directories list him as having a number of jobs, changing from year to year. In 1916 he was a gardener, in 1917 a laborer, and in 1918 a janitor.

We believe Blakiston died of tuberculosis on Christmas Day 1918. Though the California Death Index records his death as on December 26, the *San Francisco Chronicle* reported his death in its December 26 issue. The death notices in the December 27 issue cited December 25 as the date. Later, in a brief story published on the 28th, the paper wrote, "Robert J. Blakiston died at his home in this city on Christmas day."[44] He is buried at Holy Cross Cemetery in Colma, California.

SOURCES

In addition to the sources provided in the Notes, the author was aided by consulting Baseball-reference.com, Retrosheet.org, Ancestry.com, and Familysearch.org

NOTES

1   "Bob Blakiston, First of Ball Players Taken East," *San Francisco Chronicle*, February 15, 1914: 59.

2   Some sources show his name as John Robert Blakiston, but the California Death Index lists him as Robert J. Blakiston.

3   This per the 1920 United States Census, which shows Bob and his wife, Lena (Helena), living in Green Valley, Solano County, and provides us this information. John S. and Catherine were listed as Bob's parents in Bob's obituary: "Deaths," *San Francisco Chronicle*, December 27, 1918: 4. John Blakiston's city of birth was noted in his obituary. See "Died," *San Francisco Examiner*, February 1, 1901: 6.

4   David Nemec, *The Beer and Whiskey League: The Illustrated History of the American Association – Baseball's Renegade Major League* (New York: Lyons & Buford, Publishers, 1994): 53.

5   "Marriages," *San Francisco Chronicle*, February 1, 1878: 4.

6   "The Diamond Field," *San Francisco Examiner*, April 18, 1879: 3.

7   "Bob Blakiston, First of Ball Players Taken East."

8   "Bob Blakiston, First of Ball Players Taken East."

9   "Base Ball Notes," *Sacramento Weekly Bee*, March 13, 1880: 3.

10   "Base-Ball Notes," *New York Tribune*, July 23, 1880: 3.

11   "Satisfactorily Arranged," *Eureka Daily Sentinel*, September 8, 1881: 4.

12   "Victory for the Albions," *Eureka Daily Sentinel*, September 13, 1881: 4.

13   "The Diamond Field."

14   "Departing Ball Tossers," *Eureka Daily Sentinel*, January 26, 1882: 4.

15   "Bob Blakiston, First of Ball Players Taken East."

16   "General Sporting News," *Chicago Daily News*, June 14, 1882: 1.

17   "Base Ball," *Cleveland Leader*, September 22, 1882: 5.

18   "Base Ball," *New Orleans Times-Picayune*, October 26, 1882: 2.

19   "The Ball Season," *Times* (Philadelphia), March 11, 1883: 3.

20   "The Home Team: Sketch of the Men who Constitute the Local Teams," *Sporting Life* (Philadelphia), April 15, 1883: 2.

21   "The Home Team."

22   "Athletics Welcomed Home," *Cincinnati Commercial Tribune*, October 4, 1883: 3.

23   "Ball-players for 1884," *New York Tribune*, September 29, 1883: 3.

24   "Bob Blakiston, First of Ball Players Taken East."

25   "Base Hits," *Cleveland Leader*, September 12, 1884: 3.

26   "The Ball Field," *Times* (Philadelphia), August 13, 1884: 4.

27   "Base Ball: An Exhibition Game on the Athletic Grounds Won by the Champions," *Times* (Philadelphia), October 8, 1884: 3.

28   "Base Ball Briefs," *Intelligencer Journal* (Lancaster, Pennsylvania), October 8, 1884: 3.

29   "The National Game," *Denver Rocky Mountain News*, December 1, 1884: 2.

30   See "Buffalos for 1885," *Buffalo Times*, February 23, 1885: 3.

31   "Bob Blakiston, First of Ball Players Taken East." See also "news of the Diamond," *Intelligencer Journal*, June 28, 1886: 2.

32   "Caught on the Fly," *The Sporting News*, November 20, 1886: 5.

33   "Notes from the Diamond," *Cleveland Leader*, May 29, 1887: 3.

34   "Bob Blakiston, First of Ball Players Taken East."

35   "The Diamond Field."

36   "They Win at Last," *Record-Union* (Sacramento), October 31, 1887: 2.

37   "They Win at Last." Blakiston's release was reported in "Diamond Dust," *San Francisco Examiner*, February 13, 1888: 8.

38   "Stray Hits," *Oakland Tribune*, September 12, 1888: 3.

39   "Stray Hits," *Oakland Tribune*, October 3, 1888: 3.

40   "A New Target for Ball Cranks," *San Francisco Examiner*, November 2, 1888: 5.

41   "Bob Blakiston, First of Ball Players Taken East."

42   "News of the Diamond," *San Francisco Examiner*, March 3, 1890: 7.

43   "Pitched and Caught," *Boston Herald*, February 2, 1890: 18.

44   See "Deaths," *San Francisco Chronicle*, December 26, 1918: 4; "Deaths," *San Francisco Chronicle*, December 27, 1918: 4; and "Old California Ball Player Dies. Bob Blakiston, Star, Passes Away," *San Francisco Chronicle*, December 28, 1918: 10.

GEORGE WASHINGTON BRADLEY

By Brian C. Engelhardt

George Washington Bradley[1] of the St. Louis Brown Stockings shut out (or, in the baseball parlance of the time, "Chicagoed") the Hartford Dark Blues by a score of 2-0 on July 15, 1876. Aside from their being Chicagoed, the Blues also failed to get any hits in the process (although Bradley did walk two) establishing this game as the first no-hitter in the history of the recently formed National League. Bradley's nickname, "Grin," came from the constant smile he showed to batters as he pitched. It apparently made a striking impression. Years after he retired, an article in *The Sporting News* mentioned that "no one before ever had such a tantalizing smirk."[2]

While being the architect of the National League's inaugural no-hitter is Bradley's most noted accomplishment, during that same 1876 season besides shutting out the Dark Blues, he did the same to 15 other teams – a total of 16 shutouts in the season: a record that was matched only by Grover Cleveland Alexander in 1916 (it must be those presidential names). Referring to Bradley as the "Chicago King," baseball historian David Nemec suggested that the term may have arisen because Bradley's first shutout victim that season was the Chicago White Stockings, who succumbed 1-0 on May 5.[3] The unlikelihood that this record will ever be surpassed is underscored by the fact that since Juan Marichal threw 10 shutouts in 1965, only three pitchers have reached double figures: Bob Gibson with 13 in 1968, Jim Palmer with 10 in 1975, and John Tudor with 10 in 1985.

Bradley's professional career extended over 15 years, including 11 seasons with nine different teams in four different major leagues – in many ways mirroring Organized Baseball's state of flux at the time. Appearing in 347 games as a pitcher, Bradley compiled 171 victories. He played in 269 other games as a position player – mostly at third base, where his fielding skills were quite accomplished. In addition to his major-league travels, Bradley played for eight minor-league teams.

Born in Reading, Pennsylvania, on July 13, 1852, to George and Margaret Bradley,[4] George was the first native of the city to play in the major leagues.

George Bradley.

Although references to Bradley in Reading newspapers during his career occasionally mentioned his having been "born and raised in Reading," there is otherwise little information available about his life before he started playing in Philadelphia in 1872, the same year in which he married Philadelphia native Charlotte Heavener.

Early in the 1874 season, while playing for Philadelphia's Modoc club (described as a "third-rate amateur club"[5]) against an independent team from Easton, Pennsylvania, Bradley showed skills that caught the eye of Easton's manager, Jack Smith, who signed him as an infielder who would also pitch batting practice. When Smith observed that Bradley's new teammates couldn't handle his pitches during batting practice, he tried him out as a starting pitcher. That experiment went so well that that Smith, who had been the starting pitcher, benched himself in favor of Bradley. Bradley and catcher Tom Miller developed a fine relationship, which would lead to their both playing for the St. Louis Brown Stockings the next season. The chemistry between the two was noted by the *Easton Daily Express* after a 14-0 Easton victory over the Collins Club of Philadelphia in August. "Bradley and Miller worked together like a charm, many people remarking that it was their best game this year," the paper said, also describing Bradley's pitches in the game as "lightning bolts."[6]

Later that month Bradley returned to his hometown of Reading when Easton came to play the semipro Reading Actives. Before a crowd of about 4,000, Easton won the game, 11-6, in what the *Reading Eagle* described as "one of the most closely contested (games) that either club has ever played." With the score tied, 4-4, Easton broke the game open with five runs in the eighth inning. (*The Reading Times* account attributed the rally to Easton "doing some heavy batting,"[7] while the *Eagle* found Easton's runs to be the product of "bad luck, overthrows and a general demoralization"[8] on the part of the home team.) Although no statistics on the 1874 Actives or its players can be found, must have been a good one; the game account in the *Eagle* was headlined "Actives' First Defeat."[9] The account related that Bradley's "balls came in very swiftly and during the first part of the game were not hit."[10]

The *Eagle* said the Easton club was "regarded by knowing professional players to be the very best club in the country not on the professional lists,"[11] and said Easton clearly came to town as "enemy" in the eyes of the Reading locals. The *Easton Daily Express* complained that followers of the Actives "were in danger of life and limb from the blackguards and roughs of Reading, (unable) to praise the Eastons without being insulted and threatened."[12]

In a return match a few weeks later, Easton again won, 34-18, with the *Express* declaring that Reading did not appear "to get the hang of Bradley until the ninth inning."[13]

In early August Easton lost at home in front of a crowd of 2,000 to the National Association Brooklyn Atlantics by 30-11 in a game in which Bradley gave up 19 hits but was victimized by 16 Easton errors that resulted in only 4 of the Atlantics' 30 runs counting as earned runs.[14] At the end of the season Easton achieved consecutive exhibition victories over three National Association teams: the Atlantics in a rematch, then the Philadelphia Whites and finally the Philadelphia Athletics. As a result, Bradley was invited to pitch for the Athletics in an October exhibition against the Boston Red Stockings. In the game he impressed enough that St. Louis signed him after the season.

The 1875 Brown Stockings were managed by 39-year-old shortstop Dickey Pearce, and its roster included a number of players besides Bradley with Easton connections, starting with his batterymate Tom Miller, who had played four games with the Athletics near the end of the 1874 season. Also signed from the 1874 Easton team were third baseman Bill Hague, a light hitter known for his strong throwing arm and light-hitting outfielder Charlie Waitt. Browns second baseman Joe Battin played for Easton in 1873 before signing with the Philadelphia Athletics, where he spent the 1874 season.

Bradley's major-league debut was as the Opening Day pitcher on May 4, 1875, pitching the team to a 15-9 victory over the St. Louis Red Stockings. Two days later, on May 6, Bradley became an instant St. Louis fan favorite, shutting out the hated Chicago White Stockings, 10-0, in front of 8,000 fans at Grand Avenue Park in St. Louis, with another 2,000 peeking through knotholes or perched in trees outside the park.[15]

On June 2 Bradley suffered his first loss of the season, 10-3 to a Boston Red Stockings team that went an amazing 71-8 that season. Boston's lineup featured future Hall of Famers Harry and George Wright, Al Spalding, Orator Jim O'Rourke, and Deacon White, who would hit a league-leading .367. Also in the Boston lineup were White's closest competitors in the batting race, Ross Barnes (.364) and Cal McVey

(.355). The Red Stockings' victory boosted their record so far to 25-0.

Three days later Bradley avenged the loss by handing the Red Stockings their first defeat as he pitched St. Louis to a 5-4 win. The *Boston Globe* said that Bradley and "the 'Brown Sox' were carried off the field on the shoulders of their friends."[16]

On June 7, with St. Louis in a frenzy over "Brown Stocking fever," a crowd described by the *Globe* as "the largest ever seen on a ball field in this city, about 8,000"[17] saw the Red Stockings pound Bradley for 24 hits (he was said to be suffering from an attack of vertigo), with Spalding holding the home team to six hits as the visitors won, 15-2.

Just as was the case during their season in Easton, Bradley worked well with Miller, the duo being credited for much of the Browns' success. A contemporary commentator wrote that the two constituted "the main strength of the club," adding, "They are not supported by a first class field but, if their work of to-day is a criterion, they do not need one. The field(ers) were called upon to do but the easiest kind of play… and scarcely a ball was struck that would bother an ordinary player."[18] The leading hitter on the team was outfielder Lip Pike, while outfielder Jack Chapman exhibited such skill in the field that he earned the nickname of "Death To Flying Things."

A number of factors contributed to Bradley's success on the mound. At 5-feet-10 and 175 pounds, he was a big man for the times (in 1876 he was the fourth-tallest pitcher in the National League) and he used his size to power his delivery. Equally imposing from a psychological standpoint was the "smile" Bradley showed batters. In his analysis of Bradley's pitching technique, baseball historian Neil MacDonald declared the rather innocuous moniker of "Grin" to be a nickname that "belied a serious, savagely determined … man who wanted to play and win as much as any man alive."[19]

MacDonald wrote that Bradley combined the abilities of a "straight pitcher like Al Spalding, considered to be the best in the game, with the ingenuity of a breaking ball specialist like Candy Cummings, the consummate chucker of curves."[20] An additional factor contributing to Bradley's success during the 1876 season involved a new tactic learned from Browns teammate Mike McGeary: crushing game balls in a vise.

On October 26, 1875, Bradley returned to Reading with the Browns for an exhibition game against the semipro Reading Actives. Bradley and catcher Tom Miller were featured in ads in the *Times* and the *Eagle* referring to him as "THE FAMOUS BRADLEY" and proclaiming, "The old foes are coming. Bradley and Miller – St. Louis professionals versus Actives."[21] Upon Bradley's arrival in Reading the day before the game, the *Eagle* described him as "the best looking ballplayer in the profession."[22]

The next day the Browns defeated the Actives 18-11 in a sloppy game in which the Actives committed 20 errors and the Browns 12. Bradley entered the game in relief of the Browns backup pitcher, Pud Galvin, who surrendered eight runs in five innings, allowing the Actives to pull ahead at one point, 8-7. Bradley quieted the Actives' bats and the Browns erupted for 11 runs in the final four innings. (The *Eagle* headlined its game story "One of the Worst Games Yet,"[23] but failed to provide the score. Without the *Reading Times's* game account, posterity would never have known the score.)

The 18-year-old Galvin had been signed at the start of the season to back up Bradley after he had pitched impressively for the Niagara amateur team of St. Louis in a preseason game against the Browns.[24] Galvin pitched in three games in a row in late May, winning two, when Bradley was sidelined with health

Bradley with the St. Louis Brown Stockings in 1875 or 1876.

problems. Bradley returned the lineup on May 29, after which Galvin made only four more pitching starts. On his way to becoming baseball's first 300-game winner, over the next 17 years Galvin won another 361 games en route to his induction into the Baseball Hall of Fame.

The National Association of 1875 suffered from a great disparity between the haves and have-nots. The Browns finished in fourth place with a record of 39-29, a distant 26½ games behind the Red Stockings. As the winning pitcher in all but six of the Browns' victories, Bradley finished his rookie season with a record of 33-26, starting 60 games and finishing 57, with 5 shutouts. In 535⅔ innings pitched, Bradley struck out 60 and gave up a remarkably low 17 walks.

During the tumultuous offseason that followed, the National League was created, the National Association dissolved, a number of former National Association teams (the Browns among them) joining the new league, and a multitude of players moving to new teams. Although Bradley remained with the Browns, his surrounding cast underwent changes, the most dramatic being catcher Tommy Miller contracting a disabling illness over the winter from which he died on May 29, 1876.[25] Miller's replacement, Honest John Clapp, was signed away from the Philadelphia Athletics in the offseason and is viewed as one of the most talented catchers in baseball at the time. Despite the success Bradley enjoyed over the two seasons Miller was his batterymate, at least one commentator credited Clapp for helping Bradley go from very good in 1875 to superlative in 1876.[26]

Other changes to the Browns lineup included Bill Hague and "Death To Flying Things" Chapman both signing with Louisville, and 40-year-old Dicky Pearce being replaced as shortstop by Denny Mack. Pearce and as manager by Mase Graffen. (With superior fielding skills, Pearce returned as the starting shortstop later in the season even though he was 14 years older than Mack.)

Also moving on was Pud Galvin, leaving his role as Bradley's understudy to become the primary pitcher with the St. Louis Red Stockings, an unaffiliated team made up mostly of members of the team's 1875 National Association entry. Galvin was not replaced as Bradley's backup, or change pitcher; during the 1876 season Bradley threw every inning for the Browns except for four innings of relief pitched by Joe Blong.

On April 25, 1876, just before the start of the season, the *Louisville Courier-Journal* declared that Bradley was the hardest man in the profession to bat against.[27] This did not appear to be the case at the season's outset, as the Browns and Bradley lost the first two games of the season to a bad Cincinnati Reds club that won only seven more games that season. As the season progressed, Bradley did his best to confirm the *Courier-Journal's* analysis. During a series in late May against the New York Mutuals, he threw only 24 balls in 27 innings.[28] A 17-0 shutout of the Athletics on June 1 was his sixth of the year. He pitched two more shutouts in June, four in July, three in August, and one in September on his way to setting the record of 16 in a season.

In early July Bradley signed a contract with the Philadelphia Athletics for the following year. When word of this came out, the St. Louis press criticized him for "treachery," and the *Chicago Tribune* speculated that he would not try to win games in a coming series against the Hartford Blues. Bradley's response to this was to shut out Hartford three times in five days, culminating with the 2-0 victory on July 15 in which the Dark Blues failed to get a hit. The *Tribune* ran a retraction.[29]

Appreciation of no-hitters was in its nascent state at the time, and most accounts of the game focused on Hartford's poor hitting, with little attention given to the fact that Bradley had not allowed a hit, with some accounts not even mentioning that it was a no-hitter.[30]

On May 23 Boston's Joe Borden had shut out the Cincinnati Reds, giving up only two walks, which were recorded as hits consistent with scoring rules at that time. Bradley's gem has been considered the first no-hitter in the National League. (The previous season Borden, pitching for the Philadelphia Pearls in the National Association, threw the first major-league no-hitter, 4-0 against the Chicago White Stockings.) As for his 1876 shutout of Cincinnati, sportswriters and league officials disagreed over categorizing as walks as hits, but, as Neil W. McDonald wrote, "Enough doubt has been cast on Borden's efforts against Cincinnati to erase his honor of tossing the first National League no-hitter. Only God and the ghosts of '76 know if Borden was sinned against."[31]

Along with Bradley's range of pitches, pinpoint control, having the best catcher in the league, and having a withering grin, an unseemly side to his success in 1876 involved gamesmanship (or cheating, depending upon one's view). According to Bradley's former manager Frank Bancroft, the pitcher learned from teammate Mike McGeary how to steam open the sealed box containing the new ball to be used for the game, put the ball in a vise to crush it, and then reseal the box, creating a new mushy ball.[32] Aside from the process enhancing Bradley's curve, the ball usually lost its shape over the course of the game, allowing a crafty pitcher like Bradley to alter its plateward course with more trickery.[33]

With the Browns in third place for much of the season behind Chicago and Hartford, on August 17 Bradley shut out the visiting White Stockings, 3-0, culminating a stretch in which the team went 14-3 and moved past Hartford into second place, six games behind Chicago. The Browns took another game from Chicago and moved within five games of first, the closest they would get that season. (They finished in second place also with a record of 45-19, six games behind the White Stockings.) Bradley pitched 573 innings, all but four innings of the St. Louis season, and every decision was his. In addition to his record-setting 16 shutouts, he had a league-low 1.23 earned-run average. He also led the league with 34 wild pitches.

Although Bradley had signed with Philadelphia for the 1877 season, the A's were expelled from the National League for failing to complete their full schedule, and Bradley was able to nullify the contract. Instead he signed with Chicago, but tried to avoid burning bridges in St. Louis, sending the following letter to the *St. Louis Globe-Democrat* (published October 18, 1876), expressing his sentiments to St. Louis fans:

To the Editor of the Globe-Democrat:

Dear Sir: In leaving St. Louis I think it due to myself to make a few remarks in explanation of contracting in Chicago when I did so. I had a private misunderstanding with some of the officers of the St. Louis Club, this being the prime cause of my signing in Chicago.

I desire to say that my relations in St. Louis have been of the most pleasant character and to the hosts of warm friends I have acquired I desire to leave the most sincere expression of gratitude for the kind appreciation of my poor services. I shall always remember St. Louis with the liveliest feelings of respect and can never readily forget the generous treatment I have received in this city, where my professional reputation has to a great extent been made

Yours, etc. G.W. Bradley[34]

The plan with the White Stockings was that Bradley would succeed Al Spalding as the pitcher, with Spalding moving to first base. The plan didn't work out well. Bradley finished the season with a disappointing 18-23 record, with Chicago making no attempt to keep him for the next season. Reasons advanced for the falloff in Bradley's performance were that his former teammate McGeary, who had taught him the crushed-ball ploy, warned other teams of the trick,[35] and that the White Stockings made the mistake of not signing John Clapp to catch Bradley.[36]

After his season with the White Stockings, Bradley set out on an odyssey that would see him switch teams 16 times over the next 12 seasons, playing in 16 cities in various major and minor leagues. Bradley began the 1878 season with New Bedford of the fledgling International Association (which was meant to rival the National League but never did), signed by its manager, Frank Bancroft. When things didn't work out with the league to Bancroft's satisfaction, after just three games he pulled the club from the league and instead played an independent schedule for the season.[37] The team played 130 games against teams on the East Coast, with Bradley logging in more than 760 innings.[38]

The next season (1879) Bradley pitched for the last-place Troy Trojans of the National League, posting 13 wins to go with a league-leading 40 losses. In 1880 he moved to the Providence Grays of the National League, where he alternated playing third base and pitching with John Montgomery Ward. After signing with the Detroit Wolverines of the National League for 1880, he was released because of health issues after playing one game at shortstop. He then signed with the Cleveland Blues, but negotiated a release that resulted in his being sold for $500[39] to the Philadelphia Athletics of the American Association (Bradley's third major league) in June of 1883.[40]

With the A's Bradley won 16 games as the team's primary backup pitcher to Bobby Mathews; when not pitching he played third base. In September, when Mathews was out with arm problems, Bradley and Jumping Jack Jones put together a string of pitching performances that enabled the A's to win seven in a row on their way to the pennant. Despite his heroics, Bradley was released after the season, telling one interviewer, "They sent me adrift, just as you would a broken down horse. But that was strictly business, you know.[41]

The next year Bradley signed with the Cincinnati Outlaw Reds of the ill-fated Union Association, which existed only in 1884 (Bradley's fourth and final major league). His record was 25-15 as the team's primary pitcher. After the dissolution of the UA, for his playing in that league and jumping his contract with the Philadelphia, Bradley found himself blacklisted from other major-league teams for the 1885 season. Adding financial insult to career injury, Bradley never received what the Cincinnati team agreed to pay him, leading him to sue the defunct team. He eventually settled for $1,500 in cash, considerably less than what he was owed, since the team had gone bankrupt.

In 1886 Bradley signed with the Philadelphia Athletics again, as a shortstop, but was released after 13 games with an average of .083. Despite letting him go, Athletics manager Bill Sharsig called him "the hardest working and most conscientious player for his club that we ever had."[42] Despite these fine intangibles, Sharsig said, Bradley's hitting was too weak to keep him on the team.

Over the remainder of 1886 and the next four seasons Bradley played for seven minor-league teams, beginning with Nashville of the Southern League. At the outset of the next season he not only played for Nashville, but managed the team as well, where he played third base, and also envisioned making a pitching comeback.[43] Replaced as manager at the end of May,[44] he moved on to play with the New Orleans Pelicans of the same league, then appeared briefly with the Baltimore Orioles of the American Association before finishing the season with Danville in a league in Illinois.[45] In 1888 he played third base and first base for the New Orleans Pelicans of the Southern League. When the league disbanded in July, New Orleans joined the independent Texas League. Bradley moved north for the 1889 season, playing third base (and pitching one inning) for the Sioux City Corn Huskers of the Western Association. In 1890 he went full circle and finished his career in Easton of the Eastern Interstate League, playing 21 games at third base and batting .299.

With his baseball career over, Bradley first worked as a night watchman and then joined the Philadelphia police force. His son George W. Jr. apparently showed some baseball talent, and in 1907 Bradley talked of his son's growing abilities, referring to him as a, "keeper" (who) …will make good either at third-base or behind the bat.[46] No records could be found relating to a baseball career for George Jr.

In 1915 Bradley made an appearance at a revival in Philadelphia conducted by the former major leaguer Billy Sunday, whose career overlapped Bradley's. Seeing Bradley, on duty and in uniform, Sunday encouraged him to come forward, calling out to him, "Brad, God bless you, old scout."[47] An account of the event described how Bradley "gulped hard as he transferred his mace to his left hand and reached up to grip the reaching hand of his former rival. Then … said simply, 'Bill, I feel better now. Thanks.'"[48]

Bradley retired from the police in 1930.[49] He died of liver cancer on October 2, 1931, and was buried in Norwood Cemetery in Philadelphia. He was survived by his wife, Charlotte; his daughter, Lottie Crouse; and three sons, George W. Jr., John, and Morris. His obituary in the *Philadelphia Inquirer* called him "a close friend of many prominent men connected with big-league baseball today."[50] His hometown *Reading Eagle* ran a brief item noting that he pitched the first no-hitter in the National League, with no mention of his local connection.[51]

SOURCES

In addition to the sources cited in Notes, the author accessed Bradley's player file from the National Baseball Hall of Fame.

Some of the material in this article was also used were used in "Days of Grin and Heck: Berks County's First Two Major Leaguers," which appeared in *The Historical Review of Berks County,* Summer, 2014, Volume 79, Number 5.

Thanks to David Nemec for information and guidance in correspondence with the author, April 21, 2014.

NOTES

1   Not to be confused with George H. "Foghorn" Bradley, a former umpire who won nine games for the 1876 Boston Red Stockings, who, like the subject of this article, is buried in Philadelphia.

2   *The Sporting News,* April 23, 1892, quoted in David Nemec, *Major League Baseball Profiles 1871-1900, Vol. I,* (Lincoln: University of Nebraska Press, 2009), 18.

3   David Nemec, *The Great Encyclopedia of 19th Century Baseball* (New York: Donald I. Fine Books, 1997), 86.

4   "The Boys Stock Up Again," *Reading Eagle,* September 2, 1876: 1.

5   John David Cash, *Before They Were Cardinals* (Columbia, Missouri: University of Missouri Press, 2002), 26-35.

6   "Baseball – Eastons Again Victorious – Reading Disgraced," *Easton Daily Express,* August 1, 1874.

7   "An Exciting Game Yesterday Between the Eastons, of Easton, Pa., and the Actives of Reading," *Reading Times,* August 4, 1874: 1

8   "Actives First Defeat," *Reading Eagle,* August 4, 1874: 1.

9   "Actives First Defeat.".

10 "Actives First Defeat.".

11 "An Exciting Game."

12 "Baseball," *Easton Daily Express,* August 4, 1874.

13 "Baseball – Easton – Reading," *Easton Daily Express,* August 14, 1874.

14 "Baseball," *Easton Daily Express,* August 19, 1874.

15 Cash, 35.

16 "Summer Sports: The Bostons Defeated by St. Louis Club," *Boston Globe,* June 7, 1875: 5.

17   "Bat and Ball: The Bostons Slaughter the Brown Stockings,"
      St. Louis Daily Globe-Democrat, June 8, 1875: 8.

18   Quoted in David Nemec, *Major League Baseball Profiles 1871-
      1900, Vol. 2* (Lincoln: University of Nebraska Press, 2009), 295.

19   Neil W. McDonald, *The League That Lasted: 1876 and the
      Founding of the National League of Professional Baseball Clubs*
      (Jefferson, North Carolina: McFarland and Co., 2004), 143.

20   McDonald, 149.

21   "St. Louis Team in This City," *Reading Eagle,* October 26, 1875: 1.

22   "St. Louis Team in This City."

23   "One of Worst Games Yet," *Reading Eagle,* October 27, 1875: 1.

24   Jeffrey Kittel, "This Game of Games, Bradley vs. Galvin, October 3,
      2009. thisgameofgames.blogspot.com/search/label/Pud%20Galvin.

25   Nemec, Vol. 2, 296.

26   Section on Clapp written by Peter Morris in Nemec, Vol. 1, 222.

27   McDonald, 105.

28   McDonald, 105.

29   Jeffrey Kittel, "This Game of Games, Bradley's Gratitude," April 27,
      2010. thisgameofgames.blogspot.com/search/label/George%20Bradley.

30   McDonald, 152.

31   McDonald, 152.

32   Nemec, Vol. 1, 18.

33   Nemec, Vol. 1, 15.

34   Jeffrey Kittel, "This Game of Games, the 1876 Brown Stockings: The
      Clubs Might Have Played Until the Resurrection, January 20, 2010.
      thisgameofgames.blogspot.com/search/label/George%20Bradley.

35   Nemec, Vol. 1, 18.

36   Nemec, Vol. 1, 222.

37   Nemec, Vol. 2, 117.

38   Chapter by Jim Rygelski in Frederick Ivor-Campbell, Robert
      L. Tiemann, and Mark Rucker, eds, *Baseball's First Stars*
      (Cleveland: Society for American Baseball Research, 1996), 9.

39   John Shiffert, *Baseball in Philadelphia* (Jefferson,
      North Carolina: McFarland, 2006), 108.

40   "Bradley Obtains His Release," *Cleveland Leader,* May 19, 1883.

41   Ivor-Campbell, Tiemann, and Rucker, 9.

42   Rygelski.

43   "The Smiling Nashville Manager Talks About His Club, "
      March 9, 1887, Article in unidentified newspaper in
      Bradley's file at the National Baseball Hall of Fame.

44   "Baseball Notes," *Philadelphia Times,* May 23, 1887: page 1.

45   "Baseball Club Disbanded," *Decatur Herald,* September 13, 1887: 3.

46   "Brad the Second," *Sporting Life,* May 25 1907: 6.

47   "Sunday Converts Another Player," *Pittsburgh Press*, February 4, 1915: 24.

48   "Sunday Converts Another Player."

49   "Old Time Hurler Is Retired as Officer," *Lewiston
      Evening Journal,* October 2, 1930: 7.

50   "First No Hit Pitcher Struck Out by Death,"
      Philadelphia Inquirer, October 3, 1931.

51   "First No Hit No Run Pitcher Passes Away,"
      Reading Eagle, October 4, 1931: 13.

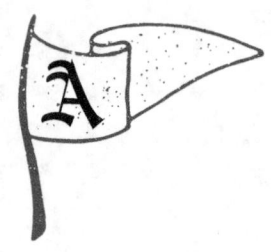

FRED COREY

By Richard Riis

In his seven seasons in the major leagues, Frederick Harrison Corey played every position on the diamond, appearing in 237 games at third base, 93 as the pitcher, 46 in right field, 38 at shortstop, 29 in center field, 11 at second base, 8 in left field, 7 at first base, and one at catcher. Before his career was cut short by a gunshot injury to his eye, Corey played a total of 432 games, batting .246 with seven home runs. As a pitcher, he made 74 starts, completing 59, for 656⅓ innings, and producing a 27-46 won-lost record and an ERA of 3.32. It was said that Corey was "one of the first to use a curve ball successfully."[1]

Corey was born in Coventry, Rhode Island, in 1855; the exact date of his birth is unrecorded. He was the fifth of eight children of Job Corey, a railroad-track layer, and Elizabeth (Tourgee) Corey. The family moved to Providence before 1865, where young Fred took up amateur baseball, playing for the local Olympics and Dexters. In 1876 the 21-year-old right-hander was invited to join the semipro Rhode Islands of the New England Association. Playing alongside future major leaguers Tom "Oyster" Burns and Ned Hanlon, Corey impressed enough in a 10-game stint as pitcher and utilityman to be invited back the following season.

Although individual records for the New England Association are scant, Corey was considered a valuable addition to the club in 1877. Sharing pitching duties with future major leaguer Hugh "One Arm" Daily, Corey "puzzled" hitters with his "peculiar curve."[2] It was remarked that "there was hardly a club that visited Providence last summer that got over six base hits off his delivery in a game."[3] Perhaps his finest pitching effort of the year came in a nonleague game on September 20, when he held a Boston amateur nine scoreless on two hits and struck out seven,

winning 10-0. Typically playing center field when not pitching, Corey "was the heaviest and surest batter of the nine."[4] Despite this, the Rhode Islands finished with a record in league games of 11-29.

The two-year-old National League, dropping the Brooklyn-Hartford franchise after the 1877 season, awarded a replacement franchise to Providence, and Corey jumped the Rhode Islands to play in the major leagues with the Grays. In a preseason warmup in Providence on April 22, Corey, pitching against an aggregation of top local amateurs and Brown University players, including future major-league pitcher Lee Richmond, tossed a one-hitter, striking out nine and winning 7-0.

Before the start of the season on May 1, 1878, the *Boston Globe* declared that Corey's "arms are said to be quite lame from over practice."[5] If so, it wasn't apparent as the Grays debuted at home against the defending NL champion Boston Red Caps. Despite losing 1-0, Corey appeared to be in good form, holding Boston hitless until the fifth inning and scoreless until the seventh.[6]

Corey benefited from significantly better run support in his second start, when the Grays hammered Boston, 24-5, but in his third start, on May 25, after pitching a scoreless first inning, he was removed from the game for reasons of a "lame arm."[7] When he started again three days later, Corey's arm "gave out at the end of the third inning."[8] It was a month before Corey started again, on June 27 in Milwaukee; this time he failed to get past the first inning.[9] In July it was reported that Corey had resigned from the team due to a sore arm, "a ligatural sprain of the elbow caused by over-practice in the gymnasium."[10] Box scores, however, show Corey in the lineup at second base for the Grays as late as August 15.[11]

The Providence Grays finished in third place in their initial season in the NL, posting a 33-27 record, eight games behind pennant-winning Boston, but Corey's first major-league season was a lost one. He played in only seven games for Providence, five of them as the starting pitcher, posting a won-lost record of 1-2, with a 2.35 ERA over 23 innings. He showed his versatility by playing in one game at first base and two at second, but contributed little at the plate, batting only .143 in 21 plate appearances.

But the season wasn't over for Corey. In September it was reported that "Cory [sic], late pitcher for the Providence club,"[12] had joined the New Bedford Clam-Eaters of the New England League to fill in for first baseman and future Athletics teammate Harry Stovey. Stovey had injured his leg in a game on August 17 and was disabled for a month; when he returned to the lineup, manager Frank Bancroft kept Corey in the lineup at second base.[13] In postseason exhibitions, Corey played second base for the International Association's Providence club.

During the offseason, it was reported that Corey "made a peculiar play last summer, and this winter was married to a young girl belonging to an adjoining town. ... The babe is expected before the ball season opens."[14] The young woman's name was Annie; their son, Harrison, was born in February 1879.

Corey signed for 1879 with the Capital Citys of the National Association. He pitched – and completed – the opening game of the season, giving up eight hits in a 3-0 loss. Less than a month into the campaign, the financially troubled club shifted from Albany to Rochester, becoming the Hop Bitters. Corey pitched regularly for Rochester until July, when they dropped out of the league and embarked on a five-month cross-country barnstorming tour. Accounts of the games show Corey most often in the lineup playing second base.

Corey returned to the majors in 1880, joining Stovey on the first-year Worcester Ruby Legs of the National League. Employed as the "change pitcher" for the club's primary hurler, former Brown University star Lee Richmond, Corey started 17 games, and relieved in eight. In 148⅓ innings, Corey compiled a 2.43 ERA, ninth best in the NL among those with at least 105 innings pitched, but won only eight games. He played an additional 29 games in the outfield, and divided five others among first base, third base, and shortstop. In all, Corey appeared in 41 games for fifth-place Worcester, batting .174 in 142 plate appearances.

The highlight of the club's season, and perhaps the National League's, came on June 12, 1880, when Richmond tossed the first perfect game in major-league history, retiring 27 consecutive Cleveland Blues in a 1-0 masterpiece. Corey was in the lineup that day, playing in center field and making a putout on one of only two batted balls Richmond permitted out of the infield.

On September 23, against Boston, Corey hit his first major-league home run – sort of. Failing to touch third base as he scrambled around the bases on the inside-the-park drive, Corey was called out at third and credited with only a double.[15] Despite the gaffe, Worcester won the game, 9-4, behind the tandem pitching of Corey and Richmond.

Back with the Ruby Legs in 1881, Corey started 21 games as pitcher and entered twice more in relief. He pitched poorly, however, posting a dismal 6-15 won-lost record and an ERA of 3.72. Playing 24 games in right field, 7 at shortstop, and one in left field, Corey appeared in a total of 51 games, batting .222.

For the second time in as many years, Corey lost what would have been his first major-league home run, when batting in the ninth against Cleveland on September 17. Again, he failed to touch third while rounding the bases on a bid for an inside-the-park home run, was called out, and credited with a two-base-hit.[16] Worcester nevertheless won, 7-2.

FRED COREY

Public domain.

Fred Corey.

Overall, Worcester struggled in 1881, finishing in last place with a 32-50 record. The Ruby Legs were worse in 1882, winning only 18 of 84 games. Splitting shortstop duties with Arthur Irwin, Corey appeared in 64 games, hitting .247, the third-highest average on a weak-hitting squad, and finished tied for second on the team in runs scored (33) and runs batted in (29). Among his 63 hits were a surprising 12 triples, tied for the second-highest in the NL. As a pitcher, Corey was a hard-luck case, coupling a club-best 3.56 ERA with a 1-13 won-lost record. He amassed 139 innings in his 21 turns in the pitcher's box.

Worcester's attendance figures were no better than their on-field performance and the franchise was dropped from the NL after the season. Corey secured a spot on the Philadelphia Athletics, second-place finishers in the inaugural season of the new NL rival American Association. Pre-season accounts suggested Corey would pitch on days when veteran Bobby Mathews was rested, citing Corey's "puzzling delivery" and "perfect command of the ball."[17] His all-around versatility was noted, the *Times* of Philadelphia describing him as a "hard hitter and a good base runner, [who] in a pinch can acceptably fill any position on the infield."[18]

Pitching in a preseason warm-up against a champion amateur team, Corey was sharp, posting a three-hit, 18-0 shutout. In his next exhibition start, he pitched well as the Athletics battered a minor-league nine from Trenton, 19-2. When the season started, however, Corey was at second base as Mathews shut out the Alleghenys, 4-0. Corey did pitch the following day, again in Pittsburgh, scattering 11 hits to win, 8-1.

The Athletics were quick out of the gate, winning 18 of 21 in the month of May, but eventually settled into a nip-and-tuck pennant race. Corey delivered what may have been his most valuable performance of the season on June 21 in Cincinnati. After the Athletics lost three games in a row to the Red Stockings to fall from first place, Philadelphia manager Lon Knight called upon Corey to pitch. Corey surrendered four runs in the first inning on a pair of hits and two errors by George Bradley at third, then was virtually unhittable the rest of the way, finishing with a four-hit, 14-5 victory. "The Cincinnatis could do nothing with him," it was observed.[19] The win snapped Philadelphia's losing streak and elevated them back into first place.

Playing second base against the Alleghenys on July 30, Corey excelled in the field, playing "a great game … making three spectacular catches and accepting every chance offered."[20] Corey's fielding was, in the words of one observer, "the finest ever seen in the city."[21] His achievement included a ninth-inning, rally-killing double play, spearing a line drive and throwing to first to catch a runner off the bag. Corey also made an impact with his bat, collecting three hits and driving in three runs.

After the two near-misses in 1880 and 1881, Corey hit a third-inning solo shot for his first major-league home run, off Cincinnati right-hander Will White, on September 16, being sure to touch all the bases in a 10-inning, 13-12 win at Cincinnati.

The Athletics nipped St. Louis by a single game to take the 1883 American Association pennant. As a pitcher, Corey started only 16 times, hurling twice more in relief, but did well enough with his opportunities, winning 10 of 17 decisions with an ERA of 3.40 in 148⅓ innings. As a measure of his utility, he played 34 games at third base, 14 in the outfield, 9 at second, and one each at catcher and shortstop. At bat, he hit .258 with 16 doubles. In a postseason exhibition against their crosstown rivals, the NL's Philadelphia Quakers, the Athletics won handily, 13-3, with Corey playing third base while scoring three runs and driving in two.

Corey's best season came in 1884. Pitching not at all that year, he hit third or fourth in the lineup as the Athletics' regular third baseman. His .276 average looks better when the league's average of .240 is taken into consideration, and his 16 triples tied for sixth-best in the American Association. Five of Corey's seven career home runs came in 1884, the second-highest total on the Athletics and tied for 10th in the league. Among the five was a line drive grand slam over the left-field wall off Washington's John Hamill in a 12-0 win at Philadelphia. The Athletics played well that year, but so did half the American Association, and the club's 61-46 record was only enough for seventh place in the 13-team league.

A newspaper article reporting on the winter activities of the Athletics players, identified Corey as working at "heeling shoes in Lynn [Massachusetts.]"[22]

The Athletics' record fell to 55-57 in 1885 as they finished fourth in the slimmed-down eight-team AA. Corey was again the club's regular third baseman, playing a career-high 94 games but batting only .245. He did pitch in one game, starting against the New York Metropolitans on June 30 and giving up 18 hits and 7 earned runs, but coming away with a complete-game 15-9 victory. Corey missed several weeks in August with a wrist injury suffered when a pitch from Cincinnati's Bill Mountjoy struck him and splintered a bone.[23]

In November 1885 it was reported that Corey had married for the second time, to a Philadelphia woman; whether he was previously widowed or divorced is unknown.[24]

While hunting on his honeymoon near Westerly, Rhode Island, Corey was accidentally shot by a companion, receiving about a dozen grains of shot in his cheek and one in his left eye, damaging his vision.[25] Although he recovered his vision, at a trial with the Athletics at the start of the following season, he "played miserably,"[26] and was released. "In the five years in which we have been at the head of the Athletic club," owner Bill Sharsig said in a statement, "we have never been called upon to perform such a painful act. Corey has been with us for four years, and in all that time he has been one of the hardest workers we ever had. … Fred was not only a natural ballplayer, but he was a thorough gentleman as well. I know that I feel a great deal worse over his release than he does himself. …"[27] Corey's teammates raised $100 in donations[28] and organized a pair of exhibition games on July 5 for his benefit. Despite Sharsig's glowing testimonial, the club charged Corey $100 for the use of the grounds.[29]

In February 1887 the Hastings (Nebraska) Hustlers of the Western League signed Corey to manage the team. One month into the season, however, Corey resigned, his vision "very bad."[30] It was reported in August that "Fred Corey, the invincible third baseman of the Athletics … is in Philadelphia, partially paralyzed."[31]

A 1889 newspaper article stated that Corey "was entirely recovered, but will never rejoin the professional ranks."[32] In the account, Corey was said to be working as a clerk in Providence.

On July 9, 1892, Corey was given another benefit in the form of an exhibition game in Philadelphia between former professionals and old-time amateurs. On the side of the professionals were Corey's former Athletic teammates Bobby Mathews, who pitched the game, and receiver Jack O'Brien, along with old American Association opponents Fred Dunlap, Joe Mulvey, Hardie Henderson, and Matt Kilroy.

Nothing is heard of Corey thereafter. The 1910 US Census shows Corey widowed, living in Cranston, Rhode Island, and working as a lather.

In 1912 he moved back to Providence, taking up residence in a lodging house. On the evening of November 27, 1912, Corey lit the gas lamp in his room and settled into bed with a book. He apparently nodded off while reading, a draft extinguished the flame, and he died of asphyxiation in his sleep.[33] Corey was 57 years old. He was buried at the North Burial Ground in Providence.

SOURCES

In addition to the sources cited in the Notes, the following was used:

Soos, Troy. *Before the Curse: The Glory Days of New England Baseball, 1858-1918*, Rev. Ed. (Jefferson, North Carolina: McFarland, 2006).

NOTES

1   "Westerly Gets 17 Licenses," *Norwich* (Connecticut) *Bulletin,* November 30, 1912: 6.

2   "The Rhode Islands Capture the Fall Rivers in a 10-Inning Game," *Boston Globe*, June 23, 1877: 5.

3   "Base Ball for '78," *Rhode Island Press* (Providence), December 29, 1877: 2.

4   "Base Ball for '78."

5   "An 11-0 Game at Providence," *Boston Globe*, April 19, 1878: 2.

6   "The Bostons Win the Game at Providence Yesterday," *Boston Globe*, May 2, 1878: 2.

7   "The Boston Reds Defeat the Providence Grays," *Boston Globe*, May 26, 1878: 5.

8   "Milwaukee 12, Providence 4," *Boston Globe,* May 29, 1878: 1.

9   "A Good Game: The Milwaukees Defeated, Seven to Six," *Milwaukee Daily News*, June 28, 1878: 4.

10   "Notes and News," *Fall River* (Massachusetts) *Daily Herald*, July 27, 1878: 1.

11   "The Providence People Delighted," *St. Louis Post-Democrat*, August 15, 1878: 5.

12   "Odds and Ends," *Chicago Tribune*, September 8, 1878: 7.

13   "Base Ball Notes," *Fall River Daily Herald*, September 26, 1878: 1.

14   "Providence Notes," *Cincinnati Enquirer*, February 10, 1879: 8.

15   "Skill and Speed," *Boston Globe*, September 24, 1880: 2.

16   "Worcester vs. Cleveland," *Chicago Tribune*, September 18, 1881: 6.

17   "The Ball Season," *Philadelphia Times*, March 11, 1883: 3.

18   "The Ball Season."

19   "Sporting News," *St. Louis Post-Dispatch*, June 22, 1883: 3.

20   "Base Ball," *Philadelphia Inquirer*, July 31, 1883: 2.

21   "Heavy Work at the Bat," *Philadelphia Times*, July 31, 1883: 4.

22   "What Players Do in Winter," *Philadelphia Times*, November 16, 1884: 7.

23   "Around the Bases," *Boston Herald*, August 18, 1885: 5.

24   "Base Ball Notes," *Cleveland Leader*, November 9, 1886: 3.

25   "Accidental Shooting of Fred Corey," *Delaware Gazette and State Journal* (Wilmington), November 12, 1886: 6.

26   "The Athletics Releasing Players," *New York Herald*, May 10, 1886: 9.

27   "Bradley and Corey," *The Sporting News*, June 7, 1886: 5.

28   "Hits and Tips," *Boston Globe*, May 18, 1886: 2.

29   "Base Ball Notes," *Boston Globe*, July 5, 1886: 3.

30   "Base Ball Notes," *Cleveland Plain Dealer*, May 20, 1887: 6.

31   "Doings on the Diamond," *Wilkes-Barre Sunday Leader*, August 21, 1887: 6.

32   "Ball Gossip," *St. Louis Post-Dispatch*, January 5, 1889: 8.

33   "Westerly Gets 17 Licenses."

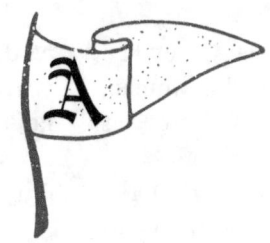

BILL CROWLEY

By Dalton Mack

According to his obituary in 1891, Bill Crowley was "at one time, one of the best ball players that donned a uniform."[1] A 5-foot-7, 159-pound right-handed outfielder, Crowley often played bigger than his size, and was considered one of the heaviest and hardest hitters of his time.[2] Crowley was known primarily for his defensive prowess, especially his arm. Crowley recorded four outfield assists on May 24, 1880, and repeated the feat three months later, eventually tallying 23 on the season.

Crowley's career was marked by inconsistency, owing in large part to troubles with his throwing arm

and his alcoholism, which got him banned from the National League in 1881, and kicked off a minor-league club in Toledo later in the decade. When Crowley was at his best, though, precious few outfielders could combine his fielding ability with his strong and accurate throwing arm. His peak lasted from 1879 to 1884, primarily playing with the National League's Buffalo and Boston clubs. Modern metrics suggest that he was 11 percent better than the average hitter in his leagues during this span (via OPS+), which when coupled with his proficient defense, made him one of his era's most well-rounded ballplayers. His only league championship came with the 1883 Philadelphia Athletics, but Crowley was released in the thick of the pennant race and thus could not celebrate with his hometown team.

William Michael Crowley was born in Philadelphia on April 8, 1857. The son of Irish immigrants, he worked in a print factory in his hometown of Gloucester, New Jersey, and in a mill in Washington, New Jersey, before signing with the National Association's Philadelphia White Stockings in 1875. Census records of the time do not give the identity of Crowley's father, but his mother, Mary, worked as a housekeeper. His older brother, Francis, and his younger brother, Joseph, also worked in the print factory. His sister, Sarah, worked in the cotton mill. Eight days shy of his 18th birthday, *The Times* of Philadelphia described Crowley as of "fine physique" and "remarkable judgment."[3] Crowley, 18 years old, was the Association's youngest player, and served primarily in a utility role, splitting time between third base and center field. He struggled at the plate, batting .081 (3-for-37) in his rookie campaign, but was praised for his "fine catches" in center field.[4] His third-base defense was considered weak,[5] and Crowley shifted

Bill Crowley with the 1878 Buffalo Bisons.

permanently to the outfield for the majority of his career.

After missing the 1876 season, Crowley was signed by the Louisville Grays of the National League for the 1877 campaign. That season he had his first brush with the less than savory elements of the game: Four of his teammates – shortstop Bill Craver, left fielder George Hall, third baseman Al Nichols, and star pitcher Jim Devlin – were banned from baseball after the season for throwing games. The 20-year-old Crowley acquitted himself well in Louisville, batting .282 in a league-leading 61 games played.

Crowley slipped out of the major leagues after 1877, and linked up with Buffalo of the International Association in 1878. He played a handful of games behind the plate, forming a battery with baseball's first 300-game winner, Pud Galvin.[6] More often, though, Crowley played in the outfield and continued to establish himself as a reliable hitter. Buffalo joined the National League in 1879, and Crowley settled into an everyday right-field role. His steady play during his two years with the Bisons was quite the change of pace for the Buffalo club, which had a 46-32 record in 1879 but slipped to 24-58 in 1880. Despite the poor showing from his club, Crowley again was an above-average hitter, and his 23 outfield assists ranked fourth in the league.

In Buffalo Crowley met one of his lifelong best friends, third baseman Hardy Richardson. Richardson became one of the game's early superstars, batting over .300 seven times and leading his league in home runs twice.

As 1880 drew to a close, Crowley received a $1,000 offer from the Boston Red Stockings, and jumped at the chance to play for future Hall of Famer Harry Wright, who carried six pennants to his name as the skipper of both the National Association and National League's Boston clubs.[7] Unfortunately for Crowley and Boston, the 1881 team fared poorly, and weathered three separate six-plus-game losing streaks. Crowley's offense took a bit of a downturn; he batted .254 with eight fewer extra-base hits than the year prior.

The 1881 season was pivotal in Crowley's career, and not to his benefit. He was banned from the National League for what was labeled "general dissipation and insubordination" by League President William Hulbert. In all, Crowley and eight others, including Lip Pike, were barred, likely due to drunkenness and suspected game fixing.[8] The newly formed American Association respected the ban; Crowley lost an appeal in March and did not play in professional baseball in 1882.[9]

The ban was lifted in 1883 and Crowley signed with his hometown American Association team, the Philadelphia Athletic Club. Philadelphia sportswriters were protective of their favorite son, declaring that his blacklisting was for "no known cause."[10] Crowley's first appearance with his new team came on April 7, when he helped the team christen its new grounds at Twenty-Sixth and Jefferson Streets in an exhibition game against Yale. Crowley wasted no time making an impression, rapping a pair of doubles from the number-three position in the lineup, and making a spectacular catch, complete with a pair of somersaults.[11]

This would be one of few bright spots for Crowley in the early part of 1883; he was hitless his other four games in April, ending the month with an .087 batting average (2-for-23).[12] Crowley's performance reached a low point on April 25, when he went 0-for-5 against a minor-league nine from Camden, New Jersey, that folded by July.[13]

May treated the 26-year-old a bit better, as he batted .279 with several clutch hits and turned in stellar fielding. However, as the month drew to a close, Crowley had a rare lapse in fielding proficiency when he muffed a key fly ball in a May 30 tangle with Cincinnati, leading to the Reds taking the victory in extra innings in front of a "howling mass of humanity."[14] This game was dubbed "one of the greatest struggles for supremacy that has ever taken place on the ball field," and was played before an estimated 15,000 fans, so many, in fact, that they could not help but interfere with several foul balls.[15]

The spotlight would continue to betray Crowley in 1883, when the surehanded outfielder made four errors in front of 12,000 fans during a July 1 tilt with the St. Louis Browns.[16] Crowley played infrequently during the summer, with young catcher Jack O'Brien and backup outfielder Bob Blakiston getting playing time in center field.[17]

A couple of days into September, Crowley was no longer a member of the Athletics, having been released while the team was in the thick of a pennant race. The Athletics must have had its issues with Crowley, as they decided that they would rather have center field patrolled by out-of-position players or weak bench options, all while tied with the Browns. It appeared that the club made the correct call: The Athletics rattled off eight wins in their next nine contests, including a series victory over the impressive Browns. But the

Athletics wound up winning the American Association crown.

Crowley soon found another home, playing the remainder of the 1883 season with the Cleveland Blues of the National League. There he found his stride quickly, notching seven hits in his first three games.[18] Crowley was likely aided by batting sixth in the lineup, with stars Fred Dunlap and Jack Glasscock helping to take the pressure off the beleaguered outfielder.[19] While his bat was lively, his once powerful arm began feeling the brunt of long throws from center field (ballparks of the day typically exceeded 450 feet in dead center), and he was pulled from a September 20 game.[20]

In October the Beaneaters once again came calling, having apparently forgiven Crowley for his past indiscretions and offering him an $1,800 contract, which Crowley spurned.[21] A month later the Beaneaters upped the offer to $1,900 and Crowley was Boston-bound.[22] The *Times-Democrat* in New Orleans reported in February 1884 that "Bill Crowley says his arm is well, and he threatens to play great ball for the Bostons this season."[23]

Great ball he did play, posting his best batting season to date, belting six home runs and tying for the team lead with 61 runs batted in.[24] Two of those home runs came in the span of a week against Old Hoss Radbourn of the Providence Grays, who was in the midst of his historic 60-win season, one baseball historians consider a prime candidate for the greatest pitching season of all time. On the negative side, on June 7 Crowley struck out to end Charlie Sweeney's 19-strikeout game, a record that stood for 102 years until it was broken by Roger Clemens in 1986.[25]

Crowley primarily played right field for the Beaneaters, and was considered to be one of the finest fielders to ever grace the South End Grounds. This was no small feat, as the right-field foul pole at the Grounds was 255 feet from home plate, with 440 feet to the fence in right-center. Two years after his death, the *Boston Globe* claimed that "Jack Manning, Bill Crowley and Tom McCarthy are the only players that ever mastered the trick of playing right field on the Boston grounds."[26]

Boston held the league lead as late as August 6, with a 50-20 record, a half-game ahead of Providence, but middling performance from the Beaneaters (23-18) and dynamic play from the Grays (35-8) down the stretch gave the National League crown to Boston's close rival.

In November the *Boston Globe* reported that Crowley had signed with Buffalo, a decision that he claimed was due to being under the influence of alcohol and one he apparently regretted.[27] Crowley shifted from right to left field, likely due to the arm issues that continued to plague him. The move failed to fully keep Crowley healthy, as he reportedly missed time due to the "old complaint" in the summer of 1885.[28] With his arm deteriorating, and his bat going quiet – his .241 average in 1885 was the worst full-season mark of his career – Crowley (and the Buffalo Bisons for that matter) never played in the major leagues again.

Buffalo was bought out by the Detroit Wolverines, who now owned the rights to Crowley. His defense a far cry from where it was when he graced the South End Grounds, he was released by Detroit so he could negotiate with other clubs.[29] A club from Macon, Georgia, showed interest, but Crowley was not keen on going south and believed he could find a better contract offer.

Nothing north of the Mason-Dixon line materialized, and Crowley indeed headed south to play for the Charleston (South Carolina) Seagulls of the Southern Association. He occasionally dazzled fans with phenomenal defensive plays,[30] but his batting continued to decline and he was released in a cost-cutting measure by the end of July after batting .236 in 83 games.[31]

Crowley returned home to Gloucester, New Jersey, and did not receive an offer until April of the following year, when he was offered contracts by the Mobile Swamp Angels of the Southern League, and the Eastern League's New Haven Blues.[32] Crowley, familiar with New England and bearing an aversion to the South, opted to join the Blues, where he was named team captain.[33]

Crowley batted .350 for New Haven but reportedly was plagued by his reliance on alcohol. After the season a local paper reported that he was currently working in the oyster business, but "would like to sign again in some good town where intoxicating liquors are not sold."[34]

Ten years after last playing in the International Association, Crowley was back, this time playing for the London (Ontario) Tecumsehs.[35] The 1888 London club was made up of a few misfit parts, including diminutive hurler Larry Corcoran, who, like Crowley, had his best days behind him and a taste for liquor. By June 11 both were suspended for drunkenness, which assuredly hampered their play (Crowley batted .196 in 24 games, Corcoran posted a team-worst 5.36 ERA in 42 innings).[36] The next week, the pair were sent packing.[37]

Within two weeks, Crowley had caught on with the Toledo Maumees of the Tri-State League where he played left field.[38] His stay with Toledo did not last long, as he fell ill in mid-August, and returned home to New Jersey.[39] His stint with Toledo was the last of his baseball-playing career, although he did manage and occasionally play in exhibition games with the Gloucester club, playing for one last time in April of 1890 against the Philadelphia Players League squad.[40] A report from the time called Crowley "quite a sick man"[41] and his name was rarely printed again until his death.

Much like former teammate Larry Corcoran, Crowley's heavy drinking caught up with him, and he died of Bright's disease (now commonly known as nephritis) at the age of 34 on July 14, 1891, at his home in Gloucester. Crowley was buried at St. Mary's Cemetery in Bellmawr, New Jersey. He was never married and fathered no children. He was eulogized in the *Philadelphia Inquirer* as "a favorite with all ballplayers and managers," and his funeral was said to be well-attended.[42] The *Buffalo Courier* stated that "Crowley was a fine batsman, superior outfielder, a good catcher, and one of the best long and line throwers in the profession."[43]

SOURCES

In addition to the sources cited in the Notes, the author consulted Retrosheet.org, Baseball-Reference.com, and Ancestry.com

NOTES

1   "Gloucester City Gleanings," *Courier-Post* (Camden, New Jersey), July 15, 1891: 4.

2   "Catcher Crowley Dead," *Philadelphia Inquirer*, July 16, 1891: 3.

3   "Base Hits," *The Times* (Philadelphia), April 10, 1875: 4.

4   "The Baseball Field," *The Times*, May 20, 1875: 4.

5   "Philadelphia vs. Boston," *The Times*, May 12, 1875: 1.

6   "Base-Ball," *Buffalo Morning Express*, May 6, 1878: 4.

7   "Sporting Notes," *Buffalo Commercial*, November 17, 1880: 3.

8   Hal Bock, *Banned: Baseball's Blacklist of All-Stars and Also-Rans* (New York: Diversion Books, 2017), https://books.google.com/books/about/Banned.html?id=78sBDgAAQBAJ&printsec=frontcover&source=kp_read_button&newbks=1&newbks_redir=1#v=onepage&q=crowley&f=false

9   "Convention at Philadelphia," *Cincinnati Enquirer*, March 14, 1882: 2.

10   "The Athletic Nine: The Other Players," *The Times*, March 11, 1883: 3.

11   "The Athletic Club wins a game over Yale," *The Times* April 8, 1883: 2

12   "Athletic Averages," *The Times*, May 6, 1883: 2.

13   "The Athletics Win," *Philadelphia Inquirer*, April 26, 1883: 2.

14   "Beaten by the Cincinnatis," *The Times*, May 31, 1883: 4.

15   "Cincinnati vs. Athletic," *Philadelphia Inquirer*, May 31, 1883: 3.

16   "The Athletics Lose," *The Times*, July 2, 1883: 1.

17   1883 Philadelphia Athletics, Baseball-Reference.com.

18   "Games To Be Played," *The Times*, September 16, 1883: 2.

19   "The Morning Games," *Cincinnati Enquirer*, September 15, 1883: 2

20   "Forty-Four Victories," *The Times*, September 21, 1883: 3.

21   "Gloucester's Latest," *Camden Courier-Post*, October 2, 1883: 1.

22   "Notes and Comments," *Sporting Life*, November 14, 1883: 3.

23   "Base Ball," *New Orleans Times-Democrat*, February 4, 1884: 2.

24   Bill Crowley, Baseball-Reference.com.

25   Ed Achorn, "June 7, 1884: Charlie Sweeney Strikes Out 19 for Providence," https://sabr.org/gamesproj/game/june-7-1884-charlie-sweeney-strikes-out-19-for-providence/

26   "Baseball Notes," *Boston Globe*, September 3, 1893: 7.

27   "Sporting Gossip," *Boston Globe*, November 7, 1884: 5.

28   "Around the Bases," *Boston Globe*, July 7, 1885: 2.

29   "Baseball Gossip," *Macon Telegraph*, April 8, 1886: 3.

30   "The National Game," *Abbeville Press and Banner* (Abbeville County, South Carolina), June 30, 1886: 2.

31   "One Base Hits," *Leavenworth* (Kansas) *Times*, July 31, 1886: 4.

32   "Diamond Dust," *St. Louis Globe-Democrat*, April 14, 1887: 5.

33   "Sports in Season," *Sunday Truth* (Buffalo, New York), June 5, 1887: 7.

34   "Will There Be a League?" *Morning Journal-Courier* (New Haven, Connecticut), December 13, 1887: 4.

35   "Local News Items," *Camden Courier-Post*, February 1, 1888: 1.

36   "Close Decisions," *Boston Globe*, June 11, 1888: 8.

37   "Base Ball," *New Haven Morning Journal-Courier*, June 18, 1888: 4.

38   "Tri-State League Notes," *The Sun* (New York), July 1, 1888: 6.

39   "Notes from Toledo," *Detroit Free Press*, September 1, 1888: 8.

40   "Sporting Notes," *Camden Courier-Post*, April 4, 1890; 1.

41   "Sporting Notes," *Pittsburgh Dispatch*, March 18, 1890: 6.

42   "Gloucester City Gleanings," *Camden Courier-Post*, July 17, 1891: 3. The "favorite" quote comes from *Philadelphia Inquirer*, July 16, 1891: 3.

43   "Diamond Glints," *Buffalo Courier*, July 24, 1891: 8.

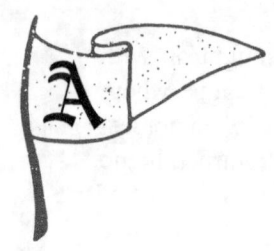

AL HUBBARD

By Richard Bogovich

When the president of the United States is in your golf foursome because you led your university to a baseball championship a quarter of a century earlier, things are going your way. That sums up a highpoint in the life of Al Hubbard,[1] who played in just two major-league games two days apart toward the end of the 1883 season. His very short professional career wasn't due to any misfortune after his collegiate championship, however. It was mostly his choice to minimize his professional sports career. After all, in contrast to so many ballplayers then, he had more lucrative options as an Ivy League graduate.[2]

Allen Hubbard was born in Westfield, Massachusetts, on December 9, 1860, to farmer George Hubbard and Clarissa Maria (Edy) Hubbard, who was sometimes called Clara. He was the second of their four children. His sister Leora was the oldest, and their two younger siblings were Agnes and George. Al was a graduate of Westfield's high school.[3]

His high school had a baseball team, at least during the spring of 1879, and Al was its captain that season.[4] He became a freshman at Yale University, in New Haven, Connecticut, during the 1880-1881 school year. His first appearance in the school newspaper may have been in March of 1881, as the catcher in a box score of a baseball game between Yale's freshmen team and "the Consolidated nine," which possibly comprised other students. He didn't exactly impress. Though he had eight putouts and two assists, he also allowed four passed balls and committed an error while going hitless at bat (as did all his freshmen teammates but one).[5]

He fared better in a rematch about a month later, with only one passed ball and one error to offset 15 putouts and an assist, plus a double and two runs scored on offense.[6] His fourth appearance in a box score was

in mid-May, when the *Yale News* devoted most of two pages to a game in which the Yale Freshmen trounced Amherst's, 14-3. That same month they similarly pounded their Harvard counterparts, 15-3.[7]

Hubbard was enrolled in Yale's Sheffield Scientific School, which had only three "classes" (freshman, junior, and senior, skipping sophomores) and thus typically awarded degrees after three years. As a freshman, Hubbard wasn't solely consumed by baseball, because he was also a member of Sheffield's Eating Club.[8]

During his second spring at Yale, in 1882, Hubbard played on the varsity team. His first action was in games on April 7 and 8 in New York against the Metropolitans, an independent team that joined the American Association in 1883. On the first date, 2,000 to 3,000 spectators went to the Polo Grounds to see the defending collegiate champions, but Yale ended up on the wrong end of a lopsided 11-5 game. The rematch was close, 8-7, but Yale lost again. Hubbard caught in both games and batted eighth. He went hitless in both games, but committed no errors (though box scores made no mention of passed balls). He did, however, figure in the second game's decisive inning. The Metropolitans trailed 7-5 after seven innings. "When the Metropolitans came to the bat Hubbard took a foul bound neatly near the ground, but the umpire did not allow it. A base on balls, a single hit, and an attempt to catch the man on third filled the bases," reported the *Yale News*. "The only wild pitch of the game, passing through a narrow passage to the rear of the grand stand was lost in the crowd, and three men scored giving the game to the Metropolitans as no further runs were made."[9]

Yale followed up those losses with games against other independent teams,[10] and finished April hosting three major-league teams. On April 22 Hubbard and Yale faced Providence of the National League, which went on to finish second in the standings that season. Hubbard batted last and went hitless against future Hall of Famer Old Hoss Radbourn, beginning with a fly or popout to short to end the third inning. On defense, the *Yale News* said, he supported pitcher Jack Jones "very well," and he logged six putouts, four assists, one error, and no passed balls. Providence won easily, 13-2.[11]

Yale then lost to the NL's Worcester team, 8-2, on April 26. Hubbard again batted last, and went hitless against Lee Richmond, who had hurled the NL's first perfect game on June 12, 1880. Behind home plate Hubbard accepted five chances without an error as such, though in the box score he was charged with a "wild throw" in addition to two passed balls.[12]

During his two years on the varsity team, Hubbard played against more than half of the National League's teams, three of which were based in New England. The American Association was the NL's brand-new rival in 1882, and though it had no New England teams, on April 29 Hubbard did get to play against the AA's Philadelphia Athletics, his future employer. Yale didn't score, but held the professionals to just two runs. Hubbard had one of Yale's five singles in three at-bats off Sam Weaver, who had a record of 26-15 by year's end. Hubbard was flawless in the field, with five putouts and three assists. He made a solid first impression in the very first inning. Philadelphia had a runner on first with one out when their third batter fouled out to Hubbard. The runner tagged up and tried for second base but "a beautiful throw of Hubbard" turned a double play, according to the *Yale News*. The game drew 500 fans, and took approximately 1 hour and 5 minutes.[13]

Yale began its collegiate league season on May 10 with a victory at home over Brown, 4-2. It ultimately won eight games and lost three against American College Base Ball Association opponents, a record good enough to win its second consecutive championship. That league was formed by Amherst, Brown, Dartmouth, Harvard, and Princeton – all later considered Ivy League institutions except the first – during the winter of 1879-1880, and Yale joined for the 1881 season (with Dartmouth not participating in 1883).[14]

On June 8 and 13, Yale had rematches against Worcester and Providence, respectively. Hubbard, who played in center field, had a single (his first hit against an NL hurler) and an RBI in three at-bats off Fred Corey in a 9-3 loss.[15] Yale's margin of defeat was a little wider against Providence: 11-3. Hubbard was back behind home plate but as a batter he was

1883 Yale Baseball Team. Daniel "Jumping Jack" Jones (standing center), with batterymate Al Hubbard seated to the left.

71

hitless off a different Hall of Famer, John Montgomery Ward.[16]

On July 11 Hubbard had a second opportunity to audition for the Athletics, in Philadelphia before more than 700 fans. This time he had two hits in four at-bats against Bill Sweeney, who went on to lead the Union Association with 40 victories in 1884. The Athletics barely won, 6-5.[17]

Hubbard was soon back home in Westfield, playing for a local team, the Firemen.[18] The captain of the Firemen was Frank Cox, who played in the NL for Detroit in 1884. On August 1 he reportedly received a telegram from Worcester manager Jack Chapman offering a job with that NL team but "Hubbard of course declined the offer as it would debar him from future playing in the college nine," reported a local newspaper.[19] Hubbard and the Firemen proceeded to play Worcester twice during the first half of August.

The first game was in Westfield on August 8, and represented the first time an NL team visited that community. Pitching for the Firemen was Hubbard's Yale teammate Jack Jones. Corey was the starting pitcher for the visitors, who won 7-4. Hubbard went 0-for-4 at bat but he was robbed by Richmond on a one-handed running catch in right field, of a likely two-run triple in what a local paper called "the special feature of the game."[20] On August 14, 500 people in Westfield saw Corey shut out the locals in a laugher, 14-0. Hubbard at least had one of his team's four hits, in three at-bats. He apparently moved from catcher to second base by the eighth inning, and on third strike in that frame, the Firemen turned a triple play that went from the substitute catcher to the third, then to Hubbard, and on to the first baseman.[21]

Hubbard was soon back at Yale, and by mid-September he was already preparing for the next baseball season, at least mentally. "It was with pleasure that men enjoying their vacation in different parts of the world received the news that Mr. Allen Hubbard, S. [Sheffield] '83 had been elected to succeed Mr. Walter I. Badger, '82, as captain of our triumphant ball nine," effused the *Yale News*. "From the time this gentleman began to play, he has won the applause of the college, not only for his superior playing, but for his even disposition, gentlemanly bearing and everlasting willingness to work for Yale."[22] About four weeks later, the paper summarized some basic American College Base Ball Association stats, noting that in the intercollegiate "games the past season, Brown had the best batting average, .295, and Princeton the best fielding, .831."

It then listed (without percentages) the best fielders by position, and Hubbard was first among catchers.[23]

Early in 1883 the *Yale News* printed an announcement for Hubbard. "All gentlemen in the university wishing to try for the University Base Ball Nine are requested to be present at 212 Durfee, Tuesday morning at 9.45," he wrote. "Everyone will be welcomed; there is an unusual number of vacant places."[24] That may have been a bit of an understatement. When the paper reported on early workouts in February, it noted that only three other players were returning from the 1882 squad, so Hubbard needed to find starters for two of the outfield spots and all of the infield positions except second baseman. In addition to Jones, one of the other returning players was Walter Camp,[25] who would become known as "the father of American football."[26]

Hubbard's squad played against six different NL teams in 1883 plus the Athletics twice. They started with the latter team on April 7 in Philadelphia and squeezed four NL teams into the second half of the month. More than 4,000 turned out for the game versus the Athletics, and Yale kept it close for seven innings, at 3-0. Philadelphia's Bobby Mathews, who won close to 300 games in the majors, eventually completed the shutout, 12-0. Captain Hubbard, who put himself in center field, managed one of Yale's four singles in his four at-bats.[27]

On April 14 Yale's second game of the spring was against Cleveland of the NL. Though they were shut out again, this time it was close, 3-0. Hubbard had one of Yale's three singles off Hugh "One-Arm" Daily.[28]

The NL's new team in New York victimized Yale twice, in New Haven on April 18 and at the Polo Grounds on April 21. In the first game he faced John Montgomery Ward for the second time in his career and this time singled against him in four at-bats. The final score was 11-4.[29] Pitching the rematch for New York was Tip O'Neill in front of about 3,000 spectators. The final score differed little, 14-3, and in four at-bats Hubbard again singled, driving in a run.[30]

Yale played a close game against Providence of the NL on April 28. The score was 2-2 after five innings, and Providence won by a whisker, 5-4. Hubbard had a hit in five at-bats off Edgar Smith and scored twice. "Hubbard fully sustained his reputation as a catcher, taking two foul tips and throwing out several men at the bases in fine style," said the *Yale News*.[31]

In May Yale's team started shifting its focus to collegiate competition. In a key game on May 12, Hubbard's charges hosted Harvard. Beautiful weather coaxed more than 2,000 fans to the game. Hubbard put himself in the leadoff spot. A coin toss resulted in Yale batting first, and Hubbard reached on an error, then stole second base. He soon scored Yale's first run, and they added two more in the inning. There was no more scoring by either side after that, and Yale had a thrilling 3-0 shutout over its big rivals.[32]

By early June, Yale had played 16 games, and Hubbard was inactive only against Boston. In those games he tied for second-most hits on his team, with 21, and was third in total bases, with 25. He played in all six college games to that point and tied for the most hits on the Yale squad, nine. Yale outscored its collegiate opponents by a wide margin, 30 runs to 10.[33]

On June 6 Yale played the Philadelphia Athletics for the fourth time in Hubbard's two years on the varsity. "About 700 people gathered at the park and occupied the grand stand and the benches," the Yale News reported. "A few carriages were drawn up about the north end of the field." Hubbard had one hit in four at-bats in his third game against Corey, and over the four games he thus had a .333 batting average. The time of that single was surely far more important to Hubbard than any statistics. Though Yale was the home team, it batted first. Neither team scored in the first inning. In the second, Yale had already scored twice when Hubbard went to bat with two outs and two men on base. His hit drove in the runners to give Yale a 4-0 lead. Yale didn't score again that day, but Jones limited the Athletics to a lone run in the third inning, and the collegians pulled off the upset.[34]

Yale almost did likewise at home again the next day, against Buffalo's NL team. Yale scored five times in the top of the first inning and Buffalo countered with two. After neither team scored in the second inning, there was a rain delay of an hour. The ball's slipperiness became an issue by the fifth inning, and Buffalo took advantage of that more than Yale did. In the end, the pro team won, 13-12. Hubbard, who played center field, contributed three runs and had a hit in four at-bats.[35]

On June 13 Hubbard's team had clinched another American College Base Ball Association pennant by beating Amherst for its seventh victory without a loss.[36] About a week later they played one more NL team, Chicago, which finished 1883 in second place. Yale lost, 7-1. Chicago used two pitchers, Larry Corcoran (who had the NL's best winning percentage and earned-run average the previous year) and Fred Goldsmith (who had the NL's best winning percentage

in 1880). Hubbard had one hit in four at-bats; his late double off Goldsmith helped prevent a shutout.[37]

On June 22 the New Haven Register ran a long article, drawn from the Boston Herald, in which it was announced that Jones and Hubbard were joining the NL's Detroit team. The very next day, the Register reported that C.H. Yates, president of the Yale Base Ball association, said Hubbard denied that he and Jones had simultaneously negotiated in bad faith with the NL's relatively new Philadelphia club. "He said Jones and Hubbard agreed to accept [Philadelphia's] proposition, but before the contract was signed Hubbard backed out, owing to the opposition of his parents," wrote the Register.[38]

In early July it was Baltimore's turn to be rejected by Hubbard. William Gittinger, secretary and treasurer of that AA team, said he offered Hubbard a salary of $600 per month and a $1,000 cash advance. "Hubbard said it was the largest offer he had received, but that he could not accept it, as his family objected to his becoming a professional ball player," reported the Baltimore Sun.[39] Jones eventually signed with Detroit, and made his debut on July 9, but Hubbard didn't join him on that club.

Hubbard's baseball career at Yale concluded with an exhibition game against Harvard in Philadelphia on Independence Day. His nine won a slugfest, 23-9.[40] In the eight official American College Base Ball Association games, he batted .314 (11-for-35), with a .963 fielding percentage.[41]

In less than a week, Hubbard was playing with the Stock Exchange team, also called the Staten Islands.[42] He also played at least twice back home, with the Westfield Firemen.[43] He kept busy with two other teams, the Cottage Citys of Martha's Vineyard, and the Company K's of Hartford, Connecticut.[44]

Jack Jones was released by Detroit after going 6-5 in 12 games, and on September 4 he won his first game for the Philadelphia Athletics, 11-1 over St. Louis.[45]

Philadelphia and Hubbard were secretive about his also joining the club, but they weren't particularly good at it. On September 11, two days before Hubbard's major-league debut, the Philadelphia Record reported on its front page that "Hubbard, the Yale college catcher, has been engaged by the Athletic club to support Jones." Back at Yale, on the day of his first game the campus paper quoted the Record's announcement. In between those two disclosures, a Cincinnati newspaper, looking forward to the Athletics visiting on September 15, noted that Philadelphia had "a new catcher, who plays under the name of West, and whom will catch Jumping Jack Jones." With that dubious phrasing, the paper may as well have just inserted "fake" before "name."[46]

Hubbard made his major-league debut in Columbus on September 13, 1883. "West, the new catcher for the Athletics, played short-stop and did some very brilliant work in the field and also at the bat," the *Times* of Philadelphia reported. He batted ninth against Frank Mountain, who was 26-33 for Columbus that year. "West" had two hits in three at-bats and scored twice as his new team won easily, 11-5.[47]

The next day was an open date, and on September 15 the Athletics were in Cincinnati. Jones started, and "West" was his catcher, but soon all pretense was off. "The Athletic catcher, playing under the name of 'West,' was recognized by Yale College men who were present as Hubbard, the Yale College catcher," noted one Philadelphia daily. "His success behind the bat was not very good – four balls got past him and he missed a third strike."[48] In fact, nobody on his team had a good day, because they were shut out, 11-0, by Will White, a 40-game winner that season and the prior one. Hubbard was hitless in three at-bats. Four of his teammates managed one hit apiece. The *Cincinnati Commercial Gazette* complimented Hubbard and Jones: "They are without a doubt the strongest college battery ever turned out."[49]

Hubbard never played in another major-league game. It might be supposed that the Athletics didn't want to retain him because of that one awful game. However, the day before that loss, a Philadelphia paper reported that the team had already signed a new catcher for the next season, Jocko Milligan, who ended up as their primary catcher in 1884.[50]

At some point in 1883, Hubbard worked briefly for J.H. Lounsbury's machine shop in Providence, and during the winter of 1883-1884 he worked as a draftsman for the Riverside & Oswego Woolen Manufacturing Company in Schenectady, New York.[51] Not surprisingly, at the age of 23 baseball was still in his blood – and the baseball world was still interested in him. For example, in February of 1884 it was projected that Jones would join the Minneapolis team in the Northwestern League after his graduation in June, and that he had already agreed to catch. In March he was noticed at the annual meeting of the Intercollegiate Base Ball Convention. In the spring, he reportedly did some coaching for Amherst.[52]

During the warmer months of 1884, Hubbard ended up splitting time among three teams. One was near his hometown, the Springfield team in a new professional league, the Massachusetts State Association. He played for Springfield at least three times during the first half of May. At home before about 1,000 fans on May 2 he helped Springfield defeat one of the seven other MSA teams, the Boston Reserves, 8-5.[53] He caught against the same team three days later in another win, 19-5, though the Springfield paper made it clear the contest wasn't official, but was merely "an exhibition game."[54] On May 10 Hubbard helped beat another MSA team, the Holyokes, at their ballpark. That contest, won 7-5, by the Springfields, drew about 1,200 spectators.[55]

In the meantime, Hubbard had been assembling a new team of his own in Westfield. On May 17 it hosted the Holyoke Reserves and won easily, 14-3. "Hubbard captained the team from center field," the *Springfield Republican* noted.[56] He played with his Westfields off and on at least through late September.[57]

During the second half of May, Hubbard started playing with another professional team, Meriden of the new Connecticut State League, which played twice weekly.[58] Jones had been recruited to pitch regularly for the team, and it was announced that Hubbard would alternate with Connie Mack and Bob Pettit as the catcher. From May 21 through June 27 Hubbard played in at least four games, all wins. The first was against Waterbury. He doubled in two runs in the second inning, and by the ninth inning Meriden led, 6-3. With one out, Waterbury had men on second and third with the tying run at bat, but on the back end of a double play, Hubbard made the game-ending putout. He then missed at least one game due to "a lame arm," as a local paper reported.[59]

Hubbard played again on June 6, at Waterbury, and contributed two hits in four at-bats toward a second win, 6-1. In a win against Willimantic on June 11, he split his finger open in the sixth inning. In the seventh he was replaced by Mack and went to right field. His final game for Meriden was a win against Hartford. All told, he had two doubles and two singles in 16 at-bats in the four games.[60] At least one paper announced the day before his finale that he and Jones had left the Meriden team, bound for Minneapolis.[61] That didn't happen.

Hubbard simply returned to his amateur team in Westfield. He caught a young local named Wilson, who struck out 22 batters of the MSA's Holyoke team in a 10-3 victory.[62] He caught or played second base for the Westfields until at least October 1, when his nine won a road game against the Amherst College team, 11-6. One of his two hits that day was a home run.[63]

From 1884 to 1888, Hubbard worked for a longtime Westfield business, the H.B. Smith Company, in its Providence branch. Late in the summer of 1887 he won the Providence tennis championship. After that, he lived and worked primarily in or near Boston.[64]

On September 23, 1896, Allen married Edna Woodruff, a musician, in her hometown of Winsted, Connecticut. Among the guests were Mr. and Mrs. D.A. "Jack" Jones.[65]

Agnes's health had been declining for a few months before her brother's wedding, and she died in October.[66] On July 27, 1897, Allen and Edna welcomed the first of their two children, Allen Jr. Their other son, Gilbert, was born on December 1, 1901.[67]

Hubbard's longest continuous service in a sporting capacity was on a committee of the Boston Athletic Club from 1895 to 1910. He became active in the club at least two years earlier, when he was player-manager of the club's baseball team.[68] His "last hurrah" as a baseball player came in 1908 among some very distinguished company. An old-timers game was organized in Boston on September 24. Hubbard was on the team of old stars from New England colleges, who were led by his old Yale teammate, Walter I. Badger. On the other team were former Boston pros. The latter team's lineup included three future Hall of Famers, Albert G. Spalding, Jim O'Rourke, and Tommy McCarthy. After the game a banquet was held, and the *Boston Herald*, for one, devoted much ink to the day. Hubbard had a single in two at-bats, plus three putouts.[69]

Not quite a year later Hubbard found himself in even more famous company, playing a sport other than baseball. At a Yale field day on September 7, 1909, one of the attendees was President William Howard Taft, six months into his term. Taft had graduated from Yale in 1878. The day include a baseball game, and one of its stars was "Rev Charles F. Carter, '78, who pitched a no-hit, no-run game against Harvard back in the '70s," noted the *Springfield Republican*. Badger also played, as did Hubbard, who "only had some 18 or 19 passed balls." Taft was asked to serve as umpire but declined, saying, "I value my life too much for such a job as that." After the first inning a group photograph was taken, with Taft in the center. Much more noteworthy was the golfing. "Mr Taft was matched with Rev Mr Carter against Samuel J. Elder, the noted Boston lawyer, and Allen Hubbard," the *Republican* reported. "The game was stopped at the 11th hole in order not to delay luncheon, and at that time the president and Mr Carter were 4 up."[70]

Hubbard died rather suddenly on December 9, 1930, at the age of 70. He was survived by his wife, two sons, sister Leora, and brother George. A large number of Yale alumni attended his funeral.[71]

In 2006 baseball historian David Nemec asserted that Hubbard and Jones were "the first college battery to perform together in a major league game." In the summer of 2012, the duo received renewed attention when Craig Breslow of the Red Sox pitched to Ryan Lavarnway. Both are Yale graduates. That hadn't happened in the majors in well over a century, since Jones and Hubbard.[72] That's a decent legacy for someone like Allen Hubbard, who could count the number of his games as a professional ballplayer with just the bruised and battered fingers of his two hands.

NOTES

1   "Taft at Yale Field Day," *Springfield* (Massachusetts) *Republican*, September 8, 1909: 9.

2   *Bulletin of Yale University: Obituary Record of Graduates Deceased During the Year Ending July 1, 1931*, December 1, 1931: 205.

3   *Bulletin of Yale University: Obituary Record of Graduates Deceased During the Year Ending July 1, 1931*, December 1, 1931: 205; also see federal census and Massachusetts birth records.

4   "Sporting Matters," *Springfield Republican*, May 9, 1879: 5.

5   "Base Ball," *Yale News*, March 24, 1881: 2.

6   "Consolidated vs. '84," *Yale News*, April 26, 1881: 2.

7   *Yale News*, May 17, 1881: 2-3. "Yale '84 vs. Harvard '84," *Yale News Supplement*, May 23, 1881: 1-2. The newspaper's coverage of the Amherst game lacked a headline; it provided an inning-by-inning account and detailed box score. In early June the Yale Freshmen won a rematch against Harvard, 21-2; see "Yale '84 vs. Harvard '84," *Yale News*, June 6, 1881: 2-3, and "College Base Ball Games," *New Haven* (Connecticut) *Daily Morning Journal and Courier*, June 6, 1881: 4. His third inclusion in a box score was against the same team; see "Consolidated vs. '84," *Yale News*, May 5, 1881: 3.

8   *The Yale Pot-pourri*, Volume XVI, 1880-81: 135. On pages 39-42 were listed freshman, junior, and senior classes without a sophomore class.

9   "Metropolitans vs. Yale," *New York Times*, April 8, 1882: 8. *Yale News*, April 13, 1882: 1-2. For a roster of the Metropolitans that identified players' prior National League experience, see *Yale News*, February 23, 1882: 1.

10 Yale's first home game was a 7-5 win on April 15 against a team called the Alaskas, according to the *Yale News*, April 17, 1882: 1-2. They then beat the Atlantics on April 19, 9-6, as reported by the *Yale News*, April 20, 1882: 1-2.

11 "An Exciting Contest Between the Providence and Yale Teams – Providence the Winner," *New York Herald*, April 23, 1882: 16. See also *Yale News*, April 24, 1882: 1-2. Hubbard was listed in the Yale newspaper's box score as playing left field, but the article made it clear that he caught at least part of the game. That box score reported how many balls and strikes each pitcher threw, and even distinguished between called and swinging strikes. The box scores later in April did likewise.

12 *Yale News*, April 27, 1882: 1-2.

13 "Athletic, 2; Yale, 0," *The Times* (Philadelphia), April 30, 1882: 2. See also "Athletics vs. Yale," *Yale News*, May 1, 1882: 2.

14 Richard Melancthon Hurd, *A History of Yale Athletics, 1840-1888* (New Haven, Connecticut: R.M. Hurd, Yale University, 1888), 95, 100; Frank

Presbrey and James Hugh Moffatt, *Athletics at Princeton: A History* (New York: Frank Presbrey Company, 1901), 35. The league was called two other names, the shortened American College Association but also the Inter-Collegiate Association on the same page of *Spalding's Base Ball Guide and Official League Book for 1882* (Chicago: A.G. Spalding & Bros., 1882): 47. However, on an unnumbered page before the Guide's preface, it was called the American College Base Ball Association in an official endorsement of the Guide.

15 "Yales vs. Worcesters," *New Haven Register*, June 9, 1882: 4; "Yale vs. Worcester," *Yale News*, June 9, 1882: 2.

16 "Providence 11, Yale 3," *Springfield Republican*, June 14, 1882: 5; "Yale vs. Providence," *Yale News*, June 14, 1882: 1-2.

17 "Base Ball," *Philadelphia Inquirer*, July 11, 1882: 2.

18 For example, at home on July 15 he played second base in a loss to a team from nearby Holyoke.

19 "Sporting Matters," *Springfield Republican*, August 3, 1882: 8. Chapman made "a flattering offer," according to "Base Ball," *Wheeling* (West Virginia) *Sunday Register*, August 20, 1882: 7.

20 "Sporting Matters," *Springfield Republican*, August 8, 1882: 8; "Worcesters 7, Westfield Firemen 4," *Springfield Republican*, August 9, 1882: 8. As in several *Yale News* box scores, this one likewise reported pitch counts.

21 "The Ball Field," *Worcester* (Massachusetts) *Daily Spy*, August 15, 1882: 4; "Sporting Matters," *Springfield Republican*, August 8, 1882: 8; "Sporting Matters," *Springfield Republican*, August 15, 1882: 5.

22 *Yale News*, September 14, 1882: 1.

23 *Yale News*, October 11, 1882: 4.

24 "Notices," *Yale News*, January 15, 1883: 2.

25 "The Ball Nine," *Yale News*, February 8, 1883: 1.

26 Warren Goldstein, "Walter Camp's Off-Side: A Tarnished Football Legacy," *Hartford Courant*, March 14, 2014, accessible at courant.com/opinion/op-ed/hc-op-commentary-goldstein-yales-walter-camp-bent--20140314-story.html.

27 "Base Ball," *Philadelphia Inquirer*, April 9, 1883: 2; "Yale vs. Athletics," *Yale News*, April 9, 1883: 1.

28 "Yale vs. Cleveland," *Yale News*, April 16, 1883: 1.

29 "New Yorks, 11; Yales, 4," *Boston Globe*, April 19, 1883: 1; "Base Ball," *New Haven Register*, April 19, 1883: 3.

30 "New York 14 – Yale 3," *Commercial Gazette* (Cincinnati), April 22, 1883: 3; "Yale vs. New York," *Yale News*, April 23, 1883: 1. The latter account mentions hits by Yale's leadoff man and Hubbard combining for one of Yale's three runs, but both hits were omitted from the box score, thus showing Yale with three hits instead of five. The Cincinnati paper's box score shows both of those batters with hits and Yale with a total of five.

31 "Providences, 5; Yales, 4," *Boston Globe*, April 29, 1883: 3; "Yale vs. Providence," *Yale News*, April 30, 1883: 1-2.

32 "Yale vs. Harvard," *Yale News*, May 14, 1883: 1.

33 *Yale News*, June 5, 1883: 1.

34 "Yale vs. Athletic," *Yale News*, June 7, 1883: 1; "Base Ball Games. The Yale College Nine Defeat the Athletics," *New Haven Register*, June 7, 1883: 2.

35 "Yale vs. Buffalo," *Yale News*, June 8, 1883: 1; "A Close Game," *New Haven Daily Morning Journal and Courier*, June 8, 1883: 2. Buffalo used at least two pitchers in the game, but box scores in these and other newspapers were inconsistent about who exactly pitched, and descriptions of the game generally didn't mention the visitors' hurlers except in passing.

36 Hurd. In late June, Princeton beat Yale and thus Hubbard's team ended with a 7-1 record.

37 "Yale vs. Chicago," *Yale News*, June 20, 1883: 1. "Base Ball – Yale vs. Chicago," *New Haven Daily Morning Journal and Courier*, June 20, 1883: 3.

38 "To Join the Detroits. Jones and Hubbard of Yale," *New Haven Register*, June 22, 1883: 1; "Yale's Battery. The Charge of Bad Faith by Jones and Hubbard Denied," *New Haven Register*, June 23, 1883: 2.

39 "Base-Ball," *Baltimore Sun*, July 4, 1883: 4. One New Haven paper printed a similar account a few days later but added, "Although he is reported to have declined, members of the Yale nine say he told them not to be surprised if he went." See "Hubbard, Yale's Catcher," *New Haven Register*, July 9, 1883: 2.

40 "Harvard Beaten by Yale," *The Times* (Philadelphia), July 5, 1883: 3; "Harvard Badly Defeated," *New Haven Register*, July 5, 1883: 4.

41 J.S. Harlan, "The Record of Averages of the Members of the Ball Nines," *Yale News*, October 18, 1883: 2.

42 "On the Diamond," *Boston Journal*, July 10, 1883: 4; "The Staten Islands Victorious," *Truth* (New York), July 17, 1883: 3; "Westfield," *Springfield Republican*, August 14, 1883; "Baseball News," *New York Tribune*, August 15, 1883: 2.

43 "Holyokes 4, Westfield Firemen 3," *Springfield Republican*, August 16, 1883: 5; "Diamond Drift," *Boston Globe*, September 12, 1883: 5. The latter mentioned that Hubbard played for Westfield in a win versus the Newtons, but two paragraphs above that the paper asked, incredulously, "How many clubs does Hubbard belong to?"

44 "Diamond Drift," *Boston Globe*, September 14, 1883: 4.

45 "A Great Day for Jones," *New Haven Register*, September 5, 1883: 1.

46 "Sporting Notes," *Philadelphia Record*, September 11, 1883: 1; "Yale Log," *Yale News*, September 13, 1883: 3; "Columbus Club Matters," *Cincinnati Commercial Gazette*. September 12, 1883; An announcement similar to the *Record's* appeared in Boston the day before Hubbard's second game as West. See "Base Ball Notes," *Boston Globe*, September 14, 1883: 4.

47 "The Association Games," *The Times* (Philadelphia), September 14, 1883: 3; the paper's box score didn't have a column for at-bats, but see "Athletics Win at Columbus," *Cincinnati Commercial Gazette*, September 14, 1883: 3.

48 "The Athletics Shut Out," *The Times* (Philadelphia), September 16, 1883: 2; "Jumping on Jumping Jack," *Cincinnati Commercial Gazette*, September 16, 1883: 7.

49 "The Athletics Shut Out," *The Times* (Philadelphia), September 16, 1883: 2.

50 "Notes," *Philadelphia Inquirer*, September 14, 1883: 2.

51 *Bulletin of Yale University: Obituary Record of Graduates Deceased During the Year Ending July 1, 1931*, December 1, 1931: 205.

52 "Tea Table Chat," *Evening Press* (Bay City, Michigan), February 4, 1884. Bay City had one of the other franchises in the Northwestern League. "Base Ball among Students," *Boston Herald*, March 15, 1884: 8; "Hampshire County," *Springfield Republican*, May 30, 1884: 6.

53 "The State Championship," *Boston Journal*, May 3, 1884: 6. His identity was confirmed when the paper asserted that "Hubbard, of last year's Yale nine, caught a good game for the home nine." The fact that the teams had played a "championship game," i.e., that it counted in the standings, was noted in "Base-Ball," *Springfield Republican*, May 3, 1884: 5.

54 "Sporting Matters," *Springfield Republican*, May 6, 1884: 5.

55 "Springfields 7; Holyokes 5," *Boston Globe*, May 11, 1884: 5. The attendance figure came from "Springfields 7; Holyokes 5," *Worcester Daily Spy*, May 12, 1884: 1. For additional information about the MSA, see baseball-reference.com/bullpen/Massachusetts_State_Association.

56 "Westfields 14, Holyoke Reserves 3," *Springfield Republican*, May 18, 1884: 1.

57 For an example not long into the team's second month, see "Westfields 16, Rockets 9," *Springfield Republican*, June 8, 1884: 1.

58   The league played on Wednesdays and Saturdays, according to base-ball-reference.com/bullpen/Connecticut_League#1884, but the first and third dates on which Hubbard played in June were Fridays.

59   "Jones and Hubbard," *Meriden* (Connecticut) *Daily Republican*, May 20, 1884: 3; "Meriden Has the Honor," *Meriden Daily Republican*, May 22, 1884: 3; "Base Ball Notes," *Meriden Daily Republican*, May 24, 1994: 3.

60   "Six to One," *Meriden Daily Republican*, June 7, 1884: 3; "Beaten in One Inning," *Meriden Daily Republican*, June 12, 1884: 3; "In Second Place," *Meriden Daily Republican*, June 28, 1884: 3.

61   "Base Hits," *Cleveland Leader*, June 26, 1884: 7.

62   "Westfields 10, Holyokes 3," *Springfield Republican,* June 29, 1884: 1.

63   "Westfields 11, Amherst College 6," *Springfield Republican,* October 1, 1884: 5.

64   *Bulletin of Yale University: Obituary Record of Graduates Deceased During the Year Ending July 1, 1931,* December 1, 1931: 205; "Hampden County," *Springfield Republican*, September 1, 1887: 6.

65   "Woodruff-Hubbard," *New Haven Register*, September 9, 1896: 1. "News Jottings," *Morning Journal and Courier*, September 25, 1896: 7; "Social Life," *Boston Herald*, September 27, 1896: 27. In the seventh column of the latter is a long paragraph that identified the Woodruff-Hubbard wedding party and mentioned Edna's musicianship.

66   "Hampden County," *Springfield Republican*, October 29, 1896: 8.

67   The dates are from Massachusetts birth records accessible online. According to the 1910 Census, Allen's sister Leora never had children.

68   "Interclub Base Ball," *Boston Journal*, March 28, 1893: 3; "BAA, 4; MIT, '96, 3," *Boston Herald*, April 30, 1893: 4. By 1897 he'd switched his baseball allegiance to the Newton Athletic Association, to the west of Boston in Newton Centre. See "Newton AA, 13; Tufts, 5," *Boston Journal*, April 20, 1897: 3. For a pencil sketch of his likeness in Newton AA attire, see "Newton's Fine Ball Team," *Boston Herald*, March 11, 1898: 12.

69   "Old Pros Put One Over Collegians," *Boston Herald*, September 25, 1908: 1, 4. Most of the latter page was reprinted in *Spalding's Official Base Ball Guide, 1909* (New York: American Sports Publishing Co., 1909), 135-139. This annual also printed a detailed box score and two pages of photos. Accounts from other Boston papers were later used by the biggest star of the day – see Albert Goodwill Spalding, *America's National Game: Historic Facts Concerning the Beginning, Evolution, Development and Popularity of Base Ball* (New York: American Sports Publishing Company, 1911), 353, 356. About five years after the game, a very large group photo of participants was printed in the *New York Times*, October 12, 1913: 36.

70   "Taft at Yale Field Day," *Springfield Republican*, September 8, 1909: 9.

71   "Death of Mrs. George Hubbard," *Springfield Republican*, January 21, 1915: 11; "Allen Hubbard Dies at Home at Newton," *Springfield Republican*, December 15, 1930: 4; "Allen Hubbard's Funeral at Newton," *Springfield Republican*, December 17, 1930: 4.

72   David Nemec, *The Great Encyclopedia of Nineteenth-Century Major League Baseball*, Second Edition (Tuscaloosa, Alabama: University of Alabama Press, 2006), 251. Gordon Edes, "Bulldog Battery Helps Sox Stop Yanks," ESPN.com, August 19, 2012, accessible at espn.com/boston/mlb/story/_/id/8281934/yale-bulldogs-alumni-craig-breslow-ryan-lavar-nway-induce-key-double-play-boston-red-sox-beat-new-york-yankees. Edes expressed some doubt that both Jones and Hubbard were Yale graduates, but that is far from debatable.

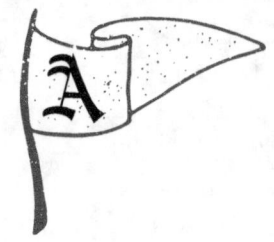

DANIEL ALBION "JUMPING JACK" JONES

By William J. Ryczek

For a player who appeared in only 19 games during part of a nineteenth-century season, Daniel Albion Jones Jr. received an inordinate amount of notoriety. Among the many cameo players who flitted briefly across the major-league scene, Jones was perhaps the most unique. He was a Yale man who sang in the college's glee club. He later graduated from both medical and dental school and maintained a dentistry practice for many years after his brief baseball career.

There were other Yale graduates and other future dentists who played major-league baseball, many of whom were more talented than Jones. What made D.A. Jones famous was his bizarre pitching motion, during which he leapt high in the air, with both feet well off the ground, like a mechanical jumping jack. What made his situation even more exceptional was that the young pitcher and his crazy jumping delivery were thrust into one of the most exciting pennant races of the nineteenth century. During the frantic month of September 1883, virtually every baseball crank in America knew about Jumping Jack Jones.

Daniel Jones was born on October 23, 1860, in Litchfield County, Connecticut to Daniel Jones Sr. and Emeline Jones. The Jones family had come to America in 1660, in the person of William Jones, a London attorney. William became a leading figure in the New Haven colony, serving as a magistrate from 1662 through 1692 and as deputy governor until 1706.[1]

By the time Daniel Jr. was born, dentistry had replaced government as the Jones family business. Daniel Sr. had his own practice and Emeline took a great interest in what her husband was doing. Being a woman, she had to pursue her interest in secret, but eventually Emeline convinced Daniel that she had sufficient knowledge and skill to work with him, and became America's first known female dentist. After Daniel Sr. died in 1864, Emeline established her own practice in order to support her two young children. For a few years she traveled through Connecticut and Rhode Island with a portable dentist chair before opening a permanent office on Chapel Street in New Haven, Connecticut.[2]

Daniel Jones Jr. attended New Haven's prestigious Hopkins Grammar School, playing for its baseball team in 1878, and then matriculated at nearby Yale College (now Yale University), where he was a member of Delta Kappa Epsilon, one of the oldest and most prominent social fraternities in the United States.

The Yale College nine played its first game in 1865 and over the next two decades the school, along with Harvard, fielded strong clubs, often playing exhibitions against major-league and other professional teams. One of Jones's Yale teammates was Walter Camp, better known for another sport and often referred to as the "Father of American Football."

Jones played baseball during each of his four years at Yale, leading the Bulldogs to Intercollegiate Baseball Association championships in 1882 and 1883. The 1882 team had a record of 14-11 against all teams and 9-3 against college teams. The following year Yale was 21-12 overall and 11-1 against college nines, losing only to Princeton in 10 innings.

During the summer Jones pitched for the Westfield Firemen in Westfield, Massachusetts. Eligibility for intercollegiate athletics was a hazy subject in the nineteenth century. The common use of aliases (or administrators simply looking the other way) allowed college players to play professionally without compromising their amateur status. Graduate students also played on the varsity nine and there were frequent disputes as to whether star athletes were actually students in good standing. Controversy and scandal in college sports are not twenty-first-century phenomena.

By the spring of 1883, Jones was one of the best college pitchers in America. En route to the IBA championship, he pitched a three-hit shutout against Harvard and yielded just a single run to Amherst in a 3-1 victory.

Meanwhile, near the shores of Lake Huron, the National League's Detroit Wolverines were having pitching problems. During the first part of the season, George "Stump" Weidman was their only reliable hurler, and they used him far too often. During May he started 14 of Detroit's 20 games, including five games in a row at one point and four in a row at another. Since backup pitcher Dick Burns was 2-12, manager Jack Chapman used Weidman whenever the latter was capable of dragging himself to the box. As Weidman predictably wore down, the Wolverines faded. After an 11-5 start, they lost 17 of their next 22 games and from June 6 through July 4 they lost 19 of 21.

As the Wolverines searched for a backup for Weidman, perhaps they recalled that in an 1881 exhibition, Jones had pitched effectively against them, although Yale lost by a respectable 4-2 score. As soon as Jones's 1883 Yale season was over, Detroit signed him for a rather lofty salary of $625 per month.

Apparently the munificent salary enabled the handsome, mustachioed Jones to dress in a style commensurate with his Ivy League background, for *Sporting Life* noted that the youngster was "said to be the best-dressed man in the league. He probably does not follow the practices of some of his colleagues, a number of whom have found it utterly impossible to support a saloon and buy anything more than jean clothes."[3]

Jones made his first start for Detroit on July 9; it was inauspicious, as he was driven from the pitcher's box after four innings, trailing 5-0. He bounced back and beat Boston in his second game, and after two more losses, reeled off four wins in a row. After a tie with Cleveland on July 28, Jones had a record of 6-5 in 12 starts, with a respectable 3.50 ERA. But Detroit President William Thompson didn't think that was a sufficient return for $625 a month. The Wolverines were far out of contention and when they acquired talented left-hander Fred "Dupee" Shaw, Thompson

decided Jones was an expensive luxury and gave him his release.

While Detroit was staggering to a seventh-place finish and looking to cut expenses, there was a red-hot race in the American Association and one of the teams fighting for the pennant had serious pitching problems. The Philadelphia Athletics were neck-and-neck with the St. Louis Browns, and at the end of August led the Browns by four percentage points. Their top pitcher was 31-year-old veteran Bobby Mathews, who'd been pitching in the major leagues since 1871. Mathews would finish the season with an excellent 30-13 record, but when August ended, he was suffering from a sore arm, a bad back, and a badly injured ankle.

The Athletics' other pitcher was George Bradley, who'd been one of the best in the National League at one time but was nearing the end of his career. In 1883 most of his time was spent playing third base, but when Mathews was injured, Bradley found himself doing more of the pitching. The Athletics desperately needed another pitcher and offered Jones $500 for the final month of the season.[4]

Jones jumped right into the fire, starting the second game of a four-game series with the Browns on September 4 before a crowd estimated at 10,000. The Athletics were a half-game behind and a win would put them in first place.

Courtesy of John Thorn.

A rendering of Jones' unique delivery style.

DAN. A. JONES.

Public domain.

Daniel Albion "Jumping Jack" Jones.

When Jones went to the box to face the Browns, it was the first time Philadelphia fans had seen him pitch[5] and they were astonished by his famous jump. The first batter Jones faced was St. Louis shortstop Bill Gleason. The first three pitches were balls. Then Jones started jumping. He jumped three straight times, Gleason took three strikes and trudged back to the bench.

The Browns had never seen anything like it. As he released the ball, Jones leapt into the air and the pitch sailed toward the batter through a mass of arms and legs. "You don't know whether Jones or the ball is coming at you," said one of the Browns.[6] Jones didn't jump on every pitch; he did it three or four times an inning, generally when he had two strikes on a batter.

Sporting Life described Jones's unusual style as follows. "He has a great variety of deliveries, hardly ever standing in the same position or manner twice. He delivers the ball without any unnecessary delay, from the centre or any corner of the box, just where he happens to stand when the ball is returned to him. Another act, which is confusing to the batsman, is a peculiar jump of about a foot in height, in delivering the ball."[7] "He has a half dozen different styles of delivery," added the *Philadelphia Times*. "His jumping act astonishes the batsmen and they forget to aim at the ball."[8]

Jumping in the air wouldn't seem to be the best way to get leverage behind a pitch, but at first it was so distracting to the batters that it didn't matter. The Browns couldn't hit Jones, and the Athletics pounded St. Louis pitcher Tony Mullane en route to an 11-1 win. If not for an error, the Athletics' new pitcher would have had a shutout.

Jones not only excelled in the box; he also contributed at the plate, collecting a single in a fourth-inning rally and running wild on the bases in the sixth. He singled in the latter inning and set out for a steal of second. On a sloppy play that included a passed ball and two wild throws, Jones came all the way around to score.

After pitching his new club into first place, Jones was carried off the field in triumph. "He ... won his way into the good graces of the audience," reported *Sporting Life,* "and when the game was over was the most popular player who ever occupied the box."[9]

Mathews was still ailing and Bradley was needed in the infield so the Athletics started Jones again the following day, before another crowd of 10,000. Jones wasn't as good as he'd been in his debut, but the Athletics survived a ninth-inning Browns rally to win 5-4. Their lead was now 1½ games.

Browns owner Chris Von der Ahe was not a man who took defeat lightly. He was also a man who spoke English with a heavy German accent, and reporters loved to quote him phonetically, and often apocryphally. After the second defeat, the *Philadelphia Times* claimed that Von der Ahe exclaimed, "Oh, it was that tam 'Jumping Jack' pitcher, that settles it. Dot was all right, but by tam, Von der Ahe will have two 'Jumping Jack' pitchers ven he gets back mit Cent Lewis."[10]

Bradley won the final game of the series, and the Athletics then swept four games from Columbus, giving them a seven-game winning streak and a 3½-game lead over the Browns. Jones won two of the victories in Columbus, giving him a record of 4-0. Then the magic seemed to disappear, as Cincinnati pummeled him in an 11-0 loss. In that game, Jones's catcher was his former Yale batterymate Al Hubbard, who had been signed by the Athletics to give Jones a familiar face and hands to pitch to. Apparently it didn't work.

With Mathews healthy enough to play, it was a full week before Jones pitched again, taking the box for the second game of another critical series against the Browns. Although he suffered his second straight loss, the Athletics took two of the three games to maintain the 3½-game lead. Strangely, Jones didn't jump at all during his loss to the Browns.

Jones's next start, his last in the major leagues, was on the 28th against fifth-place Louisville. The Athletics had a 1½-game lead with two to play, and a win would clinch the title. Mathews and Bradley had lost the two previous games, and it was up to Jones to bring the Athletics home. The fall semester at Yale had started, but senior Daniel Albion Jones Jr. was not in New Haven. He had another engagement.

Jones, who was relatively fresh, was opposed by Louisville's Guy Hecker, who by the end of the season had logged 469 innings. The Athletics pounced on the weary hurler and took a 5-2 lead. But Jones, who was jumping again, couldn't hold it, giving up four runs in the seventh, which put Louisville in front, 6-5. The Athletics tied the game in the eighth and it went to extra innings.

Jones retired the Eclipse in the top of the 10th and the Athletics scored in the bottom half of the inning, bringing Philadelphia its first championship since the old Athletics sat atop the National Association standings at the end of the 1871 season. The improbable hero was a rookie pitcher from Yale with a very strange delivery.[11] Jones finished his one-month stint with the Athletics with a record of 5-2 and a 2.63 ERA.

Jones rode in the gala victory parade, and many along the route waved toy jumping jacks. The jumping jack is little remembered today other than as a nickname, but it was a very popular nineteenth-century toy, defined in the *World Encyclopedia of Puppetry Arts* as follows: "The jumping jack is an articulated, flat or sometimes three-dimensional puppet. Its limbs are manipulated using strings. These are grouped and attached to a single string, situated below the figure and the basic movement of the jumping jack is produced by pulling on this string which causes the arms and legs to move up and down. It is also possible to have jumping jacks operated by one or more strings located above or to the side."[12] A human jumping jack named Jones had made the toy one of the most popular in Philadelphia.

Jones returned to Yale to complete the fall semester, and during the winter there was a great deal of speculation as to where he might pitch the following season. First, despite the fact that he had played professionally, he said he wanted to pitch for Yale. Jones said that if his eligibility was questioned, he would expose other college athletes who had played professionally.

During the winter, while Jones was deciding where to play in 1884, he sang second tenor for the Yale glee club, and was also one of their champion whistlers. In January, while the club was touring a number of Midwestern cities, the train on which they were traveling was involved in a horrific crash. Jones was not injured, but a couple of his fellow students were, one so seriously that his leg had to be amputated. The remainder of the tour was canceled.

There were rumors that Jones would play with the Minneapolis club, but finally he decided to play for a professional team in Meriden, Connecticut, which was only about 20 miles from New Haven. Jones played with Meriden for only about three weeks, but made the acquaintance of the team's catcher, a tall, skinny youngster from East Brookfield, Massachusetts, who played under the name of Connie Mack. Jones stayed in touch with Mack for many years thereafter.

In 1885 Jones made the final four appearances of his professional baseball career, posting a 1-3 record for Waterbury of the Southern New England League. He earned a degree in dentistry from Harvard (1889) and a medical degree from Yale (1892) and opened a dental practice in East Haven, Connecticut, in 1889, the same year he married Emma Aurelia Beadle, a 32-year-old New Jersey woman. Jones served as secretary and treasurer of the State Dental Society and continued to practice until his health failed in 1935. (Emma died in 1908.) He moved to the Masonic Home in Wallingford, Connecticut, where he died on October 19, 1936, just four days short of his 76th birthday. He is buried in East Lawn Cemetery in East Haven, while his wife is buried in Quinnipiac Cemetery in Southington, Connecticut.

SOURCES

In addition to the sources cited in the Notes, the author consulted:

Achorn, Edward. *The Summer of Beer and Whiskey: How Brewers, Barkeeps, Rowdies, Immigrants and a Wild Pennant Fight Made Baseball America's Game* (New York: Public Affairs, 2013).

findagrave.com

New York Clipper

Retrosheet.org

NOTES

1   Biography of Daniel A. Jones, from "A History of the Class of Eighty-Four, Yale College, 1890-1914," edited by Leonard M. Daggett, class secretary, published for the Class of 1884 by the Tuttle, Morehouse and Taylor Company. Thanks to Sam Rubin of Yale for providing the information.

2   A good summary of the career of Dr. Emeline Jones can be found on the Connecticut Women's Hall of Fame website cwhf.org/inductees/science-health/emeline-roberts-jones#.XTTQtfJKiUk and at daily-nutmeg.com/2018/03/20/emeline-roberts-jones-oral-history/.

3   *Sporting Life*, August 27, 1883: 3.

4   Jones's salary was reported at $650 a month or greater in some
     sources, including the *Boston Globe*, September 6, 1883.

5   Jones had pitched for Detroit against Philadelphia's
     National League club, but the game was in Detroit.

6   "Won by the New Pitcher," *Philadelphia Times*, September 5, 1883: 4.

7   "Games Played, Tuesday, September 4," *Sporting Life*, September 10, 1883: 5.

8   "Won by the New Pitcher."

9   *Sporting Life*, September 10, 1883: 5.

10   "St. Louis Beaten Again," *Philadelphia Times*, September 6, 1883: 4.

11   Jones was also a decent hitter for a pitcher, stroking six hits in 25 at-bats for
     the Athletics and batting .209 for the season, including his time with Detroit

12   World Encyclopedia of Puppetry Arts wepa.unima.org/en/jumping-jack/.

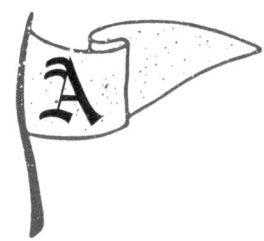

LON KNIGHT

By Chris Jones and Paul Hofmann

Lon Knight's career was one of firsts. He threw the first pitch in National League history, was likely the first player of Italian descent to play professional baseball, and was the first to hit for a natural cycle in major-league history. So who better to lead the Athletics into the 1883 season than the Philadelphia native and veteran of prior Athletics teams from both their National Association and early National League days? A homecoming to the Quaker City was welcome for Knight and the Athletics, and he was a key cog in leading the melting pot of talent that captured the 1883 American Association pennant.

Alonzo P. Leti (also spelled as Letti, Lettie, Lette) was born in Philadelphia on June 16, 1853. He was the second of three sons born to Amos and Maria Leti. His father was a boilermaker who made metal tanks for converting water to steam, and his mother was a dressmaker. The family lived in the northern section of Philadelphia. When Alonzo was 9 years old, his father died of typhoid fever. That same year, his younger brother, William, died of rubella. Undoubtedly, the work ethic that Knight learned growing up in nineteenth-century Philadelphia, as well as the challenges that he and his family faced, helped produce the man who would lead the Athletics later in life. Soon after the passing of his brother, he was sent to study at Girard College. It was at Girard that he took the last name of Knight.

Girard College was formed by an unprecedented act of philanthropy shown by French immigrant and merchant, Stephen Girard. At his death in 1831, Stephen Girard was the richest man in America and his endowment for Girard College was, up to that point, the largest private charitable donation in American history. In his will, Girard directed the city of Philadelphia to use his money to build a boarding school for poor,

orphaned, or fatherless white boys so that they might be prepared for the trades and professions of their era. Girard College opened its doors in 1848.[1]

According to SABR biographer Ralph Berger, Lon was a below-average student, with just a 6.64 out of 10 academic average. His conduct was an appalling 2.64. Perhaps that could be attributed to the atmosphere at Girard in the 1860s, which was said to be a "dreary station for a young boy."[2] At that time, there was a housemaster, a former military man who meted out harsh punishment to the inmates, as they were identified in census records. There was a punishment room for those who were considered out of line. It was a

Lon Knight with the Rochester Maroons in 1886.

dark and foreboding place, and Lon at one point found himself sequestered there. One trip to the punishment room was apparently enough, as Knight learned to watch his behavior carefully and graduated from Girard without further incident.[3]

Baseball was a saving grace for many young men at Girard, and the school established a tradition of having solid baseball teams. Lon, like many of his classmates, found baseball to be an outlet from an otherwise difficult experience at Girard and developed into a quality ballplayer. By the mid-1870s, Girard had produced an abundance of professional and semiprofessional players, but Knight was the first Girard product to play at the major-league level.[4]

Knight did not go straight from Girard to the ball field, though. After graduation from Girard in 1870, he became apprenticed to an accountant. To maintain his baseball skills, after working hours he would practice pitching. The practice must have kept him sharp enough, because in 1875 he pitched for the Shibe Club, the amateur champion of the city of Philadelphia.

It was apparent to Knight that it was time to move his full-time work to the baseball diamond. Signing with the Philadelphia Athletics of the National Association, Knight debuted with that team on September 4, 1875. For the season he started and completed 13 games with a 6-5 slate and a 2.27 ERA; his hitting was less than impressive, just 6 hits in 47 at-bats for a meager .128 average.

Knight found his way into the record books only a year later. The first game in National League history took place on April 22, 1876, at the Philadelphia Athletics' Jefferson Street Grounds. Knight, who was the starting pitcher for the Athletics, had the distinction of throwing the first pitch in the NL. After retiring the game's first two hitters, he gave up the first hit in NL history when Jim O'Rourke singled. He was opposed by Boston right-hander Joe Borden, author of major-league baseball's first no-hitter a year earlier. The crowd of 3,000 was treated to a competitive, albeit sloppy, inaugural contest. With the game tied, 4-4, Boston pushed across two runs in the top of the ninth to take a 6-4 lead. Knight, who was the victim of 16 Athletics errors, led off the ninth with a double that reached the left-field wall, stole third, and came home on a fly ball by shortstop Davy Force.[5] That was all the offense the Athletics could muster in the ninth and the Red Caps hung on for a 6-5 victory. Knight thus added the first loss in NL history to his growing collection of firsts.

Knight, splitting the pitching duties with veteran right-hander George Zettlein – winner of 125 games in the National Association – finished the season with a record of 10-22 and a 2.62 ERA. While his won-lost record was certainly disappointing, it is more impressive when considering that the Athletics were just 14-45 before the team refused to finish the season by making a late-season road trip. The Athletics' failure to finish the 1876 season led to their expulsion from the National League. Forced to find another employer, Knight caught on with the Lowell (Massachusetts) club, which competed in the League Alliance in 1877 and then moved to the International Association in 1878. In Lowell, Knight moved away from the mound and was instead used primarily as an outfielder (mostly right field) and infielder.

In 1879 Knight was recruited by Frank Bancroft, who most recently had operated a team in New Bedford (Massachusetts), to come to Worcester and play with the Grays in the National Association. Bancroft was a successful entrepreneur who had capitalized on the increased demand for hotel accommodations and theater entertainment and now saw the money-making potential in running a baseball team.[6]

Knight appeared in a team-high 50 games for the Grays and hit .367, the second highest on the team behind ace pitcher Lee Richmond's .369. Other notable teammates in Worcester included Charlie Bennett, Doc Bushong, and Arthur Irwin.

In December, Bancroft organized a team named the Hop Bitters, which included Knight and many of his Worcester teammates. The team headed south and eventually made its way to Cuba, the first known American professional team to visit the Island. While the trip was cut short because of the lack of profitability of the games, the Hop Bitters enjoyed their brief stay with some sightseeing and passed the evenings with impromptu concerts that featured "[Curry] Foley's Irish eccentricities, Bushong's ballads, and a quartet composed of Knight, (Art) Whitney, Irwin, and Bushong."[7] After leaving Cuba, the team went to New Orleans and began what would amount to an extended spring training before heading north for Worcester. Meanwhile, early in 1880, the National League Board of Governors voted unanimously to admit Worcester into the league. The team changed its name to the Ruby Legs and Knight found himself back in major-league baseball, this time as a right fielder.

Knight's name became etched in the nineteenth-century baseball folklore in May 1880. Visiting Troy for a three-game set with the Trojans, the Ruby

Legs traveled to nearby Albany during an open day on May 21 and played an exhibition game against that city's National Association team at Albany's Riverside Park. The story is told that Lipman Pike hit a ball over the right-field fence and into the river. Knight, who was playing right field for the Ruby Legs, is said to have gone after the ball in a boat before giving up. While there is undoubtedly some fictitious element to the story, it does illustrate the fact that few parks had ground rules about giving the batter an automatic home run on a ball that cleared the fence.[8]

On June 12 Knight once again became a footnote to history when he factored prominently into left-hander Lee Richmond's perfect game, the major leagues' first. "Leading off the fifth inning, Cleveland first baseman Bill Phillips slapped a Richmond left-handed delivery into right field for an apparent base hit."[9] Knight, who was playing shallow in right field, fielded the sharply hit ball and fired to Chub Sullivan at first for a 9-3 putout. Richmond went on to retire the final 14 Blues hitters to complete the gem. Such individual exploits notwithstanding, the Ruby Legs finished in a disappointing fifth place with a record of 40-43, a distant 26½ games behind the runaway National League champion Chicago White Stockings. Knight, for his part, batted .239 with 21 RBIs.

The 1881 season took Knight to yet another location; he donned the uniform of the Detroit Wolverines. On July 30 Knight hit his first major-league home run, a first-inning, two-run shot to left off future Hall of Famer Pud Galvin at Detroit's Recreation Park. Buffalo beat the Wolverines that day, 7-6. Overall, Knight appeared in 83 games with the Wolverines, 82 of them in right field, and batted .271 while driving in 52 runs, second on the team to Charlie Bennett's 64. The right-handed-hitting Knight slumped in 1882. In 86 games, primarily as the Wolverines' right fielder, he hit.207 with 24 RBIs.

Knight returned to his hometown in 1883 when he signed on as player-manager of the revamped Philadelphia Athletics. The Athletics also added veteran National League performers Harry Stovey, George Bradley, and Bobby Mathews to become one of the favorites for the American Association title. In its 1883 season preview, which profiled each member of the team, *Sporting Life* described Knight as follows:

"This gentlemanly and popular player will be the general manager for the club this year, a position for which his intelligence and varied experiences in base ball affairs peculiarly [*sic*] fits him." *Sporting Life* went on to say, "Knight is considered one of the very best right fielders in the profession and is also a good batsman and fine base runner."[10]

On July 30, 1883, Knight had the most productive offensive day of his career. In a game against the Pittsburgh Allegheny, he went 5-for-5, hitting for a natural cycle in the process. Knight started off with a single, then added a double and a triple in his next two at-bats. He completed the cycle with an inside-the-park home run, but also added a double for good measure in his final at-bat. The Athletics won, 17-4. July 30 proved to be an auspicious day for Knight. A year later to the day, Knight went 6-for-6 with five singles and a triple to lead the Athletics to a 19-11 win over Washington. Overall, Knight hit .252 in 97 games during the Athletics' championship season.

The Athletics could not repeat their success of 1883. They finished the 1884 season in seventh place in the expanded 13-team American Association with a record of 61-46, 14 games behind the pennant-winning New York Metropolitans. For Knight, though, it was perhaps his finest offensive year. He led the Athletics in games played, plate appearances, and at-bats, matching his career-high .271 average with 94 runs scored. The end of the season also marked the end of Knight's major-league managerial career. In two seasons at the helm of the Athletics, he finished with a record of 127-78, a .620 winning percentage.

In 1885 Knight was replaced as the Athletics manager by Harry Stovey, but remained as a player. With a revamped roster that included only six members of the 1883 championship team, the Athletics fell to 55-57 and finished in fourth place. Knight, who turned 32 during the season, saw his playing time diminish. He was hitting just .210 with two extra-base hits and 14 RBIs when he was released by the club.

In late August Knight was reunited with Frank Bancroft when he signed with the Providence Grays, who were visiting Philadelphia for a three-game set against Philadelphia's National League entry. Knight played in 25 games with the Grays and hit .160 with 8 RBIs.

After the 1885 season, it was rumored that Knight was headed to Troy to manage a minor-league team.[11] However, this did not come to fruition. Knight followed Bancroft and spent the 1886 season with the Rochester Maroons of the International League. For at least part of the season, he was the player-manager. He played in 92 games with the Maroons and batted .259.

In 1887 Knight played for the Binghamton Crickets of the International Association. Again he was the player-manager for part of the season, after replacing

Henry Ormsbee. While no statistics exist for that season, it was Knight's last as a player in Organized Baseball.

After the 1887 season, Knight was hired as an umpire by the American Association. The *Brooklyn Eagle* opined, "Mr. Knight is not only a veteran ball player and captain, but he has shown himself eminently fitted for the important position to which he has been assigned."[12] By all accounts, Knight was a fairly opinionated and influential umpire.

For example, the American Association held a conference in Cleveland in the spring of 1888 in which rules-related instruction was provided for the coming season. Hot topics included the stance a pitcher could take before delivering a pitch, the balk rule, and whether or not a batter hit by a ball would take his base. Outspoken on many of the umpires' interpretations of the rules, Knight's explanations of the outcomes of the meeting to a *Boston Herald* reporter are evidence of his rising stock as an umpire and the evolving nature of the game.

In regard to a pitcher's stance and delivery of the ball, Knight provided a detailed explanation of what he believed was a legal delivery, stating, "Now in the case of a right-handed pitcher, he will stand with his right foot on the rear line of his position. This, you will observe, will enable him to stand in a three-quarter position and yet show the umpire and batsmen his whole front. This is what the umpire will exact. The ball, too, must be in plain sight all the time. It cannot be hidden behind the back or upon the hip. Of course, the pitcher will wing his arm back before the last motion is made to deliver the ball. This will be allowable, but when the ball is delivered both feet must be upon the ground. The pitcher can step forward one step in delivering the ball, and he can even be out of his box after the ball has finally left his hand and his delivery is completed without incurring a penalty."[13]

Knight also opined on changes to the balk rule, which at the time awarded the batter first base as well as permitting baserunners to advance.[14] He said such calls would be "the hardest for the umpire to decide, and the balk question is where our greatest difficulty will come in."[15] Finally, Knight (albeit in a roundabout way) clarified the misunderstanding surrounding the dropped fourth strike rule. "I will give you a simple rule that will cover all cases: A man will be declared out on four strikes if the catcher does not hold the fourth strike in all cases where there is a chance to force out. For instance, with men on first base, first and second, first, second and third base, the batsman

will be declared out should the catcher fail to hold the fourth strike: but if the fourth strike does pass the catcher in any of these instances, the base-runners will be entitled to as many bases as they can get. With none on bases, or men on second, or third, or on second and third the catcher will have to hold the fourth strike.

"Suppose a batsman has four balls and the pitcher wants to save a hit by hitting the batsman with a pitched ball, we have been instructed to defeat the scheme and call the balls ball five."[16]

Knight also umpired in the National League during the 1889 season and in the Players League in 1890. It is unclear when he retired from umpiring, but he was doing it through 1890.

After retiring from baseball, Knight returned to Philadelphia. In addition to working as an umpire he worked various jobs including hanging wallpaper and working as an inspector. There is no record of his ever being married.

Knight died in Philadelphia on April 23, 1932, of toxic asphyxiation after inhaling gas while preparing breakfast in his home.[17] He was 78 years old. He is buried in an unmarked grave in Laurel Hill Cemetery in Philadelphia.

While Knight's career statistics would not place him in the company of some of the game's better-known stars, there is no doubt that he left an indelible mark on baseball, and Philadelphia baseball in particular. His ability to find success at baseball's highest level as a player, manager, and umpire demonstrated his unique blend of fortitude and ability. And in the city that raised him and had a front-row seat to many of his professional successes, Knight will forever be a champion along with the rest of his 1883 Athletics.

SOURCES

In addition to the sources cited in the Notes, the authors relied on Baseball-reference.com and Retrosheet.org.

NOTES

1   "Girard College: History, Our Founding," Retrieved from girardcollege.edu/about/history/.

2   David Nemec, "Sam Kimber," in Bill Nowlin (ed.), *No-Hitters* (Phoenix: Society for American Baseball Research, 2017), 52.

3   Ralph Berger, "Lon Knight," Retrieved from web.archive.org/web/20070202211957/http://bioproj.sabr.org/bioproj.cfm?a=v&v=l&bid=715&pid=7644.

4   Eight Girard alumni played in the majors, including Harry Davis and Jocko Milligan.

5   "Base Ball: The First Championship Game of the Season – Boston and Athletic," *The Times* (Philadelphia), April 24, 1875: 4.

6   Charlie Bevis, "Frank Bancroft." SABR BioProject.
     sabr.org/bioproj/person/frank-bancroft/.

7   'The American Nine in Cuba," *New York Clipper,* January 3, 1880. Retrieved
     from agatetype.typepad.com/agate_type/2007/12/the-first-ameri.html.

8   "Charlton's Baseball Chronology – 1880," BaseballLibrary.com.

9   John R. Husman, "Baseball Perfection," In Bill Felber (ed.), *Inventing
     Baseball: The 100 Greatest Games of the Nineteenth Century*
     (Phoenix: Society for American Baseball Research) 2013, 120.

10   "The Home Clubs: Sketch of the Men who Constitute the Local
     Teams," *Sporting Life* (Philadelphia), April 15, 1883: 2.

11   "Assists and Putouts," *Boston Globe,* September 29, 1885: 2.

12   "Byrne's Goal: The Championship of the American
     Association," *Brooklyn Eagle*, March 31, 1887: 1.

13   "An Umpire's Interpretation: Lon Knight Tells How the Association
     Umpires Are Instructed," *Sporting Life* (Philadelphia), April 6, 1887: 1.

14   Berger.

15   "An Umpire's Interpretation."

16   "An Umpire's Interpretation."

17   "Alonzo Knight," *Hartford Courant*, April 24, 1932: 8.

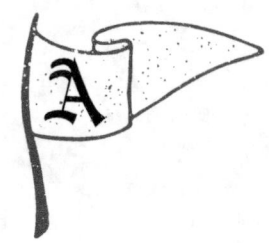

BOBBY MATHEWS

By Brian McKenna

Bobby Mathews, nearly forgotten today, was one of the top pitchers of the early professional era despite his small stature (5-feet-5½-inches tall, weight about 140 pounds). Between 1871 and 1887, he won nearly 300 games, 297 to be exact – more than any other pitcher not inducted into the National Baseball Hall of Fame. His exclusion is perhaps based on the fact that the bulk of those victories were accrued in the National Association and the American Association, leagues often brushed aside by Hall of Fame voters.

Mathews was the best native Baltimore player before Babe Ruth. Besides the highs normally attributed to the diamond exploits of a top athlete – which include being one of the first to master the curveball and throwing the game's first spitball, Mathews' career was also beset with a few negatives. He was known to have "careless habits,"[1] which most would assume meant excessive drinking and poor conditioning. It does, but it could also have extended connotations. For one, he was a member of the controversial New York Mutuals, who had a reputation for gambling-related offenses. Mathews' reputation did not emerge unscathed from this association. Secondly, he suffered complete and rapid mental deterioration, a malady that was likely attributable to syphilis, soon after leaving the big leagues.

Robert T. Mathews was born on November 21, 1851, in Baltimore, Maryland, the only son of Irish natives John and Mary Mathews. He learned to play ball as a teenager on the Belair Market lots in the Old Town section of the city.

At the age of 16, Mathews, a right-hander, joined the junior team of the Marylands of Baltimore in 1868. Junior, or reserve squads typically included younger players or those otherwise looking to compete for slots on the senior nine. In August 1869 he moved to the senior club, replacing Elias Cope as the club's main pitcher. The Marylands were formed in 1867 as an amateur club. Two years later, they declared themselves as professionals when the ruling body of the day, the National Association of Base Ball Players (NABBP), officially allowed teams to do so. Mathews made his first start as a pro on August 19 against the Orientals of New York, a 28-15 victory. The Marylands were not among the elite clubs of the NABBP; Mathews and third baseman Tom Carey were the only two whose careers would stretch into the National League era. But the roster was eventually strong enough to form

Bobby Mathews.

the crux of one of the initial franchises in the game's first professional league, the National Association.

In late July 1870, the Marylands embarked on a Western tour that took them to Washington, D.C., Indianapolis, Cincinnati, Rockford, and Chicago, among other stops. It wasn't a successful tour by any means. Of the four league games they played, the Marylands won only one. On August 8 and 9, they played the Kekiongas of Fort Wayne, Indiana, defeating them 28-10 and 19-6. The Marylands then left for Pittsburgh but soon the Kekiongas reached out and poached the Baltimore club for Mathews and Carey. First baseman Tom Forker, infielder-catcher Frank Sellman, and Mathews' batterymate, Bill Lennon, soon followed. The group played out West into November.

By the end of the year, the game was changing. The NABBP had run its course, torn apart by competing interests of amateurism and professionalism. Fort Wayne chose professionalism and set about to join the new National Association (NA). Over the winter, the club's secretary, armed with an agenda and cash, raided Baltimore clubs for several more players. The Marylands were forced to disband, and the local Pastime club was severely damaged as well.

Fort Wayne's Opening Day roster in 1871 included five Maryland club players: Mathews, Lennon, Carey, Wally Goldsmith, and Ed Mincher. On that day, May 4, Mathews, just 19 years old, pitched and won the first game in National Association history – some might call it the first major-league game. It was one of the cleanest, most competitive baseball games any fan had seen to that point. Mathews allowed only five hits and struck out six in the 2-0 shutout. It was the lowest-scoring game anyone could ever remember. The opposing pitcher, Al Pratt of the Cleveland Forest Cities, gave up only four hits. The *New York Herald* declared it "the finest game of baseball ever witnessed."[2] The *Fort Wayne Gazette* agreed: "This is undoubtedly the best game on record."[3]

The game was still in its genesis in 1871. It was played barehanded, and the style of pitching was underhanded from 45 feet. The previous winter, standout catcher Nat Hicks had gone to Baltimore to work with Mathews. Historian Peter Morris surmises that this was the point at which the pitcher developed, or perhaps gained control of, a curveball. Only one other pitcher in the game, Candy Cummings, could make that claim. (Cummings maintained that he invented the pitch, but historians over the years have put forward other "inventors.")

Fort Wayne included several other Baltimore players: Robert Armstrong, Charles Bierman, Bill Barrett, and Henry Kohler. The club was formed as a cooperative, meaning that the players shared in the gate receipts in lieu of a salary. Dwindling attendance plagued the team nearly from the start. A Fort Wayne game scheduled for Washington on July 8 was moved to Baltimore in order to spark interest and increase the gate. On July 25 Bill Lennon, Mathews' primary catcher since he turned pro, and Frank Sellman were released for excessive drinking and related offenses. The players' bitterness over this and the meager paydays took its toll on team morale. Meanwhile, the Baltimore Pastimes reorganized under manager Albert H. Henderson, who quickly signed Lennon, Mincher, and Sellman. Henderson also added Bill Stearns from the Washington Olympics and George Hall from the Brooklyn Atlantics. At the end of August, the Kekiongas disbanded amid financial troubles. Mathews had started and completed all the club's 19 games. He joined the Pastimes with Carey and first baseman Jim Foran. The men played out the season in and around Baltimore.

The Pastimes reorganized administratively again in 1872, now calling themselves the Lord Baltimores. From the previous year, Mathews, Carey, and Hall were retained as the ballclub joined the National Association. The team adopted a colorful black, white, and bright yellow uniform, which led some to call them the Baltimore Canaries. Well-known ballplayers Bill Craver, Davy Force, Dick Higham, and Lip Pike, among others, were brought in to fill out the roster. Cherokee Fisher was hired to sub for Mathews in the box. The *Baltimore Sun* wrote, "Great care has been taken and considerable expense undergone to form for the city a first-class professional nine, with suitable playing grounds."[4] (It's interesting to note that Baltimore included Hall, Craver, and Higham, three people who would become the center of National League game-fixing scandals.)

The Canaries finished second in the National Association to the extremely strong Boston Red Stockings. Mathews led the league in strikeouts. He started 47 games, for a 25-18 won-lost record, to Fisher's 11 starts. The latter, though, performed ably and posted a 10-1 mark. In September, Mathews re-signed with Baltimore, but didn't rejoin the team the following spring. Instead, he essentially traded places with Candy Cummings, who was the main pitcher for the New York Mutuals. Mathews took his batterymate, Dick Higham, to New York. Higham split the catching duties with Doug Allison and Mathews' old training partner Nat Hicks.

The Mutuals were run as a cooperative but Mathews and first baseman Joe Start were guaranteed salaries to assure their continued loyalty to the club. Mathews started all but one game for New York in 1873, amassing a 29-23 record as the team finished in fourth place. He landed in the top three in the league in wins, strikeouts, and earned-run average. On July 3 he tossed a two-hitter against Washington in a rain-shortened six-inning contest. Mathews knocked a triple and scored the tying run in the 2-1 victory.

Researcher Daniel Ginsburg unearthed some alleged game-fixing scandals involving Mathews. Though generally complimentary, he wrote, "Unfortunately, Mathews' name was brought up a number of times in connection with some of the New York Mutuals scandals."[5] The scandals involved the pitcher's time with the Mutuals, a club with a long history of suspicious play. Two specific games received the most attention. On August 9, 1873, the Mutuals lost to the Brooklyn Atlantics, 12-2, amid heavy betting. Mathews pitched a poor game, sparking numerous accusations – especially after the Atlantics went up 4-1 in the first inning.

The second game was played on August 5, 1874, in Chicago. The Mutuals lost, 5-4. The *Chicago Tribune* was particularly incensed: "For the first time in the history of baseball in Chicago the national game has been disgraced by palpable and unblushing fraud. ... This dirty piece of business was left to a club [Mutuals] which has, for the past six or seven years, enjoyed a doubtful repute for unvarying honesty. As long ago as 1868 it used to be said and believed of the Mutuals of New York that they were governed by a long ring of gamblers, and games were won or lost according as the gamblers had placed their money."[6]

The *Tribune* charged that an unnamed, "prominent" Mutual was seen in the company of a local gambler and that the odds shifted before game time in the favor of Chicago despite the fact that New York had defeated the White Stockings five times without a loss up to that point in the season. The particular charge against Mathews was that he appeared to be in perfectly good shape but had to leave the game after the fifth inning because of a lingering groin injury. Despite the fact that Mathews was leading 4-2 at the time, the *Tribune* believed that he left to appease the gamblers. He was supposedly doing too well and the fans hissed as Mathews left because it meant "[John] Hatfield, an inferior pitcher, taking his place."[7]

Amid the charges, the Mutuals produced a doctor's note after the game that certified that Mathews went to the box despite a doctor's warning. It was also learned that Chicago had been told before the game that Mathews might not be available. As a consequence, the shifting of odds might be attributed to this fact.

Daniel Ginsburg also noted that the overall accusations against Mathews were contradictory. While still with the Mutuals, now in the National League, in July 1876, the pitcher unilaterally turned over a suspicious telegram from a gambler that was sent to him. A sting was then put in place that lured further damaging telegrams. The league published all the telegrams in the *New York Herald* in an attempt to embarrass and hopefully stymie future game-fixing attempts.[8] These efforts combined with the harsh treatment the following year of accused game-fixers on the Louisville Grays helped clean up the game. Mathews certainly played a positive role toward the league's goals.

The Mutuals finished second to Boston in the National Association in 1874. Mathews, starting every game for the team, placed second in the league in wins with a 42-22 record and also placed second in ERA. On June 18 he pitched in one of the most lopsided games in the history of the majors. Mathews and the Mutuals defeated Chicago 38-1. The right-hander allowed just two hits, while the Mutuals collected 34, and only one of his teammates had fewer than three hits. To boot, Chicago committed 21 errors. The *Chicago Tribune* commented, "Nearly every man in the White Stockings nine seemed utterly demoralized. They could neither bat nor field."[9] It's interesting to note that Mathews performed so skillfully under extreme weather conditions. "The wind was blowing a perfect hurricane during the entire game," the *Tribune* said.[10] On September 1 he shut out Hartford, 14-0, on a three-hitter.

Mathews was a small guy, nicknamed Little Bobby; he couldn't overwhelm the batters with a blazing fastball. As a consequence, he relied heavily on the curveball, alternating it with a fastball, changeup (called a "slow ball" at the time), and even a spitter. Like all good pitchers, he delivered each pitch with the same fluid motion, ensuring that the batter wasn't tipped off. *Sporting Life* claimed, "Robert Mathews was the first to introduce a slow raise [a rising changeup], as far back as '72."[11] He was one of the few to master the various deliveries as the rules of the game changed over the years: underhand, side-arm, and overhand. Throughout his career, he consistently posted strikeout-per-nine-inning ratios that were among the best in the league; he was in the top two in 1871-73, 1879, 1882-83, and 1885.

Mathews relied a great deal on psychology, intellect, and confusion, strong pitching weapons. For one, Henry Chadwick noted in the *New York Clipper* that Mathews had a "habit of throwing away the first ball to each striker by tossing it over the batsman's head."[12] Second, *Sporting Life* noted, "Bobby hid the ball under his arm before pitching and turned his back to the batsman. It was a feat to be remembered." The weekly went on to comment, "Matthews pitched with his head as well as with his arm, and that explains in a large measure why he lasted so many years. There never stood in the box a cooler and nervier man than Matthews. In a tight place he had no equal, because there never has been a pitcher yet who had as good a pitching head upon his shoulders as did the subject of this sketch. As a strategist he was a marvel."[13]

Mathews summed up his own philosophy this way: "Good, straight pitching, thorough command over the ball, a good 'out-curve' and a good 'in-shoot' are what the great pitchers are working with today, and I, for my part, don't believe in anything else."[14] James Hart described another reason for Mathews' effectiveness for the *Chicago Tribune*: "He had the most remarkable memory for a batter's weaknesses of any pitcher who ever lived. … He was quick to size up a batsman. … He had perfect control, and this enabled him to put them up just where a fellow didn't want 'em. … Another thing about Matthews, he could pick up tricks of other pitchers quicker than anybody you ever saw. And there wasn't any trick of pitching that he couldn't pick up. If he saw you doing something new one day he would be doing it the next – that is, if he wasn't doing it the same day. He was one of the really great pitchers of the profession."[15]

It's thought that Candy Cummings and Bobby Mathews were the only two professionals to have mastered the curveball through the 1873 season. (Others soon cropped up.) Mathews said he learned the curve by watching Cummings. The Hall of Famer George Wright told *Sporting Life* in 1911, "Robert Mathews was the next after Cummings to get a perceptible curve on the ball. He did not, however, get a genuine curve until 1879, when he went to Worcester and changed his delivery."[16] Cummings, during his efforts to identify himself as the originator of the curveball, said, "The first man to get the curve after myself was Bobby Mathews of Baltimore, and as long as he lived he never claimed to have invented the curve, but always told all who asked that he learned it off me."[17]

Albert G. Spalding offered this perspective in his work *America's National Game*: "Arthur Cummins [*sic*], of Brooklyn, was the first pitcher of the old school that I ever saw pitch a curved ball. Bobby Mathews soon followed. This was in the early seventies. Both men were very light, spare fellows, with long, sinewy wrists, and having a peculiar wrist-joint motion with a certain way of holding the ball near the fingers' end that enabled them to impart a rotary motion to the ball, followed by a noticeable outward curve."[18]

After the spitball came into vogue in the early twentieth century, several baseball men stepped forward to claim that it was not, in fact, a new delivery. While it is true that Mathews never claimed to have been the original spitball pitcher (he died before it became an issue), quite a few did, including Cap Anson, Jim Corbett, 1880s pitcher Ted Kennedy, umpire Billy Hart, Phonney Martin, Tim Murnane, Hank O'Day, and William Rankin. O'Day wrote in an article in *Baseball Magazine* in May 1912, "There is no doubt it was employed by such a veteran as Bobby Matthews. He would certainly spit on the palm of his hand and rub the ball in the moisture. In the course of two or three innings, the ball would be perfectly black except in the spot where it was rubbed and there it would be perfectly white. Matthews was a very effective pitcher … and he was clever enough to cover this up and keep the batsman in a quandary [as to] what it was that made him so successful."[19]

Mathews started all but one of New York's 71 games in 1875. He and the club had a poor record, though, with the pitcher posting a 29-38 mark. He was a workhorse, leading the league in starts, complete games (69), and innings pitched (626⅔). Two consecutive games in May stand out. On the 21st, he dueled Cummings, of Hartford, with the latter emerging victorious, 1-0. The *Hartford Courant* reported that an error was the deciding factor: "[Jack] Remsen scored for the Hartfords on the muff of [Jim] Holdsworth. This was the only run scored and the game may be said to be one of the finest of the season. The great feature was the pitching and catching on both sides."[20] The next day, Mathews topped Brooklyn, 4-0, on a one-hitter. An error-free day allowed the pitcher to face only 28 batters.

Mathews' 131 wins in the National Association rank third behind Al Spalding of Boston (205) and Dick McBride of Philadelphia (149), quite a feat considering that the latter two played for stronger clubs (the only pennant winners) while Mathews' nines were typically weak with the bat. Over the final four

National Association seasons, Mathews amassed more than 2,050 innings on the mound. He was the career National Association leader in strikeouts and strikeouts per nine innings.

Mathews remained with the Mutuals as the club moved into the upstart National League in 1876. It was a poor club, though. He started all but one of the team's games, accruing 516 innings and a 21-34 record. On July 8, Mathews took a 5-1 lead into the ninth inning against Louisville but gave up four runs to push the game into extra innings. The game was called after 15 innings with no further scoring. Mathews and Jim Devlin pitched the entire contest. Two days later, the same pitchers dueled in the next contest between the nines. This one went 16 innings. The Mutuals scored four times in the 16th to finally claim a victory.

New York refused to finish its schedule, ignoring a road trip in mid-September, and was consequently ousted from the league over the winter. Mathews then joined Cincinnati with his batterymate Nat Hicks for 1877. The club was extremely poor and folded in mid-June. Amid financial trouble, the owner refused to pay for an impending road trip. Mathews was 3-12 in 15 games. The team reorganized a couple of weeks later but Mathews departed. Candy Cummings was brought in to man the box. Mathews wouldn't become the main pitcher on a major-league club again until 1883. At the end of the 1877 season, Cincinnati was expelled from the National League for refusing to pay its dues. Mathews then joined Janesville in the League Alliance.

Opening Day of 1878, April 20, found Mathews with the independent Brooklyn Chelseas, a club that had been in the League Alliance the previous season. On May 17 he jumped the club. According to the *St. Louis Globe-Democrat*, "The Brooklyn nine has lost the services of its pitcher and catcher, Mathews and [Ed] McGlynn, who, being offered good terms by the Worcester club manager, left Brooklyn."[21] On June 1 Worcester and the Lynn Live Oaks of the International Association essentially merged. The new club, the Worcester Live Oaks, remained a member of the International Association. Mathews continued with Worcester but in July he was expelled for drunkenness, a malady that was plaguing the team. On the 11th, stellar African American pitcher Bud Fowler, who had pitched earlier in the year for Lynn, was brought in to help replace Mathews. He pitched that day, thus integrating the club. Mathews soon returned, though excessive drinking was still a problem on the club. Management challenged the players and, as the *St.*

Louis Globe-Democrat wrote, "The members of the Worcester nine voluntarily signed the temperance pledge."[22]

On August 15 Mathews tossed a two-hit shutout over Boston of the National League. After the August 30 game, Worcester withdrew from the league. In 20 games, Mathews posted an 8-12 record. The men continued to play but soon abandoned Worcester, the city, altogether. They hopped to Mathews' hometown, Baltimore, and played under the name Waverlys. (Baltimore native Bill Smiley was also on the club.) The Waverlys played a few games around Baltimore and Washington, and then disbanded. On October 15 Mathews signed with the Providence Grays, headed back to the majors. Orator O'Rourke was also added the same day.

Providence won the National League pennant in 1879 under manager George Wright by five games over Boston. Mathews won 12 and lost 6 subbing for John Montgomery Ward (47-19) on the mound. As a strategy, Ward also finished 10 of his colleague's games. Mathews joined the club in mid-June, initially playing in right field. On June 27, he hit the only home run of his career, a two-run shot off Tommy Bond of Boston. Mathews made his first start on July 19 and started 25 of the club's remaining 46 games.

In May 1880, Mathews joined the San Francisco Stars of the independent Pacific League. It was a poorly designed league with only three area clubs, the Eagles, Renos, and Stars, and folded in July. Mathews roomed with The Only Nolan and Honest John Kelly. In December Mathews re-signed with Providence. He started 14 games between May 3 and July 13, 1881, alternating in the box with Monte Ward and Hoss Radbourn. In mid-July, Providence management became fed up with the excessive drinkers on the club. Mathews, Radbourn, and substitute catcher Emil Gross were particularly singled out. Mathews and Gross were released. The former then joined the Boston Red Stockings, but not as a pitcher, at least initially. He played 18 games in the outfield. Mathews made only one start for Boston, a 10-3 victory over Cleveland on September 28; he relieved in four other contests.

Boston's rotation changed in 1882. Mathews alternated with Jim Whitney. Bobby had 32 starts, Whitney, 48. Mathews raised his total innings pitched to 285 from his anemic totals of recent years. The pair won 43 games as Boston finished in third place. On September 18 Mathews fanned four Buffalo players in one inning.

Mathews' career took an upward turn in 1883 when he joined the Philadelphia Athletics in the American Association, a rival major league in its second season. Immediately, he reassumed his ace status after six years, at age 31. The specifics of how Mathews joined the Athletics shed some light on the secret workings of the game at the time. Philadelphia owner Bill Sharsig later told the *New York Telegram*, "In 1882 when the Association was just making itself felt, and there was no National Agreement, there was a demand for players. I met Matthews in the Bingham House (in Philadelphia) during August that year, and made an arrangement with him by which he agreed to play with the Athletic club next season. I then gave him $1,000 to bind the bargain."[23]

Mathews started 44 games for the Athletics in 1883, pitching 381 innings, and posted a 30-13 record. He was happy in Philadelphia, which wasn't far from his Baltimore hometown, and played out his career there. He won 30 games in each of his first three seasons with the Athletics, pitching 1,234 innings. Philadelphia took the pennant in 1883 behind Mathews' right arm. The battle was close as the Athletics nipped St. Louis by a mere game. Winning two of three from the Browns in late September sealed the pennant, despite the fact that the Athletics went on to drop three of four to Louisville. Philadelphia finished in the middle of the pack in 1884 and '85. On September 30, 1885, Mathews struck out four men in an inning again. From 1882 through 1885, Mathews' strikeout-to-walk figures were outstanding. He led the league in the category three of those years, with a total of 928 strikeouts to 159 walks, or 5.84 to 1. Perhaps, as George Wright noted, Mathews had successfully tweaked his curve in the minors.

In January 1886 it was announced that Mathews was returning to San Francisco, but it didn't pan out. Instead, he coached the pitchers at the University of Pennsylvania and returned to the Athletics. Mathews' arm started giving him trouble and he lost his starting job to Al Atkinson; he was benched for ineffectiveness and started only two games after July 21. Philadelphia docked his pay, an act that led to a holdout in 1887. Despite his troubles, he posted a 13-9 record in 24 games that season.

Mathews held out in the spring of 1887, demanding that the $541 deducted from his salary the previous year be restored. He coached at the University of Pennsylvania again. The two sides settled in March, agreeing on a $2,650 salary, but the pitcher's career was rapidly coming to an end. His arm was ailing.

The *Baltimore Sun* reported in late April, "One of the first surprises of the season is the announcement that the Athletic club of Philadelphia is about to dispense with the services of Bob Matthews. [The press sometimes spelled his name with two t's.] To hear of the Athletics without a Bob Matthews will be a novelty that it will take some time for the baseball public to get used to. He has been with the team many years, and was at one time considered not only the best pitcher of the Athletics, but one of the best in the country. … But the Athletics now have a long list of pitchers, and Matthews very likely has to make room for some younger blood."[24]

Philly asked waivers on Mathews, intending to ship him to Cleveland, but Baltimore claimed the pitcher, and in the end no deal was worked out. Mathews started on May 26 and 31 and again on June 13, winning two of the games, but was then sent home by the club. He returned to Baltimore and pitched for a local amateur nine. Rumors placed him with the Salem club, but that never panned out. When July 15 rolled

Public domain.

Bobby Mathews.

around and he hadn't received his monthly paycheck from Philadelphia, Mathews filed suit. Two weeks later, the *Baltimore Sun* announced, "It is said that Bob Matthews, and the Athletic management have made up, and that he will again pitch for the club."[25] He started again on August 2 and 19, two humiliating defeats, and was again bumped from the rotation. He reappeared on October 7 to start two of the final three games of the season, winning one and losing one. The October 10 game was his last active appearance in pro ball.

Mathews gained a stellar reputation coaching college pitchers. After the 1886 season, he talked about creating a training school for pitchers and probably instructed young pitchers privately. One reader sent a question to *Sporting Life* in late 1888 asking, "Where can an amateur get instructions in pitching?" The reply was, "Go to some professional and ask him to instruct you. If you live in Philadelphia you can get instructions from Bobby Matthews."[26] As his career wound down, he started focusing on his coaching skills for future employment. In fact, he may have been the first professional coach in major-league history.

Mathews was concerned that his arm was quickly failing. He had made a deal with Athletics president (and field manager for the end of 1886) Bill Sharsig to stay with the club in 1887 and help coach the team's pitchers if his arm didn't hold up. Sharsig then hired Frank Bancroft to oversee the club. Bancroft didn't approve of the deal and it was nixed. As noted, Mathews had a rocky relationship with the club in '87, falling off the roster twice. Sharsig reassumed the field manager's role in 1888 and brought Mathews back in the spring to help coach his young pitching corps, which included Gus Weyhing, Kid Gleason, Ben Sanders, Henry Long, and others. The additional hope was that Mathews could also get his arm back in shape, but that wasn't in the cards. Mathews was given control over Philadelphia's reserve squad and played for that team as well. *Sporting Life* shows him playing second base on April 14. Mathews helped coach the club for much of the season. He was with the team at least through August and even played in the outfield and pitched in some exhibition games. The following March, he filed yet another lawsuit against the Athletics – for $600 in unpaid coaching fees. In 1889 Mathews coached a couple of amateur squads in Lebanon, Pennsylvania, made up of employees of the Cornwall Railroad Company. He also pitched for the main club at times.

Like many players during the era, Mathews was called upon to umpire throughout his active career.

He did so in 25 games over four years in the National Association and for 17 games in three National League seasons. In 1888 he worked four games in the American Association. He sought an umpiring post in the American Association in 1889, even refusing "several offers from minor-league clubs" to do so.[27] He was eventually offered that post but at $1,200, a salary less than that of any other umpire. He declined, saying it wouldn't be fair to all umpires to drag the salary level down. Late that year, he joined the new Players' League. According to *Sporting Life* in November, "The veteran pitcher, Bobby Matthews, is an out-and-out Brotherhood man, and is using his influence in securing the signatures of [National] League and [American] Association players to Brotherhood contracts. Bobby is already slated as a Brotherhood umpire."[28] However, he was let go after 71 games in July 1890. *Sporting Life* wrote, "Bobby Matthews has been released for neglect of duty in leaving the New Yorks and Chicagos without an umpire in New York a couple of weeks ago in order to visit a sick friend in Philadelphia."[29] In 1891, Mathews found another slot in the American Association but was again replaced in mid-June after 37 games.

After his umpiring career ended, Mathews, who never married, moved around the East Coast from job to job. He belonged to the Mountain League, a social organization for professional ballplayers based in Philadelphia. There were a few such groups around at the time in different cities; it's not a leap to say that there was more drinking and reminiscing going on than actual social organizing. The club did have events from time to time, though. In December 1891 *Sporting Life* found Mathews still living in Philadelphia: "Bobby Matthews, the old pitcher, has joined in the tug-of-war craze and is forming an American team for the Philadelphia tournament."[30] By early 1892, he was living in Trenton, New Jersey, not far from Philadelphia, hitting the race track almost daily. Wrote *Sporting Life*: "Lon Knight and Bobby Matthews are side-partners at the Gloucester horse races."[31] A year later, in April 1893, *Sporting Life* noted, "Bobby Matthews, the veteran ex-pitcher, is [still] one of the regular attendants at the Gloucester race track"[32]

By the middle of 1895, Mathews was virtually penniless, living and working at a roadhouse outside Providence owned by his ex-teammate of six years Joe Start. In May 1897 the first indication that Mathews was ill was found in *Sporting Life*: "According to the veteran, George Wood, that once famous pitcher, Bobby Matthews, is at Joe Start's roadhouse, near Providence, a physical wreck."[33] In July, he was moved to Maryland General Hospital under the care of Dr. T.P. Lloyd for a brain disorder. Lloyd held out no hope for his recovery, proclaiming that he was "suffering from organic brain trouble, not paresis [a sexually-transmitted disease,]" as had been rumored.[34]

Mathews was suffering from delusions, believing that the nurses were trying to kill him, and having run-ins with the other patients. His memory faded and he couldn't hold long conversations. Dr. Lloyd moved him to the Spring Grove Hospital for the Insane in Catonsville, Maryland, that month. Mathews' aged mother told the press that she couldn't financially care for her son. Baseball men across the country started a collection and benefit games were arranged to help finance Mathews' care.

In late August, Mathews was invited to and attended a game at the behest of the Baltimore Orioles. *Sporting Life* regretfully announced, "Bobby Matthews attended one of the last Baltimore-Cincinnati games. The veteran has lost one of Dame Nature's priceless jewels – memory – and is but a wreck of his old self. He did not even recognize the old war horse, Frank Bancroft, and asked: 'What club are you with now?' Alas, poor Horatio!"[35] In October the *Baltimore Sun* proclaimed, "Matthews is entirely harmless and for some time has been failing very rapidly, until he has become so feeble that he can hardly move about. His malady is incurable and as the physicians hold out no hopes of his lingering very long in his present condition, his mother desired that he should spend the remainder of his life at home."[36] He was taken to his parents' tiny home at 513 Bloom Street in Baltimore on October 5.

On April 17, 1898, Bobby Mathews, 46 years old, died at home "after a long and painful illness."[37] The funeral service was held at his cousin's house and a Catholic Mass was celebrated at St. Gregory's Church. He was buried in New Cathedral Cemetery in Baltimore, near other famous Baltimore baseball men Ned Hanlon, John McGraw, and Wilbert Robinson.

SOURCES

In addition to the sources cited in the Notes, the author consulted Ancestry.com, Baseballchronicle.com, Baseballlibrary.com, Baseball-reference.com, Retrosheet,org, and a number of additional newspapers. Books that helped provide context include the following:

Bready, James H. *Baseball in Baltimore: The First 100 Years* (Baltimore: The Johns Hopkins University Press, 1998).

Egan, James M. Jr. *Baseball on the Western Reserve: The Early Game in Cleveland and Northeast Ohio, Year by Year and Town by Town 1865-1900* (Jefferson, North Carolina: McFarland, 2008).

James, Bill, and Rob Neyer. *The Neyer/James Guide to Pitchers: An Historical Compendium of Pitching, Pitchers, and Pitches* (New York: Simon and Schuster, 2004).

Morris, Peter. *Catcher: How the Man Behind the Plate Became an American Folk Hero* (Chicago: Ivan R. Dee, 2009).

Nemec, David. *The Great Encyclopedia of 19th Century Major League Baseball* (New York: Donald I. Fine Books, 1997).

Ryczek, William J. *When Johnny Came Sliding Home: The Post-Civil War Baseball Boom, 1865-1870* (Jefferson, North Carolina: McFarland & Company, Inc., Publishers, 1998).

Spalding, John E. *Always on Sunday: The California Baseball League, 1886 to 1915* (Manhattan, Kansas: Ag Press, 1992).

Wright, Marshall D. *The National Association of Base Ball Players, 1857-1870* (Jefferson, North Carolina: McFarland & Company, 2000).

NOTES

1 Robert L. Tiemann and Mark Rucker, eds. *Nineteenth Century Stars* (Cleveland: Society for American Baseball Research, 1989), 144.

2 "The Game in Indiana – The Finest Game Ever Played," *New York Herald*, May 9, 1871: 4.

3 "A Splendid Victory for Fort Wayne," *Fort Wayne Gazette*, May 5, 1871: 4.

4 "Local Matters," *Baltimore Sun*, April 4, 1872: 1.

5 Daniel E. Ginsburg, *The Fix Is In: A History of Baseball Gambling and Game-Fixing Scandals* (Jefferson, North Carolina, and London: McFarland and Company, Inc., 1995), 33.

6 "Base Ball. Chicago vs. Mutual," *Chicago Tribune*, August 6, 1874: 8.

7 "Base Ball. Chicago vs. Mutual."

8 *New York Herald*, July 23, 1876. Reprinted in the *Chicago Tribune*, July 26, 1876: 5.

9 "The White Stockings Meet Their Waterloo in New York," *Chicago Tribune*, June 19, 1874: 8.

10 "The White Stockings Meet Their Waterloo in New York."

11 "National League News," *Sporting Life*, March 2, 1907: 3.

12 "Baseball," *New York Clipper*, August 14, 1875: 157.

13 "Matthews No More: The Once Great Pitcher has Passed Away," *Sporting Life*, April 23, 1898: 1.

14 Peter Morris, *A Game of Inches: The Stories Behind the Innovations That Shaped Baseball, The Game on the Field* (Chicago: Ivan R. Dee, 2006), 137.

15 "Praises 'Bobby' Mathews," *Chicago Tribune*, April 19, 1898: 4.

16 T.H. Murnane, "The Curve Ball: Convincing Testimony that the Famous Arthur Cummings Was the Bona-Fide Inventor of the Delivery That Revolutionized the Pitching Art," *Sporting Life*, March 11, 1911: 3.

17 Candy Cummings, "More Baseball History: Close of Mr. Cummings' Reminiscences," *The Cottager* (Baldwinville, Massachusetts), August 1898, from the Cummings player file at the National Baseball Hall of Fame, per David L. Fleitz, *Ghosts in the Gallery at Cooperstown* (Jefferson, North Carolina: McFarland, 2004).

18 Albert G. Spalding, *America's National Game* (Lincoln and London: University of Nebraska Press, 1992), 484.

19 Henry O'Day, "Baseball Old and New," *Baseball Magazine*, May 1912: 58.

20 "The Hartfords Defeat the Mutual in Brooklyn 1 to 0 – A Splendid Game," *Hartford Courant*, May 22, 1875: 2.

21 "Diamond Dust," *St. Louis Globe-Democrat*, May 15, 1878: 5.

22   "Diamond Dust," *St. Louis Globe-Democrat,* August 28, 1878: 8.

23   "Diamond Dust," *St. Louis Globe-Democrat,* January 12, 1887: 5, attributed to the *New York Telegram.*

24   "Athletic to Give Up Matthews," *Baltimore Sun,* April 28, 1887: 6.

25   "Base-Ball Notes," *Baltimore Sun,* July 28, 1887: 6.

26   "Questions Answered," *Sporting Life,* November 7, 1888: 6.

27   "Local Jottings," *Sporting Life,* March 13, 1889: 6.

28   "News Notes and Comments," *Sporting Life,* November 27, 1889: 5.

29   "News Notes and Gossip," *Sporting Life,* July 26, 1890: 5.

30   "Base Ball: Local Jottings," *Sporting Life,* December 26, 1891: 10.

31   "Personal Mention," *Sporting Life,* February 6, 1892: 2.

32   "Local Jottings," *Sporting Life,* April 1, 1893: 3.

33   "News and Comment," *Sporting Life,* May 22, 1897: 5.

34   "Stricken Matthews: Condition of the Unfortunate Player Unchanged – Movements for His Financial Easement," *Sporting Life,* October 16, 1897: 6.

35   "News and Comment," *Sporting Life,* September 11, 1897: 5.

36   "Failing Matthews. The Famous Ex-Pitcher Has Not Very Long to Live," *Elkhart* (Indiana) *Weekly Truth,* December 9, 1897: 6.

37   *Baltimore Sun,* April 19, 1898: 4.

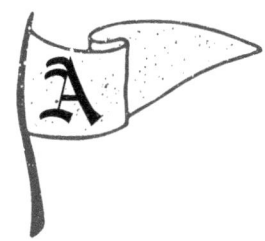

MIKE MOYNAHAN

By Pamela A. Bakker

Michael "Mike" Moynahan was a versatile player who played for a number of baseball clubs during his seven-year career. Standing at 5-feet-9 and weighing 165 pounds, the redheaded Moynahan was a jack of all trades, who played shortstop, second and third base, and the outfield. It was as a shortstop that he excelled with his brilliant right-handed throwing and catching, called "pretty stops at short"[1] by one newspaper, along with his cooperative work with his team against opponents. In its 1883 season preview, *Sporting Life* referred to him as "a heavy left-handed batter and clever base runner" who would occupy the shortstop position for the Philadelphia Athletics.[2] Moynahan proved to be one of the catalysts of the team as he led the American Association champions in hitting.

Moynahan was born in Chicago in 1856. The young city was growing with a large influx of immigrants from a number of countries. Irish Catholics, many of whom had journeyed to America during or after the 1845-1849 potato famine in Ireland, settled happily in the city, which offered plenty of factories, steel mills, and meat-packing plants, providing ready employment. The English-speaking Irish were willing to work long hours for low pay. The 1860 US census has a Michael Monahan Sr., which may be one of the spellings of Moynahan. Michael, age 49, and his wife, Bridget, 35, were born in Ireland. They had five children. A daughter named Bridget, age 17, was also born in Ireland, and the rest of the children were born in Chicago: Jane, 15; Patrick, 11; Michael, 4; and Thomas, 3. Michael's age of four on the census would place his birth in 1856 like Michael Moynahan. There are two Michael Moynahans listed in the Chicago marriages and births as married at age 18 in 1874. One married a Hana Callaghan and one married a Margeret Sullivan with a child named Alice, baptized in November, but

it is unclear if either of these is the ballplayer. By 1860 Chicago had the fourth-largest Irish population in the United States; the 1871 Great Chicago Fire left much of the city in ashes, including the courthouse with its many family records.

According to the *New York Clipper*, Moynahan began playing baseball for an amateur club in the Chicago area in 1877, when he was 21.[3] *Sporting Life* lists his first club as the Franklins. There were a number of independent clubs in the Chicago area in the 1870s, all inspired by the 1876 formation of the National League.

Mike Moynihan.

Between 1878 and 1879 Moynahan moved to Iowa to play shortstop for the Davenport Brown Stockings under manager J.W. Green. The Davenports, as they were called, had formed in 1877 on what was called by the *Rock Island* (Illinois) *Argus* "a pasture." The team played a number of amateur clubs like the Springfields, Peoria Reds, and the Burlington Club that year.[4]

The Davenports were listed in the *Chicago Tribune* on October 27, 1878, as having played 45 games from May 15 to September 28 with 33 wins and 12 losses. They scored 440 runs to 219 by their opponents. Moynahan played shortstop in 18 of those games; he made 23 putouts, had 70 assists, committed 11 errors, and had a .358 batting average in 87 at-bats. He is reported to have earned third place in the professional batting averages that year.[5] In October there was speculation that he might play third base in 1879 for the Milwaukee Club but that did not happen.[6]

The Northwestern League was formed in 1879 with four clubs: the Davenport Brown Stockings, Dubuque Red Stockings, Omaha Green Stockings, and Rockford White Stockings. The league began with high hopes, adhering to the rules of the National League, using a Spalding baseball, and refusing clubs that were financially irresponsible. The thought process was that because the clubs were reasonably close to one another, their expenses would be lower, and that the natural rivalry between the towns should bring in thousands of spectators, making the league financially viable.[7] A number of the players from the Northwestern League went on to play for major-league teams.

The Davenports' season was to run from May 1 to September 1. The *Rock Island Argus* declared that the Davenports felt they would "whip the world,"[8] but the league began to unravel under the strength of play of the Dubuque team and because of infighting about things like the choice of umpires. By July the league was suffering financial trouble. Three clubs left the circuit, leaving the championship-winning Dubuques alone. The *Chicago Tribune* reported on the Davenports' breakup:

"On their way back from Omaha they left [L.H.] Hayes and [Bid] McPhee at [Council] Bluffs [Iowa]. Thursday evening [Harry] McCaffrey and Moynahan left for Detroit –where they are now playing – and Mason for Philadelphia, his home. The others, [Charlie] Bohn, [Rudy] Kemmler, and [Samuel] Kelly,[9] are still in town. It is said that Bohn and Kemmler, after having a settlement with the Association, will go to Council Bluffs. Thus three of the clubs are disposed

of and it is an easy matter to surmise what will become of the remaining one, the Dubuques."[10]

The *Detroit Free Press*, as reported in the *Chicago Tribune*, went further, stating that the Davenports disbanded after the July game because their treasurer ran off with receipts totally three games, resulting in the players leaving.[11]

The Davenports (5-15) finished last, disbanded and did not return until 1888, which left Moynahan free to pursue offers from other clubs. There are no classifications for this year but Moynahan's batting average was listed as .400.[12] According to the *Tribune*, Moynahan finished the season at Detroit, which had been initially declined membership by the league because of financial irresponsibility toward players' salaries. It had played against clubs in the league, however. As the Northwestern League floundered, the Detroit Club, Hollinger's Nine, was one of the teams recorded in papers like the *Detroit Free Press* as filling in engagements with the remaining Dubuques.[13] Their home field was at Recreation Park and they were considered the first play-for-pay baseball team in Detroit.[14]

But Hollinger's Nine had its problems. Its owner, William Hollinger, was attacked by the *Chicago Tribune* for "personal speculation" and "arrears to players." The paper wrote, "Any nine under the management of Hollinger or Jack Chapman [manager] is sure to be a distinguished failure."[15] Hollinger argued that he had promises of working capital, but by June the *Cincinnati Daily Star* listed the club as "dead-broke," needing a money order to get home from Iowa.[16] Moynahan did not play many games with the team.

During the 1880 season 24-year-old Mike Moynahan moved east for his first big break, covering shortstop for the Buffalo Bisons of the National League. The team had joined the league in 1879 after two years of independent games and would remain in the league until 1885. Manager Sam Crane oversaw the 1880 Bisons, who played at the Riverside Grounds.

In 1880 the reserve clause imposed by the National League held players to very tight contracts which were always in the favor of the club owners. Salaries were kept low and they were not free to sell their talents on the open market.

Daniel Stearns, Hardy Richardson, and Moynahan seemed to work particularly well together in the field and the Bisons were credited with playing "a fine fielding game."[17] Moynahan was also praised for his batting in a September 1 game between Buffalo and Providence in which he was one of those who "carried off honors."[18] Even though the Buffalo team lost 6-3, the report captured some of the excitement of the game:

"In the fourth inning [Jack] Rowe led off with a safe hit, [Joe] Hornung fouled out, Moynahan got in a safe liner which sent Rowe to second, [Dude] Esterbrook went out on a fly to Start, [Dan] Stearns sent a hot grounder to [Mike] Dorgan, who attempted to throw Moynahan out at third, but threw wild and Moynahan followed Rowe home, while Stearns reached third base. [Davy] Force's baser allowed Stearns to score."[19]

In 27 games and 100 at-bats, Moynahan hit a strong .330 with an on-base percentage of .368, a slugging average of .400, 12 runs scored and 14 RBIs. His fielding percentage as a shortstop was .862. The *New York Clipper* reported that Moynahan had "led his team in batting and ranked fifth in that area in the League averages."[20]

The Bisons did not fare well and finished seventh in the eight-team National League with a record of 24-58, with 3 ties. The Bisons were financially strapped at the end of the season and required a pledge from Albert Spalding, secretary of the Chicago White Stockings of the National League, to help it out for the following year.[21] Chicago (67-17) led the league. The *Batavia* (New York) *Daily News* listed Moynahan among those who were without engagement for the 1882 season and would most likely be shelved.[22]

Leaving Buffalo, Moynahan moved around between clubs in 1882. He played third base, left field, and outfield most of the season for the National League Cleveland Blues under manager Mike McGeary and John Clapp. Clapp earned the name "Honest John" that year when a man named Woodruff attempted to bribe him into throwing games. Clapp reported him to the police and the man was arrested.[23] The club played at Kennard Street Park, also called National League Park.

The Cleveland Blues were part of a new configuration in the league; the Cincinnati Reds had been dropped and the Detroit Wolverines added. The *Chicago Tribune* at the beginning of the season reported that the Cleveland Blues appeared stronger than the prior season.[24]

Moynahan's batting average fell to .230 in 1881, in 34 games with 139 at-bats. He scored 13 runs and had 8 runs batted in. Moynahan played in the outfield in 32 games with an .883 fielding percentage. He played third base in one game for three innings with one chance taken and one error. Moynahan played in one game at third base with the Detroit Wolverines. He went 1-for-4 at the plate in a 12-inning game.

In an August article, a teammate described Moynahan as the one who "told tales."[25] This gives a small insight into his relationship within the clubhouse fraternity. The Blues (36-48-1) finished seventh. Chicago (56-28) earned first place once again.

Now 26 years old in April of 1882, Moynahan traveled back east to play for the Philadelphia Phillies in the two-team League Alliance at Recreation Park at 24th Street and Ridge Avenue. The League Alliance – the other team was the New York Metropolitans – was the National League's attempt to address the threat of the International Association of Professional Base Ball Players of 1877 with its many independent teams, luring away top players who were seeking better pay and more freedom. Besides Moynahan, the Phillies, managed by Horace Phillips and Billy Barnie, had many future National League players, including Jack Manning, Tim Manning (not related), Bill McClellan, Jack Neagle, Arlie Latham, and Charlie Buffinton.[26]

On May 8, 1882, in a game against the Metropolitans at the Polo Grounds, Moynahan was noted for doing "fine work at short-field." He and Pop Corkhill were credited with a double play each and Moynahan was one of two said to have led in batting.[27] It was not an easy year for Moynahan; in May he severely injured his hand and was sent to the outfield, "where he astonished everyone by his brilliant catches."[28] According to one historian, Moynahan ignored the pain and "picked up the ball and threw a runner out at third base before leaving the field."[29] The forefinger of his left hand had been so badly broken that it required amputation of the first joint.[30]

He may have also had prior damage from his early years in baseball when players did not use protective gloves. Those who did use gloves in the 1880s received minimal protection, resulting in many broken fingers and badly bruised palms. The Phillies played 144 games that year and finished with a record of 72-64 with 6 ties. Sixty-five of the games were played against League clubs; they won 16 and lost 44, with 5 ending in a tie.

Nursing his injury, Moynahan eventually recovered enough to play shortstop again. In 1883, he moved to another Philadelphia club, the Athletics of the American Association, replacing Lou Say. The team played at the Jefferson Street Grounds. Lon Knight was the field manager and captain. Co-owners were Billy Sharsig, Lew Simmons, and Charlie Mason, with whom Moynahan had played in Detroit.

One highlight of Moynahan's 1883 season was his lone major-league home run. On July 28 he hit a two-run, inside-the-park home run off Pittsburgh Alleghenys right-hander Jack Neagle at the Jefferson Street Grounds. The Athletics won the game 11-2. But what was to come made this a banner year for the club and the very pinnacle of Mike's career.

Moynahan's 10th-inning walk-off single against the Louisville Eclipse on September 28 secured the Association championship for the Athletics. The *New York Clipper*, reporting on the game, noted, "He has done clever work in his home-position of short-stop, besides batting remarkably well, especially at critical points. ..."[31] Baseball historian Edward Achorn gave a fuller description:

"It was up to Mike Moynahan. He had enjoyed a fine day, going 2-for-4 at the palate and making nine assists at shortstop, with only one error. Hecker held the ball, stared at the plate, took a run, and fired. Moynahan swung and connected. At the crack of the bat, left fielder Pete Browning and center fielder Leech Maskrey dashed for the ball as it shot between them. Harry Stovey, who led the American Association with 109 runs, stumbled home, wincing with number 110."[32]

The victory meant the Athletics had won the pennant by one-game over St. Louis. The Athletics finished the season with 66 wins and 32 losses.

Moynahan played in 95 games in 1883, all at shortstop. In 400 at-bats, he hit a team-leading .310, scored 90 runs and drove in 67 (second only to Jack O'Brien's 70). In the Association, he ranked second in walks (31), third in on-base percentage (.360), fourth in RBIs, sixth in batting average, sixth in slugging percentage (.413), and seventh in hits (124). His work at bat in particular was remarkable considering the fact that he had undergone the partial amputation of his left forefinger. The stress of that would begin to show in his playing ability on the field. He made 76 errors, for a fielding percentage of .833, as his throwing grew more erratic.

Philadelphians went crazy with enthusiasm after the team's win. They celebrated, decorated and draped buildings, and illuminated streets. "Broad Street was so choked that the players could scarcely reach their carriages. The club was received by the mayor after the procession to Independence Hall."[33] They were honored in Harrisburg, the state capital.[34]

The Athletics ownership enjoyed unprecedented attendance during the 1883 season. In 51 home dates, the club drew more than 300,000 fans to Recreation Park.[35] The players reportedly earned a yearly salary

of $4,000. The club offices, on the second floor of Charles E. Mason's Cigar Store on 130 North 8th Street in Philadelphia, was filled with photos and trophies.[36] It was a year of triumph with players enjoying every minute of their win and national fame.

There is little information on the personal life of Mike Moynahan but there is a report in *Sporting Life* in January of 1884 of the birth of his son.[37] That is one of the rare references to him as a family man. The year would be a year of transition at many levels. He began the season patrolling center field for the champion Athletics. Papers like the *New York Clipper* felt that the club would be even stronger this season and mentioned improvements to the field and stands with a toilet-room added for ladies. The club was called "temperate and intelligent."[38] However, Moynahan played in only one game with the Athletics He was released on May 17. He returned to the Cleveland Blues of the National League.[39] Given the severity of his hand injury in 1882, his vagabond existence in 1884 may have been a sign of how deeply his injury was affecting him.

For Cleveland Moynahan played in only 12 games under manager Charlie Hackett and batted .289. After a game in Buffalo, a local paper credited him with "good work in right field,"[40] but later, when playing in Cleveland, criticized him with an "inexcusable pass of Richardson's grounder."[41]

Cleveland (35-77) finished in seventh place. Moynahan played six games at second base, three at shortstop, and three in the outfield, committing 10 errors in 52 chances. He played his final major-league game was June 21. He was released.

Never to cry defeat, Moynahan finished the season playing third base and shortstop for the minor-league Milwaukee Brewers of the Northwest League. The Brewers played at Borchert Field, also called Athletic Field and were managed by Tom Loftus and Charlie Cushman. *Sporting Life* unkindly described Moynahan as a player the Athletics and Clevelands "did not want."[42] However, in a game against Fort Wayne in July, the local press noted that it had been "well fielded," and they recorded his appearance at bat as follows:

"So sure were the Milwaukees of victory that the bats were all carried into the club room when the tenth inning began. Moynahan made his appearance with blood in his eye. His throw had lost the game to all intents, and he seemed determined that he would get it back again, and stepping to the plate he landed against the first ball pitched and drove it far out to the left field fence for two bases. [Steve] Behel was thrown out from the pitcher to first. Griffin hit to the shortstop, who duplicated Moynahan's throw, and Mike scored, Griffin reaching third."[43]

In 1885 Moynahan moved once again, to finish out his professional career, covering the outfield and shortstop positions for the Utica Pent-Ups. The Pent-Ups were in the New York State League, and had a number of former major-league players on the team.[44]

In 1886 the Pent-Ups played in the reorganized International League. It picked up clubs from Toronto and Hamilton in Canada. The Pent-Ups offered their players some of the highest wages in baseball, higher than some of the major-league teams offered. Moynahan, now 30 years old, signed with the club in March of 1886. In June he and two others were released.[45]

There is no record of Moynahan playing baseball anywhere after 1886. He lived in Chicago and quietly worked his last few years as a butcher, a field that would have welcomed a strong man. He was now described as a widower, with no listing of his wife's name.[46]

The journeyman shortstop died in Chicago on April 9, 1899. He was 43. His passing was so unnoticed by baseball people that Alfred H. Spink, founder of *The Sporting News,* thought he was still alive in 1911.[47] He had been quietly interred on April 11, 1899, at Mount Olivet Catholic Cemetery on Chicago's south side.[48] An infant, Michael, presumably his son (born in 1887 and died March 1, 1887), was also buried in this plot.

Moynahan's versatility as both a fielder and batter are reflected in career statistics. In 169 major-league games he batted .294, with a .339 on-base percentage and a .379 slugging percentage. His 202 base hits included 30 doubles, 13 triples, and one home run. He played 125 games at shortstop, 36 in the outfield, 6 at second base, and 2 at third.

SOURCES

In addition to the sources cited in the Notes, the author consulted Baseball-Reference.com and Retrosheet.org

NOTES

1   The *Buffalo Morning Express* used this term for Moynahan's fielding while writing about a game between Buffalo and Cincinnati. "High Kicking," *Buffalo Morning Express,* September 11, 1880: 4.

2   "The Home Team: Sketch of the Men who Constitute the Local Teams," *Sporting Life* (Philadelphia), April 15, 1883: 2.

3   "Athletics Baseball Club: Mike Moynahan," *New York Clipper,* October 13, 1883 cited in Jean-Pierre Caillault, *The Complete New York Clipper Baseball Biographies* (Jefferson, North Carolina: McFarland and Co., Inc., 2009), 27. *Sporting Life,* April 15, 1883: 2, identifies his first team as the Franklins in 1878 but he may have played for the club in 1877 as per the *New York Clipper.*

4   *Rock Island Argus,* May 19, 1877: 4. The *Argus* also carried game scores for the clubs playing this year on June 20, 1878: 4; June 13, 1877: 4; July 25, 1878: 1.

5   *New York Clipper,* October 13, 1883.

6   *Chicago Tribune,* October 13, 1878: 7.

7   *Chicago Tribune,* February 16, 1879: 10.

8   *Rock Island Argus,* January 22, 1878: 1

9   Baseball-Reference spells his last name Kelley.

10 *Chicago Tribune,* July 16, 1879: 5.

11 The *Detroit Free Press* is quoted in the *Chicago Tribune,* July 6, 1879: 7.

12 Statistics in this article were provided by Sports Reference LLC. "Mike Moynahan," Baseball-Reference.com-Major League Statistics and Information, baseball-reference.com/, accessed March 6, 2019; and by Baseball Almanac, baseball-almanac.com., accessed March 6, 2019.

13 *Cincinnati Star,* June 14, 1879: 2, mentioned Detroit filling engagements in the Northwestern League.

14 This assertion that Hollinger's Nine were the first play-for-pay baseball club in Detroit is referenced on the "Before They Were Tigers," article on detroitathletic.com/.

15 *Chicago Tribune,* March 30, 1879: 10; April 5, 1879: 5; and June 22, 1879: 7.

16 *Cincinnati Daily Star,* June 27, 1879: 1.

17 "The Bashful Blonde Batted Badly – Buffalos 19, Cincinnatis 2," *Buffalo Evening Republic,* September 13, 1880: 1, and September 17, 1880: 3.

18 "The Pennant 'Problem,'" *Buffalo Evening Republic,* September 2, 1880: 3.

19 "The Pennant Problem."

20 *New York Clipper,* October 13, 1883.

21 *National Republican* (Washington), June 10, 1881: 1.

22 *Batavia* (New York) *Daily News,* January 26, 1881: 1.

23 *True Northerner* (Paw Paw, Michigan), June 3, 1881: 2.

24 *Chicago Tribune,* April 29, 1881: 6.

25 *Cleveland Leader,* August 30, 1881: 2.

26 John Shiffert, *Base Ball in Philadelphia: A History of the Early Game, 1831-1900* (Jefferson, North Carolina: McFarland and Company, Inc., 2006), 146.

27 *New York Clipper,* May 13, 1882.

28 *New York Clipper* in David Nemec, *The Beer and Whiskey League* (Guilford, Connecticut: Lyons Press, 2004), 45.

29 Edward Achorn, *The Summer of Beer and Whiskey* (New York: Public Affairs, 2006), 77.

30 Shiffert, 110.

31 *New York Clipper.* October 13, 1883.

32 Achorn, 227.

33 The press release was wired to a number of papers; this one appeared in the *Mineral Point* (Wisconsin) *Tribune,* October 25, 1883: 2.

34 *Wheeling* (West Virginia) *Daily Intelligencer,* October 4, 1883: 1.

35 Achorn, 243.

36 *Wilmington* (Delaware) *Daily Gazette,* October 18, 1883: 1.

37 *Sporting Life,* January 23, 1884: 4.

38 *New York Clipper*, March 15, 1884.

39 *Buffalo Evening Republic*, May 29, 1884: 4.

40 *Buffalo Evening Republic*, June 13, 1884: 4.

41 *Buffalo Evening Republic*, May 31, 1884: 4.

42 *Sporting Life*, July 23, 1884: 7.

43 *St. Paul Daily Globe*, July 16, 1884.

44 Richard Worth, *Baseball Team Names: Worldwide Dictionary, 1869-2011* (Jefferson, North Carolina: McFarland and Company, Inc. Publishers, 2013), 311.

45 *Oswego* (New York) *Daily Palladium*, June 15, 1886: 4.

46 George Berz on Familysearch.org lists Moynahan as a widower and butcher at the time of his death and the address shown for him matches the address given the author by the cemetery.

47 Alfred H. Spink, *The National Game* (Carbondale, Illinois: Southern Illinois University Press, 2000 edition of the 1910 original), 72.

48 Burial information was provided to the author by Thaddeus M. Dronski, manager of St. Casimir Cemetery of the Archdiocese of Chicago on March 12, 2019.

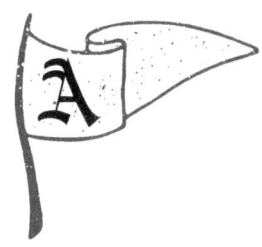

JACK O'BRIEN

By Joel Rippel

A hard-luck catcher with a strong bat, Jack O'Brien was a fan favorite among Philadelphia baseball fans during the 1880s. *Sporting Life* described him as a catcher with "a great pluck and sure catch," who struggled with throwing.[1] He was often injured, earning the reputation of being a luckless player whose career was summed up as follows: "O'Brien has but one fault and that is getting hurt in almost every game in which he takes part. … [L]ong ago, he was put down as the unluckiest man in the profession."[2]

Jack O'Brien was born John K. Byrne to Francis and Mary Byrne on June 12, 1860, in Philadelphia. He was the second of seven sons known to be born to Francis and Mary, who had emigrated to the United States from Ireland. Both the 1860 and 1870 censuses list his father as a laborer.

It is not clear when John began using the surname O'Brien. He likely started using the name Jack O'Brien when he began playing baseball as a teenager for the Yeager Amateur Club in Philadelphia.

On June 29, 1878, O'Brien, who had just turned 18, and the Yeager team "took part in one of the early day classics."[3] Yeager played at Girard College High School. It took 21 innings, and four hours, for Yeager to defeat the "Orphans," 10-7. At the time it was longest high-school baseball game ever played.

O'Brien and his teammate Bill Sweeney went west in 1879. The batterymates joined the "California" team, one of three teams based in San Francisco in the four-team California Base Ball League. (The fourth team was based in Oakland.) The teams were scheduled to play a 21-game "championship" schedule, primarily on Saturdays and Sundays.

In early April 1879, O'Brien and Sweeney were named as starters for the Californias. An early season matchup between the California and Athletic clubs drew a lot of interest, reported the *San Francisco Examiner*: "At the new Oakland Grounds, on Sunday next, will be played a game which has been looked forward to by base ball players with great interest that between the Athletic and California Clubs. The former club was an unapproachable champion last year and contains some remarkably good players. The California Club, however, has secured some new players, and from all appearances the game will probably be the most exciting one played this season."[4]

The Athletic club, which won the Pacific Base Ball League title the previous year, defeated California, 8-2. The game drew a crowd estimated at 3,000 at the Oakland Base Ball Grounds. According to an account of the game, it was a "sad disappointment to the friends of the California Club, as the nine did not seem to play well together. Much had been expected of the (California) nine as they have recently imported three or four noted experts from the East."[5]

The account mentioned both O'Brien and Sweeney: "O'Brien, the catcher, is a poor thrower, being otherwise very brilliant. Sweeney, the new pitcher, has an accurate and swift delivery, but is inferior in his management."[6]

Things improved for the Californias. On May 26 O'Brien had a hit and scored a run in its 3-2 victory over the Mutuals in a game that was "one of the most closely contested games of base ball ever played on this coast."[7]

Two weeks later, O'Brien scored three runs in the Californias' 28-7 victory over the Athletics.

Through games of August 24, the Californias had an 11-3 record. In October, the club played exhibitions against the Cincinnati and Chicago National League teams, who traveled to California after the NL season.

Cincinnati defeated California, 3-0, on October 12. On the 19th, Chicago defeated California, 13-0.

After the season O'Brien returned to Philadelphia. He was a glass worker during the offseason, and joined the Philadelphia Athletics. In 1880 the Athletics were an independent team. In 1881 they joined a new minor league, the Eastern Championship Association. The roster included Jud Birchall, Cub Stricker, and Charlie Mason, three players who would factor prominently in the Athletics' 1883 championship season.

The Athletics finished in second place in the ECA with a 42-50 record. That record included games against National League, college, and independent teams. After the season, the Athletics "sought major league status by joining the NL or aligning with an organization that would rival that League."[8]

After being turned down by the National League, the Athletics joined the newly formed American Association for the 1882 season. In their debut, on May 2, 1882, O'Brien and the Athletics made an immediate impression.

Playing at Oakdale Park, the Athletics defeated Baltimore, 10-7, before a crowd of 2,500. O'Brien, sixth in the batting order, was 1-for-3 with a double. He walked once and scored a run. And he was praised for his toughness.

"O'Brien was struck in the stomach by a wicked foul tip in the eighth inning, but he courageously held the ball until the umpire made a decision, then he fell senseless to the ground. He regained consciousness a few seconds later and after a few minutes rest resumed play amid great applause."[9]

O'Brien, considered to have above-average power for the era, hit his first major-league home run in the bottom of the seventh inning of a game against Louisville on May 17, 1882. The two-run homer came off Eclipse pitcher John Reccius in the Athletics' 11-4 victory.

O'Brien demonstrated his signature toughness again in the Athletics' 7-1 loss to Cincinnati on June 2 in Philadelphia. Playing in front a crowd of 2,000, he was injured in the fourth inning.

"(Cincinnati catcher-manager Pop) Snyder threw (O'Brien) out at second, and in trying to get back to the base he fell and the spikes of (Bid) McPhee's shoe ran into his right cheek, breaking several teeth. He laid unconscious for over an hour but had recovered sufficiently last night to leave with the nine on their Western trip."[10]

Two days later, the resilient 5-foot-10 O'Brien, listed at 184 pounds, was back in the lineup. After a

travel day, the Athletics opened their road trip with a 2-1 loss to the Louisville Eclipse in Louisville. O'Brien had one of the Athletics' eight hits.

The Athletics finished the American Association's inaugural season in second place with a 41-34 record, 11½ games behind the first-place Cincinnati Red Stockings (55-25). O'Brien played in 62 of the Athletics' 75 games and led the team's regulars in batting average (.303), on-base percentage (.339), and slugging percentage (.419). He also led the team in doubles (13) and home runs (3) and was second in RBIs (37). As a team, the Athletics hit only five home runs.

The Athletics and O'Brien got off to a good start in 1883. Through games of June 30, they were in first place with a 27-11 record and O'Brien was leading the American Association with a .337 batting average.

The Athletics (66-32) won the American Association title by one game over the St. Louis Browns (65-33). The Athletics lost six of their last 10 games and the Browns won six of their last eight games, but the Browns' two losses in that span were to the Athletics in St. Louis.

O'Brien played in 94 of the Athletics' 98 games and finished with a .290 batting average and a team-leading 70 RBIs. He also tied for the team lead with 10 triples.

In 1884 O'Brien was limited to 36 of the Athletics' 108 games because of a lengthy bout with pneumonia. He finished with a .283 batting average while the Athletics (61-46-1) slipped to seventh place, 14 games behind the league champion Metropolitans (75-32-5). The league, which had eight teams in 1883, added four teams for the 1884 season – Brooklyn, which had won the Interstate Association in 1883; Toledo, which had won the Northwestern League in 1883; Indianapolis; and Washington.

O'Brien spent the 1885 season as a semi-regular, appearing in 62 (of the Athletics' 113 games). He batted .267 with two home runs and 30 RBIs. The Athletics (55-57-1) finished in fourth place, 24 games behind the first-place St. Louis Browns (79-33).

O'Brien returned to regular duty in 1886, appearing in 105 of the Athletics' 139 games. He showed his versatility by being used at catcher, all four infield positions, and in the outfield. He batted .253 with 56 RBIs. The Athletics (63-72-4) finished in sixth place, 28 games behind the champion Browns (93-46).

Late in the season O'Brien was mentioned in trade rumors.

"There is talk of the Athletics trading O'Brien for (Pop) Corkhill of Cincinnati," reported the *Times* of Phildelphia. "The latter would make a good first-baseman, just what the Athletics need, and O'Brien would strengthen Cincinnati behind the bat."[11]

Shortly after the season ended October 15, O'Brien was released by the Athletics.

"The release of O'Brien may have occasioned some surprise to the general public, but to those who knew the strained relations he had held with one of the proprietors for several years the event came no sooner than was expected," said the *Times*.[12]

Any strained relations between O'Brien and management may have begun in the 1884 season, when he reportedly was not paid while he was sidelined with pneumonia.[13]

O'Brien was offered a contract for 1887 by the Association's Brooklyn entry. The team finished third in the in 1886 with a 76-61-4 record. O'Brien signed with the Brooklyns and was their Opening Day catcher.

The *Brooklyn Daily Eagle* praised him: "Brooklyn's new player, O'Brien, is proving to be a valuable acquisition to the team, not only by his splendid catching, but by his judgment in batting and base running, not to mention his ability play an infield position up to a high mark. He is also an excellent coach and thoroughly up in the points of the game."[14]

Injuries hampered O'Brien again in 1887; he appeared in just 30 of Brooklyn's 138 games. He batted.228 with one home run and 17 RBIs. He was released after the season, and eventually signed with Baltimore.

O'Brien was again limited by injuries in 1888. He appeared in 57 of the Orioles' 137 games, just 37 of them behind the plate. He hit a career-low .224 with 18 RBIs. The Orioles finished in fifth place with a 57-80 record, 36 games behind the champion Browns (92-43-2). O'Brien was released after the season. He sat out the 1889 season. A newspaper report said he had "retired permanently, and now he wants to be an umpire."[15]

The offseason between the 1889 and 1890 seasons was tumultuous. A third major league, the eight-team Players' League, was formed and lured many players from the National League and American Association. Six members of the 1889 Philadelphia Athletics jumped to the new league, so the team, with a new front office, persuaded O'Brien to make a comeback.

"The Athletics made a ten strike when they signed Jack O'Brien for first base," the *Philadelphia Inquirer*

declared. "There is no doubt about Jack's ability as a hitter and a general player, and he only needs to pull off some of his superfluous flesh to be as good as he ever was."[16]

Healthy the entire season, O'Brien played in a career-high 109 games as the Athletics' regular first baseman. In a career-high 433 at-bats, he hit .261 with career highs in home runs (4), triples (14), RBIs (80), runs scored (80), and stolen bases (31). He also matched his career high with 113 hits.

O'Brien and the Athletics got off to a great start, winning 21 of their first 30 games. A doubleheader sweep (4-1, 9-7) of Columbus at home on July 4 left the Athletics with a 40-20 record and a six-game lead over second-place Louisville. But the success came to an abrupt halt. The Athletics lost 15 of their next 19 games and dropped to third place.

Jack O'Brien's Old Judge card while with the Baltimore Orioles in 1888.

Courtesy of T. Scott Brandon.

The final month of the season was marred by the team's financial difficulties. In early September, the franchise was hit with several claims over unpaid bills and O'Brien was one of nine Athletic players to file suit against the franchise for unpaid salaries. The club announced that it was bankrupt.[17]

After the Athletics lost to Baltimore, 5-1, on September 16 in a game shortened to seven innings because of rain, the franchise, which was $17,000 in debt – $2,650 owed to the players – gave the players their unconditional releases.[18] The Athletics were 54-57 at the time. They were able to secure enough players to finish out the season, but they didn't win another game. They finished the season with a 22-game losing streak.

After the season, the club's property was auctioned off and in late November, the American Associated voted the team out of the league.

Having made it through the 1890 season without an injury, O'Brien decided to play again in 1891. He signed with the St. Paul Apostles of the Western Association. As in 1890, O'Brien's 1891 season was interrupted by financial issues.

In early June the Apostles franchise, which was struggling financially, was sold to a group in Duluth, Minnesota. The team remained based in St. Paul and was still referred to as St. Paul until the middle of the month. St. Paul had a 16-34 record on June 17. Between June 18 and July 4, the team played road games in Minneapolis, Omaha, Lincoln, Denver, and Kansas City. The team finally played its first home game in Duluth on July 5.

Despite the distractions, O'Brien was having a solid season. "Jack O'Brien continues to put up a fine game for St. Paul," wrote the *Minneapolis Tribune* on June 21.[19]

On August 20 the team was disbanded. "Manager (Bill) Watkins said this evening the victim would be Duluth," the *Omaha Bee* reported. "The citizens of Duluth, he said, had failed to raise the $3,000 to pay the players' back salaries for thirty days, and the club would have to go to the wall. Mr. Watkins has arranged to transfer six of his players to the new Minneapolis team, most of the players of which have deserted during the past week."[20]

Duluth finished with a 37-62 record. For the second consecutive season, O'Brien stayed healthy. Appearing in 97 games, he led the team's regulars with a .317 batting average. He had six home runs and 22 RBIs.

For O'Brien, who was 31, his professional career was over. In eight major-league seasons, he had a batting average of .266, with 106 doubles, 42 triples, 11 home runs, and 308 RBIs.

O'Brien remained in Philadelphia and worked as a pressman. He continued to play semipro baseball locally.

O'Brien died of Bright's disease, a kidney ailment, on November 20, 1910. He was 50 years old. At the time of his death, he was said to be a widower with a young daughter. Little information is known about his wife or family, but it is believed the couple had two daughters. He was buried at Mount Moriah Cemetery in Philadelphia under the name John Byrne.

SOURCES

In addition to the sources cited in the Notes, the author consulted Ancestry.com, Baseball-Reference.com, Findagrave.com, Newspapers.com, and Retrosheet.org.

NOTES

1 "The Home Clubs: Sketch of the Men Who Constitute the Local Teams," *Sporting Life* (Philadelphia), April 15, 1883: 2.

2 David Nemec, ed., *MLB Profiles, 1871-1900, Volume 1: The Ballplayers Who Built the Game* (Lincoln: University of Nebraska Press), 266.

3 Nemec, 265.

4 "Ballomaniacs," *San Francisco Examiner*, April 11, 1879: 3.

5 "Base Ball. Two Interesting Games Played at the Oakland Grounds," *Oakland Tribune*, April 22, 1879: 1.

6 "Base Ball. Two Interesting Games Played at the Oakland Grounds."

7 "Base ball," *Oakland Tribune*, May 27, 1879: 3.

8 Robert D. Warrington, "Philadelphia in the 1881 Eastern Championship Association," *Baseball Research Journal*, Spring 2019: 83.

9 "On the Field and Track," *Times* (Philadelphia), May 3, 1882: 1.

10 "Base Ball," *Philadelphia Inquirer*, June 3, 1882: 2.

11 "Base Ball notes," *Times*, October 10, 1886: 10.

12 "The Athletic Club," *Times*, November 7, 1886: 11.

13 "Base Ball," *Times*, June 4, 1884: 4; "Notes," *Cincinnati Enquirer*, July 7, 1884: 8.

14 "Storm Bound," *Brooklyn Daily Eagle*, April 19, 1887: 1.

15 "Notes of the Diamond Field," *Philadelphia Inquirer*, June 17, 1889: 6.

16 "Base Ball Comment," *Philadelphia Inquirer*, January 19, 1890: 6.

17 "The Bankrupt Athletics," *Philadelphia Inquirer*, September 7, 1890: 3.

18 "A Base Ball Club Disbands," *Philadelphia Inquirer*, September 17, 1890: 1.

19 "Base Ball Notes," *Minneapolis Tribune*, June 21, 1891: 11.

20 "Will Start Over," *Omaha Daily Bee*, August 20, 1891: 2.

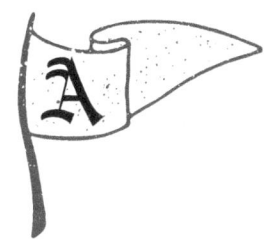

ED ROWEN

By Bob LeMoine

Ed Rowen was a backup catcher and outfielder on the 1883 Philadelphia Athletics squad, which won the American Association pennant. Although Rowen was not a key factor in the championship season – playing in only 49 games – he was 30-game-winner Bobby Mathews' personal catcher. He fielded poorly that year, possibly due to a hand injury. Like many nineteenth-century backstops who did not enjoy the benefits of gloves or modern protective equipment, Rowen often played banged up. His career was brief: three major-league seasons and only 136 games altogether. There isn't much more to his story, either, as Rowen died just a decade later while still in his 30s.

W. Edward Rowen was born on October 22, 1857, in Bridgeport, Connecticut, to John and Mary Rowen, immigrants from Ireland. John was identified as a harness maker in the 1860 census and worked in a carriage shop by the time of the 1870 census.[1] Edward had an older brother, George, and younger brothers John, Anthony, Joseph, and Peter.

In 1876 Rowen played for the semipro TBFUS or The Bridgeport Friendly United Social Club, alongside future major leaguer John O'Rourke.[2] In 1877 he debuted as a professional with the Fall River (Massachusetts) club of the New England League (also called the New England Association). Opening Day was on June 28 against Manchester (New Hampshire), a game that went 14 innings until Fall River prevailed, 1-0. Rowen "received due applause," according to the *Boston Globe*.[3] The *Spalding Guide* listed Rowen as having a .216 batting average and an .848 fielding percentage that season. The club was managed by Jim Mutrie, and future manager and Hall of Famer Ned Hanlon was a teammate. Fall River had a decent season, finishing with a record of 51-34, but Lowell (Massachusetts) won the pennant.[4]

Rowen played the 1878-79 seasons with the Manchester club and batted .206 in 35 games and .218 in 31 games, respectively.[5] Manchester belonged to the 13-team International Association in 1878 and the National Association in 1879. These Manchester teams were loaded with future major leaguers, but the 1879 club disbanded in July. Part of the dysfunction on the club was attributed to the conduct of Rowen's batterymate, Jack Leary. Both Rowen and Leary were expelled by the National Association, Rowen for refusing to play without pay.[6] Both expelled players joined a newly created team in Rochester, New York, called

Ed Rowen with the Athletics ca. 1883 or 1884.

the Flour Citys, later known as the Hop Bitters.[7] This club had taken over the National Association spot of the Capital City of Albany team, which disbanded earlier in the season. The unique team name came from club owner Asa T. Soule's patent medicine called Hop Bitters, which promised to cure anything that ailed you.[8] Club owners disputed Rochester's claim to a franchise in the league, so Soule's team went independent in July, then went on a Western road trip. Rowen and Leary traveled with the club to California.[9] "The Rochester nine is said to be one of the strongest in the United States," hyped the *Oakland Tribune*, "having defeated all the best clubs wherever they played."[10]

Rowen and Leary stayed on the West Coast for the 1880 season, to the delight of the fans.[11] They both joined the Bay City club of the California League, made up of four teams in San Francisco that scraped by to survive financially. Rowen moved on to the Californias club when Bay City dissolved.[12] In 1881 Rowen played for Oakland, one of the three teams in the New California League. But this Western adventure also was a financial disaster. According to the *Oakland Tribune,* "Rowen, their best player, it is understood, has refused to play with the Oaklands. He has not received anything this season for his services, and the funds appear to have been directed toward other players. The managers of the club may not see it, but it is perfectly apparent to the spectators that Rowen has won more than one game for Oakland this season. To antagonize him was a most foolish move."[13]

Rowen went to work in the mines to make ends meet. One day he was contacted by the superintendent of a mine in Eureka (most likely California, although some later accounts say Rowen played in Nevada) who offered him $4 a day for his services. "Eureka is agitated with baseball fever, there being two rival clubs upon whose merits the miners back their opinions heavily," wrote the *Oakland Tribune*. "Rowen, being an 'honest miner' now, will undoubtedly pop up as catcher on one of the teams. He is, by all odds, the best general player on the coast, and is a quiet little gentleman of excellent deportment."[14] He is listed as having been 5-feet-6 and 155 pounds. It is not known if he was right-handed or left-handed.

Rowen traveled back east in January of 1882 and signed with the Boston Red Stockings of the National League, serving as captain/manager John Morrill's change catcher, as backups were called at the time.[15] He made his major-league debut on Opening Day, May 1, 1882, playing shortstop for Boston in place of an injured Ezra Sutton. He collected two hits in a 6-5

win.[16] Sam Wise eventually took over the shortstop role and Rowen spent most of his 83 games either at catcher or in right field. He batted .248 with 43 RBIs.

On June 9 Jim "Grasshopper" Whitney spun a 4-0 shutout against Cleveland, striking out 13. "Rowen supported him behind the bat in splendid style," reported the *Boston Globe*. Rowen went 3-for-5 in a wild 14-13 win over Chicago six days later. He slammed his only career home run off one-time 45-game winner and future Athletics teammate George Bradley in Cleveland on June 22 and went 3-for-4 with a triple in a 13-8 win at Buffalo on June 27. Rowen also had a 3-for-5 game on July 18 in a 9-7 win to keep Boston within four games of first place, but the Red Stockings fell off the pace thereafter and finished 10 games back in third place (45-39).[17]

By this time, Rowen had built a strong reputation as a solid catcher supporting the masterful pitching of Mathews, who enjoyed a bounce-back year with a record of 19-15 and a 2.87 ERA. "He is perfectly familiar with that pitcher's delivery and methods," wrote *Sporting Life*, "which is a great point in effective battery work. Rowen is particularly adept at catching sharp foul tips, in which respect he achieved a reputation."[18]

Both Rowen and Mathews, whom the *Globe* referred to as "two of the most popular members of the Boston nine in 1882," jumped to the Philadelphia Athletics of the American Association for 1883.[19] The Athletics offered Rowen a salary of $1,800 in an attempt to protect their investment in Mathews' right arm by ensuring that the pitcher "would feel comfortable in Philadelphia.[20] However, in October of that year it was reported that Rowen had actually signed contracts with both the St. Louis Browns and the Athletics. The Association awarded Rowen to the Athletics because they filed his contract with the league office before the Browns.[21]

Rowen caught only 44 games in 1883 because of a split thumb he suffered in May.[22] Whether or not the injury was to blame, his 54 errors (third in the league) and 60 passed balls (fifth) were among the league's worst at the position, and even more glaring considering that they occurred in just 44 games. The pitching of Matthews (30-13, 2.46) helped propel the Athletics to the Association pennant, but Rowen's defense and limited offense undoubtedly hurt the team, as his -0.6 WAR dictates. He hit only .219 with 21 RBIs.

Swimming in money after their pennant-winning season, the Athletics gave Rowen a $400 raise to $2,200. However, he played in only four games with the Athletics in 1884. Despite his limited time behind the plate, he still managed six errors and four passed balls. He was released in June. In his last game he went 4-for-4 on May 12 in a 13-3 loss to the Baltimore Orioles.[23] This raised his season average to an even .400 (6-for-15). The New York Gothams (later Giants) of the National League quickly signed Rowan, but he did not appear in any non-exhibition games.[24]

After his playing career, Rowan returned to his hometown of Bridgeport. From time to time his name appeared in local papers as an umpire in the Eastern League and also for local games in Bridgeport.[25]

Rowen experienced an unimaginable tragedy on February 21, 1888, when his wife, Catherine, was killed in a train accident at the age of 29. She had been visiting a sick relative and was returning home. She was walking along the tracks of the New Haven Railroad at the Sterling Street crossing in Bridgeport. She dodged an oncoming train by moving onto another set of tracks, unaware of an approaching freight train. The *Post-Star* of Glens Falls, New York, described the gruesome detail. "She was struck by the engine and literally torn to pieces by the wheels, portions of her body being scattered along the track for a distance of nearly a mile."[26]

Edward Rowen died in Bridgeport nearly four years to the day after his wife's death, on February 22, 1892, after suffering "general debility and hemorrhages of the lungs." He was 34. The couple was not mentioned as to having any children. His funeral was "largely attended."[27] He is buried in St. Michael's Cemetery in Stratford, Connecticut.

SOURCES

In addition to the sources provided in the notes, the author was aided by the following:

Baseball-reference.com

Familysearch.org

Helander, Brock. "The Western Baseball Tours of 1879," sabr.org/research/western-baseball-tours-1879. Retrieved April 22, 2019.

Lent, Cassidy. Reference librarian at the A. Bartlett Giamatti Research Center, Cooperstown, New York, provided Rowen's file.

Retrosheet.org

NOTES

1 The family's name appears as Roan in the 1860 census.

2 Michael J. Bielawa, *Bridgeport Baseball* (Portsmouth, New Hampshire: Arcadia Publishing, 2003), 67.

3 "An Extraordinary Game at Fall River," *Boston Globe*, June 29, 1877: 5.

4 *Spalding's Official Base Ball Guide 1878* (Chicago: A.G. Spalding & Bro., 1878), 27, 35-36.

5 *Spalding's Official Base Ball Guide 1879* (Chicago: A.G. Spalding & Bro., 1879), 35; *Spalding's Official Base Ball Guide 1880* (Chicago: A.G. Spalding & Bro., 1880), 109.

6 "Sporting News," *Buffalo Commercial*, March 3, 1880: 3; "The National Bulletins," *New York Clipper*, August 2, 1879: 149.

7 "Baseball Notes," *New York Clipper*, July 19, 1879: 13.

8 Samuel Hopkins Adams, "To the Greater Glory of Hop Bitters," *The New Yorker*, August 15, 1952.

9 "Notes and Gossip," *Boston Globe*, July 14, 1879: 4.

10 "Noted Ball-Tossers," *Oakland Tribune*, September 24, 1879: 3.

11 "Base-Ball," *San Francisco Examiner*, May 11, 1880: 3.

12 "Baseball," *San Francisco Chronicle*, September 20, 1880: 4; "Baseball Notes," *New York Clipper*, August 7, 1880: 157.

13 "Base Ball," *Oakland Tribune*, July 11, 1881: 3.

14 "Rowen in Luck," *Oakland Tribune*, July 16, 1881: 3.

15 "The Boston Base Ball Team for 1882," *Boston Globe*, January 7, 1882: 2.

16 "The League Season," *Boston Globe*, May 2, 1882: 1.

17 "Sporting Matters," *Boston Globe*, June 10, 1882: 2; "Bat and Ball," *Boston Globe*, June 16, 1882: 5. "Yesterday's Sports," *Boston Globe*, June 28, 1882: 2; "Stories the Scores Tell," *Boston Globe*, July 19, 1882: 4.

18 "The Home Clubs," *Sporting Life*, April 15, 1883: 2.

19 "The Athletics," *Boston Globe*, October 1, 1883: 1.

20 Edward Achorn, *The Summer of Beer and Whiskey* (New York: Public Affairs Press, 2006), 74.

21 "Base Ball: Items from the Diamond," *New Orleans Times-Picayune*, October 24, 1882: 8.

22 "Two Good Games," *Philadelphia Inquirer*, May 30, 1883: 2; "The Athletic Club," *New York Clipper*, October 13, 1883: 490.

23 "Base Ball," *Philadelphia Inquirer*, May 13, 1884: 2.

24 "Diamond Chips," *St. Louis Post-Dispatch*, June 10, 1884: 5; *Buffalo Commercial*, June 19, 1884: 3.

25 "The Eastern," *Sporting Life*, April 13, 1887: 1; *Hartford Courant*, April 28, 1887: 3.

26 "Cut to Pieces on the Rail," *Glens Falls* (New York) *Post-Star*, February 24, 1888: 1; "Along the Sound," *New York Tribune*, February 23, 1888: 8; *Bridgeport Morning News*, February 23, 1888: 4.

27 "Edward Rowen," *New York Clipper*, March 5, 1892: 862.

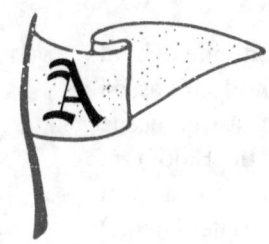

HARRY STOVEY

By Paul Hofmann

There exists a long list of forgotten nineteenth-century baseball stars who played during the game's formative stages and under relative anonymity besides being a name in a newspaper. While the game was fundamentally the same, it was evolving in an era that saw many rule changes and ballparks with vastly varying dimensions. There were no bright lights or television, and record-keeping was inconsistent. One of the greatest players of the nineteenth century was Harry Stovey.

Stovey was "one of baseball's first dual threats" in the judgment of Matt Kelly at the Baseball Hall of Fame.[1] He possessed a rare combination of power and speed that set him apart from other nineteenth-century players. He was also an innovator on the basepaths, introducing sliding techniques to the game that had never before been seen. Yet, despite the enshrinement of many of his contemporaries in the Baseball Hall of Fame, Stovey remains a forgotten star who, more than 120 years after his playing career ended, continues to be overlooked by those guarding the gates of Cooperstown.

Captain Harry Stovey with the Athletics.

Harold Duffield Stow was born on December 20, 1856, in Philadelphia.[2] He was the eighth of nine children born to John and Rachel (Duffield) Stow (or Stowe by other accounts).[3] The Philadelphia almanac that year lists John's profession as a watchman. Census and other records identify him as a shoemaker. The Stows and Duffields traced their origins to England and both sides of the family had long histories in the United States dating back to at least the early eighteenth century. The Stows had notable Philadelphians in their family tree.

Harry Stow was a direct descendant of an earlier John Stow, a Philadelphia founder who along with his partner John Pass, is credited with recasting the Liberty Bell after it cracked. At Stow's foundry on Second Street, the bell was broken into small pieces, melted down, and cast into a new bell. The two founders found that the metal was too brittle, and augmented it by about 10 percent, using copper. The bell was ready in March 1753, and Norris reported that the lettering (which included the founders' names and the year) was even clearer on the new bell than on the old.[4] The Stow surname, along with the surname Pass, appears on the upper rim of bell. This is significant as it is one of a few pieces of evidence that point to the proper spelling of the family's surname.[5]

While relatively little is known about Harry's early childhood and education, his early life was certainly shaped by the events surrounding the Civil War. Philadelphia during the Civil War was an important source of troops, money, weapons, medical care, and supplies for the Union.

The Stow family resided in the eastern section of the Kensington District, a working-class community known for its large Irish Catholic and English-American communities.

The Stows, like many of the area families, contributed to the war effort. Harry's older sisters worked in Kensington's wool mills and his older brother John joined the 90th Regiment of Pennsylvania Infantry, a unit made up entirely of volunteers from Philadelphia.[6] It was also during this time that Harry lost his older brother Edwin. On June 14, 1862, Edwin unexpectedly died of an intussusception, a bowel obstruction, at the age of 13.

Harry loved baseball from an early age and as a youngster he spent what his parents considered an abnormal amount of time playing the game, and the more he played, the better he got.[7] In fact, his mother abhorred the game and strongly disapproved of Harry playing. Her hope was that Harry would dedicate his time to learning a trade. When he was not on the sandlots the adolescent Stovey, like many of his contemporaries, learned a trade. He apprenticed and was trained as a cooper.[8]

Stovey began his ballplaying career as a pitcher with the Defiance Club of Philadelphia in 1877 in the League Alliance. In an effort to conceal his ballplaying from his mother, Harry played under the name of Stovey to avoid the name Stow being used in accounts of local baseball games.[9] After enjoying success with Defiance, Stovey joined the Philadelphia Athletics club, which had been expelled from the National League at the end of the 1876 season and also was in the League Alliance.

He spent the next two seasons playing minor-league ball for the New Bedford Clam-Eaters under their nomadic manager, Frank Bancroft. Stovey took a liking to New Bedford and a young woman named Mary Walker. Stovey and Mary were married in July of 1879 and New Bedford would become Stovey's adopted home.[10]

In 1880 Bancroft was hired as manager of the National League's Worcester Ruby Legs and took Stovey along with him. Stovey made his major-league debut on May 1, 1880. Two-and-a-half months later, on July 17, he hit his first major-league home run when he connected off the Cleveland Blues' Jim McCormick, who led the National League with 45 victories that year. On September 21 Stovey collected four hits, including two home runs, off right-hander Mickey Welch as the Ruby Legs routed the Troy Trojans, 17-2. Four of Stovey's six home runs that year came at the expense of Welch.

Splitting time between first base and the outfield, the 23-year-old right-handed-hitting Stovey enjoyed a productive rookie campaign. While his .265 batting

Courtesy of T. Scott Brandon.

Harry Stovey with the Athletics in an 1887 Kalamazoo Bats image.

average may not have been that awe-inspiring, Stovey did lead the league with 14 triples and tied Boston's Jim O'Rourke for the lead in home runs with six. He also added 21 doubles, sixth most in the league, and finished second in the league in runs scored (76) and total bases (161).

Early in 1880 Stovey and his wife welcomed their first daughter, Elizzia, who would go by Lizzie. During the offseason, Stovey supported his young family by working as the night clerk at the Bancroft House in New Bedford.[11] The Ruby Legs manager, who had interests in the local theater and entertainment industry, had opened the Bancroft House to meet the needs of "managers, agents, and [theater] companies visiting New Bedford."[12] Bancroft would apply the same skills and abilities that made him successful in the theater industry – specifically his ability to recognize new trends – to the growing popularity of baseball.

The Ruby Legs finished in fifth place during their first season. However, the team was struggling financially. The club's board of directors concluded that a professional manager like Bancroft was not worth the investment.[13] Bancroft found employment as manager of the National League's newest team, the Detroit Wolverines, in 1881. The move signaled the start of

Stovey as depicted in the New York Clipper, *August 7, 1880.*

precipitous decline for the Ruby Legs' fortunes in Worcester.

With Bancroft no longer at the helm, a rift occurred between player-manager Mike Dorgan and star pitcher Lee Richmond, who a year earlier had authored major-league baseball's first perfect game. The conflict caused Richmond to quit the team. On August 17 with the team in seventh place with a 24-32 record, the Ruby Legs suspended Dorgan (who immediately signed with Bancroft's Wolverines) and named Stovey manager for the remainder of the season. The Ruby Legs were 8-18 under Stovey and finished the season in last place, 23 games behind the pennant-winning Chicago White Stockings.

Stovey's power numbers dipped slightly in 1881. He finished the year with a .270 batting average, 25 doubles, 7 triples, and 2 home runs. His OPS dropped from .742 the previous year to .696. It was the last year his OPS would dip below .750 until 1892. Defensively he appeared in more games at first base than he did in the outfield.

Throughout his career it was often said that Stovey had sure hands and a strong, accurate arm with great range. Statistically, he was an above-average first baseman. He finished in the top four in the league in range factor from 1881 to 1885 and in the top five in fielding percentage during the same years. As of 2019,

his 165 career outfield assists place him in the top 100 all-time.

The 1882 season was the final one for Stovey and the Ruby Legs in Worcester. The team continued its free fall in the National League standings and finished in last place with an 18-66 record. Things got so bad that the team's regular-season finale at the Agricultural County Fair Grounds on September 29 drew a crowd of just 25 patrons, an improvement over the day before, when they drew just six.[14]

Despite playing for poor teams – the Ruby Legs had a meager .361 winning percentage during their three NL seasons – Stovey continued to develop into one of the game's most exciting young players. He improved his batting average to .289 and scored 90 runs as his reputation as a daring baserunner grew. He also hit five home runs, which tied him for fourth best in the circuit.

After Worcester disbanded, Stovey was lured back to Philadelphia by Athletics owners Lew Simmons, Billy Sharsig, and Charlie Mason, who reportedly offered him a salary of $2,000, a 60 percent raise over what he was earning with the Ruby Legs.[15] His signing was a coup for the American Association. Philadelphia was one of the cities in which the Association was in direct competition with the National League and the articulate, well-mannered, handsome, and home-grown 5-foot-11, 175-pound Stovey gave them a decided advantage in winning the hearts and loyalties of Philadelphia baseball fans over the cellar-dwelling Quakers of the National League.

Stovey and fellow National League imports Lon Knight and pitcher Bobby Mathews joined an Athletics team that went 41-34 and finished in second place in the American Association's inaugural season. The 26-year-old Stovey quickly established himself as the game's premier baserunner and power hitter, proving to be the offensive sparkplug the team needed to win the Association championship. Stovey led the league in runs scored, doubles, home runs, total bases, and slugging percentage. He was also considered the best baserunner in the game.[16]

In fact, Stovey was an innovator on the basepaths. He is credited with inventing sliding pads to protect the often bruised and scraped hips he suffered while sliding on the crudely manicured nineteenth-century fields. He is recognized as one of the first baserunners to slide feet-first into bases and mastering the technique of the pop-up slide, a revolutionary method of going into a base that put added pressure on the defense.[17] However, Stovey's aggressive sliding led to many leg injuries during his career.

Despite his aggressiveness on the basepaths, Stovey was often referred to as "Gentleman Harry" for his clean play. Alfred Henry Spink, author of *The National Game*, wrote of Stovey in 1910: "He always slid feet first but was not 'nasty' with his feet in the way of trying to hurt the baseman, as some of his imitators were."[18]

According to Edward Achorn in *The Summer of Beer and Whiskey*, on the 1883 American Association season, Stovey and many of the Athletics were banged up as they limped toward the finish line for the Association pennant. Stovey was suffering from a sprained ankle that "had turned him into a sad parody of himself on the base paths."[19] Achorn chronicled the last half-inning of the Athletics' pennant-clinching victory on September 28 in which Stovey fittingly scored the pennant-winning run. The Athletics and the Louisville Eclipse were tied, 6-6, and right-hander Guy Hecker was on the mound as the Athletics came to bat in the bottom of the 10th inning.

Now Harry Stovey pulled a bat from the box at the end of the bench and limped to home plate. ... Hecker, either wary of Stovey or incapable of controlling his pitches at this point, kept the ball away from the plate, finally walking the batter. When an exhausted Hecker followed with a wild pitch, Stovey hobbled down to second base – not quite scoring position, this time, given the runner's lame ankle.

Captain Lon Knight stepped to the plate. Throughout the pennant stretch he had repeatedly made clutch plays that kept the Athletics alive. Now he ripped a single to left field.

Stovey barely made it to third.

It was up to Mike Moynahan. He had enjoyed a fine day, going 2-for-4 at the plate and making nine assists at shortstop, with only one error. Hecker held the ball, stared at the plate, took a run and fired. Moynahan swung and connected. At the crack of the bat, left fielder Pete Browning and center fielder Leech Maskrey dashed for the ball as it shot between them. Harry Stovey who led the American Association with 109 runs scored stumbled home, wincing, with number 110.[20]

When the team returned to Philadelphia, a great victory celebration was held. At a banquet each Athletic player was presented with a gold badge bearing his name and the inscription "Athletic Base Ball Champions of 1884" (denoting their reign until the end of the next season).[21] Mason, one of the Athletics

owners, also presented Stovey, whose "extraordinary grace and drive had sustained the club during its crucial final six weeks," with a gold watch and chain to commemorate his leadership.[22]

Stovey, who became the first major leaguer to hit 10 home runs in a season, set the single-season home-run record with 14 during the Athletics' championship run, out-homering five of the other seven Association teams.[23] However, his record lasted only one year. In 1884 Ned Williamson and three of his Chicago White Stockings teammates (Fred Pfeffer, Abner Dalrymple, and Cap Anson) surpassed Stovey. Williamson nearly doubled Stovey's mark with 27.[24]

There was more to Stovey's year than setting home-run records and contributing to a championship season with his hometown Athletics. In 1883 he and Mary welcome their second daughter, Susan. Two years later a third daughter, Harriett, was born.

Building on his success of the previous year, Stovey enjoyed an even better season at the plate in 1884. One highlight of the season came on August 18 when Stovey had three triples and two singles in the Athletics' 20-1 thrashing of the Baltimore Orioles. Two of his triples came in the eighth inning. He was the third major leaguer to hit two triples in an inning.[25]

In 104 games played that season (all at first base), Stovey hit .326 with 22 doubles, a league-leading 23 triples, 10 home runs (second to Cincinnati's John Reilly who clouted 11), and 83 RBIs. He also recorded a career-high .545 slugging percentage. Despite his offensive output, the Athletics failed to defend their Association title. The team finished in seventh place with a 61-46 record in the 13-team league, 14 games behind the champion New York Metropolitans.[26]

After the disappointing finish in 1884, the first real signs of unrest among the Athletics' triumvirate ownership group became apparent. In November Lew Simmons announced that he was taking over as field manager in 1885 because the team had lost $20,000 in 1884. He blamed Stovey for the team's slump. Simmons cited an incident in which he asserted that Stovey arrived at the ballpark too drunk to play, a common-enough claim in the 1880s. In fact, there were numerous reports of heavy drinking among the Athletics, and the owners expressed concerns about almost all their players. The club imposed rules that among other things addressed the problems of hard living associated with the team and the American Association.[27] However, the upstanding Stovey was never linked to the social ills that plagued the Athletics.

But co-owners Sharsig and Mason were quick to come to Stovey's defense, praising him for his performance on the field and his leadership. Stovey defended himself in a letter to *Sporting Life*. The letter read:

Dear Sir:

In your last issue you published an interview with Lew Simmons, in which that individual expresses himself altogether too freely concerning the occurrences of the past season, and in which he particularly singles me out as an "awful example." Permit me to say that Mr. Simmons is so bold in his utterance because he knows I am at a safe distance and cannot just now defend myself, and he embraces the opportunity to assail me. I wish to say that the scaffold accident did really happen at the time mentioned, and that I was really injured by the falling of the same can be easily proven. I was not intoxicated, as Mr. Simmons states, and I beg that you will do me the favor to publish this public contradiction. I shall shortly have a personal interview with my "*friend*" Mr. Simmons, concerning this matter.

He says he is going to be the manager next season, and further that he will make the boys play ball or he will fine and expel them. I think he is "shooting off his mouth" altogether too previously, and a short experience will convince him that that is not the way to get good work out of his men, for they cannot and will not play with any heart under apprehension of being fined for every error they make. In my estimation he will make what I may call, in the expressive slang of the day, a "dub" of a manager; and I will frankly state right here that I would prefer my release to playing under him. Trusting that I have not encroached too much upon your valuable space,

I remain. Very truly yours,
HARRY D. STOVEY[28]

The end result was that Stovey was appointed manager-captain for the 1885 season and Simmons was, albeit temporarily, relegated to low man on the ownership's totem pole.

Stovey established two significant milestones in 1885. In a game on July 16 at Sportsman's Park I, Stovey hit the 45th home run of his career, off the Browns' Jumbo McGinnis. The two-run clout made him the major-league career leader in home runs. On September 28 Stovey hit his final home run of the season, and the 50th of his career, off Pittsburgh Alleghenys rookie hurler John Hofford. Stovey was the first player to hit 50.

Stovey finished the season batting over .300 for the third consecutive year. Playing in a league-leading 112 games, the Athletics' player-manager finished with a .315 average, 130 runs scored, 27 doubles, 9 triples, 13 home runs, and 75 RBIs. His runs scored and home run totals led the Association. With Stovey at the helm, the Athletics finished in fourth place with a 55-57 record, 24 games behind the champion St. Louis Browns. Stovey never managed a major-league team again and finished his big-league managerial career with a 63-75-2 mark.

On the last day of the 1885 season, Stovey's older brother John Jr., who had served in the Union Army during the Civil War, died. John, who was unmarried, was buried in Cedar Hill Cemetery, where Stovey's parents and his sister Sarah would later be buried.[29]

Desperate to remain competitive in the American Association and with their crosstown National League rivals, the Athletics made another managerial change. Co-owner Simmons, who a year earlier blamed Stovey for the team's troubles, emerged as the new manager to start the 1886 season. The team was mired in sixth place with a 41-55 record before co-owner Sharsig stepped in to lead the team to a 22-17 finish over its last 39 games. The team finished in sixth place.

Stovey's offensive production dipped in 1886. Splitting time between center field, right field, and first base, he batted .294 with 28 doubles, 11 triples, and 7 home runs. But the 29-year-old Stovey led the Association with 68 stolen bases in the first in which stolen bases were an official statistic.

For 1887 the Athletics turned to Stovey's first manager at Worcester, Frank Bancroft. The addition of Bancroft had little impact on team's success. The Athletics had a record of 26-29 and were in fifth place when the manager was fired and replaced by Mason, the third Athletics owner to manage the team in as many years.

Stovey enjoyed a relatively productive year. In 124 games, the majority in the outfield, he batted .286, scored 125 runs, hit 31 doubles, and stole 74 bases. He hit only four home runs and before the end of the season he was passed by Detroit Wolverines first baseman Dan Brouthers as the leader in career home runs. It was the only season in which Stovey didn't lead the American Association in at least one major offensive category.[30]

On August 2 Stovey lost another member of his family. John Sr., Stovey's father, succumbed to a heart attack at the age of 77.[31]

The Athletics' revolving door of managers continued as Sharsig returned to guide the team in 1888. Stovey was the everyday left fielder for the 81-52 Athletics, who finished in third place 10 games behind the St. Louis Browns. Stovey finished with a .287 batting average, 127 runs scored, 25 doubles, a league-leading 20 triples, 9 home runs, 65 RBIs, and 87 stolen bases. On May 15 he hit for the cycle in a 12-3 victory over Baltimore Orioles.

That season the strong-armed Stovey participated in a long-distance throwing contest sponsored by the *Cincinnati Enquirer.* Stovey's heave of 123 yards 2 inches on the fly was good enough for second place, behind Ned Williamson,[32] who won the competition with a throw of 133 yards 11 inches.[33]

The Athletics repeated their third-place finish under Sharsig in 1889, a season that was one of Stovey's finest. Playing all 137 games in left field, he batted .308 and recorded career highs in runs scored (152), doubles (38), home runs (19), and RBIs (119). (His home-run total was considered a greater accomplishment by many baseball historians than Williamson's 27 in 1884.) Stovey regained the record for career home runs when he slugged his 80th and 81st against Lee Viau at Cincinnati's League Park on August 13. Stovey joined Charley Jones as the only players to hold the career record for home runs at two different times.

War broke out in major-league baseball after the 1889 season when the Brotherhood of Professional Base Ball Players announced the creation of the Players' League for the 1890 season. Stovey was a hot commodity and was courted by the new league's Boston Reds. He found the prospect of playing closer to his wife's hometown of New Bedford too appealing to pass up and signed with the King Kelly-managed Reds, ending his seven-year stint in the Association.

Despite playing only seven of the circuit's 10 campaigns, Stovey's 76 home runs and 883 runs scored are the most in American Association history. He also ranks in the top 10 of nearly every other category, including games played, batting average, slugging percentage, total bases, hits, and stolen bases.

Stovey was the Reds' everyday right fielder in 1890 and hit .298 with 26 doubles, 13 triples, and 12 home runs, the third highest total in the Players' League behind Hardy Richardson (16) and Roger Connor (14). He drove in 88 runs, scored 145 runs, and had a career-high 97 stolen bases, helping the Reds to an 81-48 record as the team finished in first place 6½ games ahead of the Brooklyn Ward's Wonders and captured the Players League championship. On September 3

Stovey became the first player to hit 100 home runs when he hit one off former Athletics teammate Jersey Bakley in Boston.

After the collapse of the Players' League after the 1890 season and the subsequent ratification of the new National Agreement, it was presumed that Stovey would return to the Athletics and resume his record-setting Association career. The new National Agreement stated that "everyone was supposed to return to the teams that had reserved them in 1889."[34] However, an administrative error on the part of the Athletics left Stovey and former Athletics teammate Lou Bierbauer unprotected and declared free agents.

Stovey opted to accept the National League's Boston Beaneaters' offer of $4,200 a season, the highest salary of his career.[35] The Beaneaters, led by manager Frank Selee, were coming off a fifth-place finish in 1890 and were confident the aging star could help them capture the National League championship.

On April 1, 1891, three weeks before the start of the season, Stovey and his wife welcomed their fourth daughter, Rachel. The infant, who also had a twin sister who was stillborn, did not survive infancy and died on June 6.

Despite the loss of his infant daughter, Stovey played a key role in the Beaneaters' run to the National League Pennant – his third championship team in three different leagues. Stovey was primarily used as a corner outfielder (39 games in left field and 96 games in right field). In 134 games he hit .279 with a league-leading 20 triples, 16 home runs, 271 total bases, and a .498 slugging percentage. He had a team-leading 95 RBIs and 57 stolen bases.[36] It was the last great season of Stovey's career.

Stovey started the 1892 season in one of the worst slumps of his career, and on June 20 he was released by the Beaneaters. At the time of his release he was hitting an anemic .164 with no home runs and 12 RBIs. Nearly three weeks later, the 35-year-old Stovey was signed by the last-place Baltimore Orioles. On July 21 he repeated his 1884 feat of hitting three triples in a single game during a 10-3 victory over Pittsburgh. In 74 games with the Orioles, Stovey rediscovered his hitting stroke and batted .272 with 4 home runs and 55 RBIs.

Stovey also started the 1893 season slowly. After hitting only .154 in eight games, he was released by Baltimore. Three days later, on May 25, the 35-year-old Stovey signed with Brooklyn Grooms. In 48 games with the Grooms, he hit .251 with one home run and 29 RBIs. Time and injuries had taken its toll on the one-time slugger. On June 8 he hit the final home run of his career in the Grooms' 7-6 victory over the Browns. It was his 122nd career home run, the major-league high. He played in his last major-league game on July 29.

Stovey's record lasted until 1895. Stovey was third on the list all-time home run list (behind Roger Connor and Sam Thompson) as late as 1920, the year Babe Ruth began to single-handedly usher in the live-ball era.

His major-league career behind him, Stovey was reunited with King Kelly when he played briefly for Allentown in the Pennsylvania State League. Then he became the player-manager for New Bedford of the New England League.

After retiring from baseball, Harry Stovey ceased to exist. The ex-player resumed use of the name he was born with, Harry D. Stow. In 1895 he joined the New Bedford police force and served for 28 years. While patrolling his beat along the city's waterfront one day in 1901, Officer Stow spotted a seven-year-old boy who had fallen between two piers and was struggling in the water. He dived in and saved the boy's life.[37] Soon afterward he was promoted to sergeant for bravery and became a captain in 1915. In 1922 his wife of 43 years, Mary, died. He retired from the police force in 1923.

Stovey died at his daughter's house in New Bedford on September 20, 1937. He was 80 years old. He is buried in New Bedford's Oak Grove Cemetery next to his wife and two of his daughters, Harriet and Rachel. At the time of his death, few New Bedford residents knew that Officer Stow was Harry Stovey, one of the greatest baseball stars of the nineteenth century.

Whether or not Stovey belongs in the Hall of Fame has been a topic of conversation among baseball historians for years. In 1936 he received six votes for the Hall of fame, the only year he appeared on the ballot. He outpolled both Kid Nichols and Jim O'Rourke, both of whom were later inducted into Cooperstown.[38] In 1983 a poll of SABR's nineteenth century research committee voted Stovey and Pete Browning as the two players of that era most deserving to be in the Hall (excluding those already enshrined).[39] In 2011 SABR members selected Stovey as the Overlooked 19th Century Base Ball Legend.[40]

Statistically, a strong case can be made for Stovey's enshrinement in the Hall of Fame. In addition to being an early home-run king – Stovey finished in the top four in home runs 10 times, leading the league in five of those seasons – he was one of the early game's great doubles and triples hitters. Stovey finished his 14-year major-league career with 348 doubles and 176 triples. He had 912 RBIs, an impressive number considering he often batted in the leadoff position early in his career.

As of 2019, Stovey's 509 stolen bases ranked 35th all-time. However, no stolen-base statistics exist for the first six years of his career.

Stovey is also one of only three players to have played in a minimum of 1,000 games and averaged more than one run scored per game. Billy Hamilton and George Gore are the others.[41] Stovey scored 1,495 runs in 1,489 games, including nine seasons of 100 or more runs scored.

Throughout his career it was often said that Stovey had sure hands and a strong, accurate arm with great range. Statistically, he was an above-average first baseman. He finished in the top four in the league in range factor from 1881 to 1885 and in the top five in fielding percentage during the same years. As of 2019, his 165 career outfield assists placed him in the top 100 all-time.

Modern sabermetrics provide a less definitive case for Stovey's inclusion in the Hall of Fame. His black-ink and gray-ink scores of 56 and 210, respectively, are favorable.[42] Stovey led his league in important offensive categories more than 20 times, including extra-base hits five times, runs scored and triples four times, slugging percentage and total bases three times, stolen bases twice, and doubles and RBIs once. However, his WAR scores are less definitive. Stovey's career WAR of 45.2 and seven-year peak WAR of 31.1 are considerably below the average of the 20 left fielders in the Hall of Fame as of 2019. The average career WAR and seven-year peak WAR for left fielders are 65.5 and 41.6, respectively.

Stovey's omission from the Hall of Fame may also be a consequence of revisionist history. Early scoring rules differed and box scores and game accounts offered comparatively little information by today's standards. Later baseball historians went back and revised the American Association's statistics, resulting in a lowering of many the jaw-dropping statistics that were once attributed to Stovey.[43] This, coupled with the fact that the Association, though recognized as a major league, was considered inferior to the National League, may be one reason why Stovey has yet to be elected to the Hall of Fame.[44]

Regardless of whether or not Stovey is eventually enshrined in Cooperstown, he should be remembered as one of the early game's great power hitters and an innovative baserunner who helped revolutionize the national pastime.

SOURCES

In addition to the sources cited in the Notes, the author also relied on Baseball-reference.com and Retrosheet.org.

NOTES

1 Matt Kelly, "19th Century Star Harry Stovey," baseballhall.org/discover-more/stories/pre-integration/stovey-harry Retrieved March 3, 2019.

2 Edward Achorn, *The Summer of Beer and Whiskey.* (New York: Public Affairs, 2006), 76.

3 US Census Records lists the family as both Stow and Stowe. Some records include the family as both Stow and Stowe in the same census. There may have been other children at some point, but nine appear in census records.

4 "CAST: Liberty Cast and Recast." Retrieved from castartandobjects.com/blog/2017/7/4/liberty-cast-and-recast

5 Harry first appeared in US Census Records in 1860 with the surname Stow. The surname on the family headstone in Oak Grove Cemetery in New Bedford, Massachusetts, is Stow. Unhappy with the sound of the bell, Stow and Pass recast the bell as second time in June 1753.

6 "United States Civil War Soldiers Index, 1861-1865," database, *FamilySearch* (familysearch.org/ark:/61903/1:1:FS3M-L28 : 4 December 2014), John P. Stow, Corporal, Company E, 90th Regiment, Pennsylvania Infantry, Union; citing NARA microfilm publication M554 (Washington: National Archives and Records Administration, n.d.), roll 119; FHL microfilm 882,454.

7 Buddy Thomas, "Stovey: City Man Changes the Game," *New Beford Standard-Times,* April 8, 2006. southcoasttoday.com/article/20060408/news/304089946.

8 A cooper is a person trained to make wooden casks, barrels, vats, buckets, tubs, troughs, and other staved containers.

9 Matt Kelly, "19th century star Harry Stovey." Retrieved from baseballhall.org/hall-of-famers/pre-integration/stovey-harry.

10 There are multiple records of the Stoveys' marriage. One lists the date as July 21 and others as July 23.

11 "Diamond Dust Early Blown," *Boston Globe,* January 16, 1881: 2.

12 Benjamin McArthur, *Actors and American Culture, 1880-1920* (Philadelphia: Temple University Press, 1984): 7-11, cited by Charlie Bevis in "Frank Bancroft," SABR BioProject. Retrieved from sabr.org/bioproj/person/48535bb7.

13 Charlie Bevis, "Worcester Nationals ownership history," Retrieved from sabr.org/research/worcester-nationals-ownership-history.

14 Philip Lowry, *Green Cathedrals* (New York: Walker & Company, 2006), 243.

15 Achorn, 77.

16 Stolen bases did not become an official statistic until 1886.

17 Peter Morris. *Game of Inches: The Stories Behind the Innovations that Shaped Baseball. New, Revised and Expanded One-Volume Edition.* (Chicago: Ivan R. Dee, 2010), 188.

18 Alfred Spink, *The National Game* (St. Louis: National Game Publishing Company, 1910), 186.

19 Achorn, 226.

20 Achorn, 226-227. Some accounts of the game report that Stovey scored the winning run on a wild pitch. According to his obituary in *The*

Sporting News, he single-handedly sealed the championship for the Athletics in the final game of the season against Louisville when, in the 10th inning, he singled, stole second, went to third on an infield out, and scored on a wild pitch thrown by pitcher Guy Hecker.

21 Achorn, 240.

22 Achorn, 240.

23 William McNeil, *The King of Swat: An Analysis of Baseball's Home Run Hitters from the Major, Minor, Negro and Japanese Leagues* (Jefferson, North Carolina: McFarland & Company, Inc., 1997), 36.

24 Williamson's 27 home runs in 1884 were largely attributed to the fact that in White Stocking Park (a.k.a. Lake Front Park), the field's dimensions were 180 feet down the line to left, 280 feet to left-center, 300 feet to dead center field, 252 feet to right-center, and 196 feet down the line to right. The right-handed-hitting Williamson hit 25 of his 27 home runs at White Stocking Park and never hit more than nine home runs in any other season.

25 As of 2019 only 11 major-league players had hit two triples in one inning. The feat was most recently accomplished by the Colorado Rockies outfielder Cory Sullivan on April 9, 2006.

26 The American Association expanded to 13 teams for the 1884 season. The league contracted back to eight teams in 1885 and then played its final two seasons (1890 and 1891) with nine teams.

27 Paul Hofmann, "Jud Birchall," SABR BioProject. Retrieved from sabr.org/bioproj/person/8ab5cdb7.

28 Harry Stovey, "Harry Stovey Expresses Himself," *Sporting Life,* December 3, 1884: 3.

29 "Pennsylvania, Philadelphia City Death Certificates, 1803-1915," database with images, *FamilySearch* (familysearch.org/ark:/61903/1:1:JNLH-M3F : March 8, 2018), John P Stow, 09 Oct 1885; citing 797, Philadelphia City Archives and Historical Society of Pennsylvania, Philadelphia; FHL microfilm 2,070,684.

30 John Shiffert, *Base Ball in Philadelphia: a History of the Early Game* (Jefferson, North Carolina: McFarland & Company, Inc., 2006), 132.

31 "Pennsylvania, Philadelphia City Death Certificates, 1803-1915," database with images, *FamilySearch* (familysearch.org/ark:/61903/1:1:JKS5-M3X : 8 March 2018), John P. Stow, 02 Aug 1887; citing 257, Philadelphia City Archives and Historical Society of Pennsylvania, Philadelphia; FHL microfilm 2,078,809.

32 George Tuohey, *A History of the Boston Base Ball Club: A Concise and Accurate History of Base Ball from Its Inception* (Boston: M.F. Quinn & Co., 1897), 217.

33 "Baseball Records: Long Distance Throwing," *World Almanac 1892:* 227.

34 Shiffert, 153.

35 Thomas. After his retirement, Stovey claimed he never earned more than $2,400 per year playing baseball.

36 Billy Nash also recorded 95 RBIs to tie for the team lead.

37 Achorn, 245.

38 David Nemec, *The Beer and Whiskey League: The Illustrated History of the American Association – Baseball's Renegade Major League,* (New York: Lyons & Buford, Publishers, 1994): 238.

39 Lew Lipset, "Grandpa Was Harry Stovey," *The National Pastime,* Vol. 4, No. 2 (Cooperstown, New York: Society for American Baseball Research, Winter 1985): 84.

40 "Overlooked 19th Century Base Ball Legends." Retrieved from sabr.org/overlooked-19th-century-baseball-legends. Browning was selected in 2009 and Deacon White, who was elected to the Hall of Fame in 2013, was selected in 2010.

41 Gabriel Schechter, "Harry Stovey: Forgotten Five-Tool Star," The National Pastime Museum, May 9, 2013. Retrieved from thenationalpastimemuseum.com/article/harry-stovey-forgotten-five-tool-star.

42 The Black-Ink Test is named so because league-leading numbers are traditionally represented with **Boldface** type. The score is a measure of how often a player led the league in a variety of "important" stats. Similarly, the Gray-Ink test measures a player's appearance in the top 10 of the league in "important" stats. It is important to note that Stovey played during an era when 8 to 10 teams were typically the norm. These two comparative measures disadvantage modern players who played in 14- to 16-team leagues.

43 For decades after his retirement, Stovey was credited with having a career batting average of .321 and setting the single-season stolen-base record of 156 in 1888.

44 Schechter.

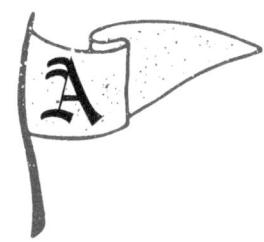

CUB STRICKER

By Chris Jones

Cub Stricker was a nineteenth-century second baseman who played for seven different clubs over an 11-year major-league career (1882-1885, 1887-1893). Affectionately referred to as Cub because of his diminutive stature – he was 5-feet-3 inches tall and weighed between 135 and 140 pounds – the right-handed-hitting and -throwing Stricker was considered an average hitter with fair speed who covered a great deal of ground defensively.[1] Stricker's feisty style of play personified the grit and determination that the 1883 Philadelphia Athletics exhibited on their run to the American Association title.

John A. Stricker was born on June 8, 1859, in Philadelphia to William and Rachel Stricker. According to the 1870 Federal Census, William worked as an "iron moulder," while Rachel stayed home, "keeping house." John was the youngest of what is believed to have been six children in the household, although records are unclear on this subject. The family lived in the eastern part of the 17th Ward of Philadelphia. John did not attend college, and began his professional baseball career in 1882 with the Athletics.

In Stricker's debut, on May 2, 1882, the Athletics defeated the Baltimore Orioles 10-7 in Philadelphia's Oakdale Park. Stricker batted eighth and walked twice, stole a base, and scored two runs. The stolen base came at a particularly opportune time, in the eighth inning with the Athletics trailing 7-6. After stealing second, Stricker took third on a muff of the throw and then proceeded to score the tying run. Wrote the *Philadelphia Inquirer,* "The game was full of errors, many of them being excusable from being sharp hit and bounding balls, which were very difficult to judge."[2] That was a generous description of the contest, as the teams combined for 23 errors. The game also included a scary moment: Athletics catcher Jack

O'Brien was briefly knocked unconscious after being struck in the neck by a foul tip but "after a short recess, O'Brien pluckily resumed his position and played the game out."[3] The newspaper aptly described the game as "very exciting."[4]

Overall, the 22-year-old Stricker had a solid if unspectacular rookie season in professional baseball, batting .217 with no home runs, 18 RBIs, and 34 runs scored. He made 52 errors at second base and appeared in two games as a relief pitcher, totaling seven innings pitched and a 1.29 ERA. While he continued in future seasons to commit a high number of errors by today's

Courtesy of T. Scott Brandon.

Cub Stricker.

119

standards, he completed his career with a fielding percentage of .907 as a second baseman and was known as one of the more accomplished second basemen of his time. The Athletics finished the 1882 season in second place, with a 41-34 record.

Stricker improved significantly in his sophomore season, batting .273 with one home run and 40 RBIs in 89 games. The 1883 Athletics also saw an uptick in their performance, and won the AA pennant with a record of 66-32, one game ahead of the St. Louis Brown Stockings. Stricker continued to play with the Athletics through the 1885 season before joining the Atlantas of the Class-B Southern Association in 1886. Eight teams made up the league – Atlanta, Augusta, Charleston, Chattanooga, Macon, Memphis, Nashville, and Savannah.

Blondie Purcell managed the Atlantas, who finished in first place. As for Stricker, the *Atlanta Constitution* reported, "The playing of Stricker at second base could not be equaled. His batting and base running was the finest ever seen south."[5] Another time, the newspaper called Stricker "unquestionably the best second baseman ever seen in Atlanta."[6] For the season, Stricker played in 85 games and recorded a .243 batting average with 50 runs scored, 58 stolen bases, and 4 home runs. He also pitched 7⅔ innings in two games and compiled a 1.17 ERA. Besides winning the pennant, Atlanta became the first team to play a game without an error, and Stricker hit the first home run in the league.[7] The league lasted just one season. *The Times* of Philadelphia, reporting on September 5 that the league had folded, called it "a disgrace to base ball this year," saying a number of players had caused trouble related to issues such as drunkenness, and adding that the reputation of some umpires was less than stellar.[8]

On November 7 two American baseball teams left for Cuba to give enthusiastic Cuban baseball players lessons about playing the game. There were three baseball clubs in Havana, which played in a championship series in February. The American teams, named "Philadelphia" and "Athletic," gave their lessons at Matanzas and Cienfuegos. Stricker played second base for the "Philadelphia" team.[9]

From 1887 to 1889 Stricker played for the Cleveland Blues. The Blues played in the American Association in 1887-88, then moved to the National League in 1889 as the Cleveland Spiders. Stricker was the captain of the team in 1887, and on June 14, in a return to his old stamping grounds in Philadelphia, fans showed their affection for him when they gave him a standing ovation and a basket of flowers with an eagle topping the basket. The Spiders defeated the Athletics, 6-4. Stricker batted leadoff and got a hit, stole two bases, and scored a run.[10] For the season Stricker batted .264 with two home runs and a career-high 86 stolen bases. The Spiders, however, concluded the season in eighth (last) place with a record of 39-92.

Stricker followed his debut season with Cleveland with another solid campaign in 1888, playing in 127 games and amassing 115 hits for a .233 batting average with 60 stolen bases and a career-high 12 innings pitched. He committed 57 errors at second base, an improvement from the 80 errors he made at the position in 1887. The Spiders fared marginally better as a team in 1888, finishing with a 50-82 record and in sixth place in the American Association. When the team joined the National League in 1889, it was greeted with skepticism. The *St. Louis Post Dispatch* lamented, "What on earth will the League do with Cleveland? It once proved a failure as a League city, and is a no better ball city now than then."[11] This sentiment proved to be well founded; the Spiders stumbled to a sixth-place finish with a 61-72 record. But they were noted for a strong infield and the *Press Herald* of Pine Grove, Pennsylvania, identified Stricker as a bright spot, writing in July that he "so far has outplayed all the League second basemen."[12] The *Salt Lake Herald* also touted Stricker's defensive abilities:

The star of the infield is Stricker, known also as the "Cub," for the reason, no doubt, that he is 30 years old and rather short in stature. … He is a fair batter, a most marvelous fielder, and a base runner of the first grade. In his position he has no superior. He always plays a magnificent game.[13]

The 1890 season brought with it great strife and change within the game. A third major league, the Players League, was formed as a protest of what players believed had been unfair treatment by team owners. Stricker wanted to jump to the league's Cleveland Infants for the 1890 season, but the Spiders sued him, declaring that the reserve clause in his contract bound him to them.[14]

Many other clubs filed lawsuits against players attempting to enjoin them from jumping to the Players League. However, multiple court rulings refusing to enjoin player movement on these grounds, most notably in the case of Brotherhood leader John Montgomery Ward, convinced teams to no longer pursue such suits as they related to the 1890 season and Stricker was permitted to play for the Infants. The *Boston Globe* referred to Stricker during the season as "one of the most outspoken brotherhood players in the country."[15] The Infants finished in seventh place in 1890 with a 55-75 record. Stricker turned in a .244 average in 127 games, with a career-high 65 RBIs.

Lack of financing doomed the Players League after one season, and Stricker was once again looking for a new home. He found it with the Boston Reds of the American Association, who used manager Arthur Irwin to recruit Stricker.[16] With the Reds, he continued to be recognized as a superior second baseman. The *Boston Globe's* early-season appraisal: Stricker "is every ounce a ball player and a pound or two over. His great work at second gained him the applause of the afternoon, and his head work on several instances could only be appreciated by thorough cranks of the game."[17] Stricker's play contributed to a championship season as the Reds' 93-42 record surpassed the second-place St. Louis Browns by 8½ games. Stricker played in 139 games and hit .216 with 54 stolen bases.

Just a year after navigating the folding of the Players League, Stricker once again was forced to change teams when the American Association went out of business after the 1891 season. He was assigned to the St. Louis Browns, where he was named the team captain.[18] He lasted only 23 games with the team, however, and was stripped of his captaincy after he jumped into the stands and punched a fan who had been heckling the team.[19] He was quickly traded to Pittsburgh for pitcher Pud Galvin.[20] Stricker never played for the Pirates; he was again quickly dealt, this time to the Baltimore Orioles for pitcher William "Adonis" Terry.[21] The Orioles finished dead last with 46 wins and 101 losses, 54½ games behind the pennant-winning Boston Beaneaters. Though the Orioles played poorly, Stricker posted his highest batting average since 1887, hitting .264 during his time with the Orioles.

A lowlight of Stricker's season occurred on the night of August 4 in the reading room of the team hotel in Boston, the United States Hotel. Stricker and outfielder William "Jocko" Halligan had been good-naturedly razzing each other when the substantially larger Halligan left the room, returned, and without warning struck Stricker in the face.[22] Stricker later claimed that the fight was as much his fault as it was Halligan's, but it was Stricker's right cheekbone that was broken and Halligan who was suspended without pay for the remainder of the season.[23] Despite the injury, Stricker was advised to sit out only one game, which the Orioles lost 6-4. Club Vice President John Waltz acknowledged, "Without Stricker we are without a head."[24]

After the season Stricker packed his baseball suitcase once again, joining the Washington Senators for the 1893 season. It was an abbreviated season for Stricker, who played in only 59 games and once again proved unable to avoid controversy. On August 5 the Senators were in Philadelphia to take on the Phillies. A contingent of fans in the right-field stands had been heckling Stricker for much of the game, and a faux cheer arose from the crowd after he made a nice catch of a difficult fly ball. This was apparently the last straw for the second baseman turned outfielder. Stricker attempted to scare the fans by throwing the baseball at the fence in front of them, but the ball skidded over the railing and struck fan William Wright, breaking his nose and knocking him out. Stricker was "quietly arrested and taken to an adjoining station house, where he was subsequently released on his own recognizance."[25] At the end of October, the case went before Philadelphia's Common Pleas Court, where it turned out that Wright was not exactly a model citizen. The court denied the request to have Stricker arrested again and decided that he should pay no court costs.[26]

The lowly Senators struggled through a miserable season themselves, finishing in last place with an anemic 40-89 record. They ended 46 games behind Boston. For Stricker, his final major-league season was unquestionably his worst, even without considering his legal troubles. He hit only .179, managing only

Cub Stricker.

Public domain.

39 hits in 218 at-bats. Stricker was not yet ready to give up the game, however, and joined Providence of the Eastern League for the 1894 season. The club finished in first place with a 78-34 record. In 108 games, Stricker batted .282 and recorded 123 hits, 88 runs scored, and 52 stolen bases. He stayed with the team in 1895 as well, continuing to provide solid second-base play.

In 1896, Stricker was released by Providence and caught on with Pottsville of the Pennsylvania State League. Stricker was the team captain. He also played a short stint for the Springfield Maroons in the Eastern League, even playing through a broken finger so that he would continue to be paid. Toward the end of the season, he played for a third team, in Norristown, Pennsylvania. Despite his ever-advancing age, Stricker bounced around Pennsylvania with a number of amateur teams for years in such places as Philadelphia and Norristown. When he played with the Philadelphia Professionals in 1904, he stole four bases on April 30. Stricker also got a hit, and his team won by a score of 15-8. He even played second base in Cumberland in 1912 at age 52![27]

Throughout his baseball career, Stricker was well known for bunting, as a place hitter, and for his speed in completing double plays.[28] He was also notorious for convincing umpires to call a runner out despite only having bluffed a tag. After one game where four visiting runners had been called out going to second base when "to everybody in the stands, it looked as if Cub never got within 10 feet of a man," Stricker was asked how many of the runners he actually touched. He replied, "What's the use of touching 'em and running the risk of getting spiked. ... All you got to do is to make a pass at 'em and then roll the ball back to the pitcher. Honest, there ain't an umpire in this league who can see further than his nose."[29]

After another game in which Harry Stovey, whom Stricker called "the best base stealer that ever lived," was called out three times at second base, Stricker said, "I'll hold up my right hand today and swear that I didn't come within six inches of touching him once."[30] He added, "[W]hat a snap the infielders had back in my day. Why, I didn't put the ball on one out of four of the base stealers when I was playing second, but I almost always got the decision."[31]

Stricker worked as a milk wagon driver during the offseason for a number of years during his playing days, and continued to do so even after leaving professional baseball. The 1910 US Census lists Stricker as a real estate agent. In 1890, at age 30, he married a woman named Hannah, age 42. Stricker and Hannah had no children, and lived in Huntingdon Pike, Rockledge, Pennsylvania. This Census also listed Mary Meister, Hannah's widowed sister, as living in the couple's home.

Stricker died at age 77 on November 19, 1937, from a combination of bronchopneumonia, generalized arteriosclerosis, and myocardial degeneration. He is buried at West Laurel Hill Cemetery in Bala Cynwyd, Pennsylvania, as is Hannah, who died from a cerebral hemorrhage at the age of 90 on January 26, 1939.

SOURCES

In addition to the sources cited in the Notes, the author consulted Retrosheet.org, Ancestry.com, and Baseball-Reference.com. I would also like to acknowledge the research of Michael Wagner and Paul Hofmann, which contributed greatly to this piece.

NOTES

1   "The Home Team: Sketch of the Men who Constitute the Local Teams," *Sporting Life*, April 15, 1883: 2.

2   "The Athletics Win the First Game from the Baltimores – Other Contests," *Philadelphia Inquirer*, May 3, 1882: 3.

3   "The Athletics Win the First Game from the Baltimores – Other Contests."

4   "The Athletics Win the First Game from the Baltimores – Other Contests."

5   "The Atlanta's Victory," *Atlanta Constitution*, April 16, 1886: 8.

6   "A Good Game," *Atlanta Constitution*, May 18, 1886: 8.

7   "First on Records for 1886," *Boston Globe*, April 14, 1886.

8   "Base Ball News."

9   "Base-Ball," *Chicago Tribune*, November 7, 1886.

10 "Today's Games," *Star Tribune* (Minneapolis), June 15, 1887.

11 "Base Ball Brevities," *St. Louis Post-Dispatch*, October 20, 1888: 7.

12 "The National Game," *Press Herald* (Pine Grove, Pennsylvania), July 19, 1889: 1.

13 "The Diamond Field," *Salt Lake Herald*, August 20, 1889: 2.

14 Gossip of the Ball Field," *Sun* (New York), March 2, 1890: 5.

15 "'Spiders' in Town," *Boston Globe*, May 16, 1890: 3.

16 "Stricker for Second," *Boston Globe*, February 11, 1891: 7.

17 "Orioles Warble," *Boston Globe*, April 24, 1891: 9.

18 "Over 13,000 Persons See the Cleveland-Cincinnati Game," *Boston Globe*, May 2, 1892: 5.

19 Mike Eisenbath, *The Cardinals Encyclopedia* (Philadelphia: Temple University Press, 1999), 361.

20 "Stricker Traded for Galvin," *Chicago Tribune*, June 15, 1892: 6.

21 "Juggling Over Player Genins," *Chicago Tribune*, June 16, 1892: 7.

22 "Halligan's Quick Anger," *Washington Evening Star*, August 5, 1892: 8.

23 "Halligan's Quick Anger."

24 "Halligan's Quick Anger."

25 "Stricker Lost His Temper."

26   "Cub Stricker's Capias," *Times* (Philadelphia) October 28, 1893: 6.

27   "New Cumberland Wins," *Philadelphia Inquirer*, July 5, 1912: 12.

28   "John Stricker," *Boston Globe*, August 14, 1904.

29   "Hot Air Is Cooled by Water Pitcher," *Oklahoma News*, December 10, 1906: 3.

30   "Foxy Ball Player Was 'Cub' Stricker," *Evening Star*, September 5, 1908: 9.

31   "Foxy Ball Player Was 'Cub' Stricker."

SELECTED GAMES

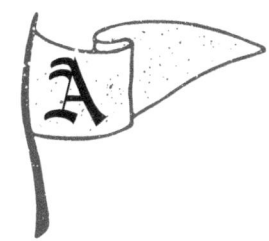

AN OPENING DAY WHITEWASH

MAY 1, 1883: PHILADELPHIA ATHLETICS 4, ALLEGHENYS OF PITTSBURGH 0, AT EXPOSITION PARK II, PITTSBURGH (UPPER FIELD)

By John Zinn

Many of the Athletics faithful in the crowd of over 10,000 who watched the final exhibition game of the spring between their American Association heroes and the new Philadelphia team in the National League must have left the Jefferson Street Grounds in Philadelphia not knowing quite what to make of their team's prospects for the coming 1883 season.[1] Clearly management had upgraded the roster, especially with the addition of first baseman Harry Stovey and pitcher Bobby Mathews. Indeed, so talented was the team's lineup that *Sporting Life* anointed the Athletics as the "strongest [club] in the American Association."[2] Yet this supposed juggernaut had lost three straight exhibition games to the upstart Quakers, of whom very little was expected in their first season in the National League, before rallying to take the final three contests.[3] Perhaps even the Athletics themselves weren't sure what to expect as they headed for the train station for the long ride to Pittsburgh for the 1883 season opener against the Alleghenys at Exposition Park.[4]

Since the Athletics spent the evening hours on the train, the players were not tempted to test management's 11:30 P.M. curfew designed to curtail carousing. Even without such a restriction, however, the Philadelphia team was probably in better condition than the Alleghenys, who were "reputed to be the hardest drinking team of all-time."[5] Nor were the Pittsburgh club's concerns limited to the condition of their players because there was so much water on the field from spring rains that the game was at risk.

But Exposition Park had two fields and the upper one was sufficiently water-free to allow the game to be played. An estimated crowd of between 1,500 and 2,500, a fairly good crowd by Allegheny standards, turned out to watch the game played under mostly cloudy skies with temperatures in the low to mid-60s.[6] Hung over or not, the Allegheny players had to face the Athletics' new ace pitcher, 31-year-old veteran right-hander Bobby Mathews. Entering his 11th major-league season, Mathews was coming off a bounce-back season in 1882 with the Boston Red Stockings. Mathews went 19-15 with a 2.87 ERA as he overcame arm trouble that had plagued him for five seasons. Although he was only 5-feet-5 and 140 pounds, Mathews effectively changed pitches and speeds to confuse batters whose weaknesses he knew all too well.[7] Mathews' repertoire included a curveball and a spitball, both of which he used to hold the home team scoreless for the first four innings.[8]

The Athletics were equally stymied by southpaw Denny Driscoll of Pittsburgh. Driscoll, who had posted a 13-9 season with a league-leading 1.21 ERA in 1882, held the Athletics scoreless through four innings. Philadelphia's fortunes changed for the better in the fifth, however, aided by some sloppy fielding by the home team. Fred Corey reached first base on a

THE BALL SEASON OPENS.

The Times (Philadelphia), *May 25, 1883.*

A DISPLAY OF POOR BATTING.

The Alleghenys Whitewashed Yesterday by the Athletics.

Subhead from the Pittsburgh Daily Post, *May 2, 1883.*

throwing error by third baseman Joe Battin and that miscue was followed by a wild pitch by Driscoll and a bad throw to second by Jackie Hayes, the Pittsburgh catcher. With the door to home plate thus set ajar, consecutive singles by Ed Rowen, Bob Blakiston, and Mathews himself sent three runs across the plate.[9] The Athletics added another run in the eighth when Jack O'Brien doubled to drive in Mike Moynahan, who had singled.[10] In fact, all, but one of Philadelphia's runs were superfluous as Mathews shut out the Alleghenies on four hits. Hayes, Pittsburgh's catcher, had two of those hits, including a double that made him the only Allegheny to reach second. (He advanced no farther.)[11] Mathews did walk one opposing batter (he may have been helped by the fact that it took seven balls for a walk at this time in baseball history), but struck out seven while benefiting from one double play behind him.[12] Mathews also collected two hits, as did Moynahan, O'Brien, and Blakiston. Stovey, who reportedly "could do everything on a ball field, and do it better than almost anyone else," was held hitless, but on this day, at least, he wasn't needed.[13]

Mathews received accolades from the *Philadelphia Inquirer,* which noted that the "Alleghenies could not understand Mathews' manipulation of the sheep skin,"[14] while the *Times* (of Philadelphia) called it a "walk-over" because Pittsburgh didn't have "the ghost of a chance against Matthews' pitching."[15] Apparently when the home team did have a baserunner, he ran the bases poorly, which both papers cited as an additional reason for Philadelphia's victory, although they provided no details.

The shutout was the 15th of Mathews' long career (he would have five more), but his Opening Day whitewash of the Alleghenys was the only one the Athletics recorded in 1883. Back home in Philadelphia, the result must have made those worried about the team's prospects feel somewhat more confident, at least for one day. And those inclined to bet on their local heroes could take additional comfort from the *Times's* conclusion that unless Pittsburgh improved, "Philadelphia people can bet on a certainty in the remaining games on their own club."[16] This proved to be sage advice as the Athletics dominated the Alleghenys and won 12 of the 14 games between the two teams.

SOURCES

In addition to the sources cited in the Notes, the author consulted Baseball-Reference.com and Retrosheet.org.

NOTES

1 "The Athletics Third Victory," *Philadelphia Inquirer*, May 1, 1883: 3.

2 "The Home Team: Sketch of the Men who Constitute the Local Teams," *Sporting Life*, April 15, 1883: 2.

3 David Nemec, *The Beer and Whiskey League: The Illustrated History of the American Association – Baseball's Renegade League* (Guilford, Connecticut: Lyons Press, 2004), 44-46.

4 *Philadelphia Inquirer*, May 1, 1883: 3.

5 Nemec, 48-49.

6 Philip J. Lowry, *Green Cathedrals: The Ultimate Celebration of Major League and Negro League Ballparks* (New York: Walker Publishing Company, 2006), 184; *New York Clipper*, May 12, 1883: 117; *National Republican* (Washington, DC), May 2, 1883: 1; *Pittsburgh Post-Gazette*, May 2, 1883: 4A.

7 John Shiffert, *Baseball in Philadelphia: A History of the Early Game, 1831-1900* (Jefferson, North Carolina: McFarland & Co, 2006), 108; Brian McKenna, "Bobby Mathews," SABR BioProject. sabr.org/bioproj/person/e7ad641f.

8 McKenna; *Pittsburgh Daily Post*, May 2, 1883: 4.

9 *Pittsburgh Daily Post; New York Clipper.*

10 *New York Clipper.*

11 *Pittsburgh Post-Gazette*, May 2, 1883: 2.

12 *Cincinnati Enquirer*, May 2, 1883: 2.

13 Shiffert, 107.

14 *Philadelphia Inquirer*, May 2, 1883: 8.

15 *Times* (Philadelphia), May 2, 1883: 1.

16 *Times* (Philadelphia).

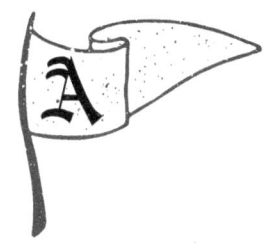

ATHLETICS EXTEND SEASON-LONG WINNING STREAK TO 10 GAMES

MAY 14, 1883: PHILADELPHIA ATHLETICS 11,
NEW YORK METROPOLITANS 1,
AT POLO GROUNDS (1), NEW YORK

By Eric Miklich

"United! Brooklyn and New York by the Great Bridge. The Mighty Structure Completed," loudly proclaimed the *Brooklyn Daily Eagle* on May 24, 1883.[1] Extensive accounts of the history of the formation of the New York Bridge Company on April 16, 1867, including the peaks and valleys of the massive project, were detailed for three days by the *Eagle*. Upon the Brooklyn Bridge's opening, it was reported that over 150,000 people crossed over the East River.[2] While the celebration over the bridge continued, so did the business of baseball.

Major-league baseball had been absent from America's largest city since 1876, when the Mutual Club was suspended from the National League for failing to complete its final Western road trip in September. New York rejoined the fray when the Metropolitans entered the American Association in 1883 and the Gothams joined the NL the same year.

Philadelphia, America's second largest city, had its 1876 NL club suspended for the same reason as the Mutuals; however, when the American Association began operations in 1882, the Athletics reemerged, and in 1883 Philadelphia placed a second club in the National League.

Baseball had survived and expanded without the money and influence of the nation's two largest cities for over five seasons. The exposure New York and Philadelphia each offered could only strengthen the business of baseball.

In 1882, the Athletics finished second to Cincinnati in the American Association, 11½ games out of first. The city of Cincinnati was also returning from a one-year hiatus from major-league baseball, when it joined the American Association. Upon the Athletics' return, they employed 24 players in 1882; however, the club retained only four for the 1883 campaign. They allowed 26-game winner Sam Weaver to seek employment elsewhere and replaced him with legend Bobby Mathews, a career 191-game winner. Mathews' résumé included four consecutive seasons of 25 wins. He was the winning pitcher in the first professional league game played in the National Association, in

THE BALL FIELD.

The Athletics Win a Sweeping Victory in New York Over the Metropolitans.

The Times (Philadelphia), *May 25, 1883.*

1871. Mathews and his Kekiongas of Fort Wayne shut out the Forest Cities of Cleveland, 2-0.

Philadelphia, with its rebuilt roster, started the 1883 season very strong, jumping out to a 13-1 record, which easily led the American Association. Cincinnati, which started out 4-0, was second at 8-5, followed by Louisville at 7-6 and New York at 8-7, 5½ games out of first place. Philadelphia's one setback was a 15-7 loss to Baltimore on May 9 in the final game of their series. Since then, the Athletics were undefeated in nine games. On the 24th, in victory number 10, it was the contributions of two holdovers from the 1882 roster, catcher Jack O'Brien and second baseman Cub Sticker, that led the way offensively

Temperatures were in the low 70s with fair skies the afternoon the Great Bridge opened and more than 10,000 spectators[3] turned up north of the historic festivities at the Polo Grounds I[4] to see if the Metropolitans of New York could end Philadelphia's good fortune.

The first game of the series featured the pitching matchup of future Hall of Famer Tim Keefe of New York and Philadelphia's Bobby Mathews. It was the third time in the young season that Keefe and Mathews faced each other, with Mathews winning both of the first two games. The right-handed Keefe, in his fourth major-league season and first in New York, entered the game with a record of 6-5. While with Troy of the NL, Keefe was a sub-500 pitcher. Mathews, a veteran right-hander, had an early-season record of 7-1.

According to the *Times* of Philadelphia, "The game was one of the poorest played here this season and was one-sided from the beginning to end."[5] Philadelphia scored a run in the second inning and three in the third inning, while holding the Metropolitans scoreless. After both teams failed to score in the fourth inning, the Athletics, aided by sloppy fielding by the Metropolitans, unloaded on Keefe and scored seven runs to open up an 11-0 lead. The Mets committed 10 errors, five of them by rookie second baseman Sam Crane.

New York was held to two hits until the sixth inning, when it got two more, including right fielder Chief Roseman's second double of the game. This brief success led to the home team scoring its only

two runs of the day. Mathews allowed only two more hits over the final three innings in the 11-2 victory. The Athletics totaled 13 hits against Keefe. O'Brien and Stricker led the way with three hits each, with O'Brien collecting a triple. Harry Stovey and player-manager Lon Knight both added a pair of hits.

Mathews went the distance and earned the victory, improving his record to 8-1. Keefe, who struck out seven Athletics, took the loss, dropping his record to 6-6. Charlie Daniels was the umpire and time of the game was 2 hours and 10 minutes.

Mathews, who struggled during the second half of the season, went on to finish with a record of 30-13. Keefe, who led the league with 68 starts, 68 complete games, and 619 innings pitched, finished the season with a record of 41-27.

Philadelphia's 10-game winning streak was the team's longest of the season. The St. Louis Browns would closely chase the Athletics for the entire season, allowing Philadelphia little chance to relax. The Athletics put together three more significant winning streaks during the season. They won six games in row twice, June 21-30 and July 28-August 4, and seven in a row September 4-13.

Philadelphia stumbled in the final week of the season but recovered to win the pennant by one game over St. Louis in what was the closest finish to that point in a major-league pennant race. New York finished in fourth place with 54 wins.

SOURCES

In addition to the sources cited in the Notes, the author relied on Baseball-reference.com and Retrosheet.org, and articles in the *Cincinnati Commercial Gazette, Philadelphia City Item, Pittsburgh Commercial Gazette,* and *Sporting Life.*

NOTES

1   "United! Brooklyn and New York by the Great Bridge," *Brooklyn Daily Eagle,* May 24, 1883: 1.

2   *Brooklyn Daily Eagle.*

3   "Athletic vs. Metropolitan," *New York Clipper,* June 2, 1883: 173.

4   David Nemec, *The Great Encyclopedia of Nineteenth Century Base Ball, 2nd Edition* (Tuscaloosa: University of Alabama Press, 2006): 272.

5   "The Ball Field: The Athletics Win a Sweeping Victory of the Metropolitans in New York," the *Times* (Philadelphia), May 25, 1883: 3.

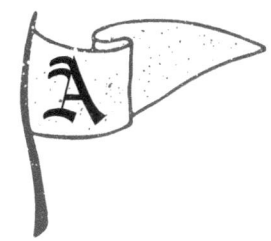

JUNE 21, 1883: ATHLETICS END SEASON'S LONGEST LOSING STREAK, RETAKE FIRST PLACE

PHILADELPHIA ATHLETICS 14, CINCINNATI RED STOCKINGS 5, AT BANK STREET GROUNDS, CINCINNATI

By Mike Huber

It had been a very long week for the Philadelphia Athletics. They had played five games from June 13 to 20 and had dropped all five, scoring a total of only nine runs while allowing 40. They had lost an extra-innings game at home to the Louisville Eclipse and had been shut out twice on the road by the Cincinnati Red Stockings.

Philadelphia was in its second season as an American Association franchise. In 1882, the Athletics had never lost more than four games in a row en route to a second-place finish. They had started the 1883 season by winning their first four games, 14 of their first 15, and 17 of their first 19. They were 18-3 in the month of May, but that month had ended. Suddenly, the Athletics pitching staff was allowing more runs, their offense wasn't scoring, and Philadelphia started the month of June by suffering defeat in five of eight games. Its lead in the American Association evaporated, and after losing the first three games of a four-game series with the Red Stockings, Philadelphia was tied with Louisville for second place, both a half-game behind the St. Louis Browns.

The defending champion Cincinnati squad, meanwhile, had also won its first four contests in 1883, but

had won only 13 of 24 leading up to this series. By taking the first three games, the Red Stockings had climbed into fourth place, but they were only a game out of first. The race for the pennant was tight.

Philadelphia and Cincinnati faced off on a Thursday afternoon in the final game of the series. The *New York Tribune* wrote, "The Athletic nine, after playing in wretched form the past week, rallied here today in their game with the champions."[1] Philadelphia's *Times* started its account of the game with, "The tables were turned this afternoon."[2] Cincinnati manager Pop Snyder sent right-hander Harry McCormick to the mound. The Red Stockings' top starter was Will White,[3] and White had started and won the previous four games for Cincinnati, so Snyder decided to rest his ace. McCormick was making just his 10th start of the year. Philadelphia's skipper, Lon Knight, countered with righty Fred Corey, a utility player who occasionally pitched. This was only his third start of the season, as Bobby Mathews was the usual workhorse on the mound for the Athletics.

GAME FOR THE ATHLETICS

The Times (Philadelphia), *June 22, 1883.*

Before a crowd of 3,200 at Cincinnati's Bank Street Grounds, Snyder won the toss and opted to bat first. The Red Stockings jumped on Corey in the first inning, scoring four runs. Hick Carpenter rolled a grounder to third base, but third baseman George Bradley missed it. Carpenter moved to second on a passed ball. Charley Jones walked and both runners advanced to third on a wild pitch and scored when Corey made a fielding error. John Reilly reached on Cub Stricker's miscue at second base and scored when Bradley dropped a pop fly by Joe Sommer. Phil Powers followed with an RBI triple to deep center, the only true hit of the inning. Powers kept going, trying for an inside-the-park home run, but he was tagged out at the plate. The fans were cheering, as their team was ahead, 4-0. After this frame, Bradley was moved to center field, switching positions with Jack O'Brien, prompting the *Times* to report, "Both men played faultlessly from that point on."[4]

In the bottom of the first inning, Jones misjudged Harry Stovey's fly ball to center. The ball bounded over Jones's head and Stovey raced around the bases all the way to third. The Athletics scored two runs on two hits and a Cincinnati error.

Three Philadelphia runners reached in the second (two hits and a walk), but none of them scored, as two were caught trying to steal second. In the third, though, Stovey again started things with a single to left. He moved to second when Sommer made a high throw back to the infield. Knight lined a pitch to Sommer in left and the outfielder misplayed it, plating Stovey. Knight reached second on a passed ball and then scored when shortstop Chick Fulmer couldn't cleanly play a grounder by O'Brien. O'Brien later came around to score. In the fourth inning, three errors and one hit (Stovey's third of the game) led to two more Philadelphia tallies, and the score was 7-4, Philadelphia.

In the top of the fifth, Cincinnati's McCormick and Jones stroked back-to-back three-baggers, getting one of the runs back, but in the bottom half, the Athletics scored twice more on Mike Moynahan's triple, a double by O'Brien, and a single by the pitcher Corey.

The Red Stockings threatened in both the sixth and seventh innings without success. For the game, they left four runners on base. Philadelphia added a solo run in the sixth (on "two hits and a couple of errors"[5]), but in the seventh, the wheels came off the Cincinnati defense. Four runs came across the plate on several more errors and just four base hits. The final two frames were scoreless. When the game ended, Cincinnati was "most serenely drubbed by the Philadelphians by a score of 14 to 5."[6]

McCormick had trouble as the Cincinnati twirler. Too often he grooved the ball where the Athletics could hit it, and "the result was the boys in the field were kept busy chasing the sphere. The visitors pounded the cover off of one ball and badly damaged another."[7] Corey held the Red Stockings to just four hits, although three of them were triples. Otherwise, he was effective as he "sent in the balls with gun-shot speed."[8] Together, the two pitchers made four wild pitches and their batterymates allowed three passed balls.

According to the *Cincinnati Enquirer*, only three of Philadelphia's 14 hits "were gained by good work. The rest were gifts from an accumulation of muffed flies, passed balls, wild pitches, fumbled grounders and wild throws."[9] Of the Red Stockings players, only Bid McPhee was solid in his defense, "the only one of the Cincinnatis who played up to the standard throughout."[10] Five Athletics players reached first on errors, either on fumbled grounders or bad throws.

Philly's Bradley was branded by the *Cincinnati Enquirer* as a dirty player. ("There is no more unpopular tosser in either association."[11]) While running to first on a grounder, Bradley hit Cincy first baseman Reilly in the mouth. It might have been an accident, but from the Cincinnati viewpoint, Bradley "can play ball, but he can't play the gentleman."[12]

When the day's other games had ended, Philadelphia found itself once again in first place. The Browns had been defeated by the New York Metropolitans. After this victory, the Athletics won their final five games in June, and they went 39-21 during the final three months, never losing more than three games in a row. Philadelphia (66-32) held on to win the pennant by one game over St. Louis (65-33), while Cincinnati finished third (61-37).

SOURCES

In addition to the sources mentioned in the Notes, the author consulted baseball-reference.com, retrosheet.org, and sabr.org.

NOTES

1   "Baseball News," *New York Tribune*, June 22, 1883: 2.

2   "Game for the Athletics," *Philadelphia Times*, June 22, 1883: 4.

3   Cincinnati's White led the American Association in wins (43), shutouts (6), and earned-run average (2.09) in 1883. Two of those shutouts came in this series against Philadelphia.

4   "Game for the Athletics."

5   "An Off Day," *Cincinnati Enquirer*, June 22, 1883: 5.

6   "An Off Day."

7   "An Off Day."

8   "An Off Day."

9   "An Off Day."

10   "A Victory for the Athletics," *St. Louis Globe-Democrat*, June 22, 1883: 6.

11   "An Off Day."

12   "An Off Day."

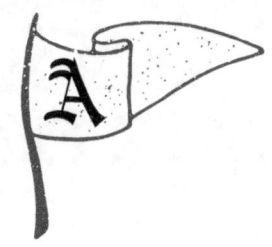

LON KNIGHT HITS THE FIRST NATURAL CYCLE IN MAJOR-LEAGUE HISTORY

JULY 30, 1883: PHILADELPHIA ATHLETICS 17, PITTSBURGH ALLEGHENYS 4
AT JEFFERSON STREET GROUNDS, PHILADELPHIA

By Mike Huber and Bill Nowlin

Through the 2021 season, there were 334 cycles hit in major-league baseball games.[1] The first one was hit by Curry Foley of the Buffalo Bisons on May 25, 1882. The second was hit by Lon Knight, the right fielder and manager of the Philadelphia Athletics, on July 30, 1883. Knight, who was a native of Philadelphia, became the first player to accomplish the rare feat that we today term a "natural cycle," meaning he got his hits in the order of total bases: first the single, then a double, then the triple, and finally the home run. In an American Association game in which Philadelphia demolished the Pittsburgh Allegheny Club, 17-4, Knight had five of his team's 23 hits to pace the attack.

The Athletics had charged out of the gate with an 18-3 record during the month of May but had dropped off the pace. Standing at 38-18, the Athletics were second in the American Association standings, 1½ games behind the St. Louis Browns and 4½ games ahead of third-place Cincinnati.

It was an ideal day for baseball. Afternoon temperatures were in the mid-70s under fair/clear skies and an unseasonably low humidity of 60 percent. The game featured "fine fielding and heavy batting" by Philadelphia.[2] There is no play-by-play available for the game, but according to newspaper accounts and the box scores, the home-team Athletics batted first, as they won the coin toss and elected to bat.[3] Approximately 6,000 spectators packed the Jefferson Street Grounds to watch the match, and "the enthusiasm was kept up throughout the game."[4] Starting for St. Louis was right-handed rookie Bob Barr.[5]

Philadelphia wasted no time and put three runs across the plate in the first inning. With one out, Harry Stovey singled and stole second. Knight followed with an RBI single to center. Knight then stole second. Barr walked Mike Moynahan and Jack O'Brien, loading the bases. Fred Corey laced a double, plating two runners.[6] Barr then worked out of the jam, holding the damage to three runs.

Right-hander Bobby Mathews pitched for the Athletics. The Athletics' diminutive 31-year-old ace, who had come over from the National League's Boston Red Stockings, was in the process of resurrecting his career, which had been sidetracked by a sore arm.[7]

The visitors put runners on base in each of the first two innings but did not capitalize. In the top of the third, Knight doubled to right field. He advanced to third on a wild pitch and came home when O'Brien tripled. The Athletics added two runs in the fourth, even though Knight popped out to Barr. In the bottom half, Joe Battin "sent the ball over [Bob] Blakiston's head for a home run."[8] The score was now 6-1, Athletics.

In the top of the sixth, Mathews reached on an error by third baseman Battin. Barr threw another wild pitch, moving Mathews up a base. Stovey doubled to left, driving in his pitcher. Knight "followed with a hit to center field for three bases"[9] and a run batted in, and then he scored on a fly out by Moynahan. Three more runs for the home team.

Stovey led off the top of the eighth with a single and trotted home on "Knight's terrific line hit to extreme left center for a home run."[10] Knight had just hit for a natural cycle. O'Brien scored on a hit by Corey. The Allegheny club posted two runs in its half of the eighth, on two hits, a passed ball, a walk, and an error.

The game was out of reach in the ninth, but Philadelphia was not finished. Consecutive singles by George Bradley, Mathews, and Jud Birchall loaded the bases. Stovey lined a single to center, and two runners came home. Knight followed with his second two-bagger, adding two more runs batted in to his line for the day. For the visitors, Ed Swartwood and Billy Taylor singled to start the last of the ninth, and Swartwood scored the game's final run on a passed ball. The game ended with a score of 17-4. Only 12 of Philadelphia's runs were earned, and only two of Pittsburgh's.

The *Philadelphia Inquirer* informed its readers that three Athletic players, Knight, Stovey, and O'Brien, starred on offense, and that Knight made "a total of eleven bases, on a home run, a three-bagger, and two doubles."[11] However, the paper's box score listed him with five hits and 12 total bases (which accounted for the missing single). The *Times*, also a Philadelphia newspaper, gave its readers the straight scoop, noting that "Knight led for the home club in work with the willow, making a single, two two-baggers, a triple-bagger and a home run."[12] In addition to accomplishing the rare feat of hitting for the cycle, Knight had scored five runs and had driven in six.

Further, "the heavy batting of the home club really demoralized the visitors and their fielding was not first-class by any means."[13] The Athletics had six runners reach because of Pittsburgh errors. Every Philadelphia player except Blakiston got at least one hit. Mathews picked up the victory. By the end of the season, Mathews had pitched 381 innings and finished with a record of 30-13, the most victories he

BASE BALL.

Defeat of the Alleghany by the Athletic— Fine Fielding and Heavy Batting.

Philadelphia Inquirer, *July 31, 1883.*

had posted in nine years. For the losers, Barr ended the 1883 campaign with a record of 6-18. One bright spot for the Alleghenys was that four batters – Swartwood, Taylor, Battin, and Frank McLaughlin – each collected two hits.

First baseman Stovey was was 5-for-6 with a double in this contest. Although he didn't homer in this game, Stovey's 14 round-trippers set a league record for the most home runs in a season, eclipsing Boston Red Stockings left fielder Charley Jones's 1879 mark of 9.[14] O'Brien, the team's catcher, was 4-for-5 with a triple.

As of the end of the 2021 season, only 17 batters have hit for the cycle in natural order, an achievement rarer than a perfect game.[15] The most recent was the Texas Rangers' Gary Matthews Jr., who accomplished the feat on September 13, 2006, in a game against the Detroit Tigers at Comerica Park. Montreal's Brad Wilkerson is the only player to accomplish a natural cycle in just four plate appearances.[16]

The 30-year-old Knight had been playing professional baseball since 1875, but this was his first season with Philadelphia's Athletic Club.[17] On a team that batted .262 for the season, Knight's .252 average was only seventh-best among the regular players. This was his only home run of the season and just the second of his eight-year career, but it was enough to hit for the cycle.[18]

The umpire was listed as John O. "Kick" Kelley and the game lasted 2 hours and 10 minutes, prolonged by the 23 base hits and two or three bases on balls collected by the Athletics.[19] The Allegheny club had nine hits. The win by the Athletic club, coupled with a 6-5 loss by the Browns to the Eclipse of Louisville, saw the Athletics take first place in the standings, by the narrowest of margins, .684 to .683.[20] They were still two games behind the Browns in wins but had two fewer losses. By season's end, the 66-32 Athletics edged the 65-33 Browns by exactly one game, five games ahead of third-place Cincinnati.

SOURCES

In addition to the sources mentioned in the notes, the authors consulted Baseball-Reference.com and Retrosheet.org.

NOTES

1   A good listing of cycles is available at baseball-almanac.com/hitting/Major_League_Baseball_Players_to_hit_for_the_cycle.shtml. Twenty-six players have hit for the cycle more than once. See a listing at mlb.com/news/players-who-hit-for-multiple-cycles-c295035814. Four are "tricyclists" – each with three cycles to his credit: John Reilly, Bob Meusel, Babe Herman, and Adrian Beltre. One cycle has been hit in postseason play – by Brock Holt of the Boston Red Sox on October 6, 2018. It was the second cycle for Holt – his first was on June 16, 2015. Christian Yelich of the Milwaukee Brewers hit for the cycle twice in a 20-day stretch (August 29 and September 17, 2018).

2   "Base Ball," *Philadelphia Inquirer*, July 31, 1883: 2.

3   "Heavy Work at the Bat," *Philadelphia Times,* July 31, 1883: 4.

4   *Philadelphia Inquirer.*

5   The Alleghenys finished in seventh place in the eight-team league, with a record of 31-67.

6   The *Inquirer* says it was hit down the right-field foul line, but the *Times* said it was the left-field foul line.

7   Mathews was 5 feet 5½ inches tall and weighed about 140 pounds.

8   "Base Ball."

9   "Base Ball."

10   "Base Ball."

11   "Base Ball."

12   "Heavy Work at the Bat."

13   "Heavy Work at the Bat."

14   Stovey held the single-season home-run record for just one year. In 1884 Chicago White Stockings third baseman Ned Williamson socked 27 home runs, a single-season mark that stood for 35 years until 1919, when Boston Red Sox outfielder and pitcher Babe Ruth hit 29. Stovey was also the major leagues' career home-run leader from 1889 through 1894, when he retired with 122.

15   Given the available play-by-play data. The 17 players who hit for a natural cycle are:

Lon Knight, Philadelphia (AA), July 30, 1883

Pete Browning, Louisville (AA), August 8, 1886

Bill Collins, Boston (NL), October 6, 1910

Bob Fothergill, Detroit (AL), September 26, 1926

Tony Lazzeri, New York (AL), June 3, 1932

Fred Carroll, Pittsburgh (NL), May 2, 1887.

Charlie Gehringer, Detroit (AL), May 27, 1939

Leon Culberson, Boston (AL), July 3, 1943

Jim Hickman, New York (NL), August 7, 1963

Ken Boyer, St. Louis (NL), June 16, 1964

Billy Williams, Chicago (NL), July 17, 1966

Tim Foli, Montreal (NL), April 21, 1976

Bob Watson, Boston (AL), September 15, 1979

John Mabry, St. Louis (NL), May 18, 1996

Jose Valentin, Chicago (AL), April 27, 2000

Brad Wilkerson, Montreal (NL), June 24, 2003

Gary Matthews Jr., Texas (AL), September 13, 2006

16   Mabry and Matthews had the four different hits in just four at-bats, but each also drew a walk in the game.

17   Knight played in 1875 and 1876, but then played on minor-league clubs in New England until he returned to the National League in 1880. He retired after the 1885 season.

18   Knight hit two home runs in a three-year American Association career and one in his five years in the National League.

19   Accounts differ.

20   retrosheet.org/boxesetc/1883/07301883.htm#1.

ATHLETICS CONTINUE DOMINANCE OF ALLEGHENYS

AUGUST 1, 1883: PHILADELPHIA ATHLETICS 19,
PITTSBURGH ALLEGHENYS 2,
AT JEFFERSON STREET GROUNDS, PHILADELPHIA

By Joel Rippel

The Philadelphia Athletics continued a season-long trend in their final meeting of the season with the Pittsburgh Alleghenys. The Athletics, who had won 11 of the first 13 games between the two in 1883 while outscoring the Alleghenys 104-55, maintained their dominance of the Alleghenys with a 19-2 victory. Athletics first baseman Harry Stovey provided an interesting footnote to the onslaught by becoming the first major-league player to hit 10 home runs in a season.

An estimated crowd of 3,000 turned out for the Wednesday afternoon game played at Jefferson Street Grounds under clear skies with afternoon temperatures hovering in the mid-80s. A gentle 10 MPH breeze blew out of the southwest toward Jefferson Street, which ran behind right field.

The Athletics, who had won the first three games of the current series by outscoring the Alleghenys 44-18, started the day in first place in the American Association with a 40-18 record and a half-game lead over the St. Louis Browns (41-20). The Alleghenys were mired in sixth place with a 20-40 record, a distant 21 games behind the Athletics.

But the series finale began with question marks for both teams. Athletics pitcher Bobby Mathews, who

had started and won the first two games of the series and had started 37 of the Athletics' first 58 games, was injured in their 16-12 victory over the Alleghenys the day before.

"In the second inning, while Mathews (who had started the game in right field) was trying to steal second, he sprained his ankle badly and had to be carried off the field," the *Philadelphia Times* reported.[1] Athletics infielder Cub Stricker was apparently battling injuries as well and was "in a crippled condition covering second base," according to the *Pittsburgh Post-Gazette*.[2]

The Pittsburgh pitching staff had to adjust when its ace left-hander Denny Driscoll, who had started 30 of the Alleghenys' first 60 games, left the team the previous day after "being called home at noon on account of the dangerous illness of his wife."[3]

Driscoll's replacement was right-hander Jack Neagle, who was with his third major-league team of the season after being released by Philadelphia of the National League and Baltimore of the AA. Neagle's

ONE ADDED TO THE SCORE
THE ATHLETICS WIN ANOTHER GAME

The Times (Philadelphia), *August 2, 1883.*

last start with Baltimore was a 7-3 loss to the Athletics on July 20.

Neagle had started two of the first three games of this series – an 11-2 loss to the Athletics on July 28 and the 16-12 loss the day before this game. The start the day before was brief – he was pulled in the second inning after he "was hit hard in the first inning."[4]

Stovey, who had doubled and hit a home run the previous day, got the carnage started in this game.

The Athletics won the toss and elected to bat first. After Jud Birchall walked to lead off the A's first inning, Stovey "electrified the audience by hitting the ball over the left-field fence, about four feet inside the foul line."[5] According to the *Philadelphia Inquirer*, "Stovey made the longest hit ever seen on the ground, sending the ball twelve feet over the left field fence, completing the circuit of the bases long before the ball was returned."[6]

Stovey, who had hit a total of 13 home runs in his first three major-league seasons with Worcester of the National League, made history with his majestic blast by becoming the first major leaguer to hit at least 10 home runs in a season. The previous record was held by Charley Jones, who hit nine home runs in 1879 while playing left field for the Boston Red Stockings of the National League. Stovey finished the 1883 season with 14 home runs, 66 RBIs, and a .304 batting average.

After Stovey's home run, the Athletics added three more runs in the top of the first. Lon Knight doubled and scored on a single by Mike Moynahan. Jack O'Brien followed with another double to score Moynahan and eventually scored on an error by shortstop Frank McLaughlin. At the end of a half-inning, the Athletics led 5-0.

The Athletics added a run in the second when Birchall singled, took third when center fielder Bob Barr let the ball get past him, and scored on a passed ball by Billy Taylor.

Leading 6-0 in the third inning, the Athletics broke the game open with six runs, aided by three errors by the Alleghenys. With two down the Athletics began to parade around the bases. George Bradley reached on an error. Stricker followed with a double, Birchall singled, Stovey walked, Knight singled, Moynahan walked, and O'Brien reached on an error.

Down 12-0, the Alleghenys scored in their half of the third when, with two out, Ed Swartwood doubled, moved to third on a passed ball, and scored on Taylor's single to center.

The Athletics added two more runs in the fourth. Bradley reached on an error by second baseman George Creamer, went to second on a bad throw by McLaughlin, and scored on a single by Stricker, who scored on another Alleghenys error to increase the Athletics' lead to 14-1.

The two teams exchanged runs in the fifth. Moynahan singled and came around to score on a wild pitch and two passed balls. The Alleghenys scored their final run of the game when Barr, Neagle, Swartwood, and Taylor put together four successive hits.

In the top of the sixth, McLaughlin relieved Neagle, who allowed 10 hits and 15 runs while throwing four wild pitches. The right-handed-throwing McLaughlin mopped up the mess and limited the Athletics to single runs in the sixth and seventh innings and two in the ninth.

Knight, Moynahan, and O'Brien each had three hits and Stricker, healthy enough to play, had two hits for the Athletics, who had 16 hits and took advantage of five walks, six passed balls, and eight Alleghenys errors. Stovey, who drew a walk in the six-run third, also singled in Philadelphia's two-run ninth. Only six of the Athletics' runs were earned. Athletics starter Bradley earned the victory by going the distance and allowing just seven hits.[7]

The loss went to Neagle, who was 3-12 with a 5.84 ERA in 16 starts for the Alleghenys. His combined season record with the three teams was 5-23 with a 5.94 ERA in 30 appearances. His 1884 season (11-26 in 38 starts with the Alleghenys), was his last.

Taylor had three hits and Swartwood had two hits for the Alleghenys. Swartwood went on to lead the Association in batting average (.357).

With the win, the Athletics increased their lead to a full game over the idle St. Louis Browns. For the Alleghenys, the 19-2 drubbing was a fitting end to the season series, which saw them defeat the Athletics, 15-2, in the third game of the season, only to have the victory not count in the standings and classified as an exhibition.[8]

SOURCES

In addition to the sources cited in the Notes, the author consulted Baseball-Reference.com, Newspapers.com, and Retrosheet.org.

NOTES

1   "Some More Big Batting," *Philadelphia Times*, August 1, 1883: 4.

2   "19 to 2," *Pittsburgh Post-Gazette*, August 2, 1883: 8.

3   "Some More Big Batting," *Philadelphia Times*, August 1, 1883: 4.

4   "Some More Big Batting."

5   "One Added to the Score," *Philadelphia Times*, August 2, 1883: 4.

6   "Batting for Runs," *Philadelphia Inquirer*, August 2, 1883: 2.

7   The box score in the *Times* gave Philadelphia 14 hits while the box score in the *Inquirer* gave 16. The newspaper accounts also differ on errors and earned runs -- giving Allegheny 10 or 11 errors. One newspaper account has 8 earned runs, the other 6.

8   According to the *Pittsburgh Post-Gazette*, "Under the rules of the American Association all championship games must be umpired by an official umpire, and as Mr. (Charles) Daniels was alleged to be sick yesterday, an exhibition game was played. It was far from satisfactory and had a suspicious look all through. ..." "If It Only Counted," *Pittsburgh Post-Gazette*, May 4, 1883: 2.

ANOTHER EASY VICTORY

AUGUST 18, 1883: PHILADELPHIA ATHLETICS 19, COLUMBUS BUCKEYES 5,
AT JEFFERSON STREET GROUNDS, PHILADELPHIA

By Paul E. Doutrich

The two teams that met at the recently renovated Jefferson Street Grounds in Philadelphia on August 18, 1883, were traveling in very different directions. The Philadelphia Athletics carried the best record in American Association. Meanwhile, the Columbus Buckeyes, in their first season in the Association, had most recently suffered a four-game sweep by the St. Louis Browns. They had lost 12 of their previous 15 games and were just 2½ games out of the league's cellar. A day earlier, in the first of a 16-game Eastern swing, the Buckeyes had been the victims of an 11-1 romp by the Athletics.

Along with the addition of the New York Metropolitans, Columbus brought the American Association in 1883 to eight teams. This would be the Buckeyes' second trip to Philadelphia. Between May 30 and June 4 they had played three games against the Athletics, dropping two. Included on the team roster was the major leagues' first deaf mute, pitcher Ed Dundon. Dubbed "Dummy," he had learned the game while at the Ohio Institute for Education of the Deaf and Dumb. Among other things, the school was known for its exceptional baseball program, which developed numerous professional players. While there, Dundon became the school's star pitcher.

With a crowd of 8,000 to 10,000 watching, the Philadelphias came to the plate first and put two runners on base but were unable to push either across the plate.[1] In the bottom of the inning, Columbus did a bit better. With one out, shortstop John Richmond

singled and went to second when Philadelphia left fielder Jud Birchall let the ball get past him. Known as an outstanding fielder, Birchall later redeemed himself with the Athletics' play of the game, a running, over-the-shoulder catch. A passed ball and a single by former Athletic Pop Smith put the Buckeyes on the board. During the previous season Smith had played 20 games for Philadelphia but his .092 batting average didn't warrant a return. Instead, he headed for Columbus and was having a fine season, leading the league in triples. His RBI gave the Columbus nine its only lead of the day.

In the top of the second inning, the Philadelphias went ahead with three runs. Third baseman Fred Corey led off with a single. Catcher Ed Rowen and second baseman Cub Stricker followed with doubles, scoring two runs. With one out, first baseman Harry Stovey, the team's most dangerous hitter and one of the best in the American Association, smacked a single to center, scoring Stricker with the Athletics' third run.

Philadelphia native Stovey had played the previous three seasons for the Worcester (Massachusetts) Ruby Legs in the National League. Born Harry Stowe, he changed his name to Stovey so that his mother, who abhorred baseball, wouldn't know he was playing professionally.[2] In 1880, his rookie season, Stovey led the league in extra-base hits, and tied for the home-run lead. A power hitter, he was also a fleet and daring baserunner who was always among the league's top basestealers. When the Ruby Legs folded after the

1882 season, Stovey moved back home and joined the Athletics. It was a move that suited him well. His first season in Philadelphia was the best of his 14-year career at bat. In 1883 he led the league in runs scored, doubles, home runs, and extra-base hits, and finished with a .304 batting average.

The Buckeyes clawed back in the bottom of the third. Right fielder Tom Brown opened with a single but was forced at second by Pop Smith. An error by first baseman Stovey got Smith to second and a wild pitch moved him to third. He came home on a ground-ball to second baseman Stricker.

With the help of numerous Columbus errors, the Athletics responded with a pair of runs in the fourth and four more in the fifth. Singles by Bradley, Stricker, and Birchall and a bad throw by the Buckeyes' catcher, Rudy Kemmler, accounted for the two fourth-inning runs. The fifth-inning tallies were aided by a slew of Columbus miscues. Kemmler let a third strike get past him, enabling the Athletics' leadoff hitter, center fielder Jack O'Brien, to hustle to second. He scored when Corey singled to left. Rowen's single scored Corey; aided by "a terrible wild throw," the Philadelphia catcher ended up on third.[3] He scored a batter later when the Buckeyes' second baseman made another bad throw to the plate on Stricker's groundball. One batter later, Stricker scored after "a spectacular over his head catch" by the Buckeyes' center fielder, Fred Mann.[4] Stovey then delivered his third single of the game and ended up on third base as a result of two more errant throws. Mercifully for Columbus, the inning ended with Stovey still at third, but the Athletics led 9-2.

In the bottom of the fifth, the Buckeyes scored twice. Left fielder Harry Wheeler opened with "a rattling hit past shortstop."[5] Richmond dropped a single to right and Wheeler scored on a bad throw to second. Richmond followed him home on a two-out single by Mann. Columbus had closed the deficit to five runs, but the worst was yet to come for the Buckeyes.

As they came to the plate in the sixth, the *Philadelphia Times* reported, the Buckeyes "appeared very tired and played the game through in a listless manner."[6] One Buckeye who should have been particularly tired was pitcher Frank Mountain. He had been on the mound through the entire 11-1 drubbing the previous day and was the recipient of the current pounding. Mountain was a well-traveled pitcher by the time he took the mound against the Athletics. Since becoming a professional in 1880 he had been with five teams, including Worcester, where he had finished the

THE ATHLETICS WIN.

The Times (Philadelphia), *August 19, 1883.*

previous season alongside Harry Stovey, Fred Corey, and Fred Mann. Though he won 26 games in 1883, he also led the American Association with 33 losses and gave up more hits, walks, and runs than any other Association pitcher.

The Athletics tacked on another run in the seventh when Birchall singled to right, stole second, and scored on Stovey's fourth hit. In the eighth inning Philadelphia further demonstrated that on this afternoon "the Athletics had their batting clothes on."[7] Twelve men came to the plate and eight of them scored. The first four hitters – O'Brien, Corey, Rowen, and Bradley – all singled and all scored. With one out Birchall doubled to left, driving in two more. He was followed by Stovey, who tripled. One hitter later, shortstop Mike Moynahan also tripled. The final run of the inning scored when Corey blasted a double, his second hit of the inning, that bounced off the left-field fence.

With the game well out of hand, the Buckeyes mounted one last effort in the bottom of the eighth inning. Not known for his hitting, Mountain drilled his second home run in two days over the left-field fence. He hit three home runs during the entire 1883 season. Mountain's shot closed the Columbus attack for the day. The Athletics finished their scoring in the top of the ninth when right fielder and team manager Lon Knight singled, went to third on another Columbus error, and scored on a long fly ball to left field.

At the end of the day the Philadelphia fans left the Jefferson Street Grounds satisfied that they had seen their hometown nine at its best. The 19-run outburst matched the Athletics' highest run output of the season. Two weeks earlier the Philadelphias had scored 19 runs against Pittsburgh. The team also solidified its league lead in runs scored. For the season the Athletics averaged 7.35 runs per game, almost two runs more than the league average. More importantly, the win kept the Athletics in first place, two games ahead of the St. Louis Browns.

SOURCES

In addition to the sources cited in the Notes, the author consulted Retrosheet.org, Baseball-Reference.com, and SABR.org.

NOTES

1   "Another Easy Victory," *The Times* (Philadelphia), August 19, 1883: 2.
See also "Sports of the Field," *Philadelphia Inquirer*, August 20, 1883: 2.
The Times reported, "The crowd numbered nearly ten thousand," while
the *Inquirer* claimed that *"about 8000 persons witnessed"* the game.

2   Matt Kelly, "19th Century Star Harry Covey" Pre-Industrial
Series (2016), National Baseball Hall of Fame.

3   "Another Easy Victory."

4   "Another Easy Victory."

5   "Another Easy Victory."

6   "Another Easy Victory."

7   "An Easy Time," *Cincinnati Enquirer*, August 19, 1883: 2.

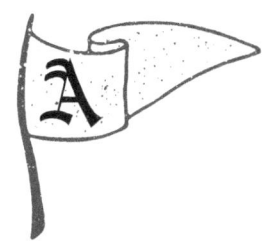

HARRY STOVEY ESTABLISHES NEW SINGLE-SEASON HOME-RUN RECORD

SEPTEMBER 18, 1883: PHILADELPHIA ATHLETICS 13, CINCINNATI RED STOCKINGS 12, AT BANK STREET GROUNDS, CINCINNATI

By Michael Wagner with Paul Hofmann

The Tuesday afternoon game at Bank Street Grounds was the middle game of a three-game set between the Philadelphia Athletics and Cincinnati Red Stockings. The two teams and the St. Louis Browns had been locked in a season-long pennant race. As the season wound down, the Athletics, with a record of 62-27, held a 3½-game lead over the Browns. The defending American Association champion Red Stockings, who had fallen off the pace in recent weeks, entered the game in third place with a record of 56-34, 6½ games behind.

The pitching matchup featured two of the American Association's greatest hurlers. Will White drew the starting assignment for the Red Stockings. The bespectacled right-hander was on his way to a winning a league-leading 43 games and leading the circuit with a 2.09 earned-run average. He was opposed by arm-weary Bobby Mathews. The Athletics reluctantly turned to the right-hander after having lost faith in Jumping Jack Jones, who had been knocked around for 11 runs and 13 hits in the series opener, and fear of overworking George Washington Bradley.[1] The Athletics' pitching staff was simply depleted by this point in the season.

The Red Stockings won the coin toss and elected to bat first. With one out in the top of the first, first baseman John Reilly tripled to left and scored on a passed ball. The Athletics responded in a "business-like manner" with five runs in their half of the frame.[2] Jud Birchall led off with a single past shortstop and moved to second on a passed ball. Harry Stovey followed with a single to left to score Birchall. Stovey stole second and scored when Lon Knight hit a ball past shortstop that Jimmy Macullar, who was playing in place of sore-armed Chick Fulmer, was too slow to reach. Mike Moynahan followed with a hot liner to second that Bid McPhee only managed to knock down as Knight advanced to second. Jack O'Brien flied out to right, allowing Knight and Moynahan to advance a base. Fred Corey sent an easy fly ball to left that Joe Sommer muffed, allowing another two runs cross the plate. One out later, Cub Stricker singled to drive in the Athletics' fifth run of the inning.

The score remained 5-1 until the top of third, when Corey sent a long drive to left-center and circled the bases for the first major-league home run of his career. This made the score 6-1 and it stayed that way until the top of the sixth.

The Red Stockings' White led the sixth off with a single that "curved out of Corey's reach" at third. The pitcher came around to score when Hick Carpenter sent a fly ball over the head of Birchall in left for a triple. "Reilly next tapped the ball down in front of the plate, but Rowen threw wildly to Stovey, and Stricker in turn fired the ball over Corey's head, and both 'Hick' and Long John came home," the *Cincinnati Enquirer* reported.[3] This cut the Athletics' lead to 6-4.

The Athletics answered with four runs in their half of the sixth. Rowan opened the inning with "a tap to Macullar, who, after fumbling it awhile threw wildly to Reilly," allowing Rowan to reach second.[4] Stricker followed with a home run to left-center that was "assisted by slow fielding."[5] After Mathews fouled out to Pop Snyder behind the plate, Macullar failed to come up with Birchall's hit and was sent to play right field, "where he had the pleasure of chasing Stovey's hit for a home-run."[6] It was the 14th and final home run of the season for 26-year-old first baseman, who earlier in the year became the first major-league player to hit 10 home runs in a season. The previous record was held by Charley Jones, who hit nine four-baggers in 1879 while playing left field for the Boston Red Stockings of the National League.

Entering the seventh inning, the Athletics appeared to have a safe 10-4 lead. However, with Mathews tiring and some shoddy Athletics defense, Cincinnati mounted a ferocious comeback. McPhee opened with a single to short center and took second on a passed ball. Macullar plated McPhee with a single past shortstop and White, who was given a second and third opportunity after Corey and Birchall missed pop fouls, singled to put runners on first and second. After Carpenter was called out on strikes, on a couple of questionable strike calls by umpire John Kelly, Knight dropped Reilly's pop fly to right field to load the bases. Jones followed with a bases-clearing triple to right to trim the deficit to 10-8. One out later, Pop Corkhill singled to right to drive in Jones. Corkhill then stole second and scored the tying run when Snyder singled and Moynahan threw wildly to the plate.

With the crowd yelling and cheering wildly, "McPhee brought the spectators up to the highest pitch of enthusiasm by a long hit to left over Birchall's

head on which he made the circuit, bringing Snyder in before him."[7] The inning came to a merciful end when Macullar was retired at first after a dropped third strike. The Red Stockings sent 11 men to the plate and when the dust settled, eight runs crossed the plate and the Red Stockings held a 12-10 lead.

Cincinnati returned the favor with subpar defense of their own in the bottom of the eighth. Mathews reached on an error by Carpenter and hits by Birchall and Moynahan loaded the bases with two outs. O'Brien, who started the game in center field and finished it behind the plate after Rowen's hands gave out, lofted "an easy fly" to right that Macullar failed to handle, allowing two runs to score. After eight innings the score was tied, 12-12.

Neither team scored in the ninth and the Red Stockings failed to push a run across in their half of the 10th. In the bottom of the inning, Stovey pushed an infield single past White and took second on a passed ball. He moved to third on a fly ball by Moynahan. When a pitch ticked off the hands of Snyder, "Stovey daringly broke for home" and outraced the catcher to the plate with the winning run.[8]

The slugfest, witnessed by a crowd estimated at 2,000, was, like many games during the era, marred by sloppy defensive work. The Red Stockings got 15 hits off Mathews and the Athletics collected 14 hits.[9] The time of the game was 3 hours.[10]

The loss all but mathematically eliminated the defending champions. With eight games remaining for the Athletics and seven for the third-place Red Stockings, the best Cincinnati fans could hope for was an improbable tie with the Athletics. The Browns edged the New York Metropolitans, 3-2, and remained three games behind the Athletics, setting up a showdown between the Athletics and the Browns in St. Louis. Meanwhile, back in Philadelphia, a mass meeting of citizens was held at the Athletics' headquarters to begin organizing a reception parade as the city prepared for a much-anticipated championship.[11]

Stovey's reign as the single-season home-run leader was short-lived. The next season Ned Williamson, shortstop for the Chicago White Stockings of the National League, slugged 27 home runs to become the new major-league single-season home-run king.[12]

SOURCES

In addition to the sources cited in the Notes, the author relied on Baseball-reference.com and Retrosheet.org.

NOTES

1   Edward Achorn, *The Summer of Beer and Whiskey*
     (New York: Public Affairs Press, 2006), 201.

2   "Stubbornly Fought," *Cincinnati Enquirer*, September 19, 1883: 2.

3   "Stubbornly Fought."

4   "Stubbornly Fought."

5   "Stubbornly Fought."

6   "Stubbornly Fought."

7   "Stubbornly Fought."

8   Achorn, 201.

9   The box score in the *Times* (Philadelphia) credits the Athletics with 13 hits.

10   The box score in the *Times* (states the time of the
     game was 2 hours and 20 minutes.

11   "The Champions: A Grand Reception to Be Given to the Victorious
     Athletics," *Philadelphia Inquirer*, September 19, 1883: 8.

12   Williamson's 27 home runs in 1884 were largely attributed to the
     dimensions of Chicago's home ballpark, White Stocking Park (a.k.a.
     Lake Front Park). In 1884 the distances were 180 feet down the line
     to left, 280 feet to left-center, 300 feet to dead center field, 252 feet
     to right-center, and 196 feet down the line to right. The right-hand-
     ed-hitting Williamson hit 25 of his 27 home runs at White Stocking
     Park and never hit more than nine home runs in any other season.

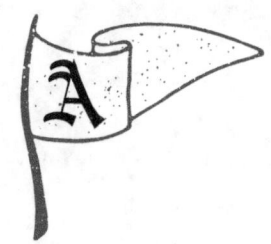

BOBBY MATHEWS WINS 30TH IN WILD GAME IN THE GATEWAY CITY

SEPTEMBER 21, 1883: PHILADELPHIA ATHLETICS 13, ST. LOUIS BROWNS 11, AT SPORTSMAN'S PARK I, ST. LOUIS

By Gregory H. Wolf

It was a battle for the American Association pennant, but "not a good game from a scientific standpoint," opined the *St. Louis Globe-Democrat*.[1] The first-place Philadelphia Athletics (63-28) arrived in the Gateway City to kick off a pivotal three-game series with the second-place St. Louis Browns (61-31). On a season-ending 13-game road swing, the Athletics needed to win just three of their final seven games to secure the championship of the American Association's second season; the Browns needed a miracle. The result was a contest that had everything, noted the *Globe-Democrat*: "home runs, loose fielding, interspersed with brilliant performances, wild throws, muffs, wrangles over points, appeals to and arguments with the umpire."[2]

Baseball fans flocked to Sportsman's Park on the city's north side to take in a Friday afternoon of baseball. The *St. Louis Post-Dispatch* reported that there were at least 8,000 spectators at the game,[3] while the (Philadelphia) *Times* described it as the "largest week-day gathering in the history of the home association" and estimated the crowd at 12,000.[4] The City of Brotherly Love was also baseball-mad. The score was shown in Recreation Park, the Athletics' home

ballpark, while "bulletin boards around newspaper offices were besieged" by fans.[5]

The game pitted two of the league's best right-handed hurlers. Scheduled to start for the A's was rookie Jack Jones, but skipper Lon Knight made a last-minute change, sending his ace, Bobby Mathews, to the rubber because he "always proved to be a terror" to the Browns, reported the *Times*.[6] Just 5-feet-5 and 140 pounds, he was in search of his 30st victory of the season and the 221st of his career, which would tie Tommy Bond for the most wins by an active player.[7] The Browns skipper, Charles Comiskey, called on emerging star Tony Mullane, who had already reached the 30-win plateau for the second consecutive season.[8]

Despite the marquee pitching matchup, the game was sloppy as "both sides exhibited great nervousness," the *Times* wrote.[9] An average of nearly 10 errors was committed in an American Association game in 1883; this game had 31, including 14 by the Browns, who had the league's best fielding percentage.[10] Only four of the game's 31 runs were earned, all of them for St. Louis.[11]

The Browns won the coin toss and chose to take the field. The game commenced at 3:13 and the A's jumped out to a 6-0 lead.[12] Jud Birchall led off with a "corking hit" through shortstop and scored three batters later on shortstop Bill Gleason's throwing error to home.[13] The A's tacked on four more runs in an error-laden third, highlighted by the league's most formidable slugger, Harry Stovey, who smacked one of his league-most 31 doubles.[14] Birchall made it 2-0 when he scored after being caught in a rundown at third. With the bases loaded, Jack O'Brien sent one to left field to plate Stovey; catcher Pat Deasley muffed George Strief's infield relay, enabling Knight and Mike Moynahan to score. In the top of the fourth, Birchall's double to left drove in Cub Stricker for a 6-0 lead. The league's most potent offense, averaging 7.35 runs per game, was cruising.

The Browns revived the "drooping spirits" of the spectators, wrote the *Globe-Democrat*, by scoring three runs in the bottom of the fourth.[15] A turning point came when first baseman Stovey sprained his knee chasing a foul ball by Strief with two men on. Moments later, Stovey attempted to complete an inning-ending double-play but his throw home to nab Hugh Nicol on Strief's grounder was late, giving the Browns their first run.[16] Unable to walk, Stovey exited the game, replaced by George Bradley, a former pitcher and third baseman. Two batters later, Bradley muffed Mullane's high popup, allowing Fred Lewis and Deasley to score. Bradley made four errors in the game, but would emerge as one of the day's heroes.

Each team scored three runs in an action-packed fifth. The A's managed just one hit (O'Brien's double to deep left), but Mullane's "delivery became very unsteady," wrote the *Globe-Democrat*.[17] He walked one and threw two wild pitches, one resulting in a run. The other two were tallied on a fly ball and first baseman Comiskey's wild throw to third attempting to complete a double play. The Browns answered with their heaviest hitting of the game. Comiskey singled, stole second, moved to third on a wild pitch, and scored on Nicol's single. The Browns hit only seven home runs all season, one of which was Lewis's two-run blast over the right-field fence to pull the Browns to within three, 9-6.

The Browns tacked on two more in the seventh inning, which also produced the game's first brouhaha. Nicol began the frame by reaching first on an error. He stole second, but suddenly three A's players, "yelling like Comanches," surrounded umpire Charles Daniels, reported the *Post-Dispatch*.[18] Daniels reversed his decision and called Nicol out, prompting the Browns bench to erupt. It looked as if Nicol and Daniels might brawl. The entire "circus" delayed the game five

THE COMING CHAMPIONS

The Times (Philadelphia), *September 22, 1883.*

minutes, continued the newspaper, and Daniels stood by his second call. Joe Quest accounted for both runs, tripling to left-center to drive in Lewis, and scoring on a passed ball to make it 9-8.

With the game's momentum shifting, the Athletics exploded for four runs in the eighth. Birchall led off with his game-high fourth hit, progressed stations on a passed ball and Mullane's wild pitch, and scored on Knight's grounder that shortstop Gleason fumbled. Run-scoring singles by O'Brien and Fred Corey and another wild pitch by Mullane resulting in a run accounted for the other three tallies to give the Athletics a 13-9 lead.

The Browns answered in the bottom of the frame with three runs. Gleason reached when Bradley (who "could not catch anything," wrote the *Times*)[19] muffed a relay throw. He moved to third on Comiskey's single and scored on Arlie Latham's sacrifice. Nicol's double plated Comiskey, then he stole third and came home when catcher Ed Rowen (who "threw the ball in all directions," lamented the *Times*),[20] fired the ball into left field, committing one of his eight errors.

With the Athletics leading 13-11 to start the ninth, a cold front moved in, dropping the temperature from around 70 at game time to the high 50s.[21] Mullane set down the visitors one-two-three. The skies grew even darker and according to the *Times*, "a regular hurricane had possession of the park and clouds of dust at times hid players from sight."[22] Several A's players surrounded the umpire and asked that the game be called. Daniels, reported the *Times*, "acquiesced and walked to the bench, as through to get his coat at leave the grounds," setting off another brouhaha.[23] The Browns' German-born owner and president, Chris von der Ahe, who had been sitting with his players on the bench, jumped up and ordered Daniels to continue the game. Players began "gesticulating" at one another while spectators were "hooting and hollering" to play ball.[24] Perhaps concerned about a possible riot, Daniels ordered the Athletics to the field, after which the club said it would play the game under protest.

Hit hard in the previous two innings, Mathews took the mound for the final inning. He "proved as invulnerable as ever," gushed the *Times*, and "by his generalship he outwitted the home team and at critical moments his cool head prevented a rattling of his forces."[25] Strief led off with a fly to right field, but the "ball was scarcely distinguishable."[26] Knight muffed the catch and Strief reached second. Mullane popped high to Moynahan at short. Gleason followed with what "seemed like best hit of the day," a blast to deep center field where the much-maligned George Bradley had been moved to start the inning.[27] According to the *Times*, Bradley "lost [the ball] in a great cloud of dust," then caught it.[28] Gleason stayed on first, claiming that he had dropped it. Daniels seemed confused, but called Gleason out. "To the surprise of all," acknowledged the *Globe-Democrat*," Bradley saved the game."[29] Comiskey hit to O'Brien to end the contest in 2 hours and 45 minutes.

The 13-11 victory moved the Athletics to within two games of the title, but the quest for those victories was tension-filled. They split the final two in St. Louis, then traveled to Louisville for a season-ending four-game series with the Eclipse. After losing the first two games, they won the third to claim the title.

Mathews' 30th victory of the season marked a stunning change of fortunes for the Baltimore native. After winning 131 games in the National Association (1871-1875), he bounced around in various independent leagues and for four teams in the National League, winning just 60 big-league games in his next seven seasons (1876-1882). He reclaimed his ace status with the Athletics in 1883, and won exactly 30 games each of the next two seasons. In 1885 Mathews set a big-league record with his 252nd victory and extended the mark until Pud Galvin overtook him in 1888.[30] Mathews retired with 297 victories (and 248 losses), the most in big-league history of anyone not inducted into the Baseball Hall of Fame.

SOURCES

In addition to the sources cited in the Notes, the author accessed Retrosheet.org, Baseball-Reference.com, and SABR.org.

NOTES

1   "A Loose Exciting Game and a Victory for the Athletics," *St. Louis Globe-Democrat*, September 22, 1883: 4.

2   "A Loose Exciting Game and a Victory for the Athletics,"

3   "The Athletics Win a Victory and the Pennant, Also," *St. Louis Post-Dispatch*, September 22, 1883: 9.

4   "The Athletics' Victory," (Philadelphia) *Times*, September 22, 1883: 2.

5   "The Coming Champions," (Philadelphia) *Times*, September 22, 1883: 2. Without radio or television, the scores of baseball games were often displayed inning by inning at many kinds of venues, from newspaper offices to stores. The *Times* noted also that "enterprising news dealers and cigar men in all portions of the city had bulletin boards up."

6   "The Athletics' Victory."

7   This claim deserves a caveat: Bond effectively stopped pitching after the 1880 season and had a record of 221-145. He made only five appearances in 1881 and 1882, losing four decisions. Technically not retired in 1883, Bond did not play big-league baseball. He returned in 1884, going 13-9 in the Union Association and 0-5 in the American Association.

8   The 24-year-old Tony Mullane finished the season with a 35-15 slate in 1883 after a 30-24 record in his first full big-league season. Bobby Mathews was a former star for the Baltimore Canaries and New York Mutuals in the National Association.

9   "The Athletics' Victory."

10   An average of 9.97 errors was committed in American Association games in 1883. The Browns made the fewest (3.96); while the A's (5.95) were ranked seventh in the eight-team league.

11   All of the play-by-play information for this game is from three sources: "A Loose Exciting Game and a Victory for the Athletics," *St. Louis Globe-Democrat*, September 22, 1883: 4; "The Athletics Win a Victory and the Pennant, Also," *St. Louis Post-Dispatch*, September 22, 1883: 9; and "The Athletics' Victory," (Philadelphia) *Times*.

12   Information about the coin toss and the game's starting time from "A Loose Exciting Game and a Victory for the Athletics."

13   "The Athletics' Victory."

14   Harry Stovey also led the AA with 14 home runs, 110 runs scored, and a .506 slugging percentage in 1883.

15   "A Loose Exciting Game and a Victory for the Athletics."

16   According to the *Globe-Democrat*, as Strief grounded to back to the mound, Nicol broke from second to steal third. Mullane's throw to Stovey dispatched Strief, but Stovey's throw to Rowen at the plate was late.

17   "A Loose Exciting Game and a Victory for the Athletics."

18   "The Athletics Win a Victory and the Pennant, Also."

19   "The Athletics' Victory."

20   "The Athletics' Victory."

21   "The Weather," *St. Louis Globe-Democrat*, September 22, 1883: 5.

22   "The Athletics' Victory."

23   "The Athletics' Victory."

24   "The Athletics' Victory."

25   "The Athletics' Victory."

26   "The Athletics' Victory."

27   "The Athletics' Victory."

28   "The Athletics' Victory."

29   "A Loose Exciting Game and a Victory for the Athletics."

30   In the history of major-league baseball, beginning with the conclusion of the first season in the National Association in 1871, only four pitchers have been the career leader in victories at the end of each subsequent season: Al Spalding (1871-1884), Bobby Mathews (1885-1887), Pud Galvin (1888-1902), and Cy Young since 1903.

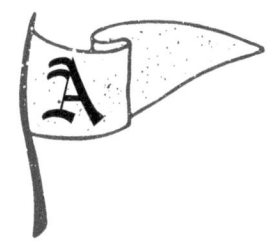

ATHLETICS CLINCH A TIE FOR THE PENNANT

SEPTEMBER 23, 1883: PHILADELPHIA ATHLETICS 9, ST. LOUIS BROWNS 2, AT SPORTSMAN'S PARK I, ST.LOUIS

By Clifford Blau and Paul Hofmann

After a season spent at or near the top of the league and the ultimate prize within sight, the exhausted Athletics arrived in St. Louis on September 20 with a 2-½ game lead over the Browns. As fans back in Philadelphia anxiously awaited news and planned a victory parade, the Athletics and Browns split the first two games. The Athletics hung on to win the series opener, 13-11, as arm-weary Bobby Mathews notched his 30th victory of the season. The Browns countered with a 9-6 victory in the second game. Knowing a victory in the rubber game would guarantee them a tie for first place, the Athletics chose a battery of George Bradley, who'd been hit hard by Cincinnati in his previous start, and Jack O'Brien. The sentiment was that Bradley was ripe to have "his eye knocked out," by the well-heeled, hard charging Browns.[1] St. Louis countered with batterymen Tony Mullane and Tom Dolan.

Unseasonably cool temperatures greeted the record-breaking overflow crowd of 16,800 fans who jammed Sportsman's Park that day.[2] The morning low in St. Louis was a record 43 degrees and temperatures warmed up only to the mid-60s by game time, approximately 15 degrees cooler than the average temperature in St. Louis for that time of year.

Sportsman's Park was one of the finest facilities in the American Association. The renovated former Grand Avenue Grounds opened in 1881 and was an innovative multipurpose entertainment facility. It included "a cricket field … a baseball diamond, cinder paths for 'sprinters,' a handball court, bowling alleys and everything of that sort."[3] Complete with a beer garden in right field and a newly constructed Bulletin Board (out-of-town scoreboard) that owner Chris Van der Ahe had installed in spring of 1883, Sportsman's Park was an oasis enjoyed by St. Louis working class and immigrant populations.

The Athletics' captain, Harry Stovey, won the coin toss and elected to send St. Louis to bat while his team took the field. After the Browns were held scoreless in the top of the first, the Athletics quickly took a 2-0 lead in the bottom half of the inning. Left fielder Jud Birchall led off with a single to right field. Stovey then smashed one into the crowd standing in right-center field. Under normal circumstances, the hit surely would have scored the speedy Birchall. However the ad hoc grounds rule in effect for the game awarded Stovey a double and forced Birchall to stop at third. With runners on second and third and no one down, right fielder Lon Knight grounded out to Arlie Latham at third to score Birchall as Stovey advanced to third.

ST. LOUIS BADLY BEATEN

THE CHAMPION PENNANT ABOUT WON

The Times (Philadelphia), *September 24, 1883.*

A wild pitch by Mullane allowed Stovey to score. The last two batters went out quietly and neither team scored over the next two innings; Fred Corey of the Athletics was the only player to reach base, with a second-inning single.

St. Louis threatened in the top of the fourth when little Hugh Nicol, considered a nineteenth-century forerunner of Ozzie Smith because of his showmanship and acrobatic antics on the field, lined a single to left-center with two out. [4] A passed ball allowed him to advance to second before he stole third. However, Joe Quest watched a third strike go by to end the inning.

In the bottom of the fifth, the Athletics added three runs. Second baseman Cub Stricker singled, stole second, and went to third on a wild pitch. Birchall followed with a slow grounder to first that St. Louis captain Charles Comiskey fielded. He attempted to throw Stricker out at the plate, but Comiskey's throw was late and catcher Dolan foolishly threw to first to get Birchall while Comiskey was out of position. The ball sailed into right field and Birchall took second. Stovey followed with a single scoring Birchall and continued to second when Dolan mishandled the throw. The Athletics plated their third run of the inning when center fielder Fred Lewis, recently reinstated after an alcohol-related suspension, dropped a fly ball off the bat of Knight. [5] At the end of five innings, the Athletics had a commanding 5-0 lead.

The Athletics tacked on another run in the sixth on Corey's walk and, belying his ninth spot in the batting order, a double by Stricker. They kept piling on in the seventh when Stovey hit another grounds-rule double and scored on two more wild pitches by Mullane. The Browns right-hander was charged with five wild pitches in the game.

The Browns, who had been silenced by Bradley on only two hits through the first seven innings, finally managed to push a run across the plate in the eighth thanks to errors by Stricker and shortstop Mike Moynahan. With one out, Mullane reached safely on Stricker's miscue at second. After the Browns pitcher stole second, Dolan sent a grounder to shortstop that was mishandled by Moynahan. Dolan also stole second to put runners at second and third. Moynahan atoned for his error on the very next play when Bill Gleason drove the ball hard up the middle. Moynahan made a "splendid stop" and threw Gleason out at first as Mullane scored the Browns' first run of the game. [6] Comiskey ended the inning when he grounded out to Corey at third, stranding Dolan.

The Athletics increased their lead to eight runs by scoring twice more in the bottom of the inning. Corey singled past shortstop to lead off the inning and center fielder Bob Blakiston followed with a single to center. Three batters later, Birchall sent a two-out double over the head of the left fielder that plated two more runs. After eight innings the Athletics lead was 9-1.

The Athletics appeared to be ready to wrap the game up and celebrate a share of the Association title when the first two Browns batters were retired to start the ninth. A hush fell over Sportsman's Park and the crowd started heading for the exits. However, true to the grit they had shown all season, the Browns failed to go quietly.

Quest singled to center field and advanced to second on a passed ball. Latham followed with what appeared to be a game-ending grounder to Corey at third, but as the remaining crowd rushed onto the diamond, Stovey dropped Corey's throw, and Quest came around to score amid the confusion. The Athletics claimed he hadn't touched third, but umpire Charley Daniels, watching the play at first, hadn't seen it and allowed the run. By this time the crowd covered the whole field in a march to the exits, and it took several minutes to clear the field so play could continue. Once play resumed, left fielder George Strief grounded out to Stricker at second to end the game, which had lasted an hour and 40 minutes.

Now with a 3½-game lead and four games to play against the second-division Eclipse, who had fallen 15½ games off the pace in the season's waning weeks, the Athletics appeared to be a shoo-in for the pennant. As it turned out, they earned it by the skin of their teeth, with only an extra-inning victory in the third game allowing them to capture the American Association flag.

SOURCES

In addition to the sources cited in the Notes, the authors relied on Baseball-Reference.com and Retrosheet. Other sources included the *St. Louis Globe-Democrat* of September 24, 1883, and the *New York Clipper*.

NOTES

1   "Sporting News: The Athletics Demolish the Local Team," *St. Louis Post-Dispatch*, September 24, 1883: 9.

2   David Nemec, *The Illustrated History of the American Association – Baseball's Renegade Major League* (New York: Lyons & Buford, Publishers, 1994), 53.

3   Edward Achorn, *The Summer of Beer and Whiskey* (New York: Public Affairs, 2006), 13.

4   Charles F. Faber, "Hugh Nicol," SABR BioProject. Retrieved from sabr.org/bioproj/person/9cdc28a3.

5   "Notes and Comments," *Sporting Life*, September 24, 1883: 6.

6   "St. Louis Badly Beaten: The Champion Pennant About Won," *The Times* (Philadelphia), September 24, 1883: 1.

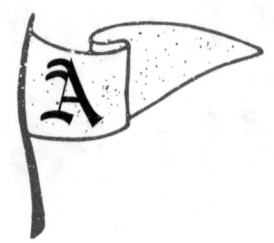

ATHLETICS SECURE AMERICAN ASSOCIATION PENNANT

SEPTEMBER 28, 1883: PHILADELPHIA ATHLETICS 7, LOUISVILLE ECLIPSE 6 (10 INNINGS), AT ECLIPSE PARK I, LOUISVILLE

By Matt Albertson

The Philadelphia Athletics arrived in Louisville for a four-game series on September 26 with a 3½-game lead over the second-place St. Louis Brown Stockings. To win the American Association pennant, either Philadelphia needed to win at least one game against the Eclipse or St. Louis needed to lose one game against the lowly Pittsburgh Alleghenys. Confident of the outcome, club executive Charles Mason left the team for Philadelphia to help prepare for a championship parade when the Athletics returned home. But the Athletics could not catch a break: Pittsburgh proved no competition for St. Louis, losing the first two games of their series, 20-3 and 6-2, while Philadelphia's pitching proved incapable of limiting the Eclipse offense.

On September 28 Philadelphia held a 1½-game lead over St. Louis. With the pennant in the balance, manager Lew Simmons sent the well-rested fan favorite Jumping Jack Jones to the pitcher's box.[1] The right-handed Jones was a late-season pickup by the Athletics, who needed to fortify their arm-weary pitching. He entered the game with a combined record of 10-7 and a mark of 4-2 with the Athletics.[2] Jones was opposed by ace Eclipse right-hander Guy Hecker (28-22).

Louisville captain Joe Gerhardt lost the toss and the Athletics elected to bat last. Philadelphia's Jones was working on five days' rest and the paltry crowd of 500 at Eclipse Park hoped he might perform his famous leap. The *Louisville Courier-Journal* noted that he "caused the spectators much amusement by his antics in the box."[3] Pete Browning led off the affair with a weak fly to left fielder Jud Birchall. Jack Gleason singled to left but was doubled up when Hecker sliced a ball to Mike Moynahan at shortstop. The Athletics were also retired quickly; Birchall flied out to Leech Maskrey in the outfield, Harry Stovey struck out, and Lon Knight was retired by Gerhardt.

The contest remained scoreless until the fourth inning, when the Athletics took the lead. Jones retired Eclipse hitters Jack Gleason, Hecker, and Sleeper Sullivan in order. Knight led off for the Athletics in the bottom of the frame and hit a weak groundball to first base. Next, Moynahan singled to left field, then stole second. With Jack O'Brien at bat, Hecker uncorked a wild pitch and Moynahan scrambled home for the game's first run. Hecker then walked O'Brien (seven balls were required for a walk in 1883). To make matters worse, O'Brien stole second and scored on Fred

Corey's single. Joe Gerhardt and Gleason were then retired to end the frame with the Athletics leading 2-0.

Not content to surrender the game without a fight, the Eclipse rallied to tie the game in the fifth inning. Jumbo Latham reached base on an error and stole second. He scored on a double by Maskrey. Chicken Wolf was then fielded out by third baseman Fred Corey. Next, Tom McLaughlin fouled out to O'Brien. With two outs and one on, Gerhardt was safe at first on an error by Stovey at first base, and Maskrey scored to tie the game, 2-2.

In the Athletics' sixth with one out, Moynahan and O'Brien reached base safely. Moynahan scored on a wild throw. Fred Corey then singled to left field. Both O'Brien and Corey scored on Bob Blakiston's single to center field. Blakiston was caught off second base for the second out. Hecker walked Cub Stricker with two outs but got out of the inning when Jones hit into a fielder's choice, with McLaughlin recording the third out at second base. At the end of six innings, with Hecker laboring to find the strike zone, the Athletics held a 5-2 lead.

The Eclipse took the lead in the top of the seventh inning as Jumping Jack began to falter. The *Philadelphia Press* noted that intense excitement abounded at Eclipse Park. Jones walked Latham to open the frame and he went to second on a single by Maskrey. Both runners scored on a double to right by Wolf. Knight fielded the ball in the outfield and the relay throw from Cub Stricker sailed over O'Brien's head, allowing Wolf to score. Unsettled, Jones walked McLaughlin for the second base on balls of the inning. Gerhardt flied out to Knight and Browning flied to Birchall. With two out and McLaughlin on first, Jones surrendered a single to Gleason. McLaughlin scored when Hecker helped his own cause with a single. Sullivan grounded out to first to end the inning with the Eclipse in the lead, 6-5.

The thousands of fans outside the *Philadelphia Press* offices fell silent each time the game was deadlocked. Now, with the Athletics down by a run in the late innings, the throng were distraught.[4] The Athletics were again on the brink of losing another opportunity to clinch the pennant as they had in the previous two games. Finally, the A's tied the game in the bottom of the eighth inning. Moynahan hit a ball to third and reached second base on an errant throw by Gleason. He advanced to third on O'Brien's fly out to Maskrey and scored on a hit by Corey that tied the game, 6-6.

Jones and Hecker made quick work of their opposition in the ninth inning and the contest moved into

THE PENNANT WON.

The Times (Philadelphia), *September 29, 1883.*

extra innings. In the bottom of the 10th, Hecker walked the hobbling Stovey[5], who limped to second when Hecker uncorked a wild pitch. Knight then ripped a ball to center, advancing Stovey to third. Moynahan strode to the plate with Philadelphia's season and pennant on the line. "Hecker held the ball, stared at the plate, took a run, and fired. Moynahan swung and connected. At the crack of the bat, left fielder Pete Browning and center fielder Leech Maskrey dashed for the ball as it shot between them." Stovey easily staggered home and plated his league-leading 110th run scored.[6]

The Athletics won, 7-6, and clinched the pennant. The *Philadelphia Press* updated the scoreboard outside its office at 6:30 P.M. to show the victorious tally. "The anxious crowd caught sight of it in a second, and when it was seen that the Athletics had won the game, such a shout as rent the heavens has seldom been heard before, round following round of cheers."[7] At the Athletic team headquarters a similar scene took place. A silk banner with the words "CHAMPION ATHLETIC" in large gold letters was hung across the street. Preparations for a victory parade were being made by the club brass as soon as the team returned home from Louisville three days later.

Philadelphia was electrified by the victory. "Upon receipt of the news of this victory in Philadelphia immense crowds blocked the streets in the vicinity of the bulletin boards displayed by the daily papers, and the excitement was similar to that with which the news of some great battle was greeted during wartime," a contemporary report said.[8] A reception committee of prominent city politicians was assembled and left Philadelphia to meet the champion Athletics in Harrisburg, where speeches were made on behalf of the club. The train stopped again in Lancaster, where excited fans cheered the wrong passenger car but stampeded to the players' car when they realized the mistake. Two bold individuals boarded the car searching for Jack Jones. The train finally pulled into Philadelphia's Broad Street Station at 7:45 P.M. and the team was met by a crush of people numbering in the thousands. "Fully ten thousand men and boys, several hundred horses and one mule … took part in the parade," the *Philadelphia Times* reported.[9] Admirers cheered until they were hoarse and the throng outside the station swarmed the city blocks surrounding the station. "So dense was the crowd that the officers for ten or fifteen minutes could not force an opening for the carriages in which the players embarked at the station door."[10]

SOURCES

In addition to the sources cited in the notes, the author consulted baseball-reference.com and retrosheet.org.

NOTES

1   The term "manager" did not mean the same thing in the nineteenth century that it does today. Lon Knight was the Athletic captain, which roughly equated to a present-day field manager. Simmons entered into the club's ownership group with Charlie Mason and Billy Sharsig late in 1881 and was made the business manager. The *Philadelphia Times* reported on September 28 issue that Mason told Knight to pitch Jones in the series' first game but that the decision was overruled and Bobby Mathews instead pitched the first game.

2   Jones was 6-5 with a 3.50 ERA for the National League's Detroit Wolverines before joining the Athletics.

3   "The Champions," *Courier-Journal*, September 29, 1883: 8.

4   Edward Achorn, *The Summer of Beer and Whiskey* (New York: Public Affairs, 2013), 226.

5   Stovey sprained his ankle badly when he slipped on the turf chasing a foul ball in a game against St. Louis on September 21. Achorn, *The Summer of Beer and Whiskey* (New York: Public Affairs, 2013), 210.

6   Achorn, 227.

7   "At the Athletics' Home," *Philadelphia Press*, September 29, 1883: 1.

8   "Base-Ball Champions," *Harper's Weekly*, Vol. XXVII, No. 1399 (1883): 654.

9   "The Base Ball Parade," *Philadelphia Times*, October 2, 1883: 1.

10   "The Base Ball Parade."

OTHER ARTICLES / PIECES

1883 ATHLETICS (PHILADELPHIA) SEASON TIMELINE

By Bill Nowlin

At a January 23 meeting of the city council, the lease of the grounds at Master and 27th Streets to the Athletics Base Ball Club was approved. The ballpark was situated between Master and Jefferson Streets, and 26th and 27th. Philadelphia newspapers of the day typically referred to the location as 26th and Jefferson. The ballpark later became known at the Jefferson Street Grounds.

The season was scheduled to start on May 1, on the road in Pittsburgh.

SOME PRESEASON GAMES

APRIL 7: ATHLETICS 12, YALE 0, AT JEFFERSON STREET GROUNDS

The first game of the year was an exhibition game against Yale and it was an uneven affair, with Bobby Mathews holding Yale to just four hits – three singles and a double. The Yale defense was perhaps subpar as well, with eight errors to the Athletics' five (three of which were by catcher Ed Rowen). The score was 3-0 through the first seven innings, but a seven-run eighth inning gave the Athletics a big boost. Only three of the 12 runs were deemed earned runs.

APRIL 11: ATHLETICS 14, MANAYUNK 2, AT THE ASHLAND CLUB'S GROUNDS

Fred Corey surrendered nine total bases in the game as Manayunk put up little resistance at a game played in Philadelphia.

APRIL 13: ATHLETICS 19, TRENTON 2, AT TRENTON

Another lopsided game, with Corey pitching again. Harry Stovey and Mike Moynahan each homered and Lon Knight himself had five base hits, one of them a triple. The game drew 1,200 people, 100 of them ladies.

APRIL 15: PHILADELPHIA 6, ATHLETICS 1, AT RECREATION PARK, PHILADELPHIA

Admission was 25 cents and the gates opened at 1:00 P.M., for a game to be called at 3:30. Drawing a large crowd of 10,000, the Philadelphia nine beat the Athletics, 6-1, but the only earned run in the game was that scored by the Athletics. The Athletics committed 10 errors, three by Blakiston at third base, and had only five base hits. "There was considerable excitement," commented the *Inquirer*, "and large sums of money changed hands on the result."[1] The crowd was said to be more or less evenly split in terms of which team

PLAYING BALL IN THE RAIN

6,000 PEOPLE SHIVER THROUGH A GAME

The Athletic Club Again Defeated by the Philadelphia Team—A Change of Batteries in Both Nines—Some Very Pretty Plays in the Field.

they favored. It was said to be the first of a three-game series between the two local clubs.

APRIL 20: ATHLETICS 16, TRENTON 6, AT JEFFERSON STREET GROUNDS

Batting sixth in the order, Corey limited Trenton to five hits. While he was without one himself, the Athletics collected 14. Third baseman Holland made two errors; he did not make the Athletics but may have been the Will Holland who played for Baltimore in 1889. Jack O'Brien's catching was said to have been a feature in the game.

A THIRD DEFEAT.

The Philadelphia Club Again Beats the Athletic After an Exciting Contest.

7,000 SPECTATORS PRESENT

APRIL 28: ATHLETICS 10, PHILADELPHIA 3, AT RECREATION PARK

Bobby Mathews pitched and Corey played center field. About 8,000 watched the game, the Athletics bettering Philadelphia both in batting and fielding. The game was called after six innings due to rain.

APRIL 30: ATHLETICS 9, PHILADELPHIA 4, AT JEFFERSON STREET GROUNDS

About 10,000 watched the Monday afternoon game. Mathews pitched for the Athletics. Philadelphia's 13 errors were costly; the Athletics committed only four.

THE CHAMPIONSHIP SEASON.

The League, American Association and Inter-State Teams to Open To-Morrow.

THE REGULAR SEASON

MAY 1: ATHLETICS 4, ALLEGHENYS 0, AT EXPOSITION PARK, PITTSBURGH

The Athletics traveled to Pittsburgh and Bobby Mathews, who had just pitched a full game the day before, shut out Pittsburgh's Alleghenys, 4-0, striking out seven. A special dispatch to the *Inquirer* said, "The

contest, although not a brilliant one, demonstrated the superiority of the Philadelphians to the home team." Three runs in the bottom of the fifth (the Alleghenys batted first) broke open a game that had been scoreless so that point. The shutout – in the first game of the regular season – was the Athletics' only shutout of the season.

MAY 2: ATHLETICS 8, ALLEGHENYS 1, AT EXPOSITION PARK, PITTSBURGH

The visitors out-hit the home-team Alleghenys, 15 to 11. The Alleghenys left 10 men on base but suffered from "poor base running, which appears to be their weakest point." Knight doubled twice, and Stovey and Bill Crowley added a double of their own. Corey pitched for the Athletics. He struck out three.

MAY 7: ATHLETICS 8, BALTIMORE ORIOLES 1, AT ORIOLE PARK, BALTIMORE

"The game was one-sided after the third inning, in which the four runs scored by the visitors somewhat disconcerted the home nine, and they lost their nerve."[2] So wrote the *Baltimore Sun*. The paper continued, "The audience was probably the largest of the season. The grand stand was thronged and the open stands and roofed spaces held an uncivil crowd, that never applauded the good plays of the Athletics, and went so far as to hiss the Baltimores once."

"Little Bobby Mathews, who was in the halcyon days of the Lord Baltimore Club, the greatest straight-arm pitcher in America, pitched a great game. He has a swift and eccentric delivery, but the Baltimore batted him eight times for a total of sixteen bases." That said, the only run the Orioles got was in the first inning on a muffed ball and a wild throw. A bases-clearing triple by Knight in the third inning gave the Athletics the lead they never relinquished.

MAY 8: ATHLETICS 8, BALTIMORE ORIOLES 5, AT ORIOLE PARK, BALTIMORE

Mathews pitched again, making his third start in a week. Neither team scored in the first two innings but the Baltimores put across a pair in the third. The Athletics got one in the third, but Baltimore then scored three more in the fourth. The Athletics answered with one more. They broke through with four runs in the sixth, giving them a 6-5 lead, adding two more in the seventh. In the sixth, Crowley hit what would have been a triple, but umpire Sommers called him out for failing to touch second base. (It still showed as a triple in the *Sun* box score.) Mathews finished the game in style and retired the last 15 batters he faced.

MAY 9: BALTIMORE ORIOLES 15, ATHLETICS 7, AT ORIOLE PARK, BALTIMORE

Perhaps Mathews should not have pitched a third day in a row. Even though the Athletics hopped out to a 4-0 lead in the first and added two more in the fourth, the Orioles scored once in the first and then had a big seven-run inning in the fourth – and then added another seven runs as the game played out. After six innings, Mathews was relieved by Stovey, Mathews going out to play left field while first baseman Stovey came in to pitch. Who then played first base is unclear. Three of the 15 runs were charged to Stovey. Two Orioles homered. Lon Knight tripled twice for Philadelphia. Of Mathews' work, the "best and most charitable explanation is that Bobby Mathews, who is a small man, is not equal to pitching three straight games, and gave out. He pitched a game that a novice on a fourth-rate amateur team could have beaten."[3]

MAY 10: ATHLETICS 2, METROPOLITANS (NEW YORK) 1, AT JEFFERSON STREET GROUNDS

Mathews, in fact, pitched for a fourth day in succession and this time he excelled, allowing just one run. He had good control as well, striking out seven and walking no one. The Metropolitans out-hit the Athletics, 7 to 5, and the Athletics committed eight errors (three by left fielder Jud Birchall) to half that many by the Metropolitans. Neither team scored through the first six innings. In the seventh, Chief Roseman hit a little squibber in front of the plate and reached first. He went first to third on a wild pitch, then scored when Birchall muffed a fly to left field. The Athletics scored twice in the eighth. With one out, Cub Stricker lined a hit to right field. He took second thanks to a wild throw by the Metropolitans catcher. Mathews grounded to shortstop, but first baseman Steve Brady dropped the ball. Birchall redeemed himself with a single to right field, scoring Stricker and sending Mathews to third base. Mathews scored the go-ahead run on a wild pitch. There were 7,000 fans present and it was said that "utmost excitement prevailed, and it was several minutes before play could be resumed."[4]

MAY 11: ATHLETICS 4, METROPOLITANS 3, AT JEFFERSON STREET GROUNDS

The Athletics jumped out to a quick lead, scoring what proved to be all their runs in the first inning. Future Hall of Famer Tim Keefe was a 41-game winner in 1883 but he took a while to settle down in this game. Birchall singled to lead off and Stovey, batting second, hit a home run over the left-field fence. It was Stovey's first home run of the year. Knight singled, followed by Moynahan hitting a triple to right field. O'Brien singled, driving in Moynahan. Each of the first five batters reached on clean base hits as the Athletics built a 4-0 lead. Keefe allowed only two more hits the rest of the game. The Metropolitans scored two in the fifth and a third run in the sixth, but 19-year-old rookie Jersey Bakley (characterized as a "West Philadelphia amateur") struck out four and had decent defense with only three errors behind him.[5] It was Bakley's first major-league victory.

MAY 12: ATHLETICS 11, METROPOLITANS 4, AT THE POLO GROUNDS, NEW YORK

The two teams traveled to New York and the Metropolitans hosted. The game was quite a long, at 2 hours and 39 minutes (perhaps the lengthiest nine-inning game the Athletic club played). The Athletics scored 11 runs and left 11 runners on base – although neither team had scored at all in the first three innings. The Athletics took the lead, but the Metropolitans scored three runs in the bottom of the sixth to tie the game, 4-4. The seventh inning saw the Athletics score four runs, on base hits by Crowley, Knight, and Stricker combining with errors by Bill Holbert, Sam Crane, and Candy Nelson, and two passed balls by the Metropolitans' catcher, Holbert.

Bobby Mathews, a member of the Mutuals of New York in the early 1870s, pitched and struck out eight to earn his fifth win of the season. Of the 15 runs scored, only one was earned, that one credited to the Athletics.[6]

A VERY CLOSE GAME.

The New York Metropolitans Again Defeated by the Athletics by One Run.

MAY 14: GAME POSTPONED

Baltimore held a 2-0 lead after four innings in a game played at the Jefferson Street Grounds, but incessant afternoon rain necessitated that the game be called.

MAY 15: ATHLETICS 8, BALTIMORE ORIOLES 7, AT JEFFERSON STREET GROUNDS

"The five thousand persons present fairly howled themselves hoarse." The Athletic club jumped out to a 5-0 lead in the first inning but the game was far from over. Baltimore scored three in the second, one in the third, and one in the fifth, and took the lead with another one in the sixth. In the seventh, Stovey singled, took second on a passed ball, and scored on a double by Crowley, who in turn scored on Moynahan's single. That gave the Athletics a 7-6 edge. They added an insurance run in the ninth and it was good they did, as the Orioles scored once, too – but only once and Mathews had himself another win. With the win, Mathews' record improved to 6-1.

THE BALL FIELD.

The Baltimore Club Again Badly Beaten by the Athletics.

MAY 16: ATHLETICS 10, BALTIMORE ORIOLES 4, AT JEFFERSON STREET GROUNDS

Bakley limited the Orioles to six hits to earn his second consecutive victory. The Athletics scored two runs in each of five different innings – the second, third, fourth, sixth, and seventh. With 18 errors in the game, 11 by Baltimore, each team scored just one earned run. The only three extra-base hits were all by the Athletics – Birchall, Stovey, and Bakley each doubled. The hits totaled Athletics 13, Orioles 6. About 3,000 fans came out for the Wednesday afternoon game.

MAY 17: ATHLETICS 13, BALTIMORE ORIOLES 6, AT JEFFERSON STREET GROUNDS

With 17 base hits (all singles) and only three errors, it's not surprising that the Athletics won handily. Baltimore got 11 hits off Bakley (3-0) and committed nine miscues. The Athletics scored six runs in the first inning, which got them off to a very good start. They added two in the third, one in the seventh, and four more in the eighth. Attendance was 2,500, including pugilist Charlie Mitchell, who sat in one of the private boxes.

MAY 18: GAME CALLED OFF

There was going to be a nonleague game between the Athletics and a Bridgeton, New Jersey, team, to be played in Bridgeton, but it was called off the day before.

MAY 19: ATHLETICS 11, ALLEGHENYS 8, AT JEFFERSON STREET GROUNDS

Some 9,000 saw a game that see-sawed back and forth. With four runs in the fourth inning the Athletics took a 5-2 lead but fell behind when the Alleghenys got to Bakley for five runs in the bottom of the seventh, taking advantage of errors by both him and his batterymate, O'Brien. It was 7-5 for the Pittsburghers heading into the ninth. The Athletics scored six times and gave back only one in the bottom of the inning. Bakley, the benefactor of the Athletics' ninth-inning explosion, improved to 4-0.

MAY 21: ATHLETICS 4, ALLEGHENYS 1, AT JEFFERSON STREET GROUNDS

The Athletics added George Bradley to handle third base. Knight moved from third base to play right field. Before the game, the Alleghenys protested that Bradley had not been officially released by the Cleveland ballclub and should not be allowed to play. He did play and was 1-for-4 without an error. In fact, the Athletics as a team committed only one error all game long (catcher Rowen) to back the steady pitching of Mathews (7-1). Each team had five hits; Rowen doubled.

MAY 22: ATHLETICS 9, ALLEGHENYS 1, AT JEFFERSON STREET GROUNDS

Knight had a four-hit game. The biggest inning was the fourth. Moynahan singled and O'Brien walked. A wild pitch enabled both to move up a base. Bradley hit the ball back to the Alleghenys pitcher and what should have been an easy out resulted in three runners – with even the batter making a complete circuit of the bases – as both the catcher and left fielder threw the ball away. Bakley got the win, to move to 5-0. He did not win another game for the Athletics that season. All five walks in the game were by Athletics batters.

The big story of the day came after the game. In the audience were three members of the Merritt club of Camden, New Jersey. The team's center fielder, Kenzil, and two others "became involved in a row on the Athletic ground, and Kenzil, who was intoxicated, was cut in the head by one of the officers. Kenzil was arrested, and it required six officers to conduct him to the station house."[7]

MAY 23: ATHLETICS 15, WEST PHILADELPHIA ATHLETIC ASSOCIATION 9, AT THE ASSOCIATION'S GROUNDS (BELMONT AND ELM AVENUES)

A nonleague game was the first one played on the Athletic Association's grounds on a site occupied by the Globe Hotel. Corey pitched, but was hit fairly hard. The Athletics, however, scored in every inning but one to win going away.

MAY 24: ATHLETICS 11, METROPOLITANS 2, AT POLO GROUNDS, NEW YORK

The Athletics extended their season record to 14-1 with an easy 11-2 victory over the Metropolitans, with Mathews on the mound. More than 10,000 witnessed the game. The Athletics out-hit the Metropolitans, 13-6. O'Brien and Stricker had three-hit games. Their fielding was better, too – the Metropolitans committed 10 errors and the Athletics only three. Five of the Athletics' runs were earned, while neither of the Mets' were. The big inning was the seven-run fifth inning. The victory improved Mathews' record to 8-1.

MAY 25: METROPOLITANS 10, ATHLETICS 4, AT THE POLO GROUNDS, NEW YORK

In the last week of May, the Athletics finally lost their second American Association game of the season, with the previously unbeaten Bakley (5-1) bearing the defeat. The four runs they scored all came in the fourth inning, earning them a temporary 4-3 lead, but the Metropolitans tied it in the fifth, scored four more runs in the sixth, and added two more in the seventh. Bradley and O'Brien each had two base hits, one of O'Brien's being a triple. The rest of the team managed only two hits in total. There were 14 base hits by the Metropolitans. And they were more effective at bringing them home. The Athletics left six on base to the New Yorkers' three.

MAY 26: ATHLETICS 11, METROPOLITANS 6, AT JEFFERSON STREET GROUNDS

The two teams traveled to Philadelphia for this game. Bobby Mathews worked before an estimated crowd of 7,000 to 8,000. The hits and errors were pretty much equal, and the Metropolitans jumped out to a 3-0 lead in the first inning before the Athletics had three big innings that put them on top. Each team had 11 base hits. The Athletics committed eight errors to the Metropolitans' seven. As the *New York*

Times noted, however, the errors by the Metropolitans "proved more costly than the home team's, as they were made at critical moments and were instrumental in swelling the score of the Philadelphians."[8]

MAY 29: ATHLETICS 2, CINCINNATI RED STOCKINGS 1, AT JEFFERSON STREET GROUNDS

The Athletics faced the reigning American Association champion Cincinnati Red Stockings for the first time in the season, and the game was a close one. Mathews pitched, and continued despite having a ball glance off his bat and into his face in the second inning. He was treated by doctors and afterward continued to earn his 10th victory of the season. The Athletics scored once in the first and once in the fourth and held Cincinnati scoreless until the ninth. An error by second baseman Stricker, a passed ball, and a single by pitcher Will White produced that lone Red Stockings run. The Athletics' first run came when leadoff batter Birchall walked. Stovey hit the ball to third base, and third baseman Hick Carpenter threw the ball over the head of first baseman John Reilly. Then Reilly fired the ball back to third, and the ball went over Carpenter's head. Knight doubled in the fourth and scored on back-to-back errors. Bradley grounded the ball to the pitcher, but when White threw the ball home, catcher Pop Snyder muffed it.

MAY 30 (FIRST GAME OF DOUBLEHEADER): ATHLETICS 8, COLUMBUS BUCKEYES 5, AT JEFFERSON STREET GROUNDS

Most of the fans of the day come out for the second game of the Decoration Day doubleheader. About 2,000 were reported to have turned out for the morning game against Columbus. Corey allowed only two hits over the first five innings, but gave up two runs in the sixth and three more in the eighth, on his way to improving to 2-0 on the season. The Athletics saw Stovey double and Bradley triple in the fifth, part of a three-run inning. In the sixth, the battery produced

THE CHAMPIONS BEATEN.

THE ATHLETICS WIN ANOTHER GAME.

The Cincinnati Club Making but Two Base Hits and One Run—Games Won by the Metropolitan, St. Louis and Louisville Teams.

another run, with O'Brien doubling and Corey hitting a single.

MAY 30 (SECOND GAME OF DOUBLE-HEADER): CINCINNATI RED STOCKINGS 10, ATHLETICS 9 (11 INNINGS), AT JEFFERSON STREET GROUNDS

With about 15,000 people gathered on the grounds for the afternoon game, standees crowded so close that there were few foul flies caught for outs. Cincinnati scored six runs in the first inning off Mathews (10-2) and, though the Athletics chipped away, it took them to the ninth inning to catch up, thanks to back-to-back doubles by Moynahan and O'Brien. The game tied, 8-8, it went into the 11th. With two outs and one on, shortstop Moynahan let a ball go right through him, letting in one run. Crowley dropped a fly ball in center, letting in another. Though the Athletics scored once, they fell one run short.

MAY 31: ATHLETICS 8, CINCINNATI RED STOCKINGS 7, AT JEFFERSON STREET GROUNDS

The Athletics scored four runs in the first inning, but by the end of five innings, the Red Stockings had a 6-5 lead. They added another run in the seventh, but the Athletics scored three times in eighth and won the game. Mathews pitched. Some 7,000 spectators watched the contest and cheered themselves hoarse. The winning runs came on a walk, a base hit by Bradley, and then three errors in succession by Cincinnati's first baseman, shortstop, and third baseman.

With the victory, the Athletics finished the month of May with a record of 18-3 and a season-high 5½-game lead over the Red Stockings and Metropolitans, who were in a virtual tie for second. The St. Louis Browns (11-10) finished the month in fifth place, seven games off the pace.

JUNE 1: ATHLETICS 15, PICKED NINE 2, AT JEFFERSON STREET GROUNDS

This was a true novelty. Pitching for the Athletics was none other than boxing champion John L. Sullivan, and he pitched quite well. When he first appeared on the grounds with Charlie Mason, he asked, "Do you employ boys to bring in the balls that are knocked over the fence?" Told there had only been one hit over the fence, he said, "I have never played here before." In fielding practice before the game, he "generally dropped" the balls thrown to him. Sullivan pitched for the Athletics, batting third in the order. The

"picked nine" against whom the Athletics played included Corey at second base, Charlie Mason in center field, Crowley in right, and Bakley at third. Mr. Ryan, who was the general superintendent of the Jefferson Street Grounds, served as Sullivan's catcher.

Sullivan struck out Corey. He got the second batter on a fly ball, then walked Mason, who stole second and scored on Crowley's base hit. Sullivan then "rubbed the ball on the sand and the next batsman went out on a fly." In his first at-bat, Sullivan may have looked at the outfield fences but, "sad to relate, he moved the ball only about ten feet, and retired at first." In the third inning, it seems, Sullivan came up to bat again and "sent a hot-liner over the third base." He "trotted leisurely" to first base, took second on a passed ball, and scored when Moynahan hit a home run to the left-field corner.

The box score shows that Sullivan allowed only four base hits, all singles. He walked two and struck out two. "After the novelty of the game had worn off," wrote the *Inquirer*, "the game was of no special interest. Sullivan in reality pitched a good game, and his support was excellent."[9]

JUNE 2: COLUMBUS BUCKEYES 8, ATHLETICS 6, AT JEFFERSON STREET GROUNDS

The Buckeyes had a six-run sixth inning and the Athletics a five-run eighth, but the Buckeyes got to Bakley (5-2) for eight runs overall as the Athletics managed only five base hits (one was a triple by Stovey) off Columbus right-hander Ed Dundon, described as "a deaf and dumb individual." He was, in fact, "the first deaf mute in major-league history."[10] Some 4,000 to 5,000 fans turned out for the game. It was a close 1-1 game through the first five innings, but that six-run inning that Columbus put up gave them the win. The runs came courtesy of a combination of defensive errors and three base hits – Stricker, Bradley, and Moynahan all committed errors and Stovey muffed a fly ball. Even down 7-1, most of the crowd still believed the Athletics would pull it out, and they did get one inning where things fell apart for the opposition. With five errors, all in the eighth inning, the Athletics scored five. Birchall singled to drive home Stricker and Bakley, both of whom had reached on errors. His base hit was the only hit; walks and errors accounted for all the other runs. The rally fell one run short. The Buckeyes added one more run in the bottom of the eighth, and won 8-6.

JUNE 4: ATHLETICS 8, COLUMBUS BUCKEYES 2, AT JEFFERSON STREET GROUNDS

Each team scored a pair of runs in the first inning. Both teams had 10 hits in the game. But after the first inning, Mathews didn't allow another run, while the Athletics scored six more. Mathews struck out eight on his way to his 12th victory of the year. The *Inquirer* reported that 3,000 attended the game, noting that the Athletics had committed only one error in the game (second baseman Stricker on a "difficult fly"), while the Buckeyes made nine. That's bound to be a recipe for a loss. The Athletics left nine on base, the Buckeyes left seven. "The visitors showed up well at the bat, but they failed to bunch their hits and their errors were mostly wild throws."

Elsewhere on June 4, a meeting was held in Cincinnati to address the claim of the Allegheny club that the Athletics victories on May 21 and 22 should be voided because they had played George Bradley before the American Association had been notified of his release by Cleveland. The decision was to let the scores stand.

JUNE 7: GAME RAINED OUT

The game against the visiting St. Louis Browns was halted with two outs in the fifth inning and called on account of rain. The score was 6-1 in favor of the Athletics after four full innings. The Athletics had scored another in the fifth before play was stopped. Mathews, in search of his 13th win of the year, pitched for the Athletics.

JUNE 8: ATHLETICS 7, ST. LOUIS BROWNS 5, AT JEFFERSON STREET GROUNDS

Mathews pitched again. Each team committed 10 errors, but there were a number of "brilliant plays" as well. The Browns put up three runs in the first inning for an early lead. The Athletics responded with two runs on an error and three base hits in their half of the first and added a tying third run in the second. Stricker walked, "trotted to second on a wild pitch, and to third on a passed ball. Mathews sent a fly to Cuthbert [in left field], who dropped it, and Stricker scored."[11] They added three more in the third and a seventh run in the fourth; it was 7-3 Athletics after those four innings and they held on for the 7-5 win. There was some excitement in the ninth when St. Louis showed some possibilities. The inning started with Birchall dropping a fly ball hit to left by Ned Cuthbert, but Birchall threw the ball in and Cuthbert was cut down trying to reach

second base. The next two batters reached base, but two more fly balls were lofted to Birchall, who handled both of them. O'Brien had three of Philadelphia's 10 base hits. The only extra-base hit of the game (the Browns had eight singles) was a double by Moynahan. Bradley and Moynahan each had two hits. Mathews improved his record to 13-2.

JUNE 9: ST. LOUIS BROWNS 3, ATHLETICS 0, AT JEFFERSON STREET GROUNDS

About 8,000 came to the grounds for what most hoped would be a win. Mathews (13-3) pitched again and held the Browns to three runs on just four hits, but the Browns' Jumbo McGinnis was better and shut out the Athletics, also allowing just four hits and striking out seven. (He struck out Cub Stricker four times.) The Browns played better defense, with only five errors to the Athletics' nine. Early in the game, some in the spirited crowd decided to take on the umpire, Ormond H. Butler, who was working just his fifth game as an Association umpire. "The right-field seats were crowded with 'hoodlums' and they began early in the action to hoot and hiss at the umpire, until the latter appealed to the Athletic management, when Mr. Simmons announced, in stentorian tones, that the decision of the umpire must be final. After this the 'hoodlums' were satisfied with making fun of Mr. Butler's fantastic costume."[12] One wonders how he was attired.

JUNE 11: ST. LOUIS BROWNS 9, ATHLETICS 7, AT JEFFERSON STREET GROUNDS

For the first time all season the Athletics had dropped two in a row. Mathews (13-4) started yet again and was staked to a 3-1 lead after the first inning, but was knocked out of the box in the fifth as the Browns pushed four runs across the plate. Bradley relieved. The Athletics mounted a threat in the eighth, scoring three runs to make the final score closer. There were nearly 5,000 fans and they were angry about some of umpire Butler's decisions; at game's end "he was surrounded by a howling mob and had to be escorted from the ground." Butler's umpiring career comprised 13 games in June, this being the sixth. His last day as an umpire was June 21; the next day he became manager of Pittsburgh's Alleghenys.

JUNE 12: ATHLETICS 8, ECLIPSE (LOUISVILLE) 2, AT JEFFERSON STREET GROUNDS

Bradley, making his first start of the season, held the Eclipse to "three scratch hits" in a game that was close until the bottom of the eighth, when the Athletics scored five times and put the game away. The game was played at a brisk pace, in 1 hour and 25 minutes. Bradley didn't walk or strike out anyone en route to his first victory of the season. There were only three errors, one of them his own. Corey's RBI double in the eighth (driving in Bradley) was the only extra-base hit by either team.

JUNE 13: ECLIPSE (LOUISVILLE) 10, ATHLETICS 3, AT JEFFERSON STREET GROUNDS

This was the first of what became a five-game losing streak, the longest of the season for the Athletics. There was a three-game losing streak in August, the only other that lasted more than two games. The 12 errors the team committed – four of them by Moynahan at shortstop – were a big part of the problem in what the *Inquirer* called "one of the worst played games of the season." Bradley started, but his fastball was too fast for the "badly overworked" catcher O'Brien, who was suffering from sore hands. So Corey came in to pitch after the third inning; the Eclipse already had a 6-0 lead. There had been some other shifting around – Corey played center field, then third base, and then pitched. Bradley (1-1) went to third base after leaving the mound. Both Blakiston and Stovey put in time in center field as well.

JUNE 14: ECLIPSE (LOUISVILLE) 6, ATHLETICS 5 (10 INNINGS), AT JEFFERSON STREET GROUNDS

This was a closely-fought game that went into extra innings, Mathews pitching for the Athletics and right-hander Guy Hecker for the Eclipse. Philadelphia scored three runs in the first and Louisville scored three runs in the third. The Athletics scored two in the sixth to take a 5-3 lead. The two runs matched by the Eclipse in the eighth. Five hundred ladies comprised about 10 percent of those who watched. Stovey homered (his second of the year), a two-run drive to left-center in the first inning. The team as a whole hit only 20 home runs all season long; 14 of them were

A GAME WITH MANY ERRORS

THE ATHLETICS BADLY DEFEATED

Unable to Hit Weaver and Fairly Outplayed at Every Point—St. Louis Again Beats the New York Metropolitans—Rain in Baltimore and Pittsburg.

by Stovey. O'Brien had quite a day. He committed four errors, and "was injured quite severely at three different times, but pluckily kept on playing." He also led the team with three of its 12 base hits. The Eclipse had only five hits, but the Athletics' 10 errors, three wild pitches, and two passed balls proved costly. The teams were tied 5-5 after nine. Jack Gleason singled for Louisville in the 10th, took second on a bad throw, and then took third on a ball hit back to Mathews. He was thrown out at the plate by third baseman Bradley, on a grounder by Joe Gerhardt, who rounded first and headed to second on the play at the plate. O'Brien's throw sailed over second baseman Stricker's head – and kept going when center fielder Corey let the ball get by him. Gerhardt had circled the bases on what started as a simple groundball to third.

JUNE 15: MERRITTS 21, ATHLETICS 10 (EXHIBITION GAME), AT JEFFERSON STREET GROUNDS

For an exhibition game, the Athletics offered one of the worst exhibitions imaginable. They out-hit the Merritt Club (from Camden), 18-10, but gave up 21 runs. One can see why: The Athletics were charged with 20 errors, and also six passed balls. Bob Blakiston served as umpire. A catcher named Corcoran played for the Athletics, but injured his finger and so Stovey finished up behind the plate. The *Philadelphia Inquirer* wrote that the game "was one of the worst exhibitions of ball playing, as far as the Athletic club was concerned, that has ever been seen in this city, and fortunately the afflicted crowd was very small."

JUNE 16: ATHLETICS 12, ROSS CLUB 4 (EXHIBITION GAME), AT CHESTER PARK. CHESTER, PENNSYLVANIA

Corey pitched for the Athletics and gave up seven hits, his game marred only by a four-run (one earned) seventh inning. There were six Athletics errors. Crowley had four of their 14 hits, and Moynahan had three. The Athletics scored one in the second, three in the third, and six in the fourth. Their catcher, "Ryan," apparently showed nicely behind the plate. The game drew an overflow crowd of 1,600, including 200 to 300 women.[13] We can probably safely assume the catcher was Rowen.

JUNE 18: CINCINNATI RED STOCKINGS 6, ATHLETICS 0, AT BANK STREET GROUNDS, CINCINNATI

The reigning champion Red Stockings scored two runs in the first inning and three more in the second.

Mathews (13-6) pitched for the Athletics and received no run support. "The Athletics were without hope," wrote Cincinnati's *Commercial Tribune*. "For the first four innings not a man of them got to first."[14]

Will White was pitching for the Red Stockings and he was on his game. The Athletics team was white-washed, shut out 6-0. White was also big on offense. Between him and first baseman John Reilly, they had seven of the team's 10 hits, three by White (including a double) and four by Reilly (one of them a triple).

There were but 2,500 people at the game, extraordinarily heavy rains in the early afternoon no doubt having discouraged many from attending. The game started 15 minutes late, at 4:15.

JUNE 19: CINCINNATI RED STOCKINGS 7, ATHLETICS 0, AT BANK STREET GROUNDS, CINCINNATI

The Athletics had been in Cincinnati for two days and still hadn't scored a run. This time they were shut out, 7-0, on a brilliant one-hitter thrown by Will White, who was pitching for the second day in a row and earned back-to-back shutouts. Bradley pitched for the Athletics and allowed three scattered runs before the Red Stockings pushed four across in the top of the ninth inning. The loss dropped Bradley's record to 1-2. But the story of the game was White. The only hit of the game for the visitors was by Birchall, a groundball that hopped over third base in the third inning. He did walk three and the Athletics left four men on base.

This was the third time in 11 days that the Athletics failed to score a run.

JUNE 20: CINCINNATI RED STOCKINGS 11, ATHLETICS 1, AT BANK STREET GROUNDS, CINCINNATI

Finally, in their third game, the Athletics scored a run. One run. In the sixth inning. The Red Stockings scored 11. Mathews was roughed up for 16 base hits (including two triples by Will White), and 27 total bases. The Athletics got only four singles off White. Two of the four were hits by Mathews. The Athletics scored their run when, with runners on first (Knight) and third (Stovey), the two baserunners pulled off a delayed double steal. Knight was out at second but Stovey scored. Mathews' record was 13-7 as the diminutive right-hander dropped his fifth straight decision.

JUNE 21: ATHLETICS 14, CINCINNATI RED STOCKINGS 5, AT BANK STREET GROUNDS, CINCINNATI

The Athletics' season-long losing streak came to an end at five games when Corey (3-0) held Cincinnati to four hits. Two errors by Bradley at third base allowed the Red Stockings, who elected to bat first, to score four runs in the first inning. O'Brien came in from center field and took over third base, Bradley going to center. Neither committed an error from that time on, and the *Times* of Philadelphia declared, "O'Brien is a magnificent third baseman."[15] Stovey hit his third home run of the season, a two-run, first-inning homer off right-hander Harry McCormick. Left fielder Joe Sommer committed four of Cincinnati's 12 errors. The Athletics scored in every inning but the second and eighth.

JUNE 23: ATHLETICS 7, COLUMBUS BUCKEYES 3, AT RECREATION PARK, COLUMBUS

Mathews snapped his personal five-game losing streak when he struck out 11 Buckeyes and the Athletics coasted to an easy 7-3 victory. Columbus scored the first two runs of the game, though, getting to Mathews in the first inning. That lead held until the Athletic club pulled even in the fourth inning. The Buckeyes took a 3-2 lead in the sixth, which held until they succumbed to the four runs Philadelphia scored off Frank Mountain in the top of the eighth. They added a seventh run in the final frame.

JUNE 25: ATHLETICS 8, COLUMBUS BUCKEYES 2 (6 INNINGS), AT RECREATION PARK, COLUMBUS

Overnight rains had flooded Recreation Park to a degree but "several loads of tan bark" were spread on the field, getting it into "passable condition."[16] The game was called in the seventh inning when the rain returned. It was another Mathews/Mountain matchup. The big inning was the seven-run fourth inning – on four hits, five errors, and a wild pitch. Despite the soggy conditions, there were only seven errors in the game, just two of them by the Athletics. Mathews struck out six and allowed only five hits to notch his 15th victory of the year.

JUNE 26: ATHLETICS 7, COLUMBUS BUCKEYES 2, AT RECREATION PARK, COLUMBUS

Corey held Columbus to two runs on eight hits to move to 4-0, and the Athletics committed only three errors. The Buckeyes made six. Moynahan and Rowen collected three apiece. "Stricker's playing was wonderful," enthused the dispatch to the *Times*. "In the eighth inning he made the finest fly catch ever seen on the grounds by running away out into centre field and taking the ball almost out of Bradley's hands."[17] The *Commercial Gazette* concurred, saying that Stricker had presented "the finale exhibition of second-base playing seen here this season."[18]

JUNE 28: ATHLETICS 3, ST. LOUIS BROWNS 1, AT SPORTSMAN'S PARK, ST. LOUIS

It was ladies day in St. Louis and "at least 8,000 fans, more than 1,000 of whom were ladies," turned out.[19] There was a lot of interest in the game and, based on whatever evidence, the *Post-Dispatch* said that there was more money wagered on this one "by the betting men than on any base ball contest ever played in the city."[20] The game started seven minutes before the scheduled start time.

Mathews gave up one run in the third, and finished with a three-hitter. The Athletics scored one run in each of the sixth, eighth, and ninth innings. The go-ahead run in the eighth was thanks to a single by Birchall and a double by Stovey. With the win, Mathews improved to 16-7.

JUNE 30: ATHLETICS 7, ST. LOUIS BROWNS 2, AT SPORTSMAN'S PARK, ST. LOUIS

A large crowd of about 8,000 took in the game. It was, oddly, a game that almost didn't happen. They needed an umpire. Charles Daniels had worked the game in Louisville on the 28th, and considerable effort was expended to get him to St. Louis – brought in by what was essentially a private train. "A special train, composed of an engine and one coach, which was arranged through … the Ohio and Mississippi Railway, left Louisville with Umpire Daniels at 3:43 a.m. and arrived here at 1:05 p.m., making the run of 322 miles in nine hours and twenty-two minutes. Everything depended on Daniels. Without him there would have been no game."[21]

Mathews worked again, allowing only four hits and not being too badly victimized by eight fielding errors. Four of the Athletics' nine base hits were doubles. The victory was Mathews' 17th.

The Athletics were 9-8 during June and finished the month with a record of 27-11, 2½ games ahead of the Eclipse of Louisville and the St. Louis Browns.

JULY 1: ST. LOUIS BROWNS 9, ATHLETICS 8, AT SPORTSMAN'S PARK, ST. LOUIS

The 12,000 people who watched the Sunday game in St. Louis were rewarded by seeing their hometown Browns beat the visitors from Philadelphia, 9-8. Tied 3-3 after five innings, the game turned into something of a see-saw battle. St. Louis took its second lead of the game, scoring once in the bottom of the sixth but then saw the Athletics score five runs in the top of the seventh to take an 8-4 lead. The Browns got three back in the bottom of the seventh to narrow the lead to 8-7, then tied it with one in the eighth and won it with one more in the ninth.

Corey pitched, dropping his first game of the year. Stovey hit the game's only home run, a solo home run in the first inning off Tony Mullane. It was his fourth of the season.

JULY 2: ATHLETICS 9, ST. LOUIS BROWNS 1, AT SPORTSMAN'S PARK, ST. LOUIS

Mathews threw a three-hitter and had a reasonably solid defense behind him (though second baseman Cub Stricker committed three errors – the only three by the Athletics) as he earned his 18th victory of the season and extended his personal win streak to five. The Browns scored their one run in the eighth, too little and too late after the Athletics had scored four in the third and five in the seventh. Many had thought the Browns had gotten back on track with the July 1 win. This game was, headlined the *Globe-Democrat*, a "shocking relapse."[22]

JULY 4: ECLIPSE 9, ATHLETICS 2, FIRST GAME OF DOUBLEHEADER, AT ECLIPSE PARK, LOUISVILLE

Some 6,000 people came out for the morning game, and another 6,000 came out for the afternoon game. The two teams split the doubleheader. Corey, who took the loss, and then Bradley pitched in the opener, giving up 14 hits. They both benefited from excellent fielding; the team committed only one error (by Bradley). Stovey doubled and tripled, but the three runs the Eclipse scored in the very first inning was enough to tide them over, and the six additional runs they got in the fifth inning allowed them to breathe much easier. It was so hot that O'Brien fell prostrate and had to be carried off. Stricker came in from second base to take over catching duties. Knight came in from right field to play second. Part-owner Charlie Mason took over in right, the only game he played for the Athletics. He did get a base hit, a single. The Athletics scored once in the fifth and once in the eighth.

JULY 4: ATHLETICS 14, ECLIPSE 9, SECOND GAME OF DOUBLEHEADER AT ECLIPSE PARK, LOUISVILLE

As in the first game, the Eclipse got 14 base hits – but this time, so did the Athletics. Much of the story of the game may be attributed to the errors – the Athletics made four, but the Eclipse made three times as many – 12. The Athletics jumped out to a 4-0 lead in the very first inning. The second and seventh innings were the only two in which the Athletics failed to score. Mathews walked nine, but struck out six, to earn his 19th victory of the year.

JULY 6 – GAME POSTPONED BY MUTUAL AGREEMENT.

There was to have been a game between the Eclipse and the Athletics on Friday, July 6, but "both teams are in a disabled condition. Stovey had hardly recovered from his injuries received in St. Louis, and Rowen and one or two others, who were affected by the heat, kept pretty quiet to-day. The heat has told on the Louisville Club as well, and the game was postponed by mutual agreement, and both clubs were glad to do it."[23]

JULY 7: ATHLETICS 4, ECLIPSE 3 (11 IN-NINGS), AT ECLIPSE PARK, LOUISVILLE

Mathews earned his 20th victory of the year, with still more than half the season to play The Athletics scored once in the third and once in the fourth, but saw the Eclipse put across a pair in the fifth. Louisville got one in the seventh and seemed in good shape until Philadelphia tied it in the top of the ninth. And won it with an unanswered run in the 11th. The Athletics won, we are informed, "by clean and hard batting" but who had the winning hits was unclear in the *Times* account.[24] All three extra-base hits in the game were by the Athletics – a triple by Crowley and doubles by O'Brien and Corey.

JULY 8 – GAME STOPPED BY RAIN

There was to have been a final game between the two teams on July 8, but it was stopped by rain during the fourth inning, with the Eclipse leading, 3-2.

JULY 10: ALLEGHENYS 11, ATHLETICS 4, AT EXPOSITION PARK, PITTSBURGH

"A miserable game," according to the *Philadelphia Inquirer.* The Alleghenys had just returned to Pittsburgh after a lengthy road trip, and showed little mercy, jumping on the Athletics for four runs in the first inning. They added another four on six hits in the fifth inning and three more later in a game that was "uninteresting because of it being so one-sided." Mathews pitched the whole game. Everyone in the Allegheny lineup had at least one base hit. The

Athletics committed a full dozen errors. In the third inning, reported the *Pittsburgh Daily Post*, Stovey hit a solo home run to deep left field off Bob Barr. It was his fifth of the season. The *Post* praised "the deportment of the visitors," even while being shellacked, which it said contrasted with their last visit "when their conduct disgusted everybody."[25] The loss ended Mathews' personal winning streak at seven and dropped his record to 20-8. It also left the Athletics with just a half-game lead over second-place St. Louis.

JULY 11: ATHLETICS 12, ALLEGHENYS 3, AT EXPOSITION PARK, PITTSBURGH

Making his first start in more than three weeks, Bradley and the Athletics turned the tables on July 11. The Alleghenys homered twice, but had only four hits total. They committed only two errors, but those two errors and two passed balls led to six of the Athletics' 12 runs. Despite the 15 runs, the game took only 1:35 to play. Bradley improved to 2-2.

JULY 12: ALLEGHENYS 9, ATHLETICS 1, AT EXPOSITION PARK, PITTSBURGH

Bradley (2-3) started again, but fared less well. He was "pounded all to pieces,"[26] with the Allegheny knocking him around for 19 base hits – at least one by everyone in the lineup and five by Joe Battin, includ-

A BALL FOR THE ATHLETICS

THE ALLEGHENY CLUB BADLY BEATEN.

ing three doubles and a triple. (Battin batted only .214 for the season.) The Allegheny committed only one error. The *Pittsburgh Daily Post* murmered that since the locals never seemed to be able to win two games in a row, they'd probably lose on the 13th.

JULY 13: ATHLETICS 4, ALLEGHENYS 1, AT EXPOSITION PARK, PITTSBURGH

Lose, the Alleghenys did, but it was a close game, not a lopsided one like the preceding three. Mathews allowed just seven hits and returned to the winning column with his 21st. The Athletics got 10 hits. Both teams fielded well, with just a pair of errors per team. Stovey hit his sixth home run of the season, off left-hander Denny Driscoll. The ball was hit so deep to center field that he was already at third base before center fielder Billy Taylor retrieved the ball. The *Post* said he had crossed the plate by the time Taylor got to it. It was "one of the finest balls ever seen on the grounds … and won for him unstinted applause."[27] The game was another quick one. It lasted just 1 hour and 35 minutes.

JULY 14: ATHLETICS 3, ALLEGHENYS 2 (10 INNINGS), AT EXPOSITION PARK, PITTSBURGH

After heavy rain in the morning, the grounds were in "shocking condition" – but 2,000 fans still came to see the game, in which each team made only three errors. Mathews allowed 10 hits, including three doubles, while the Athletics had only nine hits. The game went into extra innings and was won in the 10th. The *Times* of Philadelphia allowed that the "visitors were fairly outplayed by the Alleghenys in all material points, but the chronic bad luck of the home team at critical points, aided by an infamous decision by [umpire John O.] Kelly, which gave the visitors one run, aided in their overthrow."[28] With the win, Mathews improved to 22-8.

JULY 17: ATHLETICS 13, BALTIMORE ORIOLES 9, AT ORIOLE PARK, BALTIMORE

Baltimore batted first and scored three runs, but the Athletics answered back with five. In the third inning the Orioles tied the score by adding a pair of runs. Mathews held back Baltimore for a few innings as the Athletics scored four in the fifth, two in the sixth, and two more in the eighth. When the Orioles scored four in the top of the ninth, they were still four runs short and the game was done.

It was a game replete with errors – 24 of them. Philadelphia committed 14 errors and Baltimore committed 10. Moynahan committed four errors and Stricker and O'Brien made three each. The only two Athletics who did not make an error were the left fielder (Birchall) and the right fielder (Knight), perhaps as much as anything because they didn't have many balls hit their way. Each team had nine base hits.

JULY 18: ATHLETICS 16, BALTIMORE ORIOLES 9, AT ORIOLE PARK, BALTIMORE

Once again, the Orioles scored nine runs. And once again, that was not enough. Baltimore held a 7-3 lead after five innings, and had committed only one error in the field. But with one out in the top of the sixth, the Athletics pushed 11 runs across the plate, thanks to five singles, a double, and a pair of errors. By the time the game was over, the Orioles had accumulated 10 errors. Corey's batterymate, Rowen, was "badly hurt in the eighth inning and had to change with [second baseman] Stricker."[29] Among the Athletics, all but

Bob Blakiston got at least one base hit. And everyone – including Blakiston – scored at least one run. The *Baltimore Sun* said that Blakiston had played so badly at third base that he was sent out to center field during the fifth inning and Bradley brought in.[30] With the victory, Corey improved to 5-2.

JULY 19: BALTIMORE ORIOLES 10, ATHLETICS 9, AT ORIOLE PARK, BALTIMORE

When the Athletics scored five times in the top of the first inning, the 2,000 fans from Baltimore may well have anticipated a defeat. But it was 6-5, Athletics, after six innings. Three runs in the bottom of the ninth won the game for the home team.

Mathews gave up 16 hits, while the Athletics mustered only eight. That outweighed the fact that Baltimore committed 11 errors to five by the Philadelphia team. The loss ended Mathews' win streak at three and dropped his record to 23-9.

JULY 20: ATHLETICS 7, BALTIMORE ORIOLES 3, AT ORIOLE PARK, BALTIMORE

"The Athletics outplayed the home club and their victory is due to the fact that they bunched their hits, while the Baltimores bunched their errors." That's how the *Times* characterized the game witnessed by 3,500. The newspaper added, "The game was an uninteresting exhibition of what professionals can do and as usual was lost through the errors of the home club."[31] The Orioles committed nine errors; the Athletics but three. Bradley pitched a good game and evened his record at 3-3. Stovey had three hits, including a double.

JULY 23: NEW YORK METROPOLITANS 5, ATHLETICS 1, AT THE POLO GROUNDS, NEW YORK

Rain dampened the fans' enthusiasm and kept them away from the ballpark. Tim Keefe of the Metropolitans saw the Athletics score one run off him in the top of the first inning, but held them scoreless from that point on. Mathews (23-10) held the Mets scoreless for five innings but they finally tied the score with a run in the sixth. In the bottom of the eighth, the floodgates opened when the Metropolitans scored four runs for the final margin of difference.

JULY 25: ATHLETICS 6, NEW YORK METROPOLITANS 2, AT JEFFERSON STREET GROUNDS

Both teams made their way to Philadelphia for back-to-back grams on the 25th and 26th. Admission for the 4:00 P.M. game was 25 cents. Mathews and Rowen were the scheduled battery for the Athletics, back in town for the first time since June 14. The team had fallen out of first place on the 23rd, but only barely and for a week hovered between a half-game and a game behind the Browns. Winning this day helped them keep pace. Eight thousand watched Mathews (24-10) hold the Mets to three hits and beat Tim Keefe for his 25th victory. Rowen was not "capable of catching," so O'Brien took his place.[32] The Athletics took the lead in the first inning and never relinquished it. Birchall walked and Knight tripled, then scored on Moynahan's sacrifice fly. The Athletics had only four hits but hit for a team cycle: Corey (single), Mathews (double), Knight (triple), and Stovey (home run). Eight Mets errors and a couple of passed balls helped them get on base and advance. Stovey's home run was his seventh of the season, a solo shot in the bottom of the eighth off Keefe.

JULY 26: NEW YORK METROPOLITANS 8, ATHLETICS 1, AT JEFFERSON STREET GROUNDS

Keefe held the Athletics to five hits, all singles, with the only run coming in the first inning on an error, passed ball, and (after Knight drew a walk) an overthrow on a failed attempt at a double play. Mathews

THE DIAMOND FIELD.

The Athletics Celebrate Their Return Home by Defeating the Metropolitans.

(24-11) held the Mets scoreless through four but gave up four runs in the fifth, and two more runs in both the seventh and ninth innings.

JULY 28: ATHLETICS 11, ALLEGHENYS 2, AT JEFFERSON STREET GROUNDS

Saturday saw the Alleghenys come to town. Mathews allowed only eight hits, but was victimized by three errors. The Athletics benefited from nine Allegheny errors, two wild pitches, and a passed ball, and collected 13 hits. Both Stovey and Moynahan hit home runs. For Stovey, it was his eighth of the season, a two-run, first-inning, inside-the-park homer off right-hander Jack Neagle. Moynahan's was a two-run homer in the bottom of the eighth. The Athletics nailed down the win with seven insurance runs in the bottom of the eighth. The victory was Mathews' 25th of the season.

JULY 30: ATHLETICS 17, ALLEGHENYS 4, AT JEFFERSON STREET GROUNDS

The Athletics scored 17 runs on 23 hits for 34 total bases. By far the biggest day was Lon Knight's, with five base hits in six at-bats and 12 total bases. He drove in a run with a single in the first, doubled to right field in the third, tripled to center in the sixth, and homered to left-center in the eighth, his only home run of the season. It was the first "natural cycle" in major-league baseball history.[33] For good measure, he doubled again in the ninth, driving in two more runs. In all, Knight drove in six runs and scored five. Stovey also had a five-hit day – four singles and a double. Mathews held the Alleghenys to nine hits to earn his 26th victory against 11 defeats. With two months left in the season, Mathews was on pace to win 51 games. The team was a half-game ahead of St. Louis at day's end.

JULY 31: ATHLETICS 16, ALLEGHENYS 12, AT JEFFERSON STREET GROUNDS

The Athletics improved their slim hold on first place when the bats let loose again. Unlike the other three games in the four-game set with the Alleghenys, this one was closely contested. That said, the *Inquirer* termed it "of an indifferent character … only saved from tediousness by the heavy batting of both sides."[34] Corey (6-2) handled the mound duties, while Mathews played right field. The latter sprained his ankle early on and was replaced by Bill Crowley. The Athletics led 7-1 in the middle of the fifth, but the Alleghenys then scored two in the fifth and added four in the sixth. The game was tied, 7-7. The Athletics scored one in the seventh and five more in the eighth, enough to withstand the Alleghenys battling back with two in the eighth and three more in the bottom of the ninth. Pittsburgh out-hit Philadelphia, 16 to 15, but the Athletics had 25 total bases to 22 for the Alleghenys. Stovey hit another home run, his ninth of the season and sixth in the month of July. It was a two-run homer in the top of the ninth off right-hander Billy Taylor.

The Athletics finished July with a record of 13-7 and with Louisville eclipsing St. Louis, 7-6, the Athletics (40-18) ended July with a half-game lead in the standings over the 41-20 Browns. St. Louis had lost on both the 30th and 31st, both times in the final inning.

AUGUST 1: ATHLETICS 19, ALLEGHENYS 2, AT JEFFERSON STREET GROUNDS

It was the fourth consecutive game in which the Athletics scored in double digits, this time pulverizing the Pittsburghers, 19-2. The game was over almost as soon it began, when the Athletics scored five times in the first, one in the second, and six more runs in the third. The only inning in which they didn't score at least once was the eighth. With Mathews sidelined, Bradley (4-3) was the beneficiary of all the scoring, but solid in his own right, allowing just seven hits and walking one. He had decent defense behind him, with only three errors by the home team while the Alleghenys committed 11. Stovey homered yet again – "his usual home run," wrote the *Times*, and became the first player to hit 10 home runs in a major-league season It was a line drive two-run homer over the left-field fence, "the longest ever made on the ground."[35] Knight and O'Brien both tripled.

AUGUST 3: ATHLETICS 9, BALTIMORE ORIOLES 6, AT JEFFERSON STREET GROUNDS

The Orioles out-hit the Athletics by a considerable margin, 12 hits to 8, and led 4-1 after two innings. But they committed 11 errors to Philadelphia's four; only one Athletics run was an earned run. And Bradley (5-3) walked only one batter, while the Athletics worked seven bases on balls. The five-run fifth inning, in which Baltimore pitcher Hardie Henderson walked the first three batters, was the big one.[36] With the victory, the Athletics added a game to their lead and now led the Browns by two games

AUGUST 4: ATHLETICS 5, BALTIMORE ORIOLES 4 (10 INNINGS), AT JEFFERSON STREET GROUNDS

The Baltimores outplayed the Athletics but lost the game. They had 11 hits to Philadelphia's 6, and committed only three errors to the Athletics' seven. There was no heavy batting for the Athletics; they scored one run in each of five innings – most importantly, the 10th inning, when they scored and Baltimore did not.

Corey (7-2) pitched for the home team and had a no-hitter going through five innings, even though Baltimore had scored one run in the fourth. With two runs in the eighth, the Orioles came from behind and tied the game.

Over 8,500 attended – reported as the park's largest crowd. With two outs in the top of the 10th, the Athletics were batting. Stricker walked and ran all the way to third base on a wild throw by the catcher, Rooney Sweeney. Then Sweeney allowed a passed ball and Stricker ran home with what proved to be the winning run. The Orioles threatened, their first two batters hitting singles, but a double play provided the first two outs. Bradley dropped a foul fly but the batter,

Bob Emslie, hit the ball right to Stovey at first base for the third out, and "a perfect pandemonium reigned."[37]

AUGUST 6: BALTIMORE ORIOLES 14, ATHLETICS 9, AT JEFFERSON STREET GROUNDS

The Athletic club scored one run in the top of the first, but Bakley (5-3) was no mystery at all for the Orioles. He allowed seven runs in the bottom of the first inning before there were two outs. He swapped positions with Bradley (who came in from third base to pitch) and O'Brien (who moved from center field to third base, while Bakley went out to center field. The game was Bakley's final appearance with the Athletics. Bob Emslie of the Orioles did his part to help the Athletics, doling out nine bases on balls and throwing two wild pitches. He gave up only four hits; Athletics pitchers gave up 13. The game was, wrote the *Inquirer*, "indifferently played." Perhaps the two sportswriters had been chatting before filing; the *Times* used the same two words.

AUGUST 7: ATHLETICS 12, BALTIMORE ORIOLES 5, AT JEFFERSON STREET GROUNDS

Corey, who improved to 8-2, allowed just six base hits – one of them to Orioles pitcher Hardie Henderson, who homered over the fence in left field in the seventh inning to give Baltimore its first two runs of the game. The Athletics got 15 hits, and bunched enough of them in the first inning to score six runs. Stovey walked and then each of the next six at-bats collected hits. The Athletics led by three games in the American Association standings after the day's victory.

AUGUST 9: METROPOLITANS 14, ATHLETICS 5, AT THE POLO GROUNDS, NEW YORK

Corey (8-3) was battered around for 19 to 21 hits (depending on whether one reads the box score or the accompanying story in the *Times*). Regardless of the actual number, the Metropolitans had a lot of hits and they scored three in the second inning, five in the fourth inning, and one in the fifth to take a commanding 9-0 lead after five frames. The nine runs held up as the final margin of victory, the two teams each scoring five times in the four innings that followed. The Athletics had eight hits, with Stovey adding another home run, his 11th of year, in the top of seventh off Tim Keefe.

AUGUST 10: ATHLETICS 4, METROPOLITANS 3 (10 INNINGS), AT THE POLO GROUNDS, NEW YORK

Bradley held the Mets batters back in an evenly-matched game that was tied after nine. Two runs in the Athletics' eighth helped them overcome the 3-1 deficit they were facing. The Athletics had 10 hits; the Metropolitans had 9. The Mets committed five errors, but the Athletics only two. The game was won in the 10th when O'Brien tripled to drive in the go-ahead run. With the victory, Bradley was now 6-3.

AUGUST 11: METROPOLITANS 3, ATHLETICS 2, AT JEFFERSON STREET GROUNDS

Corey pitched a very good game as did right-hander Jack Lynch for the Metropolitans. Corey (8-4) allowed eight hits, while Lynch allowed six. The game was tied, 2-2, after the Athletics scored their second run in the eighth. The tie was broken when Lynch banged a two-base hit off the left-field wall to give the Metropolitans a 3-2 walk-off victory in the bottom of the ninth. The difference in the game, though, averred the *Times*, was "very stupid base-running" by the Athletics. They cost themselves "at least two runs."[38] In the second inning, with two outs and thus no reason not to be off with the crack of the bat, Bradley tarried at second base when the ball was hit to left field. It was dropped and so he reached third, but he could easily have scored. In the seventh, with nobody out and men on second and third, Bradley hit weakly to the Mets second baseman. Blakiston was caught off second, ran toward third and was out – Corey, feeling forced toward home as Blakiston ran to third, was thrown out at the plate.

A number of "hoodlums … massed together in the right field, seemed to be in their element, kept up an incessant volley of comments not at all complimentary to the umpire."

With wins on August 9, 10, and 11, the Browns had closed to within one game, and with a win on the 12th while the Athletics were idle, just a half-game separated the teams. The Cincinnati Red Stockings were just three games out of first.

AUGUST 13: ATHLETICS 5, METROPOLITANS 2, AT JEFFERSON STREET GROUNDS

Despite threatening weather, 5,000 to 6,000 people reportedly turned out for the game. Bradley (7-3) pitched very well, permitting only four base hits. The

Athletics scored twice in the first inning and would have scored more but for "the greatest catch ever seen on a ball ground" – made by John O'Rourke catching Knight's ball at the center-field fence, then throwing in to double up Stovey. O'Rourke later led off the sixth with a homer, his first of the season, over the fence in center for the "longest hit ever made on the ground."[39] Heavy rain delayed the game before play resumed about 15 minutes later.

AUGUST 17: ATHLETICS 11, COLUMBUS BUCKEYES 1, AT JEFFERSON STREET GROUNDS

There was a lot of scoreboard watching going on during, and after, this game. With such a close pennant race in progress (the Athletics held just a one-game lead over the St. Louis Browns, and Cincinnati just 3½ games behind the Browns entering play), results from the games of the two challengers were telegraphed to the grounds. The Athletics scored five runs in the second and two more in the third, and thus the "attention of the four thousand people on the Athletic grounds was riveted on the blackboard, and the game they were witnessing, being a foregone conclusion, only served to fill up the intervals between the dispatches."[40] The *Times* documented the changes in mood of the crowd in Philadelphia during the fourth,

CINCINNATI WINS.

The Athletics Fail to Make a Run.

fifth, and sixth innings of the St. Louis-Baltimore game, and said there was a "perfect ovation" when the news was posted that the Metropolitans had taken the lead from Cincinnati.

The Athletics committed only two errors in the game, though the base hits were fairly even, the Athletics hitting 14 to the Buckeyes' 12. Everyone but Knight had a base hit. Corey and Stricker both doubled. There was some exceptional fielding noted by several of Philadelphia's fielders. Pitcher Frank Mountain's home run was the only run Columbus scored off Corey, who won his ninth game of the season.

After the game was over, most of the crowd lingered to await the results of the other games. When the final results were announced, "[m]en threw their hats in the air and the ladies waved their handkerchiefs in the grand stand."[41] The Athletics added another game to their lead over both the Browns and Red Stockings.

AUGUST 18: ATHLETICS 19, COLUMBUS BUCKEYES 5, AT JEFFERSON STREET GROUNDS

Coming into the game with his team enjoying a two-game lead, Bradley and teammates enjoyed "another easy victory" – one pretty well in hand even before an eight-run eighth inning put the icing on the cake. They "had their batting clothes on" and pounded out 26 hits to just 7 for Columbus.[42] Birchall, Rowen, and Stricker all doubled, while Stovey and Moynahan made triples. Corey added a double. Mountain pitched

ATHLETIC'S GREAT DAY.

A BIG LIFT FOR THE CHAMPIONSHIP.

A Victory at Home and Great Excitement Over the News From New York and Balti-more—Yesterday's League and Association Games.

again for Columbus and homered for the second game in a row, his third of the season. He walked only one, but the base hits piled up, amounting to 34 total bases. Bradley won his sixth consecutive decision and improved to 8-3.

AUGUST 20: ATHLETICS 9, COLUMBUS BUCKEYES 4, AT JEFFERSON STREET GROUNDS

The differences in hits (12-9) and errors (five for Philadelphia and eight for Columbus) were more or less reflected in the final 9-4 score. It was all over in an hour and 45 minutes before a sparse crowd of about 2,000. Corey was staked to a four-run lead in the top of the first when Birchall doubled over third base and then scored when Stovey hit the ball back to pitcher Pete Fries, who threw the ball over the first baseman's head. Stovey ran all the way around to third base on the error, and scored on the very next pitch – a wild pitch. Two bases on balls and a wild pitch followed, allowing both baserunners to advance before they scored on O'Brien's single. Rowen reached on an error by the first baseman in the third inning, went to second on Bradley's base hit, and both Rowen and

Bradley scored on successive throwing errors by the third baseman and shortstop. The victory was Corey's 10th, his final victory of the season.

AUGUST 21: ATHLETICS 11, CINCINNATI RED STOCKINGS 9, AT JEFFERSON STREET GROUNDS

The Athletics captured their 50th victory (against 21 losses). It was a lengthy game, lasting 2:20, but with 20 runs scored and only two runs separating the winners from the losers, that's understandable. The anticipation was terrific: "By many it was regarded as the pivotal game on which the final decision of the American Association championship may depend. The cars leading to the grounds were packed fully three hours before the game commenced, and one hour before, every seat within the enclosure was occupied and thousands were standing. Over ten thousand tickets were sold at the gates, and the crowd, which was wild with excitement over the game, rivaled the size of the first Athletic-Philadelphia contests."[43]

The Athletics scored twice in the first inning and the Red Stockings tied it, 3-3, in the top of the fourth. The Athletics responded with three runs in the bottom half of the inning and, despite leaving the bases loaded, "were never once headed," despite four runs in the eighth and two in the ninth from Red Stockings that made a game of it. Each team had 17 hits, Bradley pitching against White and neither of them was hard to solve. Cincinnati had five doubles to Philadelphia's three. Stovey hit the game's only homer, his 12th of the season, a two-run homer in the bottom of the sixth off Red Stockings ace Will White. Moynahan, O'Brien, and Rowen each had three hits; Stricker and Stovey collected two apiece. The errors were relatively balanced; Cincinnati's six were one more than the Athletics committed. Bradley continued his winning ways and ran his record to 9-3.

AUGUST 22: CINCINNATI RED STOCKINGS 8, ATHLETICS 6, AT JEFFERSON STREET GROUNDS

A 4 P.M. game against the reigning champions turned out to be a disappointing one for the Athletics who went down to defeat. The blue-stockinged Athletics succumbed to the Cincinnatians in a game with a lot of scoring late in the game. There was a lot of energy before the game began. Eight to nine thousand turned out to the grounds. It was 3-3 through six innings, but the Red Stockings pulled away, scoring two in the seventh and three in the eighth. Mathews (26-12) returned to the mound for first time since July

30. Cincinnati had eight hits (with one walk) and the Athletics had seven (with two walks), but the story of the game was more in the errors – the Athletics committed 11 errors and the Red Stockings committed only four. The *Times* was succinct: "The Athletics lost the game by some bad playing in the field."[44] Third baseman Bradley's two throwing errors led to each of Cincinnati's first two runs. Not a single one of Cincinnati's eight runs was deemed an earned run. The *Inquirer* account repeated the words "miserable fielding" twice.[45]

The Red Stockings had an 8-3 lead after eight innings, and gave up three runs to the Athletics in the ninth, with Moynahan forced out at home on what could have been another run.

AUGUST 23: CINCINNATI RED STOCKINGS 4, ATHLETICS 1, AT JEFFERSON STREET GROUNDS

Corey (10-5) was tasked with holding the Red Stockings down, and he did a good job, allowing just four runs on eight hits. Both teams fielded fairly well – four errors apiece. The difference was that Lorenzo "Ren" Deagle pitched even better, allowing only four hits. Neither team scored for five innings, but Bradley committed three errors (one throwing and two while attempting to field the ball) in the sixth and seventh innings when the Red Stockings scored all four of their runs, three of them attributed to the hapless third baseman. The lone Athletics run came in the ninth.

The *Times* presented attendance figures for the first three games of the series with the Red Stockings, saying that 33,030 had passed through the gates, netting $8,850 in admission fees.[46] Both the *Inquirer* and the *Times* used the word "disgust" to characterize the demeanor of the fans.

The Red Stockings had fallen back in the standings but with wins on the 22nd and 23rd got back to 5½

ST. LOUIS WINS.

The Athletics Lose the Second Game of the Series to Their Rivals.

THE CHAMPIONSHIP CHANCES

Everything Favorable to the Athletics.

games out. Of greater concern to Athletics aficionados, only percentage points separated the 50-23 (.685) Athletics and the 51-24 (.680) Browns.

AUGUST 24: CINCINNATI RED STOCKINGS 8, ATHLETICS 5, AT JEFFERSON STREET GROUNDS

Hope sprang eternal as another 10,000 fans came out to the grounds, but they were disappointed once again. Cincinnati had scored three times in the bottom of the first, but the Athletics came back with three of their own in the top of the second. The *Times* said the cheers at the comeback could be heard from blocks away.[47] The mood soon turned more somber. Mathews started, but resprained his ankle in the fourth and Corey, who was charged with the loss, came in to take over. Corey (10-6) was hit hard – getting hit for four hits and (combined with two of the Athletics' 11 errors) giving up four runs. The Athletics added only single runs in the seventh and ninth. The Athletics were out-hit by the Red Stockings, 12-9, but in the errors department committed those aforementioned 11 miscues while Cincinnati committed only two.

An official statement said the four-game series had drawn 41,000 with receipts totaling $11,400.

With their victory, the Red Stockings had knocked the Athletics out of first place. The Browns led by one game in the standings. After the Browns' loss on the 25th, the winning percentage couldn't be any closer without being tied: Athletics .676 and Browns .675.

AUGUST 27: ATHLETICS 13, COLUMBUS BUCKEYES 8, AT JEFFERSON STREET GROUNDS

The *Times* declared that the August 27 game was arguably more "a burlesque than a struggle for the pennant and was only made endurable to the twenty-five hundred people present by the ridiculous errors made on both sides."[48] Each team committed 11 errors, for a total of 22. Corey made three errors at third base and so did Bradley, the pitcher. Stovey was given a short leave of absence and Bob Blakiston filled in at first base; he had two singles and a double. But those 2,500 people saw the Athletics snap their three-game losing streak and win a game. With the win, Bradley (10-3) extended his personal win streak to eight games and joined Mathews and Corey with double-digit wins.

AUGUST 28: ECLIPSE 10, ATHLETICS 8, AT JEFFERSON STREET GROUNDS

The two-run margin of victory in the 10-8 game was closer than one might have thought based on how the *Inquirer*'s game account began: "Wretched fielding on the part of Moynahan and Stricker lost the Athletics their game with the Louisvilles yesterday. Corey was put in to pitch, and was hammered all over the field."[49] The *Times* dubbed it a "miserably played" game and described the 3,000 patrons as watching in "disgust."[50] The *Times* headline was overly dramatic: "Going Fast to the Rear." True, the Athletics had lost four out of five, and they were now truly in second place, by a full game. But it is not as though all hopes to salvage the season had been dashed.

Moynahan and Stricker each committed four errors in the game; Moynahan compensated for his defensive struggles with four hits. Corey (10-7) was hit hard and was not relieved until a time in the game when it didn't make a difference. Louisville had come from behind and tied the game, 6-6, with a pair of runs in the fifth, and then scored three runs in the sixth and one in the seventh.

Stovey was still away on leave.

AUGUST 29: ATHLETICS 11, ECLIPSE 3, AT JEFFERSON STREET GROUNDS

The game was quite a contrast to the desultory play over the preceding week. Bradley pitched and held the Eclipse to four hits, not allowing even one hit through the first five innings, while improving his record to 11-3. Everyone in the Athletics' lineup had at least two hits (save Knight, who had none). Stovey was back and played very well at first base, including two one-handed catches. Blakiston played center field. The Athletics collected 19 base hits and steadily added to their lead throughout the game.

After the game, only four percentage points separated the Athletics and Browns, Philadelphia on top with a winning percentage of .675 to .671 for St. Louis. This was quite a pennant race, but there was still a month to go.

AUGUST 30: ATHLETICS 8, ECLIPSE 7, AT JEFFERSON STREET GROUNDS

The Athletics committed nine errors, but won "because the Louisvilles played still worse."[51] The Eclipse "out-erred" the Athletics, 11-9. They also out-hit them, 14 to 11, but the 5-5 tie that stood after three innings was broken when the Athletics scored one run each in the sixth, seventh, and eighth innings, and gave up only two in return. Mathews struck out six and walked two to earn his first victory of August and 27th of the season. Everyone on the Athletics but O'Brien had at least one hit. Corey was said to have played well behind the plate.

AUGUST 31: ATHLETICS 6, ECLIPSE 3, AT JEFFERSON STREET GROUNDS

Both teams scored one run at a time for each of the first seven runs of the game, the lead changing hands a couple of times. Leading 4-3, the Athletics added two insurance runs in the eighth. Bradley pitched, permitting just six hits to win his ninth game in the month of August (10th in a row overall) to improve to 12-3. Apparently Rowen found it difficult to handle his fastball, and so O'Brien took over catching duties while Rowen replaced him in center field. Moynahan doubled and tripled, and Bradley hit a double, too. Notably, the Athletics only committed one error – an error by Corey on a hard-hit ball to third base.

Coming back to win three games in a row from Louisville was significant. Despite Mathews winning only one game, the Athletics were 14-7 during the up-and-down month of August. They finished the month with a record of 54-25, just .005 ahead of the Browns, who were 55-26. Stovey, who clubbed six home runs during July, had three more in August.

SEPTEMBER 1: ATHLETICS 11, METROPOLITANS 5, AT JEFFERSON STREET GROUNDS

Mathews kept the Metropolitans in check, and the Athletics made it four in a row with a fairly easy game. Whereas Friday's game saw a total of five errors, this one had 19. Eleven of them were by the Mets. The game was a low-scoring 1-1 affair through the first four innings. Bradley and Stricker both singled to lead off the fifth; Mathews reached first base on an error to load the bases. Birchall singled and drove in two. Stovey reached on a fielding error by the third baseman, and then Moynahan singled, driving in three more. Each team had 13 hits. Mathews, matching his win total for August, improved his record to 28-12.

SEPTEMBER 3: ST. LOUIS BROWNS 7, ATHLETICS 5, AT JEFFERSON STREET GROUNDS

After an offday, the second-place St. Louis Browns came to town only half a game behind the Athletics. The crush of people trying to get into the grounds was so great that "the big gate on Twenty-sixth street was carried away, but the police force was sufficiently strong enough to hold back the people until the damages had been repaired."[52] People were allowed on the field in right and left, held back by ropes so as not to encroach too far onto the playing field. There were "hundreds stowed away against the centre-field fence."[53] An additional ground rule was implemented – any ball hit into the crowd could be for no more than two bases.

The *Philadelphia Inquirer* informed readers who were not among the 12,000 in attendance: "The Athletics threw away another game yesterday by miserable fielding. For some unaccountable reason the club has been playing wretchedly in the field for the past month, and almost every game they have lost has been a clear throwaway."[54] This was another game featuring "sloven fielding" – 11 Athletics errors to six by St. Louis. The hits were relatively even, seven for the Browns and six for the Athletics.

The Athletics led, 5-3, after five innings, but failed to score the rest of the game. Errors by Moynahan and Stricker led to a Browns run in the sixth. Errors by Stovey and Knight contributed to two more Browns runs in the seventh, and a relinquishing of the lead. Bradley (12-4) was the Athletics pitcher and suffered the loss. The *Times* averred that the fielding "would have disgraced an amateur club" and said that the "hoodlums" started "whistling the 'Dead March,'" as the seventh inning saw St. Louis take the lead.

The Athletics had taken a half-game lead on September 1, but losing to the Browns on the 3rd put them half a game behind.

SEPTEMBER 4: ATHLETICS 11, ST. LOUIS BROWNS 1, AT JEFFERSON STREET GROUNDS

"Jones, the Yale College Pitcher" was announced as the starter in an advertisement in the September 3 *Times*. Jack "DA" Jones was a right-hander who had pitched for the National League's Detroit Wolverines earlier in 1883, going 6-5 with a 3.50 ERA. A note in the *Times* said that Jones had been "playing with professional clubs during his vacation only" and "will return to his studies shortly."[55] He was the star of the game – the *Times* headline the next day read "Won by the New Pitcher."[56] Jones allowed only four base hits and all four were singles. He struck out six and walked

only one to earn the victory in his Athletics debut. St. Louis committed nine errors, three by center fielder Fred Lewis.

Ten thousand people came to the game. Jones's first three pitches were all wide of the plate. "Then he jumped two feet in the air, and while Gleason gazed at him in astonishment the ball traveled squarely over the centre of the plate and one strike was called. 'Jumping Jack' jumped again and Gleason aimed at a ball two feet from the end of his bat. He jumped again on the next ball and Gleason was called out on strikes, and then the crowd applauded, while the 'hoodlums,' who have moved over into the sun in left field, fairly went wild.

"Jones has a wonderful command over the ball. … He also has a wonderfully deceptive delivery and, judging from the ill success of the St. Louis batsmen, he has discovered several new 'curves' and 'shoots.' He has a half dozen different styles of delivery. His jumping act astonishes the batsmen and they forget to aim at the ball. In fact, as one of the visitors remarked, 'You don't know whether Jones or the ball is coming at you.'"[57] The newspaper said he proved a good batter (he had two base hits) and baserunner and if Stovey had not muffed a throw in the fifth inning, Jones would have had a shutout.

SEPTEMBER 5: ATHLETICS 5, ST. LOUIS BROWNS 4, AT JEFFERSON STREET GROUNDS

The Athletics ran Jumping Jack back out to the mound the very next day, and they won the game – but not easily. Jones pitched well. He allowed eight hits and walked one, but saw a 3-1 lead after five innings slip away. The game was tied, 3-3, after seven innings. In the eighth, O'Brien walked and Corey drove him in with a double. Bradley then singled to right-center to drive in Corey. St. Louis needed two to tie, but came up one run short. They scored once on a single, a wild pitch (a passed ball according to one paper), and somehow scored on a fly ball to second baseman Stricker, which he caught but fell down after catching. The box score doesn't show him charged with an error. Two more runners reached base, but the Athletics recorded the third out on a ball hit to third baseman Bradley. Again, not an earned run had been scored off Jones, who won his second game in a row.

SEPTEMBER 6: ATHLETICS 4, ST. LOUIS BROWNS 3, AT JEFFERSON STREET GROUNDS

ST. LOUIS BEATEN AGAIN.

A GAME VERY CLOSELY CONTESTED.

The Athletics Take a Commanding Lead in
the Championship Race, Much to
the Disgust of President
Von der Ahe.

Bradley pitched before another huge crowd – estimated at 12,000 – so large that "the fences along the left and right-field seats gave strong indications of giving away from the strong pressure against them."[58] The crowd was disappointed that "Jumping Jack" wouldn't be pitching, but Bradley helped give them what they came for – another win. Another one-run victory, as it happened. Bradley (13-4) held the Browns to three runs on seven hits. The Athletics had only six hits off Tony Mullane, but they were enough. The lead changed hands but the game was tied, 3-3, after the sixth. In the top of the seventh, the Athletics took the lead on back-to-back doubles by Corey and Stricker.

Winning three games in a row from the Browns made a huge difference. When St. Louis left Philadelphia for home after this day's game – the second in a row decided by just one run – the Athletics held a 2½-game lead.

SEPTEMBER 7: ATHLETICS 5, COLUMBUS BUCKEYES 2, AT JEFFERSON STREET GROUNDS

Jones was trotted out again. He allowed only five base hits and two runs, one in the second inning and one in the eighth, and both of them unearned runs. The Athletics scored three runs in the second inning on singles by O'Brien and Stricker, a double by Corey and a ball the Columbus left fielder muffed. They added two more in the in the third inning on a walk, a double by Moynahan, an error by the catcher, a single, and a second error by the Columbus catcher. The Friday game drew only 1,500, the crowd likely depressed because of the Athletics' more comfortable lead in the standings and the opponent not being a pennant-contending team.

With the win, the newly discovered phenomenon, Jumping Jack Jones, improved to 3-0.

SEPTEMBER 8: ATHLETICS 4, COLUMBUS BUCKEYES 2 (EXHIBITION GAME), AT JEFFERSON STREET GROUNDS

This game took an unexpected turn in mid-game. It began as a championship game but ended as an exhibition game. Bradley started for the Athletics and Ed Dundon for the Buckeyes. Neither team scored through the first three innings. In the fourth, the Buckeyes had a man on second base with one out. Second baseman Pop Smith was batting, and hit a foul ball that glanced off Rowen's mask and struck Michael Walsh, the umpire, on the temple. Walsh "fell senseless to the ground. He lay still for a few minutes and then went into violent convulsions, from which he recovered only after the physicians had worked with him for a considerable time."[59] He was unable to continue and was taken back to his hotel.

Without an umpire – all Association games were worked by just one umpire – the teams agreed to continue to play, but to deem it an exhibition game. Both second basemen came in as pitchers – Stricker for the Athletics and Smith for the Buckeyes. The game finished as a "burlesque" which included a member of the audience being invited to serve as umpire (his name was not recorded for posterity by the *Times*), and Stricker "set the large crowd wild by giving an imitation of 'Jumping Jack' Jones' style of delivery."[60]

Walsh, a native of Ireland, had six seasons of umpiring under his belt. He managed the Louisville Eclipse in 1884, then returned to umpiring in 1885 and 1886, and finally worked one game in both 1887 and 1888.

SEPTEMBER 9: ATHLETICS 10, COLUMBUS BUCKEYES 3, AT RECREATION PARK, COLUMBUS

Bradley (14-4) pitched on Sunday afternoon, the game played in Columbus as the Athletics began a 13-game road trip to conclude the season. The Athletics out-hit the Buckeyes, 12 hits to 7. Columbus notably made only one error in the game, and the Athletics three. The first three batters of the game for Philadelphia produced back-to-back-to-back doubles by Birchall, Stovey, and Knight. That resulted in two runs. In the fourth, Stovey walked and Knight tripled. Moynahan and Corey both drew walks, loading the bases. Blakiston singled to drive in two and a sacrifice hit to the shortstop brought in a fourth run.

On September 10, the Browns closed to within 2½ games. They didn't get any closer until September 27.

SEPTEMBER 12: ATHLETICS 7, COLUMBUS BUCKEYES 5 (10 INNINGS), AT RECREATION PARK, COLUMBUS

Jones gave up his first earned runs – three of them – but hung on to win a very close game that was settled in the 10th inning. Columbus committed only three errors, while the Athletics made six. The Athletics collected 12 base hits; Columbus had 10. Philadelphia scored one in the first inning and one more in the second. The Buckeyes then took the lead with three runs in the third and another in the fourth. It was 5-3, Columbus, after six innings. The Athletics tied it with Stovey's two-run homer off right-hander Ed Dundon in the eighth. Stovey's home run, his 13th of the season, was his first in more than three weeks.

With one out in the top of the 10th, Birchall singled and moved to second on a passed ball. Stovey then singled, sending the Athletics left fielder racing around third before he was cut down at the plate. Knight followed with a triple to center field, knocking in Stovey, and Knight tagged up and scored when O'Brien flied out to center field. The Athletics held a 7-5 lead. Columbus put the two tying runs on base in the bottom of the 10th, but Jones (4-0) shut them down and the Athletics won.

SEPTEMBER 13: ATHLETICS 11, COLUMBUS BUCKEYES 5, AT RECREATION PARK, COLUMBUS

This was a makeup of a postponed game. Bradley (15-4) pitched and was hittable – giving up 11 base hits to Buckeyes hitters. Bradley collected two hits himself and his teammates added another dozen. O'Brien had three hits, while Birchall, Stovey, Corey, Bradley, and West (Al Hubbard) each had two. Birchall led off for the Athletics with a home run to the left-field fence, the only home run of his three-year major-league career.

West, described in the September 14 *Times* as "the new catcher for the Athletics," played shortstop, and "did some very brilliant work in the field and also at the bat."[61] Stovey at first base and Blakiston in center field drew exceptional praise for their fielding – "equal to any ever seen on the ball grounds." The Athletics led 6-0 after the first three innings. With the win, the season series between the two teams was over, with the Athletics winning 13 games and losing only one.

The win was Bradley's 13th in his last 14 decisions.

SEPTEMBER 15: CINCINNATI RED STOCKINGS 11, ATHLETICS 0, AT BANK STREET GROUNDS, CINCINNATI

Jones was pitching and West was catching. The Athletics were shut out for the fourth time in 1883. It wasn't even close. Cincinnati scored twice in the first, once in the second, and twice in the third, and added another five runs before the slaughter was complete. The Athletics secured only four hits. In seven of the nine innings, they sent only three men to the plate. Only once did the Athletics advance a runner as far as second base. The loss was Jones's first with the Athletics and dropped his record to 4-1.

It turns out that "West" wasn't really West. He was Al Hubbard, a batterymate of Jones from Yale. He played in only two games. He didn't get any hits in this game, allowed four passed balls, and also let a third strike get away from him. See Rich Bogovich's SABR biography of Hubbard in this volume for more.

SEPTEMBER 18: ATHLETICS 13, CINCINNATI RED STOCKINGS 12 (10 INNINGS), AT BANK STREET GROUNDS, CINCINNATI

The game seemed to be very one-sided until the sixth inning. The Athletics scored five runs in the first inning and Stovey and Stricker added home runs in the top of the sixth. For Stovey, it was his 14th and final home run of the season. Corey homered as well, the first home run of his career. For Stricker, it was the first of his career. After six innings, the Athletics led 10-4. The Red Stockings mounted a comeback and scored eight runs off Mathews in the seventh inning. Suddenly the Athletics found themselves behind 12-10. But the Athletics didn't go quietly. They scored two runs in the eighth to tie the game, 12-12. Neither team scored in the ninth. The Athletics won the game on Stovey's steal of home. Here's how the *Times* dispatch described what happened: "The game as lost by the Cincinnatis through White's failure to hold a grounder sent to him by Stovey. A wild pitch then let Stovey to second and a strike carried him to third, then he stole home."[62] Cincinnati's *Commercial Gazette*, which provided a much more detailed account of the game, wrote: "White tried to stop Stovey's grounder and missed it. … A wild pitch sent him to second. Knight's out advanced him to third, and a passed ball let him home."[63] The victory was Mathews' 29th of the season.

PLANNING A PARADE

Back in Philadelphia, a group of some 300 citizens in Philadelphia held a mass meeting at the Athletic headquarters at 159 North Eighth Street. They initiated plans for a reception parade to meet the Athletics base ball team when they returned home from the road trip, hopefully securely in possession of the American Association pennant. They established committees to deal with a hall, carriages, music, etc. It was reported that "forty base ball clubs in full uniform, forty social clubs, and ten pioneer corps and yacht clubs, with forty bands of music, and numbering fully six thousand men, had already applied for position in the line of parade."[64] During the meeting word arrived that the team had beaten the Red Stockings in 10 innings, and "the greatest enthusiasm was manifested."

SEPTEMBER 19: CINCINNATI RED STOCKINGS 12, ATHLETICS 3, AT BANK STREET GROUNDS, CINCINNATI

Most of the game was closer than the final score would indicate; the Red Stockings scored six runs in the top of the ninth inning. Bradley (15-5) pitched for the Athletics and took the loss. The Red Stockings scored first – one run in the first inning – and added three more in the third. The Athletics cut the Red Stockings' lead in half when Bradley hit a two-run homer in the third. The Red Stockings out-hit the Athletics, though, 17 to 5, with two doubles, three triples, and two home runs. Bradley homered for Philadelphia, his first of the season. It was a game of relatively few errors- three for the Athletics and only two for the Red Stockings. The *Times* observed, "The notable feature of the game was that 11 of the 12 runs by the Cincinnatis were earned runs."[65]

The Red Stockings were the only team that had a winning record against the 1883 Athletics; in 14 games, the Red Stockings held a 9-5 advantage.

SEPTEMBER 21: ATHLETICS 13, ST. LOUIS BROWNS 11, AT SPORTSMAN'S PARK, ST. LOUIS

There were 12,000 who thronged Sportsman's Park, but in Philadelphia a large number gathered around bulletin boards outside city newspaper offices to learn the scores from St. Louis as they were posted. Some of the streets were nearly impassable. When the news broke, around 7 P.M., that the Athletics had won, "[m]en threw their hats in the air and shouted themselves hoarse, and the scene was simply indescribable."[66]

It was quite a back-and-forth game, with 24 runs being scored. The base hits were close in number, too, 12 for the Athletics and 11 for the Browns. Most astonishing were the number of errors recorded in the game – 30 of them, 17 by the victorious Athletics and 13 by the Browns. "Bradley, who took Stovey's place at first, could not catch anything. Rowen threw the ball in all directions, never at his target."[67] Bradley was charged with four errors. The catcher, Rowen, was charged with eight (and one passed ball). Birchall collected four base hits.

It was Mathews' 30th win of the season.

Preparations for a parade continued, and arrangements were made for a special train that would meet the Athletics in Harrisburg and bring them back to Philadelphia.

SEPTEMBER 22: ST. LOUIS BROWNS 9, ATHLETICS 6, AT SPORTSMAN'S PARK, ST. LOUIS

There were still games to be played, however. After the game on the 21st, the Athletics had a 3½-game lead over St. Louis and six games left to play. Certainly St. Louis partisans hadn't given up yet, and they turned out in large numbers, some 13,000 of them. They were encouraged when the Browns beat Jones and the Athletics, 9-2, this Saturday. It was Jones's second consecutive loss. That narrowed the gap to 2½ games. Jumping Jack (4-2) "showed his nervousness at the start."[68] The scoring, however, was remarkably parallel; both teams scored one run in the fist, both teams scored three runs in the second, and both teams scored two runs in the third. The difference from then on was St. Louis pitcher Jumbo McGinnis, who shut out the Athletics the rest of the way. Rowen allowed four passed balls and made four errors. All in all, the Athletics committed nine errors and the Browns only two.

SEPTEMBER 23: ATHLETICS 9, ST. LOUIS BROWNS 2, AT SPORTSMAN'S PARK, ST. LOUIS

Sunday afternoon saw 16,800 come out to Sportsman's Park for the rubber game of the three-game series. They arrived via street cars, "hired hacks, private conveyances, many of the latter being express wagons, furniture wagons, milk carts and other vehicles usually allowed a Sunday repose but to-day pressed into service and groaning under the weight of their passengers." The scene at the park was chaotic: "The stands were early filled, and thousands who had purchased tickets for reserved seats and found that none were left, available, secured the park ladders and climbed to the roof of the stands, the legs of the forward ones, who sat upon the edge, dangling over the heads of those below. The strain upon the wooden structures was tremendous, but they stood it, and the day passed happily without a casualty of any kind."[69]

In Philadelphia, "a multitude of excited people" gathered outside the *Times* offices. When word was received that St. Louis had failed to score in the first inning, there was cheering. Shortly afterward, when it was announced that the Athletics had scored two in the bottom of the first, there "went up a roar that was heard blocks away and people came running from all quarters to swell the crowd."[70]

Bradley (16-5) pitched a masterful game, allowing only three hits. The Athletics scored two in the first inning and three in the fifth, and it soon became clear that there was little hope for the Browns to break through. And they did not. They didn't get their first base hit until the fourth. They scored only two runs, one in the eighth and one in the ninth. After the game, "the victorious visitors were warmly applauded. The crowd concentrated around the gate by which the players were to depart, and as the Athletics got into their carriages, the cry went up: 'Three cheers for the coming champions!' and ten thousand throats lustily shouted their hearty appreciation of the plucky and skillful Philadelphians, who showed plainly that they fully appreciated the kindly compliment."[71] The Athletics had clinched at least a tie for the American Association pennant.

SEPTEMBER 26: ECLIPSE 7, ATHLETICS 5, AT ECLIPSE PARK, LOUISVILLE

Bradley (16-6) did not have his best day. He threw four wild pitches and allowed 14 hits. There were only two Athletics errors on the field (three by Louisville). The Eclipse built a 4-1 lead over the first four innings, but a four-run fifth gave the edge to the Athletics. The Eclipse responded with two runs in the sixth and a seventh run in the top of the ninth. The game was played before a "very small audience."[72]

SEPTEMBER 27: ECLIPSE 6, ATHLETICS 3, AT ECLIPSE PARK, LOUISVILLE

The Browns beat the Alleghenys, 20-3, on September 26. With another win on September 27, they closed the gap to 1½ games and clung to the hope of tying the Athletics. The Browns had only one game left to play. The Athletics had two.

The September 27 game was again played before another very small crowd. Both teams scored once in the first. The Athletics scored another run in the third inning, but the Eclipse scored three in the fourth and added single runs in the fifth and eighth. The Athletics had just one more run in them, scoring in the seventh. Mathews pitched, his last game of the season. He allowed only eight base hits, but three of them (including two doubles) were bunched in the fourth, and two errant throws aided the Eclipse in that inning. With the loss, Mathews finished the season with a record of 30-13. Moynahan had three of the Athletics' seven hits. The Louisvillians committed just three errors.

SEPTEMBER 28: ATHLETICS 7, ECLIPSE 6 (10 INNINGS), AT ECLIPSE PARK, LOUISVILLE

That the Athletics had lost two in a row was "harrowing" to their supporters back home. And this game kept everyone on the edge. Entering the series with the Eclipse, all the Athletics needed was one win to secure the pennant, but they had lost on the 26th and again on the 27th. And this game – while lasting only two hours – seemed to take a long time to play out.

Meanwhile, excitement all over the city of Philadelphia was at a "fever pitch." The streets were packed around the newspaper offices. Even at Recreation Park, where the National League's Philadelphia Quakers were hosting the Chicago White Stockings, the crowd "gave its almost undivided attention to the blackboard," scoreboard-watching.[73]

The Eclipse lost the toss and the Philadelphians batted last. Jones (5-2) pitched for the Athletics.

The Athletics were the first to score – two runs in the fourth inning, but the Eclipse promptly matched that in the fifth. In the sixth inning, the Athletics upped the ante by scoring three runs, but the Eclipse came right back, matching those three runs and adding a fourth, taking a 6-5 lead in the seventh. The Athletics evened it up again with a run in the eighth. Neither team scored in the ninth, nor did the Eclipse score in the top of the 10th. In the bottom of the inning, Stovey earned a base on balls, then took second base on a passed ball. Knight singled, and Stovey advanced to third base. With runners on first and third, and still nobody out, Moynahan singled and won the game – and the pennant.

They had out-hit the Eclipse, 11-8, and committed only three errors to Louisville's four.

SEPTEMBER 30: ECLIPSE 10, ATHLETICS 5, AT ECLIPSE PARK, LOUISVILLE

There was no game in Louisville on the 29th. Both teams waited until Sunday the 30th to close out the season. With their win in the season's final game,

ENDING THE BALL SEASON

THE RECORDS OF THE VARIOUS CLUBS

The Athletics and the Bostons Win the Championship Pennants—Another Victory for the Louisvilles Over the Home Team—St. Louis Also Wins Again.

Louisville drew even in its season series against the Athletics, a record of 7-7. Only Cincinnati had a winning record against Philadelphia, which was 5-9 against the Red Stockings.

Bradley (16-7) pitched the season finale for the Athletics, but the game was of course anticlimactic. There were still sizable crowds who flocked to the Philadelphia newspaper offices to follow the game. It was a 10:00 A.M. game in Louisville. The Athletics took a 2-0 lead, then saw the Eclipse score one run in the fourth. The Athletics still held a 2-1 lead after seven innings, but the Eclipse scored two runs in the eighth on a single, a triple, and a wild throw. With two outs and nobody on, the Eclipse exploded for seven more runs. The Athletics scored three runs in the ninth, but were five runs short.

The Eclipse played another game later in the day, against a team from Indianapolis, winning 13-2.

The Athletics were 12-7 during September and finished the season with a record of 66-32, a single game ahead of the second-place St. Louis Browns, who finished with a record of 65-33.

The Athletics took the train to Cincinnati, there to connect with the one that would take them to Philadelphia – and the reception that awaited them.

SOURCES

Unless otherwise indicated, game information and all unattributed quotations came from the *Philadelphia Inquirer*. In general, it may be said that the *Times* of Philadelphia provided better coverage. Both Retrosheet.org and Baseball-Reference.com were consulted throughout.

NOTES

1   "Field Sports," *Philadelphia Inquirer*, April 16, 1883: 3.

2   "The Baltimores Beaten," *Baltimore Sun*, May 8, 1883: 1.

3   "The Athletics Defeated," *Baltimore Sun*, May 10, 1883: 1.

4   "The 'Mets' Beaten," *Philadelphia Inquirer*, May 11, 1883: 2.

5   "Another Close Contest," *Philadelphia Inquirer*, May 12, 1883: 2.

6   The *New York Times* box score gave two earned runs to Philadelphia.

7   "Base Ball Players Quarreling," *Philadelphia Inquirer*, May 23, 1883: 2.

8   "Base-ball: The Metropolitans Defeated by the Athletic Club," *New York Times*, May 27, 1883: 2.

9   "Base Ball," *Philadelphia Inquirer*, June 2, 1883: 2.

10   Brian McKenna, "Ed Dundon," SABR BioProject, at sabr.org/bioproj/person/92319431.

11   "Athletic Beats St. Louis," *Philadelphia Inquirer*, June 9, 1883: 2.

12   "The Association Race," *Times* (Philadelphia), June 10, 1883: 2.

13   "Ross vs. Athletic," *Delaware County Daily Times* (Chester, Pennsylvania), June 18, 1883: 3.

14   "Champion Work, Which Shut Out the Athletics Yesterday," *Cincinnati Commercial Tribune*, June 19, 1883: 2.

15   "Game for the Athletics," *Times* (Philadelphia), June 22, 1883: 4.

16   "Around the Canvas Bags," *Times* (Philadelphia), June 26, 1883: 4.

17   "Columbus Beaten a Third Time," *Times* (Philadelphia), June 27, 1883: 1.

18   "Athletics 7, Columbus 2," *Commercial Gazette*, June 27,1883: 3.

19   "The Browns Badly Outplayed," *St. Louis Post-Dispatch*, June 29, 1883: 5.

20   "The Browns Badly Outplayed."

21   "St. Louis Again Loses a Game to the Athletics," *St. Louis Globe-Democrat*, July 1, 1883: 7.

22   "A Shocking Relapse," *St. Louis Globe-Democrat*, July 3, 1883: 8.

23   "No Game in Louisville," *Times* (Philadelphia), July 7, 1833: 1.

24   "The Association Games," *Times* (Philadelphia), July 8, 1833: 2.

25   "This Is Good Enough," *Pittsburgh Daily Post*, July 11, 1883: 4.

26   "The Athletics Badly Whipped," *Times* (Philadelphia), July 13, 1883: 3.

27   "Around the Canvas Bags," *Times* (Philadelphia), July 14, 1883: 1.

28   "Won in Ten Innings," *Times* (Philadelphia), July 15, 1883: 2.

29   "Both the Home Clubs Win," *Times* (Philadelphia), July 19, 1883: 4.

30   "The Baltimores Meet the Athletics, with the Usual Results," *Baltimore Sun*, July 19, 1883: 4.

31   "Thirty-five Hundred People Witness the Defeat of the Baltimores," *Times* (Philadelphia), July 21, 1883: 4.

32   "The Diamond Field," *Times* (Philadelphia), July 26, 1883: 3.

33   For a full game account, see Mike Huber, "Philadelphia's Lon Knight Is First Player to Hit for a 'Natural' Cycle," SABR Games Project, sabr.org/gamesproj/game/july-30-1883-philadelphias-lon-knight-first-player-hit-natural-cycle.

34   "Another Defeat," *Philadelphia Inquirer*, August 1, 1883: 2.

35   "One Added to the Score," *Times* (Philadelphia), August 2, 1883: 4. The *Inquirer* agreed it was the longest ball ever hit at the park, adding that it sailed out of the park 12 feet over the fence.

36   The Orioles finished in last place in 1883, with a record of 28-68. Henderson's record was 10-32.

37   "Won in Ten Innings," *Times* (Philadelphia), August 5, 1883: 2.

38   "Another Game Lost," *Times* (Philadelphia), August 12, 1883: 2.

39   "The Athletics Win," *Philadelphia Inquirer*, August 14, 1883: 2. The *Times* concurred that O'Rourke's catch was "the most difficult catch ever seen on the ground." See "One for the Athletics," *Times* (Philadelphia), August 14, 1883: 4.

40   "Athletic's Great Day," *Times* (Philadelphia), August 18, 1883: 1.

41   "Athletic's Great Day."

42   "Another Easy Victory," *Times* (Philadelphia), August 19, 1883: 2.

43   "Wild Over a Ball Contest," *Times* (Philadelphia), August 22, 1883: 4. The reference was to the late April preseason games between Philadelphia's National League team and the Athletics.

44   "Defeated by Cincinnati," *Times* (Philadelphia), August 23, 1883: 1.

45   "The Champions Win," *Philadelphia Inquirer*, August 23, 1883: 2.

46   "No Longer the Leaders," *Times* (Philadelphia), August 24, 1883: 4.

47   "Another Ball Game Gone," *Times* (Philadelphia), August 25, 1883: 4.

48   "One Won from Columbus," *Times* (Philadelphia), August 28, 1883: 4.

49   "Another Defeat," *Philadelphia Inquirer*, August 29, 1883: 2.

50   "Going Fast to the Rear," *Times* (Philadelphia), August 29, 1883: 4.

51   "Progress of the National Game," *Philadelphia Inquirer*, August 31, 1883: 2.

52   "Two Games Played in the City," *Philadelphia Inquirer*, September 4, 1883: 2.

53   "Defeated by St. Louis," *Times* (Philadelphia), September 4, 1883: 4.

54   "Two Games Played in the City."

55   "To Correspondents," *Times* (Philadelphia), September 5, 1883: 3.

56   "Won by the New Pitcher," *Times* (Philadelphia), September 5, 1883: 4.

57   "Won by the New Pitcher."

58   "The Good Work Goes On," *Times* (Philadelphia), September 7, 1883: 4.

59   "Umpire Walsh Injured," *Times* (Philadelphia), September 9, 1883: 2.

60   "Umpire Walsh Injured."

61   "The Athletics Win the Final Games of the Series from Columbus," *Times* (Philadelphia), September 14, 1883: 3.

62   "Won in the 10th," *Times* (Philadelphia), September 19, 1883: 3.

63   "Great Sport – The Most Exciting Game of the Season," *Commercial Gazette*, September 19, 1883: 3.

64   "A Grand Reception to Be Given the Victorious Athletics," *Philadelphia Inquirer*, September 19, 1883: 8.

65   "The Athletics Beaten," *Times* (Philadelphia), September 20, 1883: 3.

66   "Athletics Will Win the Pennant," *Philadelphia Inquirer*, September 22, 1883: 2.

67   "The Athletics' Victory," *Times* (Philadelphia), September 22, 1883: 2.

68   "The Athletics' Defeat," *Times* (Philadelphia), September 23, 1883: 2.

69   "St. Louis Badly Beaten," *Times* (Philadelphia), September 24, 1883: 1.

70   "St. Louis Badly Beaten."

71   "St. Louis Badly Beaten."

72   "The Athletics Lose One," *Times* (Philadelphia), September 27, 1883: 1.

73   "The Pennant Won," *Times* (Philadelphia), September 29, 1883: 2.

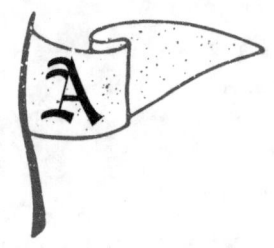

THE BASE BALL PARADE

WELCOMING THE CHAMPIONS HOME.
TEN THOUSAND ADMIRERS OF THE ATHLETIC CLUB
MARCH IN HONOR OF PHILADELPHIA'S VICTORY.
HOW MAYOR KING AND THE MULTITUDE
RECEIVED THE PLAYERS.

Mr. Moynahan, butcher; Mr. Stricker, milk wagon driver; Mr. Corey, shoemaker; Mr. Bradley, brickmaker; Mr. Birchall, weaver; Mr. Blakiston, carpenter; Mr. Stovey, ice wagon driver; Mr. Knight, pot hunter; Mr. O'Brlen, civil engineer; Mr. Rowen, Mr. Matthews and Mr. Jones, gentlemen of leisure, form the team that won the Association base ball championship for the Athletic Club, of Philadelphia. The victors returned home last night and the youth and chivalry of Swampoodle and Smoky Hollow and Kensington and other neighborhoods turned out in thousands to receive them. Fully ten thousand men and boys, several hundred horses and one mule – the antique gray which so long pulled Mr. Stricker's milk wagon – took part in the parade. They marched six miles, through streets that were literally packed with spectators, who manifested little enthusiasm after the passage of the carriages containing the champions.

Yesterday morning a dozen gentlemen in black clothes and glistening hats attracted a great deal of attention in the Pennsylvania Railroad station on Broad Street. They formed the committee appointed to receive the returning champions at Harrisburg. William B. Smith, President of Select Council; Charles Lawrence, of Common Council; George Hoffman, of Common Council, and Poor Guardian Ruhl were the leaders of the band. The off coat-tail of each gentleman bulged out in a way that excited some comment among members of the temperance party in the station. These suspicions were unjust, as the swelling of the coat-tails was caused by while cotton gloves, which, when put on, made the hands of the wearers look like unpainted Cincinnati hams.

GOING TO MEET THE CHAMPIONS.

The committee boarded the train at once and were soon whirling away toward Harrisburg. Most of the gentlemen are first-class theoretical ball players, but their knowledge of the technical teams and other fine points was limited. Mr. Ruhl affectionately referred to the Athletic team as "our eleven," Mr. Lawrence spoke of bowling and President Smith insisted on calling the difference between the runs of contending nines as "the majority" or "the majorities."

"How much majority did our boys have in the first St. Louis game?" asked President Smith of Mr. Hoffman, who was dreamily sucking an unlighted cigar.

"Bill, do you know I made the first tambourine Lew Simmons ever banged?" irrelevantly replied the Fourth ward Councilman.

THE BASE BALL PARADE.

WELCOMING THE CHAMPIONS HOME.

Ten Thousand Admirers of the Athletic Club
March in Honor of Philadelphia's Victory.
How Mayor King and the Multitude
Received the Players.

The Times

Mr. Smith's question was never answered, for the reference to Mr. Simmons' first tambourine led a fat little man in a back seat to say: "I don't know anything about his tambourine, but I have heard he's a Jonah."

"What!" chorused half a dozen gentlemen, and the question, "Is Mr. Simmons a Jonah or Mascot?" was discussed until the train reached Harrisburg. There a mob of 1,500 people surrounded the committee and admired their dazzling silk badges. An hour later an express train from Pittsburg rolled into the depot, with the Athletic and Metropolitan teams. The crowd cheered and the committee, headed by Mr. Smith, pressed forward to receive them. The heroes, however, were hungry and as they had only thirty minutes for dinner jumped from the cars and rushed for the dining room, hurriedly shaking hands with the reception committee as they went. While they ate, an enormous crowd collected in and about the depot and almost fought for positions at the windows looking into the dining room. Everyone wanted to see "Jumping-Jack Jones," and in order that that honored gentleman might eat in peace an obliging member of the reception committee went out and astounded the spectators by telling them the large, portly gentleman – Mr. Hoffman – was the renowned jumper.

RECEIVED ON BEHALF OF THE PEOPLE.

The ball-players and the committee had a special car to Philadelphia, and before the suburbs of Harrisburg were left behind the oratory began. President Smith welcomed the Athletic players, as he said, on behalf of the people of Philadelphia, and spoke of their victory and the interest everyone here had felt in the same spirit, and in pouring rhetorical treacle over the victors said. "It is a great deal better to be a good shoemaker than a poor lawyer, and better to be a good ball-player than a poor doctor."

"He said that same thing this morning," whispered Committeeman I. K. Brailler to Mr. Birchall and two or three others. "Wait until Bill (Mr. Smith) goes at it again."

If this advice was intended to put a damper on the applause it failed signally, for Mr. Lawrence's sentiments were vociferously cheered. Mr. Hoffman began speaking and the train stopped. Facetious friends declared that his voice had some strange effect on the air-brakes. After he had said several pleasant things about the victories of the Athletic Club he sat down and the train moved on. Mr. Hoffman made many other speeches and in one of them he made the astonishing announcement that "If the Association championship had depended upon the returns of the Fourth ward the Athletic Club would have been counted in long ago."

Mr. Ruhl made a few remarks and Mr. Appleton, one of the managers of the Metropolitan Club, spoke through a tunnel and all the listeners heard when the cars rushed out of the cavern was: "And I'm glad you've got it." Mr. Gilchrist appeared to be of a religious turn of mind. He ended his speech by saying: "I sincerely thank heaven you have won."

Calls were made for Jones or "Old Jumping-Jack" as some of the shouters called him, but he was comfortably curled like a spiral spring up on a seat and declined to respond.

"Call on Lynch, he's a daisy talker," suggested Mr. O'Brien.

Lynch was called on, and he may be a "daisy," but he said: "I can't open my mouth for a speech in a crowd."

THE OVATION IN LANCASTER.

An immense crowd surrounded the train at Lancaster. They cheered the wrong car, but discovered their mistake and surged to the rear of the train, where the ball-players were. Hundreds shouted for Jones, Stovey, and O'Brien. The admirers of Jones out-yelled and out-stayed the others, but their favorite sat in a dark corner of the car, smoking and fondling his little black moustache. Finally, a crowd of yelling maniacs, headed by an excited man in a brown tweed suit and a cigarette hat, charged on the colored porter who guarded the front door of the car. In the collision the Nubian and the plate glass were telescoped and the crowd pushed on over the debris into the car. Mr. Rowen and Mr. Jones occupied the last seat from where the invaders broke in. The maniac in brown tweed came swinging down the aisle, shouting, "Where is Jones?" No one replied, until the question was put direct to Jones, who said: "I guess he is at the other end of the car." Rowen turned, and, pointing to the jumper, said: "No, here he is." The tweed-covered maniac seized Jones' hands, pulled him to his feet, and with inconceivable rapidity and without pausing to draw breath, said: "Allow-me-sir-in-the-name-of-the-Ironsides-Club-of-Lancaster-and-the-people-of-Pennsylvania-to-congratulate-and-thank-you-for-your-noble-and-gallant-efforts-good-bye-sir-good-bye-sir," and he whisked out of the door and with his followers left the moving train. The train stopped again in a moment and a gray-haired man, so large that he blocked the door, roared: "Where is that Jumping-Jack?"

"The string must be out of order," shouted a man on a ladder at one of the windows. The crowd shouted at this. Jones then walked out on the rear platform and blushed and bowed to the enthusiastic crowd until the train moved off. Between Lancaster and Philadelphia two of the train hands fell asleep standing against the car door. They came from Pittsburg and Harrisburg was the end of their run, but they concluded to go to Philadelphia and witness the reception. After the parade they returned to Harrisburg and this morning started back to Pittsburg without sleep.

WAITING FOR THE CHAMPIONS.

Long before the victorious base ball players reached Philadelphia the streets for squares about the Broad Street Station were crowded with people. One shrewd chap, in order to escape the crowd in the streets, bought a ticket for West Philadelphia and with it passed through the gates. His example was followed by hundreds and before the railroad officials were able to account for the extraordinary rush of travelling to the other side of the Schuylkill the train platforms were choked with hundreds of people. Chief of Police Givin sent 125 officers to the station to control the crowd and the railroad company had 230 picked men present to protect the property of the corporation. The train bearing the Athletic players arrived at 7.45 and while they formed in line on the platform their admirers about them cheered until they were hoarse. The cheers were taken up by the crowd in the station, and the streets for blocks around echoed with shouts. The procession of players was headed by a squad of fifty stalwart policemen, who flourished their clubs menacingly and forced a passage through the dense crowd. As the players marched through the station many of them were presented with handsome bouquets, which were badly wrecked by the crush of the crowd on Broad street. So dense was the crowd that the officers for ten or fifteen minutes could not force an opening for the carriages in which the players embarked at the station door.

When the last carriage rolled off and the divisions of the procession were preparing to move there was vomited out of the station a small army of people, who had until then been held in check by police. The charge from the station carried everything before it and many people were knocked down and trampled upon. None were seriously injured. In the excitement a brass band turned the corner of Broad and Filbert streets and the steed of a gallant-looking division marshal began dancing wildly to the tune of "When Johnny Comes Marching Home Again." The marshal oscillated between the pommel and back part of the

saddle. "Whoa," whispered the marshal. "Whoa!" he murmured coaxingly. "Whoa!" he said emphatically, and, finally:" Whoa! — —you!" The crowd shouted with laughter and the marshal dismounted and led his fiery horse into the quiet of Filbert street.

THE PROCESSION.

After much trouble and lost time the legion of base ball, athletic and social clubs, with their bands, formed in line and the march began. Chestnut street was ablaze with red fire, electric and calcium lights and transparencies. "Welcome, Athletics," was the favorite motto and every banner bore it. Many persons are of the opinion that the procession was witnessed by as many people as saw the Grant parade or the Bi-Centennial pageant. Standing under an electric light in front of the City Hall Mayor King received the conquerors and bowed respectfully to the occupants of each carriage. Behind him stood 'Squire McMullen and a number of politicians, to whom the Mayor once turned and, referring to the parade, said: "I guess they are all Democrats."

THE DINNER.

The Metropolitan, the Athletic and the Baltimore teams, with the invited guests, filed out of the procession on Broad street, near Brown, and, escorted by the marshals, drove to Mercantile Hall, on Franklin street, below Poplar, where they marched into the banquet hall. Flags dropped gracefully from the walls and posts and the tables were adorned artistically by vases of running plants and hot-house flowers.

At the signal of "Be seated, gentlemen," a band of music placed on the stage in the hall struck up a galop and from the frantic manner in which knives and forks were rattled the feasters were evidently trying to keep time with the music. After a good supper the championship banner was presented to the Athletic team by William B. Smith. Harry D. Stovey was made the recipient of a gold watch, the presentation speech being made by George Hoffman. The distribution of handsome gold badges to the victors was made by Mr. Heinaman. After the interchange of toasts and the delivering of several impromptu speeches the guests withdrew and the great base ball reception was a thing of the past.

The article is reprinted in full from *The Times (Philadelphia, Pennsylvania)* newspaper edition of Tuesday, October 2, 1883.

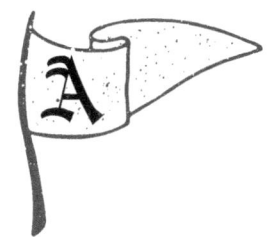

A NIGHT TO REMEMBER:
THE PHILADELPHIA ATHLETICS
1883 VICTORY PARADE

By Donna L. Halper, Ph.D.

On Friday, September 28, 1883, the Philadelphia Athletics clinched the American Association pennant, defeating the Louisville Eclipse 7-6, in a game that went 10 innings.[1] It was an exciting conclusion to a hard-fought season: the pennant was not decided till the final week,[2] and the Philadelphia fans, who had faithfully supported their team, were ready for a celebration.

And there was a lot to celebrate. Not only had the Athletics won, but base ball had won too (back then, the sport was spelled as two words, or sometimes hyphenated as *base-ball*). As *Harper's Weekly* noted, this had been a "remarkable" season, and the sport could now truly say it was America's "National game."[3]

Anyone who read the newspapers knew that *Harper's Weekly* was right: Interest in baseball was growing. In years past, it was typical to find only the scores, or perhaps a paragraph about the games. But throughout 1883, coverage of the home team became more thorough, and game stories were longer. In Philadelphia, as in most other cities, the newspapers did not have a sports page yet; but increasingly, reports about the games were given more prominence; in fact, some stories about the Athletics were placed on page 1.[4] Bylines were still rare, so we don't know the names of the reporters who wrote the stories; but the coverage now provided more details – such as highlighting the players who did well and pointing out those who didn't.

The word *fan* was also not in common use in 1883; loyal supporters of a team were often referred to as *enthusiasts* or *admirers*, and fanatical supporters were called *cranks*. But whatever you called them, the people who loved their favorite team had lots of choices for base ball news. (And by the way, *team* was not in common use either – the Athletics were often referred to as a *club* or a *nine*). In addition to reading the local newspapers (of which Philadelphia had at least 15), there was a new weekly sports publication called *The Sporting Life*, which made its debut on April 15, 1883; and the *New York Clipper* was another excellent resource for national baseball news.

Thanks to the telegraph (many ballparks now had telegraphers situated right near the reporters, so that game summaries could quickly be sent back to the local publications)[5], the late editions of your favorite paper might at least have a box score or a short summary. And when the Athletics clinched the pennant, the story appeared in newspapers from coast to coast. (Nearly every paper had an "exchange editor," who received copies of many out-of-town papers, and selected the biggest stories for re-publication;[6] that is how newspapers in cities far from Philadelphia were still able to get stories about the Athletics' exciting win, and share the news with readers.)

But as the pennant race grew more competitive, some of the team's most devoted supporters didn't want to wait for the next edition of the newspaper. They wanted to know what was happening right away; and lucky for them, the Philadelphia newspapers were ready. Most of the city's major publications were located on or near Chestnut Street, and in that era before radio and television, fans who wanted the latest scores would gather in front of the office of their favorite newspaper. Many publications had bulletin boards, and when the headlines arrived by telegraph, someone from the newspaper would write them out for the public to read. In late September, as it appeared more likely that the Athletics might win the pennant, larger and larger crowds began to gather during each road game, eagerly awaiting information about how the Athletics were doing.[7] The day of the pennant-clinching game, not even a rainshower could keep the fans from waiting for the inning-by-inning updates.[8] And when the final score arrived from Louisville, "… [Men threw their hats in the air and shouted themselves hoarse, [and] the ladies waved their handkerchiefs, and in some cases even joined in the shouting."[9]

We may never know who first came up with the idea, but on September 18, 10 days before the pennant was won, several hundred loyal fans gathered at the Athletics' headquarters, 159 North Eighth Street.[10] Confident that the club would finish in first place, they decided the Athletics deserved a victory parade when they returned home from the road.[11] The supporters formed a number of committees, including one to handle the arrangements, another to handle the finances, a music committee, a committee to hire the carriages, etc. There would also be a reception committee, to greet the players and the various dignitaries participating in the event. As might be expected, the Athletics' ownership approved of having a parade; in fact, co-owner Charlie Mason even participated in the planning,[12] and so did an influential local politician, William B. Smith, president of Philadelphia's Select Council. At the second meeting, the members of the reception committee elected Smith the chairman.[13] (While he may indeed have been a loyal fan, William B. Smith was also a candidate for mayor, and associating himself with a winning baseball club would certainly be beneficial for his campaign.)

Meanwhile, committee member William H. Heck was named chief marshal, and he was tasked with organizing the various groups that would be taking part in the parade. It was rapidly becoming a massive undertaking, as hundreds of people asked to participate – including other athletic clubs, local civic organizations, members of the military, local dignitaries, and even some local merchants. The committee decided to organize the parade's participants into four divisions, each with its own marshal. Leading the torchlight procession would be the victorious Athletics players and the club's management, displaying the championship

AT 7.25
MONDAY EVENING, OCTOBER 1,
THE
ATHLETICS
Will Arrive at Broad and Filbert Sts.

The route of the great Parade will be down Broad street to Christian; countermarching up Broad to Chestnut; thence down Chestnut past.

banner as they rode in elegant horse-drawn carriages called barouches.[14] Also in that first division would be the members of the reception committee, along with members of several other American Association clubs (the New York Metropolitans and the Baltimore Orioles) and their managers. In the second division would be numerous semipro and amateur clubs from the region; the third would comprise various social and civic clubs; and in the fourth, there would be miscellaneous participants, including some local businesses.

As for the parade route, the plan was to form the line on Broad Street, north of Filbert Street, close to the Broad Street train station, where the team was scheduled to arrive. (Broad Street Station was a major terminal for the Pennsylvania Railroad back then – it was relatively new, having been opened in December 1881,[15] and it was conveniently located in the center of the city, not far from City Hall.) According to the *Philadelphia Times* and other local publications, the assembled marchers would then "countermarch on the west side of Broad Street to Carpenter, east side of Broad Street to Chestnut, to Fifth, to Arch, to Eighth, to Girard Avenue, to Broad, to Market, and [then] dismiss."[16] This route would take the marchers past many of the city's newspapers, businesses, and stores: one merchant helpfully pointed out in a large newspaper advertisement that anyone planning to participate, whether as a marcher or a spectator, would probably need a warm coat; and luckily, there was a sale on men's all-wool winter coats at Brownings' Clothing House, Ninth and Chestnut Streets.[17]

And no parade would be complete without music: Many bands wanted to take part, but one of them stood out – a local favorite, with a long track record, previously known throughout the state as either Beck's Philadelphia Band or Beck's First Regiment Band.[18] The band now had a new patron – the *Philadelphia Evening Call* newspaper. The *Evening Call* was the newest newspaper in the city, having made its debut on September 28, the day the Athletics won the pennant.

The *Call* was owned by veteran journalist Robert Stewart Davis (who was well-known in the region for publishing a critically acclaimed literary magazine, *Saturday Night*, from 1867 to 1879). In addition to sending reporters to cover the victory parade, Davis saw an opportunity to get some positive attention for his newspaper by providing some of the music. So he hired Beck's Band and changed their name to the Evening Call Band. With popular bandleader John G.S. Beck at the helm, they made their debut the same day the *Evening Call* did, with a concert and a street parade to announce the arrival of the new daily paper.[19] (Not only did the band have a new name, but all 50 members were wearing the new uniforms Davis had purchased for them.)[20]

Now that the pennant was officially won and the Athletics were on their way home, the reception committee was finishing up with last-minute details, and preparing to meet the team. The plan was to hire a special train to meet the victorious Athletics when they got to Harrisburg and bring them the rest of the way.[21] Meanwhile, after playing a Sunday morning game on the 30th, the Athletics left Louisville at 3 P.M.; they were due to arrive in Philadelphia on Monday, October 1, at 7:30 P.M. Their train first made a stop in Cincinnati to pick up the New York Metropolitans, who rode with the Athletics to Philadelphia.[22] By the time the train reached Harrisburg, 12 members of the reception committee, dressed formally in "black clothes and glistening hats,"[23] were waiting to greet the champions and offer congratulations for a job well done. (Wasting no time, Select Council President Smith immediately gave a short speech, praising the players and telling them what their victory meant to the city of Philadelphia.)[24] In addition to the reception committee, some fans from Harrisburg were also there to welcome the Athletics and accompany them to Philadelphia.[25] And fans from other cities were planning to make the trip: For example, a large group of supporters from Wilmington, Delaware, was traveling to watch the parade.[26]

In Philadelphia, the organizers were happy to see the weather cooperating. Unlike the day before, when there had been light rain,[27] today there was no rain in sight; the forecast was for a clear but cool evening, with temperatures in the 50s. As anticipation grew, some of the newspapers engaged in guesses about how big the parade would be. The *Philadelphia Inquirer* asserted that about 10,000 people would participate (although that number didn't include groups that asked to participate at the last minute, or additional bands, or local fife-and-drum corps).[28] Several days earlier, the *Philadelphia Times* said at least 7,000 men and boys would be participating, and more than 40 bands.[29] But by the 30th of September, the *Times* agreed that 10,000 was probably an accurate number.[30] Other newspapers didn't try to guess how many people would participate: they just used adjectives like "immense" to describe the planned torchlight procession.[31] And while most of the spectators were expected to be men, there was reason to believe some women would be in the crowd. The Athletics had made attracting female fans a part of their strategy all season, designating each Thursday home game as Ladies Day; the ownership gave free admission to any woman accompanied by a ticket holder.[32] (It seemed to work: Reporters noticed that although the majority of the fans continued to be men, a small but steadily growing number of women had begun to attend the games. In early September, the *Philadelphia Times* remarked that although it wasn't Ladies Day, there were more than 300 female fans in the grandstand, cheering the Athletics on in a game against St. Louis.)[33]

The train carrying the Athletics was supposed to arrive at Broad Street Station at 7:30 P.M. on October 1; by most newspaper accounts, it was between 5 and 10 minutes late.[34] (The *Philadelphia Evening Call*, however, claimed the train was five minutes early.)[35] But whatever the correct arrival time, anticipation had been building all day, and people from all walks of life and all social classes[36] formed a massive throng on every nearby street. The *New York Clipper* described the crowd as a "veritable tidal-wave of people."[37] When the Athletics emerged from the station, Select Council President William B. Smith led them onto the street, where their carriages were waiting. Fans shouted and cheered and pointed with excitement as they caught a glimpse of players they recognized.[38] In addition to the carriages for the Athletics, there were also some for the other teams that had been invited – including the New York Metropolitans and the Baltimore Orioles. As soon as all the players and managers were seated, the parade officially began: the Great Western Band, one of the many musical groups taking part, started things off with a rousing version of "Hail to the Chief."[39] And as the carriages proceeded (slowly, because so many people were crowding the streets that any movement was difficult),[40] spectators waved and cheered, and some even threw flowers as the players rode by.[41]

All along the parade route, streets were illuminated with electric and calcium lights; storefronts and other buildings, including several of the newspapers, had colored lanterns hung in the windows. It seemed nearly every building was draped in festive bunting, and many displayed banners with messages of congratulations to the Athletics. At John Wanamaker's clothing store at 818 Chestnut Street, the decorations included flags of many nations, banners and streamers; in addition, "lights blazed from every window and an immense gas jet glittered a welcome with the words *Well done*."[42] Music was everywhere – bands played, as did fife and drum corps, and many in the crowd either sang along or simply cheered as the various carriages passed.[43] And as the marchers reached the intersection of Broad and Chestnut, there was even a fireworks display, courtesy of the Hotel Lafayette.[44]

As for the four divisions that the Reception Committee had diligently planned for, they turned out to be even larger than expected – estimates ranged from 8,000 to 10,000 marchers, in a procession that stretched for about two miles.[45] This proved to be a challenge for the several hundred members of law enforcement and the various marshals who were involved in crowd control. Fortunately, despite the massive number of spectators – estimated by the *Philadelphia Evening Call* at more than 200,000 and by the *St. Louis Globe-Democrat* at half a million, there was no rioting or vandalism. In fact, there were surprisingly few incidents of bad behavior. Pickpockets had a good night – the police later received complaints from some attendees who reported lost watches or other valuables.[46] A man brutally assaulted a woman who had asked him to stop pushing against her: He caused her serious injury by kicking her, and two police officers promptly arrested him.[47] There were also several minor injuries: A boy who was trying to get a better view of the parade fell from a tree and broke a wrist, and a woman had one of her feet crushed by the hooves of an unruly horse. And there was one fatality: A 5-year-old girl was run over by a wagon, and she died instantly.[48] But overall, the organizers, along with Philadelphia's political leaders, were pleased by how well everything turned out. As the *Philadelphia Times* editorialized the next day, "[N]othing in history has surpassed the splendor of last night, when the entire population turned out, with music and banners and fire-works … to do honor to a base ball nine."[49]

As the *Evening Call*'s publisher, Robert Stewart Davis, had hoped, the Evening Call Band was well-received,[50] and even his competitors remarked upon its presence; they also remarked upon how he hired a number of wagons to follow behind the band, so that his newsboys and other staff could ride, rather than walk, in the parade.[51] Another noteworthy feature of the parade was the large number of baseball clubs that marched – all in their team uniforms, carrying their bats. While many of the clubs were semipro, some were from youth leagues, including several teams from Camden, New Jersey; one of them, the Young Merritts, carried a banner announcing they were the champions from clubs under 16 years old.[52] *The Sporting Life*, in covering the parade, noted with amusement that most residents of Philadelphia had never seen so many baseball clubs, nor realized that such a large number existed. The publication also observed that a party atmosphere prevailed: members of local social clubs and civic organizations were marching in various costumes.[53] And one notable display from the fourth division was a float from the Arion Camping Club: it featured a replica of a camp and a fire, with several members of the club inside a tent, and others outside pretending to be relaxing on what looked like grass.[54]

When the procession finally reached City Hall, at Fifth and Chestnut, Mayor Samuel G. King was waiting there, accompanied by some prominent Philadelphia politicians. A reviewing stand had been set up for the mayor[55] so that he could offer his personal congratulations to the winning Athletics and greet the rest of the marchers. This was a more difficult task than one might think, because Mayor King was known for going to bed early. According to the *Philadelphia Times*, he didn't even stay up late on the night he won the race for mayor. On this festive occasion, however, he not only stayed up past his normal bedtime – he enthusiastically reviewed the entire parade.[56] (By some accounts, the parade took at least an hour and 10 minutes before it completely passed by the reviewing stand.[57])

But Mayor King's evening wasn't done. When the parade-goers were dismissed, about 150 invited guests, escorted by the marshals, made their way by carriage to Mercantile Hall on Franklin Street, where a banquet was being held in the Athletics' honor.[58] Among the invitees were some prominent local politicians, the mayor among them, and some business leaders. And there were also three professional teams. The victorious Athletics and the previously mentioned Baltimore Orioles and New York Metropolitans. But there was also the city's other pro team, the Philadelphia Quakers. Philadelphia's National League franchise was an interesting choice – its president and general manager was former Athletics player Alfred J. "Al" Reach. While he had some success in the early 1870s (and even hit .353 in 1871), his track record in management in 1883 was nothing to brag about – in fact, his team had a truly awful season, finishing dead last, with a record of 17-81. Throughout 1883, while the Athletics were frequently and deservedly praised, Reach's team lost so many games that it was often mocked by the local press.[59] (It is worth noting that the Philadelphia team, which some modern sources say was called the Quakers, and others claim was called the Phillies, seemed to be referred to by neither name in 1883. Most local newspapers called the team either the Philadelphias, the Philadelphia Base Ball Club, or occasionally, the Quaker City Boys.[60]) And although we do not know why the decision was made to include the club, perhaps it had to do with Reach's five years as an Athletics player, or perhaps the Athletics were just trying to give the fans of the city's other team a chance to participate in the festive occasion, even if their team hadn't provided many reasons for celebration that season.

In addition to the professional clubs, two semi-pro teams were invited to the banquet. One was the August Flower Club, which had made its debut earlier in 1883;[61] it had gotten a lot of coverage from the Philadelphia newspapers, and evidently it was now sufficiently well-known (it was even included in the first division of the Athletics' victory parade). Also part of that first division, and also invited to the banquet, was the Anthracite Club of Pottsville, Pennsylvania.[62] The Anthracite Club had undergone some serious financial struggles during 1883,[63] but managed to get through the season and then get invited to the Athletics' celebration.

Inside the banquet hall, where the tables were attractively decorated with flowers and plants, and there was also a baseball-themed centerpiece featuring "two floral baseball bats standing crosswise over a ball of red and white flowers,"[64] the celebratory atmosphere continued, as a band played an up-tempo song, and attendees tried to keep time with the music.[65] All the guests were treated to an eight-course meal, and there was a keynote address by Col. Thomas Fitzgerald, an orator, publisher, philanthropist, and the founder of the first Athletics club. (And showing that hyperbole is nothing new in public speaking, the colonel asserted that this celebration far surpassed celebrations in ancient Greece or ancient Rome; he also said that more than 750,000 men, women, and children had witnessed the parade.[66])

When it came time for the presentations, William B. Smith gave the championship banner to the team

(and also gave another speech);[67] and co-owner Mason gave slugger and team captain Harry Stovey, who had scored the winning run in the game that clinched the pennant, a gold watch and chain.[68] Several other politicians, including Councilman George W. Hoffman, made speeches in praise of the team, and each member of the Athletics received a gold badge, to commemorate their incredible season.[69] By the time the banquet ended, around 1 A.M. (much to the consternation of Mayor King, no doubt), one reporter summed up the festivities by saying this banquet was "one of the largest and most remarkable that has taken place in this city of pageants."[70]

While nearly every newspaper reporter was effusive in praise of the Athletics, as well as eager to praise the parade, and the banquet too, every event has a curmudgeon or two, and this one was no exception. An untitled editorial in a West Virginia newspaper groused about the attention given to athletes and complained that more important news was being pushed off the front pages. The writer was especially annoyed that a member of US President Chester A. Arthur's Cabinet, Postmaster General Gresham, was on the same train as the Athletics, yet he was completely ignored. Further, said the writer, most of the players aren't even from Philadelphia, so why had the local fans bonded so intensely with players who might be playing for some other team next year?[71]

But this viewpoint was in the minority. In fact, for the next few years, the city of Philadelphia continued to recall the 1883 Victory Parade fondly, and newspapers would mention it whenever there was an upcoming celebration. For example, in 1888, there was an event that honored amateur baseball in the city, and reporters expressed the belief (or perhaps the hope) that this event would be as exciting and impressive as the 1883 victory parade had been.[72] In time, of course, recollections about the victory parade faded, and many of the players did go on to other teams (or leave baseball entirely). But when Harry Stovey died in 1937, at age 80,[73] there were still some old-timers who recalled what he did for the Athletics back in 1883; and for one brief moment, memories of a very different era lived again.

SOURCES

In addition to the sources cited in the Notes, the author consulted Baseball-reference.com. The author is also grateful to the reference librarians at the Free Library of Philadelphia, who provided historical information about Philadelphia in 1883.

NOTES

1 "The Pennant Won," *Philadelphia Times*, September 29, 1883: 2.

2 "The New Base-Ball Champions," *New York Times*, October 1, 1883: 2.

3 "Base-Ball Champions," *Harper's Weekly*, October 13, 1883: 653-654.

4 For example, "Both the Home Nines Win," *Philadelphia Times*, May 16, 1883: 1.

5 In St. Louis, for example, Western Union announced telegraphers would be regularly assigned to the games, making it easier for reporters covering the 1883 season. "Diamond Dust," *St. Louis Daily Globe-Democrat*, March 27, 1883: 5.

6 "How They Do It," *Jackson* (Ohio) *Standard*, August 30, 1883: 1.

7 "The Coming Champions," *Philadelphia Times*, September 22, 1883: 2.

8 "The Pennant Won," *Philadelphia Times*, September 29, 1883: 2.

9 "Out-Door Sports," *Philadelphia Inquirer*, September 29, 1883: 2.

10 "The Champions," *Philadelphia Inquirer*, September 19, 1883: 8.

11 "The Athletic's Reception," *Philadelphia Inquirer*, September 22, 1883: 2.

12 Edward Achorn, *The Summer of Beer and Whiskey: How Brewers, Barkeeps, Rowdies, Immigrants, and a Wild Pennant Fight Made Baseball America's Game* (New York: Public Affairs, 2014), 219.

13 "Baseball Notes," *Philadelphia Times*, September 22, 1883: 2.

14 "Receiving the Athletics," *Philadelphia Times*, September 30, 1883: 2.

15 "The Broad Street Station," *Philadelphia Inquirer*, December 2, 1881: 3.

16 "Receiving the Athletics."

17 "At 7:25," *Philadelphia Times*, October 1, 1883: 4.

18 "The Fourth," *Scranton Republican*, July 10, 1878: 2.

19 "Greetings from the Philadelphia Journals to the Evening Call," *Philadelphia Inquirer*, September 29, 1883: 8.

20 "A Military Band at Last Worthy of Our Great Metropolis," *Philadelphia Times*, September 29, 1883: 8.

21 "Honoring the Champions: Philadelphia Preparing a Grand Reception for the Victorious Athletics," *New York Sun*, October 1, 1883: 4.

22 "Receiving the Athletics."

23 "The Base Ball Parade," *Philadelphia Times*, October 2, 1883: 1.

24 "The Base Ball Parade"

25 "Base Ball Players Going Home," *Harrisburg Telegraph*, October 1, 1883: 4.

26 "Notes," *Wilmington* (Delaware) *Daily Gazette*, October 1, 1883: 1.

27 "The Weather in Philadelphia," *Philadelphia Inquirer*, October 1, 1883: 8.

28 "After Many Battles," *Philadelphia Inquirer*, September 27, 1883: 2.

29 "The Last Week," *Philadelphia Times*, September 23, 1883: 2.

30 "Receiving the Athletics."

31 "Honoring the Champions."

32 Achorn, 44.

33 "On Top Again," *Philadelphia Times*, September 7, 1883: 3.

34 For example, a St. Louis newspaper said the club arrived at 7:45 P.M. "The Athletics Receive a Grand Ovation Upon Arriving Home," *St. Louis Globe-Democrat*, October 2, 1883: 6; but the *Philadelphia Inquirer* said the arrival time was actually 7:35 P.M. "The Victors Home," *Philadelphia Inquirer*, October 2, 1883: 1.

35 "Champions at Home," *Philadelphia Evening Call*, October 2, 1883: 7.

36 "The Athletics' Reception," *The Sporting Life*, October 8, 1883: 5.

37 "The Athletic Club's Reception," *New York Clipper*, October 6, 1883: 469.

38 "The Athletics Receive a Grand Ovation Upon Arriving Home," *St. Louis Globe-Democrat*, October 2, 1883: 6.

39 "The Victors Home."

40 "The Athletics Receive a Grand Ovation Upon Arriving Home."

41 "Philadelphia Enthusiastic Over the Athletics," *Pittstown* (Pennsylvania) *Evening Gazette*, October 2, 1883: 1.

42 "Champions at Home."

43 "Base-Ball Champions"; "The Athletics' Reception," *The Sporting Life*, October 8, 1883: 5; "Champions at Home."

44 "Champions at Home."

45 "The Athletics Receive a Grand Ovation Upon Arriving Home."

46 Achorn, 238.

47 "Champions at Home"; Achorn, 238.

48 "Champions at Home."

49 Editorial page, *Philadelphia Times*, October 2, 1883: 2.

50 "Champions at Home."

51 "The Victors Home."

52 "Athletics' Parade," *Camden* (New Jersey) *Daily Courier*, October 2, 1883: 1.

53 "The Athletics' Reception." See also Achorn, 237.

54 "The Victors Home."

55 "The Athletics' Reception."

56 Editorial page, *Philadelphia Times*, October 2, 1883: 2.

57 Achorn, 238.

58 "The Athletic Club's Reception."

59 Opinion page, *York* (Pennsylvania) *Daily*, July 25, 1883: 2; opinion page, *Philadelphia Times*, August 8, 1883: 2.

60 "Poor Philadelphia," *Philadelphia Times*, August 19, 1883: 2; "Base Ball," *Philadelphia Times*, October 27, 1883: 2.

61 "Baseball Notes," *Philadelphia Times*, March 18, 1883: 7.

62 "Receiving the Athletics," *Philadelphia Times*, September 30, 1883: 2.

63 "Current Comment," *Harrisburg Daily Independent*, September 20, 1883: 4.

64 Achorn, 239.

65 "The Athletic Club's Reception."

66 Achorn, 240.

67 "Champions at Home."

68 "The Athletics' Welcome Home," *Harrisburg Telegraph*, October 2, 1883: 1; Achorn, 240.

69 "The Victors Home."

70 "The Champions Home."

71 Editorial, *Wheeling* (West Virginia) *Daily Intelligencer*, October 4, 1883: 1.

72 "Base Ball: The Demonstration Arranged by the Philadelphia Clubs," *Philadelphia Times*, June 17, 1888: 16.

73 "Harry Stovey Dies, Old Baseball Star," *Philadelphia Inquirer*, September 21, 1937: 4.

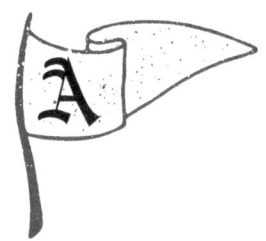

THE POSTSEASON MATCHUP
THAT WASN'T

By Paul E. Doutrich

The Philadelphia Athletics clinched the 1883 American Association championship on September 28. For five days the Quaker city had nervously watched their team's lead over the St. Louis Browns shrink, but with just one game left to play, the Philadelphias put away the pesky Louisville Eclipse and claimed their first baseball championship. Four days later the city celebrated as never before. The team "was attended with reception ceremonies unprecedented in the history of the national game."[1] A brass band played as the team arrived back home, 10,000 cheered as their heroes got off the train, and a parade followed that "was witnessed by as many people as saw the Grant parade or the Bi-Centennial pageant."[2]

The end of the season signaled the beginning of an exhibition season between National League and American Association teams. For the second year the exhibitions were expected to include a three-game series between the National League champion Boston Beaneaters and the American Association champion Athletics. *Spalding's 1884 Base Ball Guide* said the winner of the series would be recognized as champion of the United States.[3] The *Philadelphia Times* went one step further and claimed that the winner would be the North American Champion.[4]

Two days later, on October 3, the new champions played their first postseason exhibition game, against their hometown rivals, the Phillies. It had been a rough season for the Quaker City's National League representative. The Phillies ended the campaign deep in the League's cellar, having lost 81 of the 98 games they played. The two teams were scheduled to play three times. The winner would be recognized as the

Philadelphia city champion. After the excitement surrounding the Athletics' championship as well as the local significance of games, a large, enthusiastic crowd was anticipated. Instead, only between 5,000 and 6,000 fans showed up, far fewer than most expected.

The game that followed was "the slowest and most tedious of the season," wrote the *Philadelphia Times*. "There was scarcely any vim displayed by the players and the audience appeared to be in a decidedly comatose state."[5] Through the early innings "errors came thick and fast" but initially the two pitchers dominated play.[6] The teams scratched away at each other until a five-run Athletics outburst in the fourth inning put the game away. Despite the uninspired performance, the Athletic players shared half of the game's gate which came to approximately $50 each.

The next day another disappointing crowd, 2,500, came out to see the Athletics do battle with the Cleveland Blues. Cleveland had finished in fourth place in the National League, 7½ games back of Boston. The game turned into a sloppy 8-7 loss for the home team. Though Philadelphia hit well, "the contest was remarkable for the number of fly balls muffed."[7] In all Philadelphia committed 12 errors. For local fans, the high point of the afternoon came on the day's last pitch to Cleveland hitters when pitcher finally executed his unique four-foot jumping delivery.

The results a day later were even more discouraging. A crowd of only 2,000 watched "the most humiliating (defeat) sustained by the Athletics this season."[8] While Providence Grays ace Hoss Radbourn held the Athletics scoreless, allowing only three singles, his teammates, with the help of more Philadelphia errors, pummeled the Athletics ace, Bobby Mathews, for 12 runs. It was a very gloomy afternoon for the American Association champions and their fans.

The series with the Phillies resumed three days after the Providence shellacking. Through five innings the Athletics looked like champions again. Athletics pitcher George Bradley held the city rivals to a single run while Athletics hitters scored four times. Then in the sixth, the Phillies broke through with five runs, and two innings later put another two on the board. Meanwhile, the Athletics were blanked and able to scratch out only one hit over the last six innings.

Buffalo added to the Athletics' woes, trouncing them on three consecutive afternoons, October 9-11. In the first game, the home team was held to just four hits in a 7-1 loss during which "there was not much to amuse the two thousand spectators."[9] In the second meeting, the Bisons put 10 runs on the board before the Athletics scored. Throughout the game "the champions fielded in a slow and easy manner and apparently made no effort to make the contest of interest to the fifteen hundred spectators."[10] The result was a 15-5 drubbing. In the final game, both teams sprinkled their lineups with pickup players and both teams played miserably in the field. It was a different story at the plate. The Bisons roared out to an early five-run lead, which "took all interest out of the game," then coasted to an easy 9-2 victory.[11]

After the third loss to Buffalo, the Athletics management decided to cancel the postseason series with Boston even though just a day earlier local papers had reported that the series was still set for October 18, 19, and 20.[12] In justifying the decision, a club representative claimed that all the players needed a rest and several "are more or less crippled."[13] In fact, regular starter Ed Rowen had missed two games, Harry Stovey missed three, and Bobby Mathews and Jack O'Brien had missed four of the seven games played. "I don't want to see them limping around the field and spectators would not make allowances," the club spokesman said.[14]

There were additional considerations that went into the Philadelphia decision to cancel the Boston series. Obviously, the steadily shrinking audience meant steadily shrinking revenues and there was no guarantee that even a postseason series would generate more attendance. It was also clear that the Philadelphia players were anxious to rest after a long, hard-fought season. Stovey, the team's most dangerous hitter, was already headed back to his home in New Bedford, Massachusetts, and four others were scheduled to leave within a few days. Another consideration was the American Association's reputation. Since its inception in 1882, there were many who questioned the league's quality of play. During the exhibition season Association teams had not done well against their National League opponents, dropping 37 of the 55 games played. Of course, no Association team had done worse than the league's champion. The Athletics losses to the lowly Phillies were especially embarrassing. Those who argued that the American Association was an inferior league would be fortified if Philadelphia, playing without several of its best players, was swamped by Boston, which appeared likely to happen. The final factor influencing the decision was the weather. The mild days of autumn were quickly giving way to the approach of winter, further deterring potential attendance.

In Boston the cancellation was greeted with a degree of distain. The previous season the American Association champion Cincinnati Red Stockings had beaten their National League counterpart, the Chicago White Stockings. Defenders of the National League, most notably White Stockings president A.G. Spalding, claimed that the games were merely exhibition games and meant very little. Nevertheless, in its inaugural season of play, the Association's series victory was a grand success. The Beaneaters, as well as the rest of the National League, were anxious to redeem their League. The cancellation abruptly curtailed the league's anticipated revenge. "It would have been far more creditable and honorable to have completed the season, no matter how badly beaten, than to have closed the season the way they have."[15]

Despite backing out of the series with the Bostons, the Athletics did play one final game against a National League team and it was for a championship. The team was the Phillies, and the championship was the Philadelphia city championship. On a chilly, wet, and windy mid-October afternoon playing in front of only 1,500 fans who "stood about and shivered in the cold, raw wind," the Athletics, who included a couple of pickup players, lost to the Phillies one last time, 8-3.[16]

NOTES

1   "The American Season of 1883," *Spalding's Official Baseball Guide, 1884*: 54.

2   "The Base Ball Parade," *Times* (Philadelphia), October 2, 1883: 1.

3   *Spalding's 1884 Base Ball Guide*: 58.

4   "Base Ball Notes," *Times*, October 11, 1883: 3.

5   "The Athletics at Home," *Times*, October 4, 1883: 1.

6   "The Athletics at Home."

7   "The Champions Beaten," *Times*, October 5, 1883: 3.

8   "Twelve to Nothing," *Times*, October 6, 1883: 3.

9   "The Athletics Again Beaten," *Times*, October 10, 1883: 3.

10 "Beaten Again," *Times*, October 11, 1883: 3.

11 "The Last of the Season," *Philadelphia Inquirer,* October 12, 1883: 3.

12 "Base Ball Notes," *Times*, October 11, 1883: 3.

13 "The Crippled Champs," *Times*, October 12, 1883: 1.

14 "The Crippled Champs."

15 "Diamond Dust," *Boston Globe*, October 14, 1883: 6.

16 "Bat and Ball," *Times*, October 16, 1883: 4.

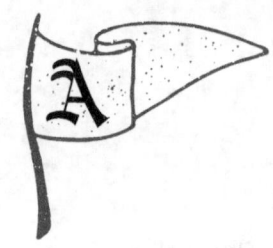

BY THE NUMBERS

By Dan Fields

1883 PHILADELPHIA ATHLETICS

0.732

Bases on balls per nine innings pitched by Bobby Mathews, best in the American Association (AA). George Bradley (0.924) was fourth in the league, and Fred Corey (1.456) was ninth.

1st

Major-league player to hit for a "natural" cycle (first a single, then a double, then a triple, and finally a home run): right fielder and manager Lon Knight, on July 30, 1883.

1.106

WHIP of George Bradley, fifth in the AA. Bobby Mathews (1.121) was sixth.

2.46

ERA of Bobby Mathews, sixth in the AA. George Bradley (3.15) was eighth.

2.88

ERA of the 1883 Athletics, third in the AA.

3.65

Ratio of strikeouts to walks by Philadelphia pitchers, best in the AA.

4-0

Score by which the Athletics beat the Pittsburgh Alleghenys on Opening Day (May 1). The Athletics did not shut out another opponent during the season.

4.795

Strikeouts per nine innings by Bobby Mathews, second in the AA.

6.548

Ratio of strikeouts thrown to walks allowed by Bobby Mathews, best in the AA. George Bradley (2.546) was seventh in the league. In 1883, a batter walked after seven balls.

9.028

Hits per nine innings pitched by George Bradley, seventh in the AA. Bobby Mathews (9.354) was ninth.

10

Consecutive games won by the Athletics from May 10 through May 24.

10

Triples each by Mike Moynahan and Jack O'Brien, tied for seventh in the AA. Lon Knight (9) was tied for 10th.

11

Home runs allowed by Bobby Mathews, second-most in the AA. George Bradley (7) was tied for fifth.

14

Home runs by Harry Stovey. This was a major-league record for only one season; in 1884 Ned Williamson hit 27 home runs. Stovey had 14 of the 20 home runs hit by the 1883 Athletics.

19-2

Score by which the Athletics beat the Pittsburgh Alleghenys on August 1. The Athletics beat the Columbus Buckeyes 19-5 on August 18.

22

Home runs allowed by the 1883 Athletics, most in the AA.

30

Wins by Bobby Mathews, fourth in the AA. It was the first of three consecutive years in which he won exactly 30 games for the Athletics. George Bradley (16 wins) was 10th.

31

Doubles by Harry Stovey, most in the AA. Lon Knight (23) was tied for third in the Association, and Mike Moynahan (18) was tied for ninth.

31

Walks drawn by Mike Moynahan, tied for second in the AA. Harry Stovey (27) was tied for fifth, and Jack O'Brien (25) was tied for seventh.

41

Complete games by Bobby Mathews, tied for seventh among AA pitchers.

44

Games started by Bobby Mathews, eighth among AA pitchers.

51

Extra-base hits by Harry Stovey, most in the AA. Lon Knight (33) was sixth, and Mike Moynahan (29) was 10th.

66-32

Record of the 1883 Athletics, best in the AA. The team was 37-14 at home and 29-18 on the road.

70

RBIs by Jack O'Brien, third in the AA. Mike Moynahan (67) was fourth in the Association, Harry Stovey (66) was fifth, and Lon Knight (53) was seventh.

95

Walks allowed by the 1883 Athletics, fewest in the AA.

95

Errors by Cub Stricker (93 as second baseman and two as catcher), most in the AA. Jud Birchall led AA outfielders with 45 errors.

97

Games played by Lon Knight, tied for sixth among AA batters.

110

Runs scored by Harry Stovey, most in the AA. Lon Knight (98) was fourth, Jud Birchall (95) was tied for fifth, and Mike Moynahan (90) was tied for seventh.

128

Hits by Harry Stovey, fourth-most in the AA. Mike Moynahan (124) was seventh in the Association.

149

Doubles by the 1883 Athletics, most in the AA.

199

Walks drawn by the 1883 Athletics, most in the AA.

203

Strikeouts thrown by Bobby Mathews, second in the AA.

213

Total bases by Harry Stovey, most in the AA. Mike Moynahan (165) was tied for eighth.

.262

Batting average of the 1883 Athletics, tied with the Cincinnati Red Stockings for best in the AA.

.300

On-base percentage of the 1883 Athletics, best in the AA.

.310

Batting average of Mike Moynahan, sixth in the AA. Harry Stovey (.304) was eighth in the Association.

.360

On-base percentage of Mike Moynahan, third in the AA. Harry Stovey (.346) was sixth and Jack O'Brien (.333) was eighth.

381

Innings pitched by Bobby Mathews, eighth in the AA.

448

At-bats by Jud Birchall, most in the AA and a major-league record for one season. Lon Knight (429) was fifth in the league, and Harry Stovey (421) was seventh.

468

Plate appearances by Jud Birchall, most in the AA and a major-league record for one season. Lon Knight (450) was third in the Association, and Harry Stovey (448) was tied for fourth.

.506

Slugging percentage of Harry Stovey, best in the AA. Mike Moynahan (.413) was sixth.

.698

Winning percentage of Bobby Mathews, second in the AA. George Bradley (.696) was third in the Association, and Fred Corey (.588) was seventh.

720

Runs scored by the 1883 Athletics, most in the AA. The team averaged 7.35 runs per game.

.852

OPS of Harry Stovey, second in the AA. Mike Moynahan (.772) was sixth.

.965

Fielding percentage as first baseman by Harry Stovey, best in the AA.

ELSEWHERE IN THE AMERICAN ASSOCIATION IN 1883

2

Games in eight days (September 12 and 19) in which John Reilly of the Cincinnati Red Stockings hit for the cycle. On September 12 he had six hits and six runs.

2.09

ERA of Will White of the Cincinnati Red Stockings, best in the AA.

3

Total hits given up by Tim Keefe of the New York Metropolitans in winning both ends of a doubleheader against the Columbus Buckeyes on July 4.

9.97

Average number of errors per American Association game in 1883.

15

Consecutive road losses by the Columbus Buckeyes, from July 14 through August 23.

17

Triples by Pop Smith of the Columbus Buckeyes, most in the AA.

33

Losses by Frank Mountain of the Columbus Buckeyes, most in the AA. He won 26 games.

43

Wins by Will White of the Cincinnati Red Stockings, most in the AA. He lost 22 games. This was the second consecutive season (and third overall) in which White won at least 40 games.

68

Games played, games started, and complete games by Tim Keefe of the New York Metropolitans, all most in the AA. He had a record of 41-27.

80

RBIs by Charley Jones of the Cincinnati Red Stockings, most in the AA.

.357

Batting average of Ed Swartwood of the Pittsburgh Alleghenys, best in the AA. He also led the league in hits with 147.

359

Strikeouts thrown by Tim Keefe of the New York Metropolitans, a major-league record for one season.

.394 and .869

On-base percentage and OPS, respectively, of Ed Swartwood of the Pittsburgh Alleghenys, both best in the AA.

619

Innings pitched by Tim Keefe of the New York Metropolitans, most in the AA.

.700

Winning percentage of Tony Mullane of the St. Louis Browns, best in the AA. He had a record of 35-15.

IN THE NATIONAL LEAGUE

1st

Game played by the New York Gothams (who became the New York Giants in 1885 and the San Francisco Giants in 1958) and by the Philadelphia Quakers (who became the Phillies in 1890). On May 1, 1883, the Gothams beat the Metropolitans 4-3, and the Providence Grays beat the Quakers 4-3.

1.84

ERA of Jim McCormick of the Cleveland Blues, best in the NL.

2

No-hitters thrown, by Charles "Old Hoss" Radbourn of the Providence Grays on July 25 against the Cleveland Blues and by Hugh "One Arm" Daily of the Cleveland Blues on September 13 against the Philadelphia Quakers.

3

Triples in a game by Buck Ewing of the New York Gothams on June 9.

4

Doubles each by Cap Anson and Abner Dalrymple of the Chicago White Stockings on July 3. Chicago beat the Buffalo Bisons 31-7.

6

Runs scored by Jim Whitney of the Boston Beaneaters on June 9. He was the first major-league player to score this many runs in a game. Boston beat the Detroit Wolverines 30-8.

10

Home runs by Buck Ewing of the New York

Gothams, an NL record until 1884.

13

Consecutive home losses by the Philadelphia Quakers from May 1 through June 5. The Quakers lost 14 consecutive games (home or away) from August 11 through September 1.

17

Triples by Dan Brouthers of the Buffalo Bisons, most in the NL.

17-81-1

Record of the Philadelphia Quakers, worst in the NL.

18

Runs scored in the seventh inning by the Chicago White Stockings on September 6 against the Detroit Wolverines. Tom Burns hit two doubles and a home run in the frame, and Fred Pfeffer and Ned Williamson also had three hits during the inning. Chicago won 26-6.

28-0

Score by which the Providence Grays beat the Philadelphia Quakers on August 21.

48

Wins (against 25 losses) by Old Hoss Radbourn of the Providence Grays. This was a major-league record until the next season, when Radbourn won 60 games.

48

Losses (against 12 wins) by John Coleman of the Philadelphia Quakers, a major-league record that is unlikely to ever be broken.

49

Doubles by Ned Williamson of the Chicago White Stockings. This was a major-league record until 1887 and an NL record until 1894.

61

Extra-base hits by Dan Brouthers of the Buffalo Bisons. This was a major-league record until 1886, when Brouthers had 66 extra-base hits.

63-35

Record of the Boston Beaneaters, best in the NL.

75

Games started by pitcher Pud Galvin of the Buffalo Bisons, to match a major-league record (set by Will White in 1879) that is unlikely to ever be broken. Galvin had 72 complete games in 1883, most in the NL.

76

Games played by Pud Galvin of the Buffalo Bisons and Old Hoss Radbourn of the Providence Grays, to match a major-league record set by Will White in 1879. The record was not broken until 1964, when reliever John Wyatt of the Kansas City Athletics pitched in 81 games.

97

RBIs by Dan Brouthers of the Buffalo Bisons, a major-league record for one season.

107

Runs by Joe Hornung of the Boston Beaneaters, most in the NL.

159

Hits by Dan Brouthers of the Buffalo Bisons, a major-league record for one season.

-216

Run differential at home by the Philadelphia Quakers, who scored 224 runs and allowed 440 runs. This was a major-league record until 2019, when the Detroit Tigers had a run differential of -221 at home.

243

Total bases by Dan Brouthers of the Buffalo Bisons, a major-league record for one season.

345

Strikeouts thrown by Jim Whitney of the Boston Beaneaters, an NL record for one season.

.374

Batting average of Dan Brouthers of the Buffalo Bisons, best in the NL.

.397/.572/.969

On-base percentage, slugging percentage, and OPS of Dan Brouthers of the Buffalo Bisons, all best in the NL.

656⅓

Innings pitched by Pud Galvin of the Buffalo Bisons, most in the NL.

.700

Winning percentage of Jim McCormick of the Cleveland Blues, best in the NL. He had a record of 28-12.

SOURCES

Society for American Baseball Research. *The SABR Baseball List and Record Book* (New York: Scribner, 2007).

Sugar, Burt Randolph, ed. *The Baseball Maniac's Almanac* (fifth edition) (New York: Sports Publishing, 2019).

baseball-almanac.com

baseball-reference.com

retrosheet.org

sabr.org

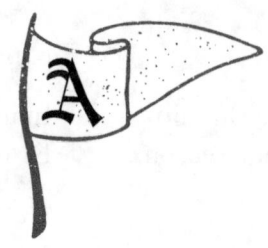

CONTRIBUTORS

Matt Albertson resides in Havertown, Pennsylvania, with his wife, Jess, and son, Garret. He joined SABR in 2015 and in 2018 was named the recipient of the SABR 19th Century Committee's Chairman's Award.

Pamela A. Bakker is a published author of history research books, articles, and historical poetry. Her books include *Eyes on the Sporting Scene, 1870-1930: Will and June Rankin, New York's Sportswriting Brothers* (Jefferson, North Carolina: McFarland Publishers, 2013); *The 104th Field Artillery Regiment of the New York National Guard, 1916-1919* (McFarland, 2014); and *McDowell Mill Fort in Markes, Pennsylvania, 1853-1840: French and Indian War to the Establishment of a New Nation* (Sunbury Press, Inc., 2020).

Clifford Blau has been a SABR member since 1983 and a Retrosheet volunteer since 1999. He serves as fact-checker for the SABR annuals and has contributed articles to the *Baseball Research Journal* and other publications.

Richard Bogovich is the author of *Kid Nichols: A Biography of the Hall of Fame Pitcher* and *The Who: A Who's Who*, both published by McFarland & Co., for whom he is finalizing a biography of Frank Grant. He has contributed to such SABR books as *Pride of Smoketown: The 1935 Pittsburgh Crawfords* and *Bittersweet Goodbye: The Black Barons, the Grays, and the 1948 Negro League World Series*. He works for the Wendland Utz law firm in Rochester, Minnesota.

Dr. Jerrold Casway is a retired history professor and social sciences dean emeritus, who lives in Cape May Court House, New Jersey. Casway has written four books, two on baseball subjects. He has also published more than 30 articles on baseball topics and has been a featured keynote speaker at the Baseball Hall of Fame in Cooperstown, New York. One of his books, *Ed Delahanty in the Emerald Age of Baseball*, was selected as one of most important books written on baseball in the last half-century. Jerrold specializes in nineteenth-century baseball and the history of the sport in Philadelphia. His latest book, *The Culture and Ethnicity of Nineteenth-Century Baseball*, was singled out as an "important and unique" overview of baseball's early years.

Paul E. Doutrich is professor emeritus at York College of Pennsylvania, where he taught American history for 30 years. He now lives in Brewster, Massachusetts. Among the courses he taught was one entitled Baseball History. He has written scholarly articles and contributed to several anthologies about the Revolutionary era, and has written a book about Jacksonian America. He has also curated several museum exhibits. His recent scholarship has focused on baseball history. He has contributed numerous manuscripts to various SABR publications and is the author of *The Cardinals and the Yankees, 1926: A Classical Season and St. Louis in Seven*.

Brian C. Englehardt is a native of Reading, Pennsylvania, where he resides with his wife, Suzanne, a good sport about any number of things. The author of *Reading's Big League Exhibition Games*, he has written several SABR biographies together with articles appearing in other SABR publications. He is also a regular contributor to *The Historical Review of Berks County*, with his subjects covering various local matters of historical note including baseball.

Dan Fields is a senior manuscript editor at the *New England Journal of Medicine* and lives in Framingham, Massachusetts. He has contributed to numerous SABR books.

Tim Hagerty is the broadcaster for the Triple-A El Paso Chihuahuas and has called professional baseball games since 2004. He has broadcast two major-league games and has been heard nationally covering various sports for Fox Sports Radio and Westwood One. He's the author of one baseball book and freelance articles for *Baseball Digest*, *The Sporting News*, the *Hardball Times*, and other publications. He resides in El Paso, Texas, with his wife, Heather, and son, Carson.

Donna L. Halper is an associate professor of communication and media studies at Lesley University in Massachusetts. She joined SABR in 2011, and her research focuses on women and minorities in baseball, the Negro Leagues, and "firsts" in baseball history. A former radio deejay, credited with having discovered the rock band Rush, Dr. Halper reinvented herself and got her Ph.D. at age 64. In addition to her research into baseball, she is also a media historian with expertise in the history of broadcasting. She has contributed to SABR's Games Project and BioProject, and has written several articles for the *Baseball Research Journal*.

Richard Hershberger has written numerous articles on early baseball history for SABR publications and *Base Ball: A Journal of the Early Game*. He is the author of *Strike Four: The Evolution of Baseball* and is currently writing a history of baseball from 1744 to 1871. He works as a paralegal in Maryland.

Paul Hofmann has been a SABR member since 2002. He has contributed to more than 25 SABR publications. Paul currently teaches in the College of Management at National Changhua University of Education in Taiwan. A native of Detroit, Paul is an avid baseball card collector and lifelong Detroit Tigers fan. He currently resides in Folsom, California.

SABR member **Michael Huber** is professor of mathematics at Muhlenberg College in Allentown, Pennsylvania, where he teaches an undergraduate course titled "Reasoning with Sabermetrics." He has published his sabermetrics research in several books and journals, including *The Baseball Research Journal, Chance, The Annals of Applied Statistics,* and *Base Ball*. Mike genuinely enjoys contributing to SABR's Baseball Games Project, especially if the games contain rare events, such as hitting for the cycle or a no-hitter.

Bill Johnson has contributed over 40 articles to SABR's Biography Project, and presented papers at the 2011 Cooperstown Symposium on Baseball and American Culture, the 2017 Jerry Malloy Negro League Conference, and the inaugural Southern Negro League Conference. He has published a biography of Hal Trosky (McFarland and Co., 2017) and most recently an article about Negro American League All-Star Art "Superman" Pennington in the journal *Black Ball*. Bill and his wife, Chris, reside in Georgia.

Chris Jones is an attorney at Phelps Dunbar, where he practices in the area of commercial litigation, with a focus on property rights, eminent domain, real estate disputes, and contract disputes. He is a lifelong baseball fan and a member of SABR since 2015. The highlight of his playing days was being drafted by the Toronto Blue Jays in the 2001 amateur draft. He resides in the Dallas/Fort Worth area with his wife and four children. For firm information visit www.phelpsdunbar.com, or contact Chris directly at chris.jones@phelps.com.

Bob LeMoine is a librarian and adjunct professor in New Hampshire. A lifelong Red Sox fan, Bob has contributed to several SABR projects and was co-editor of two SABR books: *Boston's First Nine: The 1871-75 Boston Red Stockings* and *The Glorious Beaneaters of the 1890s*.

Len Levin is a longtime newspaper editor in New England, now retired. He lives in Providence with his wife, Linda, and an overachieving orange cat. He now (Len, not the cat) is the grammarian for the Rhode Island Supreme Court and edits its decisions. He also copyedits many SABR books, including this one. He is just down the interstate from Fenway Park, where he has spent many happy hours.

Dalton Mack was a writer for *USA Today Sports Weekly* and MLB.com and has been a SABR member since 2012. Much like Bill Crowley, he grew up in New Jersey, albeit in Union instead of Gloucester County. Dalton's fondest Philadelphia baseball memory was attending Pat "The Bat" Burrell's "Bat Day" on August 3, 2003 (the Phillies, as luck would have it, lost the game in extra innings).

Michael McAvoy is associate professor of economics at SUNY Oneonta, located down the road from Cooperstown. As a child he resided in northern Illinois, where he developed a lifelong attachment for the Cubs. Lew Simmons struck a chord as he also maintained a lifelong attachment for the Philadelphia Athletics after moving to that city during the Civil War.

A Baltimore native, **Brian McKenna** has contributed over 50 works to SABR's Biography Project. His full-length projects include the biography *Clark Griffith: Baseball's Statesman*.

Eric Miklich is a member of SABR's Nineteenth Century Committee. He is the owner of 19cbaseball.com and coauthored *Forfeits and Successfully Protested Games in Major League Baseball* with David Nemec. In 2021, after appearing in over 900 matches, he retired from the Brooklyn Eckfords. He is a goaltending development leader for USA Hockey and is the organizational goaltending coach for East Islip High School. Eric lives in Islip, New York.

Bill Nowlin has enjoyed collaborating with many other researchers, authors, and editors in SABR and edited or helped edit several dozen books, as well as contributing over 1,000 articles, primarily biographies and Games Project stories. A long-ago political science professor and a co-founder of Rounder Records in 1970, he has kept busy with baseball research as the current century progresses. He's a Boston native and lifelong Red Sox fan.

Joel Rippel, a Minnesota native and graduate of the University of Minnesota, is the author or coauthor of 10 books on Minnesota sports history and has contributed to several books published by SABR.

Bill Ryczek has written seven books on baseball history, including a trilogy (*Blackguards and Red Stockings, When Johnny Came Sliding Home,* and *Baseball's First Inning*) on the nineteenth century. He has also contributed to numerous SABR publications.

John Thorn, the official historian of Major League Baseball, has been a SABR member for 40 years. In that time he has written altogether too much about baseball and other things that matter.

Michael Wagner served as a US Air Force historian for 21 years. He has been a New York Yankees fan since he was a child. Mr. Wagner self-published the 511-page book *Babe's Place: The Lives of Yankee Stadium* in 2012, and published a 620-page revised edition in 2017. *Babe's Place* is a history of the New York Yankees and the original Yankee Stadium, with great detail of the 1970s Yankee Stadium renovation. It may be purchased on amazon.com.

Gregory H. Wolf was born in Pittsburgh, but now resides in the Chicagoland area with his wife, Margaret, and daughter, Gabriela. A professor of German studies and holder of the Dennis and Jean Bauman Endowed Chair in the Humanities at North Central College in Naperville, Illinois, he has edited more than a dozen books for SABR. He is currently working on projects about Shibe Park in Philadelphia and Ebbets Field in Brooklyn. Since January 2017 he has been co-director of SABR's BioProject, which you can follow on Facebook and Twitter.

A lifelong New Jersey resident, **John Zinn** is the author of five books, including three about the Brooklyn Dodgers, as well as numerous essays and articles. He also writes a baseball history blog entitled "A Manly Pastime." John is the scorekeeper for the Flemington Neshanock vintage baseball team. He holds BA and MBA degrees from Rutgers University and is a Vietnam veteran.

SABR Books on the Negro Leagues and Black Baseball

From Rube to Robinson: SABR's Best Articles on Black Baseball

From Rube to Robinson brings together the best Negro League baseball scholarship that the Society of American Baseball Research (SABR) has ever produced, culled from its journals, Biography Project, and award-winning essays. The book includes a star-studded list of scholars and historians, from the late Jerry Malloy and Jules Tygiel, to award winners Larry Lester, Geri Strecker, and Jeremy Beer, and a host of other talented writers. The essays cover topics ranging over nearly a century, from 1866 and the earliest known Black baseball championship, to 1962 and the end of the Negro American League.

Edited by John Graf; Associate Editors Duke Goldman and Larry Lester
$24.95 paperback (ISBN 978-1-970159-41-7)
$9.99 ebook (ISBN 978-1-970159-40-0)
8.5"X11", 220 pages

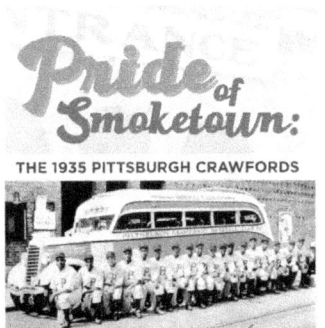

Pride of Smoketown: The 1935 Pittsburgh Crawfords

The 1935 Pittsburgh Crawfords team, one of the dominant teams in Negro League history, is often compared to the legendary 1927 "Murderer's Row" New York Yankees. The squad from "Smoketown"—a nickname that the *Pittsburgh Courier* often applied to the metropolis better-known as "Steel City"—boasted four Hall-of-Fame players in outfielder James "Cool Papa" Bell, first baseman/manager Oscar Charleston, catcher Josh Gibson, and third baseman William "Judy" Johnson. This volume contains exhaustively-researched articles about the players, front office personnel, Greenlee Field, and the exciting games and history of the team that were written and edited by 25 SABR members. The inclusion of historical photos about every subject in the book helps to shine a spotlight on the 1935 Pittsburgh Crawfords, who truly were the Pride of Smoketown.

Edited by Frederick C. Bush and Bill Nowlin
$29.95 paperback (ISBN 978-1-970159-25-7)
$9.99 ebook (ISBN 978-1-970159-24-0)
8.5"X11", 340 pages, over 60 photos

The Newark Eagles Take Flight: The Story of the 1946 Negro League Champions

The Newark Eagles won only one Negro National League pennant during the franchise's 15-year tenure in the Garden State, but the 1946 squad that ran away with the NNL and then triumphed over the Kansas City Monarchs in a seven-game World Series was a team for the ages. The returning WWII veterans composed a veritable "Who's Who in the Negro Leagues" and included Leon Day, Larry Doby, Monte Irvin, and Max Manning, as well as numerous role players. Four of the Eagles' stars—Day, Doby, Irvin, and player/manager Raleigh "Biz" Mackey, as well as co-owner Effa Manley—have been enshrined in the National Baseball Hall of Fame in Cooperstown. In addition to biographies of the players, co-owners, and P.A. announcer, there are also articles about Newark's Ruppert Stadium, Leon Day's Opening Day no-hitter, a sensational midseason game, the season's two East-West All-Star Games, and the 1946 Negro League World Series between the Eagles and the renowned Kansas City Monarchs.

Edited by Frederick C. Bush and Bill Nowlin
$24.95 paperback (ISBN 978-1-970159-07-3)
$9.99 ebook (ISBN 978-1-970159-06-6)
8.5"X11", 228 pages, over 60 photos

Bittersweet Goodbye: The Black Barons, The Grays, and the 1948 Negro League World Series

This book was inspired by the last Negro League World Series ever played and presents biographies of the players on the two contending teams in 1948—the Birmingham Black Barons and the Homestead Grays—as well as the managers, the owners, and articles on the ballparks the teams called home. Also included are articles that recap the season's two East-West All-Star Games, the Negro National League and Negro American League playoff series, and the World Series itself. Additional context is provided in essays about the effects of baseball's integration on the Negro Leagues, the exodus of Negro League players to Canada, and the signing away of top Negro League players, specifically Willie Mays. Many of the players' lives and careers have been presented to a much greater extent than previously possible.

Edited by Frederick C. Bush and Bill Nowlin
$21.95 paperback (ISBN 978-1-943816-55-2)
$9.99 ebook (ISBN 978-1-943816-54-5)
8.5"X11", 442 pages, over 100 photos and images

Friends of SABR

You can become a Friend of SABR by giving as little as $10 per month or by making a one-time gift of $1,000 or more. When you do so, you will be inducted into a community of passionate baseball fans dedicated to supporting SABR's work.

Friends of SABR receive the following benefits:
- ✓ Annual Friends of SABR Commemorative Lapel Pin
- ✓ Recognition in This Week in SABR, SABR.org, and the SABR Annual Report
- ✓ Access to the SABR Annual Convention VIP donor event
- ✓ Invitations to exclusive Friends of SABR events

SABR On-Deck Circle - $10/month, $30/month, $50/month

Get in the SABR On-Deck Circle, and help SABR become the essential community for the world of baseball. Your support will build capacity around all things SABR, including publications, website content, podcast development, and community growth.

A monthly gift is deducted from your bank account or charged to a credit card until you tell us to stop. No more email, mail, or phone reminders.

 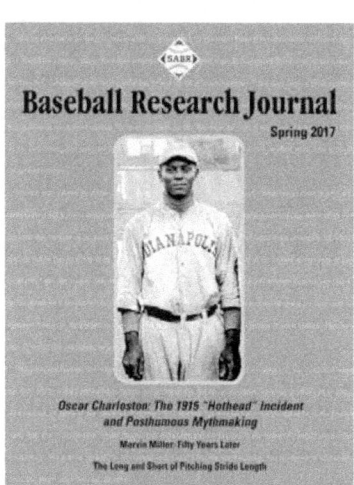 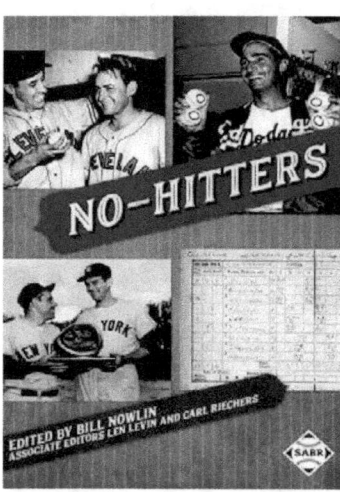

Join the SABR On-Deck Circle

Payment Info: _____Visa _____Mastercard   ○ $10/month

Name on Card: _____   ○ $30/month

Card #: _____   ○ $50/month

Exp. Date: _____ Security Code: _____   ○ Other amount _____

Signature: _____

Go to sabr.org/donate to make your gift online

Society for American Baseball Research

Cronkite School at ASU
555 N. Central Ave. #416, Phoenix, AZ 85004
602.496.1460 (phone)
SABR.org

Become a SABR member today!

If you're interested in baseball — writing about it, reading about it, talking about it — there's a place for you in the Society for American Baseball Research.

SABR memberships are available on annual, multi-year, or monthly subscription basis. Annual and monthly subscription memberships auto-renew for your convenience. Young Professional memberships are for ages 30 and under. Senior memberships are for ages 65 and older. Student memberships are available to currently enrolled middle/high school or full-time college/university students. Monthly subscription members receive SABR publications electronically and are eligible for SABR event discounts after 12 months.

Here's a list of some of the key benefits you'll receive as a SABR member:

- Receive two editions (spring and fall) of the *Baseball Research Journal*, our flagship publication
- Receive expanded e-book edition of *The National Pastime*, our annual convention journal
- 8-10 new e-books published by the SABR Digital Library, all FREE to members
- "This Week in SABR" e-newsletter, sent to members every Friday
- Join dozens of research committees, from Statistical Analysis to Women in Baseball.
- Join one of 70+ regional chapters in the U.S., Canada, Latin America, and abroad
- Participate in online discussion groups
- Ask and answer baseball research questions on the SABR-L e-mail listserv
- Complete archives of *The Sporting News* dating back to 1886 and other research resources
- Promote your research in "This Week in SABR"
- Diamond Dollars Case Competition
- Yoseloff Scholarships

- Discounts on SABR national conferences, including the SABR National Convention, the SABR Analytics Conference, Jerry Malloy Negro League Conference, Frederick Ivor-Campbell 19th Century Conference, and the Arizona Fall League Experience
- Publish your research in peer-reviewed SABR journals
- Collaborate with SABR researchers and experts
- Contribute to Baseball Biography Project or the SABR Games Project
- List your new book in the SABR Bookshelf
- Lead a SABR research committee or chapter
- Networking opportunities at SABR Analytics Conference
- Meet baseball authors and historians at SABR events and chapter meetings
- 50% discounts on paperback versions of SABR e-books
- Discounts with other partners in the baseball community
- SABR research awards

We hope you'll join the most passionate international community of baseball fans at SABR! Check us out online at SABR.org/join.

- - ✂ -

SABR MEMBERSHIP FORM

	Standard	Senior	Young Pro.	Student
Annual:	❑ $65	❑ $45	❑ $45	❑ $25
3 Year:	❑ $175	❑ $129	❑ $129	
5 Year:	❑ $249			
Monthly:	❑ $6.95	❑ $4.95	❑ $4.95	

(International members wishing to be mailed the Baseball Research Journal should add $10/yr for Canada/Mexico or $19/yr for overseas locations.)

Participate in Our Donor Program!

Support the preservation of baseball research. Designate your gift toward:

❑ General Fund   ❑ Endowment Fund   ❑ Research Resources   ❑ _____
❑ I want to maximize the impact of my gift; do not send any donor premiums
❑ I would like this gift to remain anonymous.

Note: Any donation not designated will be placed in the General Fund.
SABR is a 501 (c) (3) not-for-profit organization & donations are tax-deductible to the extent allowed by law.

Name _____

E-mail* _____

Address _____

City _____ ST_____ ZIP_____

Phone _____ Birthday _____

* Your e-mail address on file ensures you will receive the most recent SABR news.

Dues $_____

Donation $_____

Amount Enclosed $_____

Do you work for a matching grant corporation? Call (602) 496-1460 for details.

If you wish to pay by credit card, please contact the SABR office at (602) 496-1460 or sign up securely online at SABR.org/join. We accept Visa, Mastercard & Discover.

Do you wish to receive the *Baseball Research Journal* electronically? ❑ Yes   ❑ No
Our e-books are available in PDF, Kindle, or EPUB (iBooks, iPad, Nook) formats.

Mail to: SABR, Cronkite School at ASU, 555 N. Central Ave. #416, Phoenix, AZ 85004   10/19